HUMAN RIGHTS: NEW DIMENSIONS AND CHALLENGES

Human Rights: New Dimensions and Challenges

Edited by
JANUSZ SYMONIDES

v. 1

MANUAL ON HUMAN RIGHTS

Ashgate

DARTMOUTH

Aldershot • Brookfield USA • Singapore • Sydney

UNESCO
Publishing

Published by
Dartmouth Publishing Company Limited
Ashgate Publishing Limited
Gower House
Croft Road
Aldershot
Hants GU11 3HR
England

Ashgate Publishing Company
Old Post Road
Brookfield
Vermont 05036
USA

Published jointly with the United Nations
Educational, Scientific and Cultural Organization
7, place de Fontenoy, 75352, Paris 07 SP

British Library Cataloguing in Publication Data
Symonides, Janusz
 Human rights : new dimensions and challenges : UNESCO
 manual on human rights
 1. Human rights – Handbooks, manuals, etc.
 I. Title
 323

Library of Congress Cataloging-in-Publication Data
Human rights : new dimensions and challenges : UNESCO manual on human
 rights / Janusz Symonides [editor]
      p. cm.
   ISBN 1-84014-426-2 (hb). – ISBN 1-84014-430-0 (pbk.)
   1. Human rights–Study and teaching.   I. Symonides, Janusz.
 II. Unesco.
 JC571.H76967   1998
 323–dc21   98-35237
                                                                                CIP
Ashgate ISBN 1 84014 426 2 (Hbk)
        ISBN 1 84014 430 0 (Pbk)
UNESCO ISBN 92-3-103582-7

Typeset by Manton Typesetters, 5–7 Eastfield Road, Louth, Lincolnshire, LN11 7AJ, UK.
Printed and bound by MPG Books Ltd. Bodmin, Cornwall.

Contents

PART II   OBSTACLES

Preface

The necessity to develop human rights education has been underlined in numerous resolutions adopted by the United Nations General Assembly, the Economic and Social Council (ECOSOC), the Commission on Human Rights, UNESCO and other United Nations bodies and specialized agencies. The final document of the World Conference on Human Rights (Vienna, June 1993) stressed the crucial importance of human rights education, training and public information, and proposed the proclamation of a special United Nations Decade. In accordance with this suggestion, the General Assembly declared the United Nations Decade for Human Rights Education (1995–2004). The Plan of Action for the Decade placed an emphasis on the preparation of teaching aids on human rights designed for various levels of education and target groups.

UNESCO's long experience in this field goes back to 1951, when the first guide for teachers on the Universal Declaration of Human Rights was published. This can be perceived as a part of the Organization's efforts to create a comprehensive system of human rights education, embracing formal and non-formal education. While preserving its interest in promoting human rights teaching in primary and secondary schools, UNESCO has been paying greater attention in recent years to higher education. This is linked to the fact that universities have a special role in the training of specialists who then ensure both the implementation of human rights standards and the dissemination of knowledge on human rights. With this in mind, more than 30 UNESCO Chairs dealing with education for human rights, as well as for peace, democracy and tolerance, have been established since 1991 in Africa, Asia, Europe and Latin America.

The Manual on Human Rights Education for Universities has been prepared in the hope that it will serve as a teaching aid for institutions of higher education, as well as for UNESCO Chairs. This first volume is devoted to new dimensions and challenges. The choice of the content is explained by the fact that, at the end of the twentieth century, there is a need for a greater reflection on the human rights agenda for the beginning of the third millennium. This is linked with new dimensions of human rights and the recognition of their important role in the promotion and consolidation of peace, democracy and development. The still unresolved problems which the new threats and challenges pose are those concerning, *inter alia*, the responsibilities of scientists and universities.

This volume was prepared by well-known specialists coming from different regions of the world, which may be seen in itself as a confirmation of the universality of human rights. It does not provide ready solutions to all the problems but its aim is to raise public awareness and contribute to the current debate.

The editor would like to thank the authors for their constructive cooperation, and to express his gratitude to Ms. S. Bennett, Ms. J. Lebras, A. McLurg and V. Volodin who, in different ways but with the same devotion, assisted in the preparation of this volume.

The second and third volumes dealing, respectively, with international human rights standards and with international protection of human rights, are in preparation. The publication of this volume may be considered as a contribution to the commemoration of the fiftieth anniversary of the Universal Declaration of Human Rights.

JANUSZ SYMONIDES

About the Contributors

Upendra Baxi Professor of International Law. Former Vice Chancellor of Delhi University. President of the Indian Society of International Law.

David Beetham Professor of Political Science and Director of the Centre for Democratization Studies of the University of Leeds, UK.

Antonio Augusto Cançado Trindade Judge of the Inter-American Court of Human Rights; Professor of International Law at the University of Brasilia; Executive Director of the Inter-American Institute of Human Rights.

Vojin Dimitrijevic Professor of International Law and International Relations, University of Belgrade Law School Yugoslavia (Serbia); Visiting Professor, Raoul Wallenberg Institute of Human Rights and Humanitarian Law, University of Lund, Sweden; Director, Centre for Human Rights, Belgrade.

Virginia A. Leary Distinguished Service Professor, State University of New York, and Professor of Law Emeritus, Law School, State University of New York (SUNY) at Buffalo. She has taught and lectured in Australia, France, Switzerland, the Netherlands, Sri Lanka and the UK.

Patrice Meyer-Bisch Coordinator of the Interdisciplinary Institute of Ethics and Human Rights, University of Fribourg, Switzerland.

Vitit Muntarbhorn Professor of Law at the Faculty of Law, Chulalongkorn University, Bangkok. From 1990 to 1994, he was the United Nations Special Rapporteur on the Sale of Children with a global mandate under the United Nations Human Rights Commission.

Louis-Edmond Pettiti   Judge at the European Court of Human Rights. He is former *bâtonnier* (President) of the Paris Bar Association.

Janusz Symonides   Professor of International Law, Warsaw. Since 1989, Director of the Division of Human Rights, Democracy and Peace, UNESCO.

Colin Warbrick   Senior Lecturer in Law at the University of Durham, UK. Member of the Durham European Law Institute.

C.G. Weeramantry   Professor of International Law. Judge at the International Court of Justice since 1991 and its Vice-President since 1997. He was Judge at the Supreme Court of Sri Lanka from 1967–1972.

Rüdiger Wolfrum   Professor of International Law. Director of the Max Planck Institute for Comparative Public Law and International Law, Heidelberg. Member of the Council of the German Section of the International Law Association.

Claudio Zanghi   Professor of Law, Rome. President of the International Centre of Sociological, Penal and Penitentiary Research and Studies, Taormina, Italy.

1 New Human Rights Dimensions, Obstacles and Challenges: Introductory Remarks

JANUSZ SYMONIDES

The United Nations System and the Interdependence and Interrelation between Human Rights, Peace, Democracy and Development

The close relationship between peace and human rights as well as peace and development was already recognized by the Charter of the United Nations which, in its preamble, declares: 'We the peoples of the United Nations, determined to save succeeding generations from the scourge of war [...] and to reaffirm faith in fundamental human rights ...'. Article 55 adds further that, with a view to the creation of conditions of stability and well-being which are necessary for peaceful relations among Nations, the United Nations shall promote conditions of economic and social progress and development and at the same time universal respect for, and observance of, human rights and fundamental freedoms.

The analysis of international human rights instruments confirms the conviction of the international community, based on the tragic experiences of the Second World War, that respect for human rights is at the basis of peace. Therefore the phrase, 'recognition of the inherent dignity and the equal and inalienable rights of all members of the human family is the foundation of freedom, justice and peace in the world', formulated in the preamble of the Universal Declaration of Human Rights of 1948, was repeated by both the preambles of the International Covenant on Civil and Political Rights and the International Covenant on Economic, Social and Cultural Rights of 1966. A number of instruments emphasize that specific human rights violations, such as racial discrimination or apartheid, may disturb peace and threaten international security.[1]

The Proclamation of the Tehran Conference on Human Rights (1968) was the first to point out the other dimension of the relationship between peace and human rights providing that peace and justice are indispensable to the full realization of human rights and fundamental freedoms.[2] As V. Dimitrijevic states in Chapter 2, the absence of peace, either international or national, endangers the enjoyment of human rights, totally or partially. War is harmful to human rights. However, in his view, in a world of sovereign nation-states, respect for human rights does not unequivocally result in peace.

The gradual acceptance by the United Nations of a positive definition of peace understood, not only as absence of war, but also as the achievement of social justice, brings into the picture this important aspect. The Declaration on the Preparation of Societies for Life in Peace[3] uses the term, 'just and durable peace', which is described not only as freedom from oppression but also as development and cooperation of all nations. The seminar on the relations between human rights, peace and development, organized by the United Nations in 1981, reflects in the title itself the conviction that all three dimensions should be dealt with simultaneously and comprehensively.[4]

What new elements and changes can be observed in relations between human rights, peace and development at the close of the twentieth century? Can we speak about new human rights dimensions? The answer to these questions cannot but be positive.

One of the profound changes in international relations and within states is the new agenda adopted by the United Nations which finds its expression in the series of world conferences organized in the 1990s and also in new activities and programmes undertaken by the whole United Nations system.

The end of the Cold War and ideological confrontation, the wave of democratization and the fall of totalitarian and authoritarian regimes in many parts of the world have resulted in the addition to the already existing list of a new human rights dimension – democracy. The Vienna World Conference on Human Rights (June 1993) was convened to consider, *inter alia*, the relationship between development, democracy and the universal enjoyment of all human rights. The Vienna Declaration and Programme of Action adopted by this Conference, in its preamble, speaks about the aspirations of all peoples for an international order founded on promoting and encouraging respect for human rights and fundamental freedoms for all, respect for the principle of equal rights and self-determination of peoples, as well as for peace, democracy, justice, equality, rule of law, pluralism, development, better standards of living and solidarity. The Declaration further states that democracy, development and respect for human rights and fundamental freedoms are interdependent and mutually reinforcing.

There is no doubt that only democracy can truly guarantee human rights. It is a political system which best allows for the free exercise of individual rights.[5] However, there is also the other side of the linkage between democracy and human rights: democracy cannot be established without respect for human rights.

In Chapter 3, D. Beetham underlines that human rights constitute an intrinsic part of democracy, because the guarantee of basic freedoms is a necessary condition for the voice of the people to be effective in public affairs and for popular control over government to be secured. Therefore, in his opinion, civil and political rights constitute an integral part of democracy, whereas economic and social rights are in a relation of mutual dependency with democracy. As stated in the Universal Declaration on Democracy, adopted by the Inter-Parliamentary Union, in Cairo on 16 December 1997, democracy is a universally recognized ideal as well as a goal. It is thus a basic right of citizenship.[6]

For a long time governments were giving pre-eminence to economic thinking favouring most of all economic development.[7] The persistence of extreme poverty, social exclusion, vulnerable groups, unequal sharing in the benefits of development and new dramatic inequalities cannot but intervene in the debates concerning development. The United Nations Conference on Environment and Development (Rio de Janeiro, 1992) in its *Agenda 21* took into account the need to improve the situations of vulnerable groups, and underlined the necessity to satisfy basic human needs/rights: from the right to food to the right to education. The Conference used the term 'sustainable development', which covers economic development, social development and environmental protection, which are interdependent and mutually reinforcing components.

A.A. Cançado Trindade, in his chapter on 'Human rights and the environment', presents considerations on affinities in the parallel evolution of human rights protection and environmental protection, the wide dimension of the fundamental right to life and the right to health, the question of the implementation of the right to a healthy environment, and the relevance of the right to democratic participation. He concludes that the results of the conferences in Rio and in Vienna will accelerate the creation of a universal culture of the observance of human rights and the environment.

The World Summit for Social Development (Copenhagen, 1995) adopted the Copenhagen Declaration and Programme of Action which underlined the urgent need to address profound social problems, especially poverty, unemployment and social exclusion, which affect every country. The Declaration stresses: 'people are at the centre of our concern for sustainable development and ... they are entitled to a healthy and productive life in harmony with the environment'. Commitment 1 speaks about the promotion of equality and equity between women and men and full respect for all human rights, 'including those relating to education, food, shelter, employment, health and information, particularly in order to assist people living in poverty'. Participants also undertook a commitment to reinforce peace by promoting tolerance, non-violence and respect for diversity, and by settling disputes by peaceful means.

The interdependence between the observance of human rights, participatory democracy and peace became particularly evident in the 1990s as a result of the proliferation of internal conflicts. The massive and flagrant violations of human rights, discrimination against minorities and other vulnerable groups, racism, xenophobia and ethnonationalism are among the main sources of conflicts which now plague the international community. This aspect has been duly taken into account by the United Nations, which sees in the promotion and respect of human rights one of the main elements of peace keeping and peace building.[8] Peace keeping and post-conflict peace building, as well as peace agreements signed by parties to internal conflicts, foresee various actions and steps aimed at the protection and reinforcement of human rights, the conducting of free elections and the building of democratic institutions which together are seen, very rightly, as an important guarantee of peace. For this very reason, electoral assistance for new or restored democracies has become an important part of the present activities of the United Nations.

By the end of the twentieth century, the international community not only confirmed the close relations and interdependence existing between human rights, peace, democracy and development, but reinforced them and enriched them with new dimensions. The Declarations, Programmes and Platforms of Action adopted by the world conferences and summits which took place in the 1990s,[9] together with actions foreseen by international years and decades, create an ambitious agenda which, in fact, can be recognized as an agenda for the twenty-first century. It emphasizes the importance of all human rights and puts human beings and human needs at the centre of all national and international actions and efforts. This new human rights dimension is symbolically reflected in the terms which are now more and more in use, namely 'human security' and 'human development'.[10] Human dimensions of development, democracy and peace are also reflected in the discussions concerning the recognition of new human rights.

Towards Further Consolidation of the Right to Development

The development of the right to development is presented in Chapter 4 by U. Baxi, who observes that, despite the adoption of the Declaration on the Right to Development, the major task of finding concrete ways and means to develop this right is still on the agenda of states and peoples of the world. The *leitmotiv* of the Declaration is that the human person is the central subject of development and therefore an active participant and beneficiary of the right to development. In conclusion, he states that the discourse concerning this right has to be initiated at all levels of policy making and actions.

What has been done by the United Nations during the years which have elapsed since the adoption of the Declaration to strengthen and consolidate the right to development? This right was put on the agenda by all the United Nations world conferences organized in the 1990s. The United Nations Conference on Environment and Development, in the Rio de Janeiro Declaration of 14 June 1992, adopted the principle that 'the right to development must be fulfilled so as to equitably meet developmental and environmental needs of present and future generations'.[11]

The Vienna Conference reaffirmed the right to development 'as a universal and inalienable right and an integral part of fundamental human rights'.[12] It declared that states and the international community should promote effective international cooperation for the realization of this right and the elimination of obstacles to development. This also requires effective development policies at the national level as well as equitable relations and a favourable economic environment at the international level.

Among the principles and goals of the Copenhagen Declaration on Social Development (1995), the promotion of universal respect for, and observance and protection of, all human rights and fundamental freedoms for all, including the right to development, is specifically mentioned. Commitment 1 repeats the Vienna formula qualifying the right to development 'as a universal and inalienable right and an integral part of fundamental human rights'.[13] The right to development has also been reaffirmed by the Platform for Action of the World Conference on Women.

In 1993, the Commission on Human Rights established a Working Group on the Right to Development with the mandate to identify obstacles to the implementation and realization of the Declaration on the Right to Development, and to recommend ways and means towards the realization of this right. The Working Group identified several obstacles and proposed in general terms different mechanisms to implement and monitor the right to development. However, as it concluded its work in 1995, it did not have time to elaborate the strategy requested. This became a task for the Intergovernmental Group of Experts established in 1996. In its first report, the group underlined that it will take a balanced and comprehensive approach in the elaboration of a strategy to implement and promote the right to development.[14]

After years of controversy, the right to development was at last accepted as an integral part of fundamental human rights.[15] The debate focuses increasingly on substantive issues. The functions and importance of the right to development, as well as its impact on other human rights, are today more profoundly recognized and have become less controversial. In 1996, the Commission on Human Rights adopted for the first time by consensus resolution 1996/15 on the right to development. The General Assembly, in its resolution 51/99, called upon all Member States to make further concrete efforts at the national and international levels to remove the obstacles to the realization of the right to development. Indeed, it is of vital importance to move from a theoretical or political discussion to practically oriented measures. In this context, it is worth noting that the Commission on Human Rights asked the Secretary-General to provide the United Nations Centre for Human Rights with a focal unit to follow up the implementation of the Declaration on the Right to Development. The High Commissioner for Human Rights also started consultations with the World Bank concerning the right to development.

UNESCO Initiatives Aimed at the Recognition of the Human Right to Peace

In 1989, the UNESCO International Congress on Peace in the Minds of Men, held in Yamoussoukro, Côte d'Ivoire, adopted a declaration inviting states, governmental and non-governmental organizations, the scientific, educational and cultural community and all individuals to contribute towards building a new concept of peace by developing a culture of peace based on the universal values of respect for life, freedom, justice, solidarity, tolerance, human rights and equality among men and women. Responding to this request, UNESCO put forward a programme to promote a culture of peace. In 1995, the General Conference approved this project and authorized the Director-General to implement activities foreseen by it and comprising the following: education for peace, human rights, democracy, international understanding and tolerance; promotion of human rights and democracy; cultural pluralism and intercultural dialogue; and conflict prevention and post-conflict peace building.

The General Assembly welcomed the UNESCO Transdisciplinary Project, 'Towards a culture of peace', and encouraged countries, regional organizations, non-governmental organizations and the

Director-General of UNESCO to take all necessary action to ensure by this project education for peace, human rights, democracy, international understanding and tolerance.[16] A year later, the General Assembly once again called for the promotion of a culture of peace based on the principles established in the Charter of the United Nations, the respect for human rights, democracy, tolerance, dialogue, cultural diversity and reconciliation as an integral approach to prevent violence and conflicts and to contribute to the creation of conditions for peace and its consolidation.[17]

In this context the Director-General of UNESCO, in his Declaration of January 1997,[18] put forward the idea of proclaiming the human right to peace. This idea received a positive response and was discussed at an international meeting of experts held in Las Palmas, Spain, in February 1997.[19] In the final document of the meeting, the participants formulated an opinion that the human right to peace should be recognized, guaranteed and protected at the international level through the preparation and adoption of a declaration on the human right to peace.

An international meeting of experts on the human right to peace, held at the Norwegian Institute of Human Rights in Oslo in June 1997, elaborated the Oslo Draft Declaration on the Human Right to Peace, for eventual adoption by the UNESCO General Conference.[20] In its preamble, it refers to the relevant provisions of the Charter of the United Nations, the Constitution of UNESCO and the Universal Declaration of Human Rights. It notes that peace is a common goal of all humanity and a universal and fundamental value to which all individuals and all peoples aspire, and that recognition of a human right to peace can give peace its full human dimension.

The draft provides that every human being has the right to peace, and that war, armed conflicts and violence are intrinsically incompatible with this right which must be guaranteed, respected and implemented in internal and international contexts by all states and other members of the international community. It further states that every human being, all states and other members of the international community and all peoples have the duty to contribute to the maintenance and construction of peace, and to the prevention of armed conflicts and of violence in all its forms; they should favour disarmament and oppose by all legitimate means acts of aggression and systematic massive and flagrant violations of human rights which constitute a threat to peace. A culture of peace is seen as the means of achieving the global implementation of the human right to peace.

At the beginning of July 1997, the Director-General sent a letter with the text of the Oslo Draft Declaration to the heads of all Member States, in order to elicit their opinions and comments.[21] The report by the Director-General on the human right to peace was then presented in October 1997 to the 29th session of the General Conference.

During the debate, though the majority of states expressed their support for the idea of the elaboration of a declaration on this subject, some states expressed reservations. From a legal point of view, two questions deserve special attention. Is a right to peace a new right? What is the legal content of this right?

The human right to peace may be seen, not as a completely new right, but rather as the development of Article 3 of the Universal Declaration of Human Rights: 'Everyone has the right to life, liberty and security of person'. It is already formulated in a number of international instruments which, however, are of a non-binding character and have to be qualified as so-called 'soft law'.[22]

In 1969, the Istanbul Declaration, adopted during the 21st International Conference of the Red Cross, proclaimed the right to lasting peace as a human right. In 1976, the right to life in peace was recognized as a human right by resolution 5/XXXII of the Commission on Human Rights. In 1978, the General Assembly adopted resolution 33/73 on the preparation of societies for life in peace which provides: '1. Every nation and every human being, regardless of race, conscience, language or sex, has the inherent right to life in peace. Respect for that right, as well as for the other human rights, is in the common interest of all mankind and an indispensable condition of advancement of all nations, large and small, in all fields'.

The Declaration of Principles on Tolerance, adopted by the General Conference of UNESCO in 1995, in Article 1, paragraph 1, states that human beings 'have the right to live in peace and to be as they are'. It is true, however, that none of these instruments was entirely devoted to the elaboration of the right to peace.

The legal content of the human right to peace is determined by a number of already existing human rights whose implementation has direct impact on the maintenance of peace and the prevention of conflicts and violence. This applies to freedom of thought, conscience and religion, including the right to have conscientious objections to military service, freedom of opinion and expression, freedom of peaceful assembly and association and the right of everyone to take part in the government of his country. Among duties of states formulated, *expressis verbis*, in human rights instruments, prohibition by law of any propaganda for war and any advocacy of national, racial or religious hatred that constitutes incitement to discrimination, hostility or violence deserves particular mention (Article 20 of the International Covenant on Civil and Political Rights). States also have the duty to educate for peace. As formulated by paragraph 2 of Article 26 of the Universal Declaration of Human Rights, 'Education [...] shall promote understanding, tolerance and friendship among all nations, racial or religious groups, and shall further the activities of the United Nations for the maintenance of peace'. This obligation is repeated in Article 4 of the Convention against Discrimination in Education (1960), in Article 13 of the International Covenant on Economic, Social and Cultural Rights and in Article 29 of the Convention on the Rights of the Child.[23]

The human right to peace may be seen as an autonomous right but, at the same time, as a common denominator of a number of already existing human rights.[24] The debate concerning the human right to peace is not yet finished. The UNESCO General Conference asked the Director-General to convene an intergovernmental consultation in 1998 to reflect further on this subject.

Obstacles and Threats to Human Rights

Extreme Poverty and Exclusion: a Violation of Human Dignity

Although poverty has been reduced in many parts of the world, a quarter of the world's population remains in severe poverty. This, in a global economy of US$25 trillion, 'is a scandal – reflecting shameful inequalities and inexcusable failures of national and international policy'.[25] About 1.3 billion people live on incomes of less than US$1 a day. Nearly a billion people are illiterate. More than a billion lack access to safe water and over 800 million go hungry or face food insecurity. Poverty may then be described as a denial of chances to lead healthy, creative and long lives and to enjoy a decent standard of living, freedom and dignity.

The rise of poverty in regions where it had long been in decline, in the industrial countries of Western and, particularly, Eastern Europe, together with the persistence and constant worsening of the problem in parts of the developing world like sub-Saharan Africa, has brought poverty to the forefront of the international agenda.

The World Summit for Social Development (1995) recognized the goal of eradicating poverty as an ethical, social, political and moral imperative of humankind. The General Assembly declared 17 October the International Day for the Eradication of Poverty; it then proclaimed 1996 the International Year for the Eradication of Poverty and the years 1997–2006 as the United Nations Decade for the Eradication of Poverty.[26]

In the 1990s, in parallel with the international debate on the eradication of poverty, the United Nations system placed on its agenda the question of human rights and extreme poverty. The Commission on Human Rights requested in 1990 that the Sub-Commission on Prevention of Discrimination and Protection of Minorities carry out a study on extreme poverty and social exclusion. In 1992, L. Despouy was appointed special rapporteur on this question.

The Vienna Declaration, in its paragraph 2, affirmed that 'extreme poverty and social exclusion constitute a violation of human dignity'. It stressed the need to achieve better knowledge of extreme poverty and its causes in order to promote the human rights of the poorest people, and to foster their participation in the decision-making process by the community in which they live.

The General Assembly, in a series of resolutions on human rights and extreme poverty, reaffirmed that extreme poverty and social exclusion constituted a violation of human dignity and that urgent national and international action is required to eliminate them. In resolution 51/97 of 12 September 1996, it recognized that widespread extreme poverty inhibits the full and effective enjoyment of human rights and might, in some situations, constitute a threat to the right to life. The General Assembly also welcomed the final report on the question of human rights and extreme poverty presented by the special rapporteur.[27]

First of all, poverty affects economic, social and cultural rights, as it is in contradiction with the right of everyone to a standard of living adequate for the health and well-being of himself and of his family. It also contradicts the ideal of free human beings enjoying freedom from fear and want, as established in the Universal Declaration of Human Rights and the International Covenants on Human Rights. This can be achieved only if conditions are created whereby all human beings may enjoy their economic, social and cultural rights, as well as their civil and political rights. It means that treaty bodies monitoring the application of human rights instruments, as well as the High Commissioner for Human Rights, should in their activities take into account the question of extreme poverty.[28]

In Chapter 6, L.E. Pettiti and P. Meyer-Bisch write that too little attention has been paid to poverty in the logic of human rights because: 'a poor person hardly exists and can only lay claim, modestly, to "poor" rights'. Human rights instruments only indirectly refer to protection from poverty. They underline that poverty renders all human rights inoperative. To follow a new impetus created by Copenhagen, there is a need for a comprehensive approach and partnership of all debtors for the elimination of poverty.

Discrimination and Intolerance: Violation of Human Rights, Sources of Conflicts and Threats to Peace and Stability

All human beings, as stipulated by Article 7 of the Universal Declaration of Human Rights: 'are equal before the law and are entitled *without any discrimination* [emphasis added] to equal protection of the law'. Discrimination is the very negation of the principle of equality and an affront to human dignity.

The Charter of the United Nations, in Articles 1, 55 and 75, speaks three times about 'respect for human rights and for fundamental freedoms *for all without distinction* [emphasis added] as to race, sex, language or religion'. Article 2 of the International Covenant on Civil and Political Rights obliges the states parties to ensure the rights of all individuals 'without distinction of any kind, such as race, colour, sex, language, religion, political or other opinion, national or social origin, property, birth or other status'. Neither the Universal Declaration of Human Rights nor the International Covenants define 'discrimination'. A definition of this term can only be found in conventions and declarations dealing with specific types or forms of discrimination.[29]

During its 37th session in 1989, the Human Rights Committee in its general comment gave the following definition of the discrimination:

> any distinction, exclusion, restriction or preference which is based on any ground such as race, colour, sex, language, religion, political or other opinion, national or social origin, property, birth or other status, and which has the purpose or effect of nullifying or impairing the recognition, enjoyment or exercise by all persons, on an equal footing, of all rights and freedoms.[30]

The prohibition of discrimination is formulated at present not only in the Charter of the United Nations and the International Bill of Human Rights but also in the impressive number of instruments dealing with discrimination on specific grounds or directed against persons belonging to vulnerable groups, adopted by the United Nations, the International Labour Organization (ILO) and UNESCO.[31] Standards concerning non-discrimination can also be found in a series of instruments adopted by regional organizations.[32]

Implementation of conventional provisions imposing obligations on states is subject to control and verification procedures based on periodic state reports and also providing, as in the case of the International Covenant on Civil and Political Rights and the International Convention on the Elimination of All Forms of Racial Discrimination, the possibility of individual communications. The treaty bodies, that is the Human Rights Committee, the Committee on Economic, Social and Cultural Rights, the Committee on the Elimination of Racial Discrimination and the Committee on the Elimination of Discrimination Against Women, are authorized not only to consider state reports but also to formulate general recommendations.

Since 1946, all the United Nations organs dealing with human rights have been actively involved in the struggle against discrimination. Questions linked with the elimination of discrimination are permanently dealt with by the General Assembly, the Economic and Social Council, the Commission on Human Rights and the Sub-Commission on Prevention of Discrimination and Protection of Minorities. The Sub-Commission carries out studies whose aim is to ban discrimination. These studies are related, amongst others, to the right to education, the exercise of political rights, discrimination based on religion or beliefs, the elimination of racial discrimination and the rights of minorities and indigenous peoples.

The legal and administrative means against discrimination including penal sanctions, though no doubt very important for the elimination and prevention of discrimination, are not sufficient. Therefore standard-setting instruments also call for a change in traditional practices, the elimination of stereotypes and the use of education and the mass media in the struggle against discrimination. Although the duty to combat all forms of discrimination is first of all imposed on and undertaken by states, the importance of participation of the United Nations system, regional organizations, national and international non-governmental organizations, all parts of civil society, and individuals in the struggle against discrimination cannot be overlooked.

The progress achieved in the development of international protection against discrimination does not mean that this system as a whole is already fully satisfactory. The advancement of standards prohibiting discrimination of persons belonging to various vulnerable groups is uneven. In some cases the prohibition is established by conventions, in others by non-binding declarations. There are also vulnerable groups such as indigenous people or people with HIV/AIDS who are not protected by any specific instruments. The effectiveness of even the most advanced protection based on conventions is diminished by the fact that they are not ratified by all states, and that, at the moment of ratification or accession, many states parties have deposited reservations. Therefore, in the light of these remarks, a call for further development of anti-discriminatory law seems to be fully justified.

Discrimination and intolerance go hand in hand. In order to renew action for the promotion of tolerance, the General Assembly, at the initiative of UNESCO, proclaimed 1995 the United Nations Year for Tolerance and requested UNESCO to prepare for the conclusion of the Year a declaration of principles and a programme of action as a follow-up to it.

The Declaration of Principles on Tolerance, foreseen by a General Assembly resolution, was adopted by the General Conference of UNESCO at its 28th session in 1995. In Article 1, it explains:

Tolerance is respect, acceptance and appreciation of the rich diversity of our world's cultures, our forms of expression and ways of being human [...] Tolerance is harmony in difference. It is not only a moral duty, it is also a political and legal requirement.

C. Zanghi, in Chapter 8, analyses the very concept of tolerance, its historical development as well as contemporary manifestations of intolerance. He stresses that tolerance is an element of paramount importance for all democratic societies and an essential precondition for the respect of human rights.

The struggle for the elimination of all forms of discrimination and intolerance conducted by the United Nations system from the moment of its creation is a very important element in the efforts of the international community to ensure full implementation and observance of human rights. Discrimination, violation of rights of persons belonging to vulnerable groups (women, minorities, indigenous people, refugees, migrant workers and aliens) should also be seen as the cause of serious conflicts and danger for international and internal peace and stability.

The struggle against all forms of discrimination and intolerance is still far from being won. In the conclusion of Chapter 7, R. Wolfrum states that international efforts against them, with the exception of the struggle against apartheid, have so far not been successful. New forms of racism, racial discrimination and ethnic prejudice or persecution have increased. In a situation where the international community is witnessing a mounting wave of racism, xenophobia, ethnonationalism, anti-semitism and intolerance, the need to increase by all possible means the efforts of the United Nations system and regional organizations to combat all forms of discrimination and intolerance is more than evident.

Terrorism, Organized Crime and Corruption: Threats to Human Rights, Democracy and Peace

Terrorism Terrorism is not a new phenomenon in international relations. The rise of terrorist practices in the nineteenth and twentieth centuries made evident the need for international cooperation to combat it. The first step was undertaken by the League of Nations which, in 1937, adopted a special convention aimed at the punishment and prevention of terrorism. Though the convention did not enter into force, it played an important role in the condemnation of terrorism, qualifying it as an international crime.

After the Second World War, in the early 1970s, the General Assembly became preoccupied with the question of terrorism, which was included in the agenda of its 27th session in 1972 and which led to the establishment of an Ad Hoc Committee. The General Assembly examined the report of this Committee during its 34th session and, in resolution 34/145 of 17 December 1979, condemned all acts of international terrorism which endangered or took human lives or jeopardized fundamental freedoms. Since that time, the United Nations has adopted a number of resolutions which qualified as criminal and unjustifiable all acts, methods and practices of terrorism whenever and by whomever committed.

The direct linkage between terrorism and violations of human rights was recognized by the World Conference on Human Rights (Vienna, 1993). The Vienna Declaration and Programme of Action, in its paragraph 17, stipulates:

> The acts, methods and practices of terrorism in all its forms and manifestations as well as linkage in some countries to drug trafficking are activities aimed at the destruction of human rights, fundamental freedoms and democracy, threatening territorial integrity, security of States and destabilising legitimately constituted Governments.

The resolutions on 'Human Rights and Terrorism', adopted by the General Assembly after the Vienna Conference of 1993,[33] expressed serious concern at the gross violations of human rights perpetrated by terrorist groups. The same concern was articulated in the series of resolutions adopted by the Commission on Human Rights and its Sub-Commission on Prevention of Discrimination and Protection of Minorities which these two bodies have adopted since 1994.

As stated by K. Koufa in the working paper on terrorism and human rights, submitted in accordance with the Sub-Commission resolution 1996/20, terrorist acts and methods abuse the human rights of the victims and, at the same time, they provide or give an excuse for serious violations of human rights and fundamental freedoms by governments which feel threatened by terrorism.[34] There is a link between terrorism and human rights violations. Terrorism provides a severe test for the ideal of fundamental rights. It is a clear threat to the life and dignity of the individual.

The analysis of statements during debates on this subject in the General Assembly, the Commission on Human Rights and the Sub-Commission reveals the existence of conflicting views and interpretations, not only concerning the very notion or definition of terrorism but also with regard to the dividing lines between terrorism and guerrilla warfare, between nationalists and 'pure' terrorists.[35]

In Chapter 9, C. Warbrick presents the difficulties with regard to the definition of terrorism. He emphasizes that the law of human rights gives no authority to individuals to use violence against the government of a state; therefore those who resort to violence violate the human rights of their victims. At the same time, terrorism presents a serious test for those states committed to the ideals of human rights.

Organized crime   Terrorism is often linked with transnational organized crime. In 1996, the Commission on Crime Prevention and Criminal Justice established an open-ended working group to explore the links between transnational organized crime and terrorist criminal activities: a combination viewed as 'a severe threat to peace and development'. The General Assembly adopted during its 51st session the United Nations Declaration on Crime and Public Security, which states that Member States shall seek to protect the security and well-being of their citizens and all persons within their jurisdiction by taking effective national measures to combat serious transnational crime, including organized crime. They shall promote bilateral, regional, multilateral and global enforcement cooperation.

All illegal activities conducted by organized crime, such as drug trafficking or money laundering, have a bearing on human beings and societies. However, among those calling for special attention from a human rights point of view are the smuggling of migrants, trafficking in women and children. The smuggling of illegal migrants leads to various incidents of racist and xenophobic character, as well as criminal acts against them. The General Assembly[36] condemned the practice of smuggling aliens, and recognized that this practice contributes to the complexity of current international migration. It reaffirmed the need to observe fully international and national law in dealing with the smuggling of aliens, including the provisions of human treatment and strict observance of all the human rights of migrants.

Traffic in women for sexual exploitation is a distinct manifestation of violence inflicted upon women and a modern form of slavery. It entails violations of fundamental human rights. This phenomenon has gained momentum and intensity, *inter alia*, with the increasing flows of population between Central and Eastern Europe, on the one hand, and the rest of Europe, on the other. The Council of Europe has, through the work of a group of specialists, identified the most urgent areas for actors in this field. The Ninth Congress on the Prevention of Crime and the Treatment of Offenders, which took place in Cairo in 1995, placed violence against women among its topics.

Sexual exploitation of children has become another important point in the international debate. It has been discussed in the Commission on Crime Prevention and the Commission on Human Rights has already begun to draft an Optional Protocol to the Convention on the Rights of the Child dealing with the sale of children, child prostitution and child pornography, as well as the basic measures needed for their prevention and eradication. For this purpose, a special open-ended intersessional working group of the Commission was created.[37]

Corruption   Another threat to democracy, the rule of law and human rights is linked with corruption. It occurs throughout the world in old but also in new and restored democracies. With systemic corruption, social, economic and political development is endangered and can only have negative consequences for social justice and human rights. Corruption in the 1990s has become subject to the attention of international and regional organizations. It was put on the agenda of the United Nations, the Organization of American States, the Organization for Economic Cooperation and Development (which adopted a Declaration on this subject in December 1997), the European Community and the Council of Europe.

The General Assembly, as well as the Economic and Social Council, adopted a series of resolutions on this matter.[38] The General Assembly pointed to the links between corruption and other forms of crime, in particular organized crime, and stressed that, as this phenomenon crosses national borders and affects all societies and economies, international cooperation to prevent and control it is essential.[39] It also adopted an International Code of Conduct for Public Officials which is based on the assumption that a public office, as defined by national law, is a position of trust, implying a duty to act in the public interest. The Code sets global standards for good governance. It emphasizes the duty of public officials to refrain from using 'their official authority for the improper advancement of their own and their family's personal or financial interests' and calls for new requirements to disclose personal assets and liabilities. The General Assembly also addressed a particularly pernicious type of corruption – bribery in international business transactions which leads to the perpetuation by the industrial countries of the climate of corruption in the developing world.

What are the structural and cultural factors that facilitate corruption? How can it be effectively prevented and fought? What is its impact on human rights? These questions are now raised by non-governmental organizations and the human rights community.[40]

New Challenges of Science and Technology

At the dawn of the twenty-first century, the breathtaking advances of science and its applications raise serious questions concerning its impact on human rights, on human dignity and integrity. These questions have been tackled in human rights instruments from a positive point of view. As proclaimed by the Universal Declaration of Human

Rights (Article 27): 'Everyone has the right [...] to share in scientific advancement and its benefits.' The International Covenant on Economic, Social and Cultural Rights (Article 15) confirms the right of everyone to enjoy the benefits of scientific progress and its applications, adding that full realization of this right should include 'the development and diffusion of science' by the States Parties as well as respect for 'the freedom indispensable for scientific research'.

The question of the possible positive and negative effects of scientific and technological developments upon the enjoyment of human rights and fundamental freedoms was for the first time discussed in greater detail during the Tehran International Conference on Human Rights.

In the first half of the 1970s, the Secretary-General and the Specialized Agencies presented a series of reports on the positive and negative consequences of scientific and technological developments for human rights.[41] Consideration of these reports prepared the ground for the elaboration of a draft instrument designed to strengthen respect for human rights in the light of developments in science and technology. In November 1975, the General Assembly proclaimed the Declaration on the Use of Scientific and Technological Progress in the Interests of Peace and for the Benefit of Mankind. Despite repeated calls by the United Nations for measures to be applied by states and international organizations to ensure that scientific and technological developments are utilized exclusively for the reinforcement and not the endangering of human rights, the situation cannot be seen as fully satisfying.

As argued in Chapter 10 of this volume by C.G. Weeramantry, in his reflection on human rights and scientific and technological progress, the protection of the human body, human society and the human environment from the dangers created by modern technology can only be found in a holistic approach. Neither domestic nor international law alone can provide a satisfactory response to the technological challenges which pose grave new problems for both systems. There is an urgent need for an ethical code for scientists as well as the preparation, through education, of future lawyers and specialists in the life sciences. Courses on technology should be supplemented by the relevant human rights perspectives. Weeramantry stresses that, though the development of science cannot be halted, the areas of conscious choice are still available.

By the end of the twentieth century, thanks to the progress of science and technology, people have the possibility to live a better and longer life. They can use modern technologies to protect and even improve their health. They can have access to all kinds of information and data. They may, but this does not mean all of them, have or be able to utilize all these possibilities.

Though progress can be observed in all areas of science and technology, it is uneven and its impact on human rights also differs. As stated by the Vienna Declaration:

> certain advances, notably in the biomedical and life sciences, as well as in information technology, may have potentially adverse consequences for the integrity, dignity and human rights of the individual, and call for international co-operation to ensure that human rights and dignity are fully respected in these areas of universal concern.[42]

Biotechnology and Human Rights

The enormous and rapid developments in biotechnology and genetic engineering, sometimes qualified as a prerequisite for a 'third industrial revolution', have a profound impact on human rights. The progress of biomedical technology in many spheres is linked with, in particular, the transplantation of adult and foetal organs, tissues and reproductive technology.

The donation or selling of such organic materials as blood and sperm has been practised for a long time. A new, remarkable chapter in the development of medicine is linked with the transplantation of human organs. Major medical centres, mainly in the industrialized countries, carry out on a routine basis kidney, heart, liver, heart–lung or pancreas transplants. Organs and tissues used for transplantation are taken either from living persons, dead adults or foetal cadavers. This raises a number of questions linked with human rights, such as consent for the donation and transplantation, respect for the bodies of dead persons, conservation of organs and tissues, definition of death posed by the danger of premature 'harvesting' of organs which could be qualified as murder,[43] and equality of chances for a transplantation.

The progress in reproductive technology, apart from artificial insemination which has been long applied in clinical medicine as well as contraceptive technology, now embraces a wide range of non-coital reproductive methods such as the use of surrogate mothers and *in vitro* fertilization with the implantation of the embryo. New reproductive technology is giving women the freedom of personal fertility control. However, the fact that new techniques are far from being applied on a massive scale raises the question of equality. Reproductive problems of poor and disadvantaged women have not been changed by technological progress.

New technologies lead to legal and ethical debate concerning, *inter alia*, parenthood, legal identity, the rights of children born through non-coital methods, and qualifications and rights to be parents. The approach to these questions differs and is determined in various countries by cultural and religious traditions.

Genetic Engineering

Genetic engineering, which may be defined as the method of changing the inherited characteristics of an organism in a predetermined way by altering its genetic material, has a great therapeutic potential, enabling the correction of a genetic disorder or acquired disease. The analysis of a genetic code allows the prediction of the life course or degenerative brain disease and may be used in forensic medicine to identify paternity, or suspects in criminal cases. Genetic manipulation allows the use of bacteria to produce certain so-called 'recombinant' substances like growth hormones, insulin or blood clotting agent Factor VIII, so important in the treatment of diabetes and haemophilia. It also opens up possibilities to create new genetically modified plants which are more productive or resistant.

With all its positive consequences, genetic engineering raises a number of serious ethical and human rights questions. Should the alteration of germ cells which results in a permanent genetic change for the whole organism and subsequent generations be allowed? Does the reproduction of a clone organism from an individual gene, successfully used to produce mice and sheep, be allowed in the case of human beings? How to eliminate the creation of 'humanoids' (human inter-species hybrids)?[44] These questions touch the very essence of being 'human', of the dignity and integrity of the human person.

The progress of biotechnology and, in particular, genetics leads to public concern stemming from misconceptions about the nature and uses of genetic technology. This leads to requests for the limitation of research in these fields. The possible dangers of new research in this field must be weighed against the heavy costs of suffering being borne at present.[45] To attain the right levels of physical and mental health is an important human right which cannot be fully implemented without scientific progress.

However, freedom of research cannot be absolute and, if necessary, may be circumscribed. Such a necessity arises when research violates respect for human dignity which is at the basis of all human rights, including the right to scientific research. In the field of human genetics, it has already been recognized in the case of cloning of human beings.[46] Another field in which research should be limited is the creation of new biological genetic weapons.[47]

The fact that it is almost impossible to predict all conceivable outcomes of research, as even well-intended and carefully planned research may have unforeseen adverse side-effects, justifies calls for vigilance. This is particularly true of applications of unchecked biotechnologies and the introduction into the environment of new genetically modified organisms. Therefore, in the light of the rapidity of biotechnological advances, 'biovigilance', respect for the principles of bioethics, for ethical sensitivity in policy making and for raising of public awareness have become today an absolute necessity.

Bioethics

The advances in biology, medicine and genetics, and the need to provide ethical and legal guidance to prevent abuses so as to ensure that scientific and technological progress is in the service of humanity and does not encroach on human rights and fundamental freedoms have led to the development of bioethics. Bioethics takes into account the right of everyone to the enjoyment of the highest obtainable standard of physical and mental health, as well as the requirement formulated in Article 7 of the International Covenant on Civil and Political Rights that 'No one shall be subjected to torture or to cruel, inhuman or degrading treatment or punishment. In particular, no one shall be subjected without his free consent to medical or scientific experiment.'

Bioethics is developed on both national and international levels. In many countries, special national ethical committees have been created to advise, to consult and to prepare legislation on this subject.[48] On the international level, the group of advisers for ethics of biotechnology was established by the European Commission, and the International Bioethics Committee was created by UNESCO.[49] The Commission on Human Rights in its resolution 1995/82 on human rights and bioethics underlined the need to develop a life sciences ethic at the national and international levels, as well as the need for international cooperation in order to ensure that humankind as a whole benefits from the life sciences.

As requested by the General Assembly, codes of medical ethics were formulated by the Council for International Organizations of Medical Sciences (CIOMS) and endorsed by the World Health Organization (WHO). Together with CIOMS, WHO also prepared and published in 1982 the International Guidelines for Biomedical Research Involving Human Subjects. In 1991, the 44th World Health Assembly endorsed a set of guiding principles on human organ transplantation.

An active role in the promotion of bioethics is played at the regional level by the European Union and the Council of Europe.[50] In 1996, the Committee of Ministers of the Council of Europe adopted the Convention for the Protection of Human Rights and Dignity of the Human Being with Regard to the Application of Biology and Medicine. In Article 2, it provides that the interests and welfare of the human being shall prevail over the sole interest of society or science. Any intervention in the health field, including research, must be carried out in accordance with relevant professional obligations and standards. Among the principles of bioethics enumerated and elaborated in the Convention there are, *inter alia*, the requirement of free and informed consent by the person concerned to any intervention in the health field; the right to respect for private life; the principle that removal of organs or tissue from a living person for transplantation purposes may be carried out solely for the therapeutic benefit of the recipient; and the prohibition of financial gain from the human body and its parts.

The Human Genome

In its activities concerning bioethics, UNESCO has attached special attention to the human genome. On 10 November 1997, the UNESCO General Conference adopted by consensus a Universal Declaration on the Human Genome and Human Rights.[51]

The Declaration, the result of four years of deliberations and work of the UNESCO International Bioethics Committee, provides an answer to several ethical and legal concerns linked, in particular, with the threat that research on the human genome may open the door to dangerous deviations contrary to human dignity and fundamental human rights. It establishes limits on interventions in the genetic heritage of humanity and in individuals which the international community has a moral obligation not to transgress.

Among the rights of individuals, the Declaration enumerates the following: prior consent to all research, treatment or diagnosis;[52] prohibition of any discrimination based on individual characteristics; confidentiality of genetic information associated with an identifiable person; and the right to 'just reparation' for damage sustained as a direct result of an intervention affecting an individual's genome.

With regard to the crucial question of research on the human genome, it takes a balanced position, underlining that, on the one hand, no research or application concerning the human genome in biology, genetics and medicine should prevail over the respect for human rights, fundamental freedoms and human dignity. It states, on the other, that freedom of research, which is necessary to the progress of knowledge, is part of freedom of thought. However, certain practices, as stated in Article 11, contrary to human dignity, such as reproductive cloning of human beings, shall not be permitted. States, as provided by the Declaration,[53] should respect and promote solidarity towards individuals, families and population groups who are particularly vulnerable to or affected by disease or disability of a genetic character.

*The Challenges of New Information and Communication Technology
(ICT): the Information Highways*

What are the key components of the new information technology? In
general, it is the transmission of signals in a digital mode instead of
an analogical one. New technologies allow the compression of signals which enhances immensely the capacity to store, retrieve and
transmit rapidly over large distances vast amounts of information:
text, images and sound. The central component of this communication revolution is the computer married to television and
telecommunications. This marriage has given birth to the information highways: the Internet. The new information technology has
already had a profound impact on human beings, civil societies,
states and international organizations. These changes are characterized by the use of a new term, 'the emerging global information
society'. This term articulates the fact that now many areas of economic, social, cultural and political activities are influenced and
permeated by new information technologies. In the economy,
teleservices, teleshopping, telebanking, telecommuting, various data
banks and websites change traditional management (organization of
companies and banks and their *modus operandi*). The information and
communication sector is expanding at twice the rate of the world
economy.[54]

The new information technologies have a rather positive impact
on human rights. Thus interactive long-distance education and learning can strengthen the right to education and enables reaching out
and delivering education services to people in isolated countries and
localities, to provide quality education and create lifelong learning
opportunities for all, which otherwise would not be possible.

The right to participate in cultural life acquires a new dimension
with the possibility of easy access to the world cultural heritage, the
possibility of visiting, through the Internet or CD-ROM, the most
prestigious museums and exhibitions or to attend concerts of the
best orchestras and conductors. The right to benefit from scientific
progress is reinforced by rapid access to the latest results of research,
to libraries located in other countries and regions, to scientific publications and periodicals.

The information highways can bring positive results only when
they are accessible. At present the gap and inequalities between industrialized and developing countries are widening. A new type of
exclusion and poverty, information exclusion and poverty, can be
noted. Access to the Internet depends on the availability of electricity
and the existence of a telecommunication network. How can inhabit-
ants of millions of small African, Asian or Latin American villages
without electricity use computers? The dividing line between infor-

mation haves and have-nots may also be observed within states. It runs between those who can afford the cost of access and those who cannot. To ensure the participation of all states in the emerging information society, the democratization of access to new information technology is an enormous challenge for the United Nations system and for the whole international society in the next century.

Among human rights which are endangered in cyberspace are the right to privacy and the right to the protection of the moral and material interests resulting from any scientific, literary or artistic production. Computer memories contain impressive amounts of the most personal data concerning finance, health, family relations, work and career records, and so on. More data, including electronic mail, may be exposed or misused. Protection of electronic privacy and confidentiality becomes one of the most pressing requirements.

Another problem is linked to electronic piracy and the violation of the rights and interests of copyright holders. The development of information networks and digital highways requires, on the one hand, protection against unauthorized exploitation and, on the other, the facilitation of legitimate exploitation. There is also a need to achieve a balance between the interests of copyright holders and those of the public. New intellectual property rights concerning databases also await regulation.

The use of the Internet for the dissemination of pornography by paedophiles, for the advocacy of racism, xenophobia and violence raises a number of ethical and legal questions concerning the limits to the freedom of information and expression. Some countries have introduced prior registration of users, some filter rigorously the flow of data accessible to their citizens. In 1996, the United States adopted the Communications Decency Act which foresees punishment of up to two years' imprisonment and heavy fines for posting 'indecent' information on a website.

Should the Internet fall under the law of the press and mass media, or should it be governed by laws regulating private correspondence? Is cyberspace a private or a public area? Is state control and censorship justified? It seems that, in many countries, already existing legislation concerning the struggle against racism and paedophilia permits reaction to and evaluation of individual responsibilities as well as punishment for acts prohibited by law. There is no need for state censorship and preventive control. Freedom of expression and information should be a guiding principle for the Internet. This is the most effective guarantee of cultural and linguistic pluralism and diversity. Therefore the free flow of information should be fully preserved and defended.[55]

Exchange of opinions, reflection and dialogue on major ethical, legal and societal problems posed by cyberspace can gradually lead

to international consensus and agreement, without which any effective regulation will be impossible. A right step in this direction was
made by the International Congress on Ethical, Legal and Societal
Aspects of Digital Information (INFO-ETHICS) held in Monaco in
March 1997.[56] To facilitate the consultative process, UNESCO proposed the creation of a World Commission on the Ethics of Scientific
Knowledge and Technologies.

Universality of Human Rights versus Cultural Relativism

In recent debates concerning human rights, cultural relativism is
presented as a main challenge to their universality. As observed by
Z. Brzezinski:

> culture is now going to be the dividing line in the debate over the
> question of freedom and the question of human rights. We are all
> familiar with the cultural argument. It rejects the notion of inalienable
> human rights on the grounds that this notion merely reflects a very
> provincial, Western perspective.[57]

He adds that cultural relativism regarding human rights and democracy is self-defeating, parochial and just plain wrong.

The acceptance of the very idea that persons belonging to one
culture should not judge the policies and values of other cultures,
that any system of common values cannot and does not exist, indeed
undermines the very basis of the international community and the
'human family'. They cannot function without the existence of standards allowing them to judge what is right or wrong, what is good or
bad.

The World Commission on Culture and Development in its report,
Our Creative Diversity, pointed out that the logical and ethical difficulty about relativism is that it must also endorse absolutism and
dogmatism. Cognitive relativism is nonsense, moral relativism is
tragic.[58] An assertion of absolute standards is a condition *sine qua non*
of reasoned discourse concerning a code of conduct or behaviour.

Cultural relativism in its extreme interpretations may even lead to
or justify theories like that on 'conflict of civilizations' put forward
by S. Huntington. In his opinion, the globalization of the modern
world has given rise to a conflict between the basic cultural systems.
The theory of the beginning of an age of irreconcilable battles between the most powerful civilizations does not correspond to reality.
It can be rather seen, as stated by Al-Hassan bin Talal, as an attempt
to create or invent a new arch-enemy after the Cold War which could
justify huge defence budgets.[59] Cultural diversity and plurality of

cultures have to be seen as positive factors leading to intercultural dialogue. In the modern world, cultures are not isolated. They inter-act peacefully and influence each other. The intercultural dynamics is set in motion by the contemporary processes of globalization which lead, not without tension, to the emergence, consolidation or refor-mulation of specific cultural and ethical values common to the various cultural areas. Any culture in relation to and comparison with other cultures may find its own idiosyncrasies and peculiarities, its strong and its weak points.

The Rejection of Cultural Relativism by the Vienna Conference

The question of the universality of human rights was discussed dur-ing the World Conference on Human Rights (1993), an exchange of views on this subject having already taken place during its prepara-tory meetings. The African states in the Tunis Declaration, adopted in November 1992,[60] stressed that 'the universal nature of human rights is beyond question', adding however that 'no ready-made model can be presented at the universal level since the historical and cultural realities of each nation and the traditions, standards and values of each people cannot be disregarded'.

The Asian states, in the Bangladesh Declaration of April 1993,[61] underlined: 'While human rights are universal in nature, they must be considered in the context of a dynamic and evolving process of international norm-setting, bearing in mind the significance of na-tional and regional particularities and various historical, cultural and religious backgrounds.'

The analysis of statements during the Vienna Conference shows that the universality of human rights was not openly challenged, whereas cultural relativism was in fact rejected. Universality and cultural specificity were seen by many states as being fully compat-ible notions.

The delegation of Tunisia, recognizing the universal values of hu-man rights, then qualified them as a common heritage of different religions and cultures of humanity. As observed by Kuwait, all hu-mans are equal on the basis of their humanity. States stressed not only the absence of any contradictions but also the importance which Islam attaches to the universality of human rights.

In order to clarify the position of the signatories of the Bangkok Declaration, Indonesia stated: 'we have not come to Vienna [...] to advocate an alternative concept of human rights, based on some nebulous notion of "cultural relativism", as spuriously alleged by some quarters'.[62]

A similar position was taken by Iran:

Human rights are no doubt universal. They are inherent in human beings, endowed in them by the sole Creator. As such, they cannot be subject to cultural relativism. However, drawing from the richness and experience of all cultures, and particularly those based on divine religions [...] would only serve to enrich human rights concepts.[63]

The delegation of Viet Nam observed: 'Human rights are at the same time an absolute yardstick of a universal nature and a synthesis resulting from a long historical process [...] universality and specificity are two organic interrelated aspects of human rights, which do not exclude each other but co-exist and interact.'[64]

From the point of view of the universality of human rights, the most challenging statement was probably that of China:

Countries of different development stages or with different historical traditions and cultural backgrounds also have a different understanding and practice of human rights. Thus, one should not and cannot think the human rights standard and model of certain countries as the only proper ones and demand all other countries to comply with them.[65]

This was balanced, however, by the assurance that the Chinese government complies with the principles formulated in the UN Charter and the Universal Declaration of Human Rights.

The request to take into account national and regional, cultural or religious particularities has been subject to criticism. Several states, for example, Costa Rica, expressed their preoccupation with the possible adverse impact this request may have on the universality of human rights. As stated by the Netherlands, 'the Bangladesh Declaration governments have accepted a formula which seems to depart from the idea of inalienable rights'.[66]

The Vienna Declaration adopted by consensus by the World Conference *confirmed the universality of human rights and rejected the notion of cultural relativism.* The Declaration, in its paragraph 1, reaffirms the solemn commitment of all states to fulfil their obligations to promote universal respect for and observance and protection of all human rights and fundamental freedoms for all. It stressed that 'The universal nature of these rights and freedoms is beyond question'.

The problem of national and regional peculiarities is referred to in paragraph 5 of the Declaration, which provides:

All human rights are universal, indivisible and interdependent and interrelated [...] While the significance of national and regional particularities and various historical, cultural and religious backgrounds must be borne in mind, it is the duty of States, regardless of their political, economic and cultural systems, to promote and protect all human rights and fundamental freedoms.

The mention of particularities and various historical, cultural and religious backgrounds is sometimes interpreted as a sort of escape clause, as an argument for not (yet) complying with human rights standards.[67] This understanding of paragraph 5 does not take into account the last part of the formulation which underlines that states are duty-bound, regardless of their political, economic and cultural systems, to promote and protect all human rights. In line with this formulation, cultural specificities should be taken into account in the promotion and protection of human rights, therefore they should rather help to determine the most effective modalities and ways and means to overcome difficulties in the implementation of human rights and fundamental freedoms.

The results of the Vienna Conference confirm that cultural relativism is in retreat on many fronts.[68] This is important not only for the debate concerning the universality of human rights but also in a more general context for international relations. Rejecting cultural relativism and recognizing at the same time the significance of cultural specificities, the Vienna Conference intensified the discussion concerning relations between cultural values and human rights. This has been articulated, in particular, in the debate concerning the so-called 'Asian values'. Begun by the already mentioned Bangkok Declaration of 1993, animated by declarations and statements of the governments of China, Malaysia, Indonesia and Singapore, the debate quickly surpassed the governmental level and is now conducted at various seminars and in specialized literature.[69]

In the debate concerning Asian values there are various emphases and approaches. Thus for Asian governments the existence of specific values in this region resulting from special historical circumstances justifies adopting an understanding of human rights and democracy which is different from that prevailing in the West. This position has been strongly criticized by various governments, non-governmental organizations and activists (also from Asia) as an excuse for gross violations of human rights. At the end of the twentieth century, human rights cannot be seen as a 'Western product'; they were developed by and belong to the whole international community.

Though the very existence of common values in a region of so many religious traditions and languages, and of different political and economic systems, as well as the existence of any culture in a pure distinctive form, either Western or Asian (in fact all societies are multicultural and pluralistic) can be challenged, certain differences in the system of values can be traced.[70]

Are Asian values, such as respect for tradition and the elderly, strong family ties and communitarianism, and emphasis on duties and responsibilities, compatible with human rights? The answer must be in the positive. There is no contradiction between them. This being so, what then are those specific elements of Western human rights tradition which, from an Asian point of view, should not be a part of the universal concept of human rights? The West is accused of eccentric individualism, consumerism, drug addiction and violent crimes. However, neither human rights nor democracy may be blamed or are responsible for these ills, resulting from the erosive forces of the market economy and industrialization. To the contrary, the solutions may be found, not in the establishment of authoritarian governments, but by the achievement of a proper balance between the free market, individuals, society and a democratic state of law.

The existence of cultural differences should not lead to the rejection of any part of universal human rights. They cannot justify the rejection or non-observance of such fundamental principles as the principle of equality between women and men. Traditional practices which contradict human rights of women and children have to be changed!

Nevertheless, all cultures can contribute to the general discussion concerning the human rights concept. The establishment of a proper balance between rights and responsibilities, between individual rights and their collective dimension, between individuals and groups, is far from being achieved, not only in the Asian region but also in Western societies. It is not accidental that, in recent years, such attention has been given to the preparation of various declarations of human duties or responsibilities and the elaboration of a global ethics[71] which are seen, not as a rejection, but as a reinforcement of universal human rights.

Globalization, Regionalism and Nationalism: Chances and Threats

Globalization

The evolution of the modern world may be characterized by three megatrends: globalization, regionalism and nationalism. All of them have various implications for human rights but effects of globalization are the strongest as they are felt in all countries.

Globalization is the term used to characterize the processes of growing interconnection and interdependence in the modern world. It is generated by growing international economic, cultural and political cooperation and links, as well as by the need to respond together to global problems which can be solved only on a planetary scale. In the economic sphere, globalization may be desirable because of the widening and deepening of the international flow of trade, finance and information in a single, integrated global market. The world is shrinking as a result of increased human mobility, and the increasing contacts between the world's people, possibly with the aid of cheap and speedy travel, the telephone, fax and Internet. Artificial barriers have been eased with the reduction in trade barriers, the expansion of capital flow and the transfer of technology.

Although the economic dimension of globalization is the most evident and observed, globalization also has other dimensions – cultural and political: the international spread of cultures has been at least as important as the spread of economic processes.[72] Through the mass media international ideas and values are being mixed and imposed on national cultures. A homogeneous worldwide culture is developing in the process, sometimes qualified as the creation of a 'global village'. Advances of popular culture mean that throughout the world peoples are dressing, eating and singing similarly and that certain social and cultural attitudes have become global trends.

Globalization also has profound implications for states. The autonomy and policy-making capability of states is being undermined by economic and cultural internationalization.[73] Everywhere the demands to liberalize, to limit states' control over the economy and to privatize, bring a shrinking of the states' involvement in national life. Many governments see their role as not to regulate markets but to facilitate their expansion. Global and regional interactions are wiping out national borders and weakening national policies. States' sovereignty is gradually being limited, not only as the consequence of the existence of supranational political and economic organizations but, in many cases, because of the asymmetry of bargaining power between transnational corporations and small, poor developing countries.

What are the consequences of economic globalization? V.A. Leary, in Chapter 11, on 'Globalization and human rights', presents the mixed record of economic globalization: it may contribute to alleviation of poverty, to mobilization of public opinion, to calling immediate attention to gross violations of human rights; sometimes it has less beneficial consequences for the rights of workers; in particular, women workers, migrant workers and indigenous peoples. As Leary points out, globalization has been cited as a contributory factor in violations in many countries of the right to life, the right to protection of health, minority rights, freedom of association, the right to safe and healthy working conditions and the right to a standard of living adequate for health and well-being.

The benefits of globalization should exceed the cost. During 1995–2001, the results of the Uruguay Round of the GATT are expected to increase global income because of greater efficiency and expansion of trade by an estimated US$212–510 billion.[74] However, those benefits are spread unevenly. Gaps among developing countries are widening. In many industrial countries, an increase in overall income is accompanied by a rise in income inequality and in unemployment which has reached a very high level and is rapidly growing.

What is the impact of cultural globalization on human rights? The culturally homogenizing effect of globalization, the gradual process of adopting common values and behavioural patterns, reinforces the universality of human rights, establishes ties and linkages between various parts of the world and helps to eliminate certain traditional practices which may be qualified as discriminatory. However, the mixed blessings of cultural globalization are linked to its negative consequences for the cultural rights of vulnerable groups such as people belonging to minorities, indigenous peoples or immigrant workers. It also undermines existing cultural identities, weakens various ethical norms and social cohesion, as well as the feeling of belonging and, thereby, contributes to the proliferation of various internal conflicts. As stated by the Director-General of UNESCO during the 29th session of the General Conference in November 1997: 'Just as the protection of biological diversity is indispensable to the physical health of humanity, so the safeguarding of cultural diversity – linguistic, ideological and artistic – is indispensable to its spiritual health'.[75]

The limitation by globalization of the state's ability to determine national policies to intervene in economic activities also has manifold negative impacts on human rights for the implementation of economic, social and cultural rights. Weaker states may be more immune from authoritative or totalitarian deviations, but the limited governmental ability to run deficits as a result of the opening of financial markets forces them to slash social and cultural programmes, health services and food programmes. As underlined by the Secretary-General in his report presented at the special session of the 51st General Assembly in June 1997, 'Globalization affects, and sometimes reduces, the ability of governments to achieve desired outcomes. While governments continue to provide the overall framework in which the private sector must operate, many important decisions are made by the private sector, especially by companies operating in an international context.'[76]

States still bear the main responsibilities for the implementation of human rights. Markets cannot replace governments in the determination of economic, social and cultural policies, in providing social services and infrastructures, eradicating poverty, protecting vulnerable groups and defending the environment. Weak states cannot guarantee the rule of law which is *conditio sine qua non* for the full implementation of human rights.

Regionalism

The trend towards closer political, economic and cultural cooperation among the states of the same region or sub-region, leading to
economic integration and the creation of security communities, has
positive consequences for human rights. It has brought to life three
regional systems of human rights protection: the first created by the
Council of Europe based on the Convention for the Protection of
Human Rights and Fundamental Freedoms (1950);[77] the second established by the Organization of American States which adopted the
American Convention on Human Rights (1969); and the third created on the basis of the African Charter on Human and People's
Rights (1981) by the Organization for African Unity.

European and American systems provide for the existence of special courts of human rights with the possibility of presenting
individual cases of alleged violations of human rights by States Parties to regional human rights instruments.

The Vienna Declaration and Programme of Action gives a positive
evaluation of regional arrangements, noting that they play a fundamental role in promoting and protecting human rights. The regional
human rights systems reinforce universal human rights standards.
They may also advance and develop universal standards. Thus, for
example, in Europe the protection of persons belonging to minorities
as a result of instruments adopted by the Council of Europe, the
Organization for Co-operation and Security in Europe, as well as a
number of bilateral agreements, is more advanced in comparison to
instruments adopted by the United Nations system. The same may
be said of the systems for monitoring the implementation of human
rights established by American and European states.

The World Conference on Human Rights reiterated the need to
establish regional and sub-regional arrangements for the promotion
and protection of human rights where they do not already exist. The
General Assembly adopted a series of resolutions in which it affirmed the value of regional arrangement for the promotion and
protection of human rights in the Asia and Pacific region.[78]

Nationalism

Nationalism is not a new phenomenon. In fact, most modern nations
have developed gradually on the basis of common descent and ties
of ethnic, religious and linguistic character which led to the creation
of a feeling of belonging to a community, living in a certain territory.
The tendency towards nationalism was fostered mainly by various
political, cultural, economic and technological developments. As
a distinctive movement, nationalism emerged in the eighteenth

century and can be seen as an important factor in the building of nation-states. In itself, it is not necessarily a negative, phenomenon, and may also be a positive phenomenon. In this sense it is perhaps more appropriate to use the term 'patriotism', which helped to keep nations together in the most difficult periods of their history.

The end of the twentieth century brings a new challenge as nationalism changes its character and is often articulated in a pathological form of ethnonationalism (aggressive or extreme nationalism and chauvinism) which leads to internal ethnic conflicts and massive and flagrant violations of human rights such as genocide in Rwanda or 'ethnic cleansing' in former Yugoslavia. Ethnonationalism can be characterized as a tendency either to achieve a hegemonic position for a given ethnic group in a heterogeneous society or to secede from it. In order to achieve a dominant position, ethnonationalists utilize either forced assimilation, imposition of a dominant cultural identity, language and religion or exclusion of members of other ethnic groups from the national society by the denial and deprivation of citizenship or by outright ethnic cleansing.[79]

It may also have a form of discrimination directed against other groups in multicultural societies – immigrants or indigenous peoples – and is used by a state, seen as a 'property' of one ethnic group, in order to achieve greater cohesion or consolidation of a dominant ethnic group by the creation of images of 'internal enemies'. Ethnonationalistic movements have a strong irrational component which contributes to their strength but at the same time makes them less susceptible to political compromise or acceptance of the rights of other cultural groups.[80] It leads in some cases to the use of various forms of violence and terrorism.

What are the sources of the present explosion of extreme, aggressive nationalism? There are many. The collapse of communism in Central and Eastern Europe, the dissolution of the former Soviet Union and Yugoslavia, together with decolonialization, led to the emergence of new states, many of which are multi-ethnic and contain within their borders various national, religious and linguistic minorities. The end of the Cold War, profound geopolitical changes and the weakening of states have created a specific situation of destabilization, vacuums and the absence of external pressure towards moderation. This creates a chance for various ambitious groups and leaders to seek power.[81] Fomenting nationalistic feelings, due to the independent mass media, is paradoxically much easier. In some cases, ethnonationalism is caused by discrimination, by denial of rights of persons belonging to minorities and exclusion.

What are the ways and means leading to the elimination of the dangers that ethnonationalism creates for human rights, peace and human security? The first step leading in this direction is the full respecting of various cultural, national, ethnic, religious and linguistic minorities, and acceptance of multiculturalism and cultural autonomy.[82] An important role in the prevention of aggressive nationalism may also be played by intercultural, formal and non-formal education of youth and the whole of society. As ethnonationalism is often linked to claims concerning the right to internal self-determination, representation and participation in decision-making processes, in state institutions, in political, economic, social and cultural development within the democratic framework is also a *conditio sine qua non*. Last but not least, the international community, the United Nations and regional organizations should have a procedure and criteria to evaluate claims to external self-determination, to secession and independence. Among these criteria, the respecting of human rights and fundamental freedoms should have priority.

Through Human Rights Education and Public Information towards a Culture of Human Rights

The importance of education for the promotion of human rights has been recognized on various occasions by the United Nations. At the moment of the adoption of the Universal Declaration of Human Rights, the General Assembly expressed the view that this text should be disseminated among all peoples throughout the world, and recommended governments to cause it to be disseminated, displayed, read and expounded principally in schools and other educational institutions.[83]

This recommendation was respected by the Economic and Social Council when, in 1950, it invited UNESCO to encourage and facilitate reading about the Universal Declaration in schools and adult education programmes, and through the press, radio and film services. In 1971, the Commission on Human Rights urged UNESCO to examine the desirability of envisaging the systematic study and development of an independent scientific discipline of human rights, with a view to facilitating the comprehension, study and teaching of human rights at the university level and subsequently at other educational levels. Two years later, in 1973, the Commission encouraged the organization to develop education for human rights for all and at all levels. Responding to these requests, the General Conference of UNESCO in 1974 adopted the Recommendation concerning Education for International Understanding, Co-operation and Peace and Education relating to Human Rights and Fundamental Freedoms.

In Chapter 12, V. Muntarbhorn, after his introductory remarks concerning UNESCO's congresses dealing with human rights teaching and education (Vienna, 1978; Malta, 1987; Montreal, 1993) and

the World Conference on Human Rights (Vienna, 1993), presents key
challenges for human rights education: universalization, intercon-
nections, diversification and specifications. The analysis of the state
of human rights education in various regions and states leads him to
the conclusion that 'human rights education tends to be found
substantively at the tertiary level rather than at the pre-school, primary and secondary levels in formal education'. He proposes a
detailed agenda for the development of human rights education,
including a UNESCO Human Rights Education Plan of Action.

Duty of States to Develop Human Rights Education

Half a century after the adoption of the Universal Declaration, states
are duty bound to develop human rights education. This obligation
is already well established in international human rights law. The
Universal Declaration of Human Rights was the first instrument to
demand, in its Article 26(2): 'education shall be directed to the full
development of the human personality and to the strengthening of
respect for human rights and fundamental freedoms'. This formulation was repeated literally in Article 4 of the Convention against
Discrimination in Education (1960). In Article 13 of the International
Covenant on Economic, Social and Cultural Rights (1966), States
Parties agreed: 'that education shall be directed to the full development of the human personality and the sense of its dignity, and shall
strengthen the respect for human rights and fundamental freedoms'.

The Convention on the Elimination of All Forms of Racial Discrimination (1965) in Article 7 imposes on States Parties an obligation
to accept immediate and effective measures, particularly in the fields
of teaching, education, culture and information, with a view to combating prejudices which lead to racial discrimination, whereas the
Convention on the Elimination of All Forms of Discrimination Against
Women (1979), in its Article 10, requires that States Parties take appropriate measures to eliminate discrimination against women in
order to ensure their equal rights with men in the field of education.

The obligation to education for human rights is formulated in
Article 19 of the Convention on the Rights of the Child (1989) which,
apart from 'the development of respect for human rights and fundamental freedoms and for the principles enshrined in the Charter of
the United Nations', also requires the preparation of the child for a
responsible life in a free society in the spirit of understanding, peace,
tolerance, equality of sexes and friendship among all peoples, ethnic,
national and religious groups and persons of indigenous origin.

The 49th session of the General Assembly in its resolution 49/184
proclaimed the 10-year period beginning 1 January 1995 the United
Nations Decade for Human Rights Education. The resolution, as

formulated by the Montreal International Congress on Education for Human Rights and Democracy, declared that 'education for human rights and democracy is itself a human right and a prerequisite for the realization of human rights, democracy and social justice'.

Human Rights Education and the Creation of a Universal Culture of Human Rights

Human rights education in recent years is also seen as an important means for the creation of a culture of human rights. The World Plan of Action on Education for Human Rights and Democracy adopted by the UNESCO Montreal Congress in 1993 underlines that its ultimate purpose is to create a *culture of human rights* and to develop democratic societies in which individuals and groups can resolve disagreements and conflicts by the use of non-violent methods.

The Plan of Action for the United Nations Decade for Human Rights Education[84] contains the most comprehensive definition of human rights education. It stipulates that human rights education shall be defined as 'training, dissemination and information efforts *aimed at the building of a universal culture of human rights* [emphasis added] through the imparting of knowledge and skills and the moulding of attitudes'.

The new role of education as the foundation for a human rights culture was also recognized by the 44th session of the International Conference on Education, which took place in Geneva in 1994. Ministers of Education in the Declaration adopted by the Conference[85] expressed their conviction that education 'should promote knowledge, values, attitudes and skills conducive to respect for human rights and to an active commitment to the defence of such rights'.

The Plan of Action for the UN Decade for Human Rights Education and the Declaration of the International Conference on Education understand identically the very term 'culture'. A culture of human rights can be achieved not only through access to and knowledge of certain values but also by imparting and moulding attitudes and skills. Readiness to defend and follow the human rights standards in everyday life, both private and public, and the creation of peaceful non-violent behavioural patterns and skills are the ultimate indications of progress achieved in the construction of a culture of human rights. In line with such assumptions, human rights education is a much wider concept than the study of international and internal human rights standards, procedures and institutions. It has to be understood, not as instruction about human rights but as education for human rights. This means that educational institutions should become open, ideal places for the exercise of tolerance, respect for human rights, practice of democracy and learning about the diversity and worth of cultural identities. They should develop skills involving judgment and ability to arrive at fair and balanced opinions and conclusions, ability to seek solutions through dialogue and non-violent ways and means, and ability to participate actively in public life.

A universal culture of human rights is a long-term goal which can be achieved through the establishment of a comprehensive system of education, training and public information aimed at all groups of the population, especially women, children, minorities, indigenous people and the disabled, embracing all levels of education, formal and non-formal.[86] Although education has to be seen as a cornerstone in the construction of a human rights culture, it cannot be built without the participation of the media[87] which at present exert a predominant influence on the forging of attitudes, judgments and values which create images and often determine the relation to 'others': individuals, groups, religions or cultures.

A human rights culture cannot be constructed without the participation of civil society. For this very reason, the Montreal World Plan of Action on Education for Human Rights and Democracy is addressed to various social actors, from individuals, families, groups, associations and non-governmental organizations to states, intergovernmental organizations and the United Nations system. Building such a broad coalition of partners in human rights education is no doubt a great challenge. Real progress in the building of a human rights culture is also linked with the need to reach, through all means and innovative programmes, the excluded, the vast masses of the illiterate and the millions of children who do not even have an opportunity to acquire the rudiments of education. From this point of view, the emphasis on 'education for all' and 'lifelong education' as well as the promotion of 'teaching without frontiers' are of paramount importance.

Making Human Rights a Reality

Article 28 of the Universal Declaration of Human Rights provides: 'Everyone is entitled to a social and international order in which the rights and freedoms set forth in the Declaration can be fully realized.' Can we state that the present 'international order' guarantees the implementation of all human rights? Can it assure the realization of legitimate aspirations of humankind to international and internal peace, to human rights, to sustainable development, to democratization? Is the elaboration of an effective common policy to meet scientific, technological and environmental challenges possible?

More than half a century ago, the President of the United States, Franklin D. Roosevelt, while thinking about a new world order to be established after the end of the Second World War, proposed to base it on four freedoms: the freedom of speech and expression, the freedom of every person to worship God in his own way, the freedom from want and the freedom from fear. None of these four freedoms can be recognized as being already guaranteed in the existing international order.

To achieve this goal, the international system should have the possibility of dealing with the main obstacles and threats to human rights, such as extreme poverty, exclusion, underdevelopment, discrimination, intolerance or terrorism. The international community should have the ability to address real causes of conflicts. It demands further structural adjustments of the United Nations system.

Though the creation of the post of the United Nations High Commissioner for Human Rights[88] may be seen as the first step in this direction, there is perhaps a need for the establishment of a new principal organ or body with much stronger competencies and responsibilities. However, such a new role and further involvement of the United Nations in the protection of human rights are determined by the political will of Member States, their readiness to accept new legal, economic and social measures.

This means further limitations of sovereignty and the principle of non-interference in internal affairs. An agreement on actions of the United Nations Security Council in cases of gross and massive violations of human rights is also needed. However, possible coercive measures undertaken by the international community should punish those responsible for gross human rights violations and not additionally increase the suffering of victims. The creation of a Permanent International Criminal Court would be an important step in the right direction.

The new international order should include such important principles as solidarity and burden sharing: solidarity between countries and solidarity within every country in favour of the most disadvantaged. It requires actions based upon common interests and values to manage problems that respect no borders and can be solved only through international cooperation, which should cover a range of global problems, from environmental degradation and migration, to drugs and epidemic diseases. The international community needs to sustain and increase the volume of development assistance in order to reverse the growing marginalization and exclusion of the poor and to achieve progress towards goals of human development. In fact, human rights have to become a new dimension of all United Nations functions.

The progress of democratization in many parts of the world poses new questions concerning democratization of the international system. Advancement of democracy, though in many countries of rather 'low density', is to a great degree a function of the development of civil societies: participation of individuals and groups in decision-making processes, in the democratic governance of their countries. What is the place of a global society in international relations? How should non-governmental organizations, which undeniably become a *spiritus movens* of progress in the field of human rights, be represented in international structures and organs? Should individuals and groups become subjects of international law? What are the international consequences of the recognition of rights and responsibilities of individuals, groups and organs of society to promote and protect universally recognized human rights and fundamental freedoms?[89] National institutions, non-governmental organizations, academic institutions and grassroots initiatives should be fully accepted as natural human rights advocates and partners in international human rights cooperation.

The construction of an international order in which all human rights and freedoms, including economic, social and cultural as well as the right to development, can be fully realized, in which all human rights could be guaranteed for all, has become the most important human rights challenge for the twenty-first century.

Notes

1   See the preamble of the International Convention on the Elimination of All Forms of Racial Discrimination (1965) and that of the International Convention on the Suppression and Punishment of the Crime of Apartheid (1983).
2   A. Michalska and J. Sandorski, 'Right to peace as a human right. Evolution of the conception', *Polish Peace Research Studies*, 1, (1), 1998, 86. The close linkage and mutual interdependence between peace and human rights is acknowledged not only in human rights instruments but also in numerous declarations and treaties, both universal and regional, concerning international law.
3   Resolution 33/73, adopted by the General Assembly on 15 December 1978.
4   In fact, this three-dimensional approach was already in the Declaration on Social Progress and Development (1969).
5   'The Opening Statement of the United Nations Secretary-General', World Conference on Human Rights, United Nations, DPI/1394–39399, August 1993, p.17. See also Boutros Boutros-Ghali, *Agenda for Democratization*, New York, United Nations, 1996.
6   See also, T.M. Franck, 'The emerging right to democratic governance', *American Journal of International Law*, 86, 1992, 46.
7   A. Eide, 'Obstacles and goals to be pursued', in A. Eide, C. Krause and A. Rosas (eds), *Economic, Social and Cultural Rights*, Dordrecht/Boston/London, Martinus Nijhoff Publishers, 1995, p. 381.
8   Boutros Boutros-Ghali, *An Agenda for Peace, 1995*, 2nd edn, New York, United Nations, 1995.
9   To the already mentioned conferences one can add the World Conference on Education for All (1990), the World Summit for Children (1990) and the International Conference on Population and Development (1994). The Fourth World

Conference on Women took place in Beijing, from 4 to 15 September 1995. Its main theme was 'Action for equality, development and peace'. In the Beijing Declaration, adopted on 15 September 1995, governments stressed their determination to advance the goals of equality, development and peace for all women everywhere in the interest of all humanity.

10 *Human Development Report, 1997* explores the following: 'The process of widening people's choices and the level of well-being they achieve are at the core of the notion of human development. Such choices are neither finite nor static.' Nevertheless, regardless of the level of development, the three essential choices for people are to lead a long and healthy life, to acquire knowledge and to have access to the resources needed for a decent standard of living.

11 Report of the United Nations Conference on Environment and Development, Rio de Janeiro, 3–14 June 1992, Doc. A/CONF.151/26/Rev.1.

12 The Vienna Declaration and Programme of Action, June 1993, para. 10.

13 The Copenhagen Declaration and Programme of Action, World Summit for Social Development, New York, United Nations, 1995, p.14.

14 Doc. E/CN.4/1997/22, 21 January 1997. Question of the Realization of the Right to Development, Progress Report of the Intergovernmental Group of Experts, Geneva, 4–15 November 1996.

15 In this context, the idea of adding the Declaration on the Right to Development to the International Bill of Rights was put forward.

16 Resolution 50/173 of 22 December 1995, entitled 'United Nations Decade for Human Rights Education: Towards a culture of peace'.

17 Resolution 51/101 of 12 December 1996, 'Culture of peace'.

18 'The Human Right to Peace, Declaration by the Director-General', UNESCO, SHS-97/WS/6.

19 It gathered together 30 well-known specialists in international law and human rights, including judges of the International Court of Justice (M. Bedjaoui, Algeria; R. Ranjeva, Madagascar); Judge A. Cançado Trindade of the Inter-American Court of Justice; I. Nguema, Gabon, President of the African Commission of Human and Peoples' Rights; Professor E. Roucounas, Greece, member of the United Nations International Law Commission; and Dr A. Eide, Director of the Norwegian Institute of Human Rights.

20 UNESCO, General Conference, 29th session, Paris 1997. Report by the Director-General on the Human Right to Peace; Document 29C/59, Annex II.

21 The Director-General received 44 answers. For the most part, the Member States expressed their support and interest in this initiative. The adoption by UNESCO of such a declaration was also seen as an important contribution to the celebration of the fiftieth anniversary of the Universal Declaration of Human Rights. The Member States suggested changes or proposed amendments. Four Member States expressed reservations.

22 The right of peoples to peace was recognized by the African Charter on Human and Peoples' Rights which provides, in Article 23, that 'All peoples have the right to national and international peace and security'. In 1984, the General Assembly adopted, with 34 abstentions, the Declaration on the Right of Peoples to Peace which 'solemnly proclaims that the peoples of our planet have a sacred right to peace' and 'solemnly declares that the preservation of the right of peoples to peace and the promotion of its implementation constitute a fundamental obligation of each State'.

23 An analysis of all instruments dealing with education for peace is presented in J. Symonides, 'The long journey to a culture of peace', *Dialogo*, 21, June 1997, 8–9.

24 A. Rosas and M. Scheinin, 'Categories and beneficiaries of human rights', in E. Hanski and M. Suksi (eds), *An Introduction to the International Protection of*

Human Rights. A Textbook, Abo Akademi University, Turku/Abo, 1997, pp.55–6, express the opinion that the right to peace can be tackled in the context of the right to life.

25   *Human Development Report, 1997*, New York/Oxford, Oxford University Press, p.2.

26   Respectively: resolutions 47/196 of 22 December 1992; 48/183 of 21 December 1993; and 50/107 of 20 December 1995.

27   Doc. E/CN.4/Sub.2/1996/13.

28   In fact, the Committee on the Rights of the Child has already paid attention to the situation of children living in extreme poverty with a view to promoting the enjoyment by all children of all rights recognized in the Convention on the Rights of the Child.

29   Article 1 of the International Convention on the Elimination of All Forms of Racial Discrimination defines the term 'racial discrimination' as any distinction, exclusion, restriction or preference based on race, colour, descent, or national or ethnic origin which has the purpose or effect of nullifying or impairing the recognition, enjoyment or exercise, on an equal footing, of human rights and fundamental freedoms, in the political, economic, social, cultural or any other field of public life.

30   'United Nations Compilation of General Comments and General Recommendations adopted by Human Rights Bodies', HRI/GEN/1/Rev.2 of 29 March 1996, p.27.

31   See *The Struggle Against Discrimination. A Collection of International Instruments Adopted by the United Nations System*, Paris, UNESCO, 1996. See also J. Symonides, 'Prohibition of hatred, prejudice and intolerance in the United Nations instruments', *Democracy and Tolerance*, Seoul, Korean National Commission for UNESCO/UNESCO, 1996.

32   *Inter alia*, the American Convention on Human Rights (1969); the Convention on the Status of Aliens (1928); the Inter-American Convention on the Granting of Political Rights to Women (1948); the Inter-American Convention on the Granting of Civil Rights to Women (1948); the Inter-American Convention on the Prevention, Punishment and Eradication of Violence Against Women (1994); the African Charter on Human and People's Rights (1981); the European Convention on Human Rights (1950); the European Convention on the Legal Status of Migrant Workers (1977); the Framework Convention for the Protection of National Minorities (1994).

33   Resolutions 48/122 of 20 December 1993; 49/185 of 23 December 1994; and 50/186 of 22 December 1995.

34   Doc. E/CN.4/Sub.2/1997/28 of 26 June 1997, p.3.

35   Ibid., p.4.

36   Resolution 51/62 12 December 1996: 'Measures for prevention of the smuggling of aliens'.

37   Reports on the sale of children, child prostitution and child pornography are prepared personally by the special rapporteur of the Commission on Human Rights (resolution 1995/79 of 8 March 1995).

38   The first of these resolutions was resolution 45/121 adopted by the General Assembly on 14 December 1990, followed by resolution 46/152 on 18 December 1991. The Economic and Social Council adopted similar resolutions in 1992, 1993 and 1994.

39   Resolution 51/59: Action against corruption, of 12 December 1996.

40   For example, by the recent seminar on political corruption and human rights, organized by the Catholic University of Brussels (Belgium) from 11 to 12 December 1997.

41   The reports analysed, *inter alia*, the impact of scientific and technological devel-

opments on economic, social and cultural rights (the right to food and clothing, equal pay for equal work, housing, rest and leisure), the beneficial consequences of the application of electronic communications techniques, as well as the benefits which will be derived from advances in biology, medicine and biochemistry. The report presented in 1975 endorsed the harmful effects of automation and mechanization of reduction in the enjoyment of the right to work and the harmful effects of scientific and technological developments on the enjoyment of the right to adequate food. It also presented the deterioration of the human environment as a result of scientific and technological development as well as the problem of increasingly destructive power of modern weapons and the public health problems linked with atomic reaction.

42   Paragraph 11 of Vienna Declaration and Programme of Action.

43   E.B. Brody, *Biomedical Technology and Human Rights*, Paris/Cambridge, UNESCO/Dartmouth Publishing, 1993, p.109.

44   Ibid., p.149.

45   Conclusions and Recommendations of the International Symposium on the Effects on Human Rights of Recent Advances in Science and Technology, organized under the auspices of UNESCO by the International Social Science Council, Barcelona, Spain, 25–28 March 1985, Part C, Recommendations of major importance. III. Consider critically any calls to limit research particularly when it is claimed that the research would directly contravene human rights.

46   This is broadly recognized. Apart from Article 11 of the Universal Declaration on the Human Genome and Human Rights, this position was taken by the Fiftieth World Health Assembly held in Geneva, which stated in its resolution of 14 May 1997 that 'the use of cloning for the replication of human individuals is ethically unacceptable'. The Council of Europe adopted an Additional Protocol on the Prohibition of Cloning Human Beings opened for signature on 12 January 1998.

47   *SIPRI Yearbook 1995, Armaments, Disarmament and International Security*, Oxford, Oxford University Press, 1995, pp.613–15.

48   E. Deutsch, 'The functions of ethical committees', in *Onore di Guido Gerin*, Milan, Cedom, 1996, p.176; *Les Comités d'éthique*, Collection 'Que sais-je?', Paris, Presses universitaires de France, 1990. The first national ethical committee was set up in 1983 in France: 'Comité consultative national d'éthique pour les sciences de la vie et de la santé'.

49   The establishment of the International Bioethics Committee was approved by resolution 5.165 of the 27th session of the UNESCO General Conference. It is the only ethical committee within the United Nations system.

50   N. Lenoir, 'L'Europe, le droit et la bioéthique', in *Hector Gros Espiell Amicorum Liber*, Vol.1, Brussels, Bruylant, 1997, pp.6, 641–66.

51   Doc. 29C/21: Drawing up of a Declaration on the Human Genome: Report by the Director-General, UNESCO General Conference, 29th session, Paris, 1997.

52   The Declaration explains: 'If, according to the law, a person does not have the capacity to consent, research affecting his or her genome may only be carried out for his or her direct health benefit, subject to the authorization and the protective conditions prescribed by law'.

53   Articles 17–19, Part E of the Declaration: Solidarity and International Co-operation.

54   Statement on Universal Access to Basic Communication and Information Services, adopted in April 1997 by the Administrative Committee on Co-ordination (ACC); Doc. 151 EX/16, Ad. p.1.

55   During the debate in the Executive Board on 'The challenges of the information highways. The role of UNESCO', the President of the General Conference, T. Krogh said: 'we have the fundamental principles to guide our decisions on the

new information technology. They could be summarized in two central notions: promoting freedom of expression and expanding the sharing of knowledge' (manuscript, p.10).

56   Monaco proposed the continuation of these meetings and the organization of a second conference in 1998 to deal with ethical and policy issues of the new information environment. The discrimination of UNESCO took a position that, instead of a one-time event, a future UNESCO Conference on Information and Communication for Development, a more effective and economic approach could be to organize a regular, perhaps annual, series of INFO-ETHICS (Doc, UNESCO, Executive Board, 151 EX/16, Paris, 21 April 1997, p.1).

57   Z. Brzezinski, 'The new challenges to human rights', *Journal of Democracy*, 8, (2), April 1995, 4.

58   *Our Creative Diversity*, Report of the World Commission on Culture and Development, UNESCO, 1995, p.55.

59   H.R.H. Crown Prince Al-Hassan bin Talal, 'The universality of ethical standards and the governance of civil society', *Arab Thought Forum*, 4, (17), May–June 1997, 5.

60   Doc. A/CONF.157/AFRM/14.

61   Doc. A/CONF.157/ASRM/7.

62   Statement by the Minister of Foreign Affairs of Indonesia, 14 June 1993.

63   Statement by the Deputy Foreign Minister of Iran, Vienna, 18 June 1993.

64   Statement by the Deputy Minister of Foreign Affairs of the Socialist Republic of Viet Nam, 14 June 1993.

65   Statement by the Head of the Chinese Delegation at the World Conference on Human Rights, 15 June 1993.

66   Statement by the Minister for Foreign Affairs of the Netherlands, 14 June 1993. In his address to the World Conference, the US Secretary of State said: 'We respect the religious social and cultural characteristics that make each country unique. But we cannot let cultural relativism become the last refuge of repression.' (Quoted by M.J. Perry, 'Are human rights universal? The relativist challenge and related matters', *Human Rights Quarterly*, 19, 1997, 498.)

67   W. van Gemegten, 'Universality of human rights, as discussed during the 1993 World Conference on Human Rights; description and comments', in Patricia Morales (ed.), *Towards Global Human Rights*, International Centre for Human and Public Affairs, Tilburg, The Netherlands, 1996, p.44.

68   A. Etzioni, 'The end of cross-cultural relativism', *Alternatives*, 22, 1997, 177.

69   See J. Bauer, 'International human rights and Asian commitment', *Human Rights Dialogue*, December 1995; 'Three years after the Bangkok Declaration: Reflection on the state of Asia–West dialogue on human rights', *Human Rights Dialogue*, March 1996; M. Ng, 'Why Asia needs democracy', *Journal of Democracy*, 8, (2), April 1997; J. Chan, 'Hong Kong, Singapore and "Asian Values". An alternative view', *Journal of Democracy*, 8, (2), April 1997; B. Kansikan, 'Hong Kong, Singapore and "Asian Values". Governance that works', *Journal of Democracy*, 8, (2), April 1997; M.E. Hamdi, 'The limits of the Western model', *Journal of Democracy*, 7, (2), April 1996; R.R. Ty, 'The human rights debate in the southeast Asian region', *The Human Rights Agenda*, University of the Philippines Law Center, 2, (2), March 1997.

70   In studies conducted in recent years in the United States on the extent to which American and Asian values differ, D.I. Hitchcock, *Asian Values and the United States: How Much Conflict?* (Center for Strategic and International Studies, Washington, 1994), found both similarities and differences. Among similarities he listed self-reliance and hard work; as to the differences, Americans underlined more personal achievements, personal freedom and individual rights, whereas Asians emphasized the importance of learning, honesty, self-discipline and an

orderly society. A survey of the values of Asian executives conducted by Wirthlin Worldwide, *Wall Street Journal*, 8 March 1996, also confirmed the existence of differences. He found that for Asians the most important values were hard work, learning and honesty; for Americans freedom of expression, personal freedom and self-reliance. Traditional cultures and philosophies, like Confucianism, in Asian systems also differ from Western concepts. Confucianism places greater emphasis on duties in basic human relations, on the virtue of respect for the elderly and filial piety, and on mutual trust and care between family members.

71 For example, the Trieste Declaration of Human Duties, A Code of Ethics of Shared Responsibilities or the Universal Declaration of Human Responsibilities proposed by the InterAction Council; F. Lewis, 'Basic Common Ethics for All', *International Herald Tribune*, 25 April 1997; H. Küng and K.-J. Kuschel (eds), *A Global Ethic, The Declaration of the Parliament of the World's Religions*, London, 1993. It is also worth mentioning that the 29th session of the General Conference of UNESCO adopted the Declaration on the Responsibilities of the Present Generations Towards Future Generations.

72 *Human Development Report 1997*, New York/Oxford, UNDP/Oxford University Press, 1997, p.83.

73 'Contemporary influences on patterns of ethnic diversity', Ch. Inglis, 'Multiculturalism: New policy responses to diversity, management of social transformations', Policy Papers No. 4, UNESCO, Paris, 1996, pp. 3 *et seq.*

74 *Human Development Report 1997* (op. cit., note 72), p.82.

75 UNESCOPRESS, 29th session of the General Conference, N° 97–219. In his closing speech, the President of the General Conference formulated an opinion that cultural cleansing is perhaps more dangerous than a biological one. Wherever it occurs, the thermometer of intellectual competition registers a drop in temperature.

76 E/CN.17/1997/2, 31 January 1997, p.23.

77 It is worth noting that the system of human rights protection of the Council of Europe is supplemented by the human dimension system established by the Organization for Security and Co-operation in Europe.

78 See resolution 41/153 adopted on 4 December 1986; 43/140 of 8 December 1988; 45/168 of 18 December 1990. Similar resolutions have also been adopted by the Commission on Human Rights. As mentioned by K. Drzewicki, 'Internationalization of human rights and their jurisdiction', in *An Introduction to the International Protection of Human Rights. A Textbook* (op. cit., note 24), pp.35–6, with the adoption of the Arab Charter on Human Rights on 15 September 1994, a new regional system for the protection of human rights is *in statu nascendi.*

79 See A. Eide, 'Multicultural education and group accommodation in the light of minority rights', paper presented at the UNESCO Regional Conference on Human Rights Education in Europe, Turku, Finland, 18 September 1997, p.2.

80 Ch. Inglis, 'Multiculturalism, new policy responses to diversity', *MOST Publication N°5*, Paris, 1996, p.24.

81 Ibid., p.21.

82 A.H. Richmond, 'Ethnic nationalism: social science paradigms', *International Social Science Journal*, Vol. 111 'Ethnic phenomena', February 1987, p. 11 underlines the importance of the preservation of an ethnic 'cultural heritage' and the promotion of human rights including affirmative action and positive discrimination designed to compensate for past deprivations.

83 Resolution 217 (III) of 10 December 1948.

84 The Plan of Action for the Decade. Report of the Secretary-General, Document A/49/261/Add.1.

85 ED-BIE/CONFINTED 44/5, Paris, 24 October 1994.

86   Activities and programmes of the United Nations and UNESCO aimed at the creation of a comprehensive system of education for human rights are presented in a number of publications: see J. Symonides, 'United Nations and human rights education', in D. Bourantonis and M. Evrivades (eds) *A United Nations for the Twenty-First Century*, The Hague, Kluwer, 1996; J. Symonides and V. Volodin, 'Education for human rights and democracy in the new international context', *Education for Human Rights and Citizenship in Central and Eastern Europe*, Prague, Human Rights Education Centre of Charles University, 1995, pp.38–49; D. Chitoran and J. Symonides, 'UNESCO's approaches to promoting international education at the level of higher education', in J. Calleja (ed.), *International Education and the University*, Malta, Cromwell Press, 1995, pp.9–40.

87   In 1978, the General Conference adopted the UNESCO Declaration on Fundamental Principles concerning the contribution of the Mass Media to Strengthening Peace and International Understanding, to the Promotion of Human Rights and to Countering Racialism, Apartheid and Incitement to War. In Article II, para. 3, it states '... the mass media throughout the world, by reason of their role, contribute to promoting human rights'.

88   Resolution of the General Assembly 48/141 of 20 December 1993.

89   The Commission on Human Rights established a working group which is drafting a Declaration on the Right and Responsibility of Individuals, Groups and Organs of Society to Promote and Protect Universally Recognized Human Rights and Fundamental Freedoms. The 12th session of the group took place in 1997; E/CN.4/1997/92 of 25 March 1997.

PART I
NEW DIMENSIONS

2 Human Rights and Peace

VOJIN DIMITRIJEVIC

Human Rights and Peace as Sets of Values

Peace and human rights can be studied axiologically, to attempt to determine whether one or both are values, or sets of values, and which one, the one covered by the term 'human rights' or the one denoted as 'peace', is higher, that is, more desirable.

The value approach has practical relevance in terms of defining political programmes, both nationally and internationally. It is, however, complicated by the fact that, within each cluster, value choices have to be made. Students of human rights are not unfamiliar with attitudes and programmes which not only clearly indicate the order of preference for various human rights and groups of rights, but go as far as to discard some rights as undesirable or even harmful.[1] Depending on the case, the source of such discrimination may lie in ideological differences (this was characteristic of Cold War oratory) or in cultural relativism (frequently associated with the North–South divide).[2] A peace researcher will be aware of the opinions which reject certain elements that are usually subsumed under the concept of peace. One possible ground for gradation can be relevant to our theme: if human rights are part of a meaningful and desirable peace, then peace without human rights is less valuable or not peace at all.

If the meanings of peace and human rights are clear, at least in operational terms, then one of them may be posited above the other. In the peace–human rights–development debate of the late 1970s and early 1980s, groups of states in the United Nations and other international organizations were taken to be characterized by such preferences. Thus the 'West' was said to favour human rights (with the priority of the 'first generation' civil and political rights), the 'East' peace, and the 'South' development.[3] It was implied that all

47

groups, and within them the most important states, recognized the other two values as relevant, albeit secondary.

Only in more radical circles, which were not represented in government delegations and did not use diplomatic language, were some of the values totally excluded. Thus, for instance, the 'insider' official thinking of the 'real socialist' ideologues, publicly considered only to prefer peace over other values, in fact considered peace not as inherently valuable but as expeditious, as long as the Soviet Union and then the socialist camp had to 'strengthen socialism' in the hostile international environment.[4] Their preference for economic and social rights was also a diplomatic euphemism used by those who wanted to involve them in international efforts to promote human rights: the indisputable fact that socialist states provided relatively stable social security and health care did not mean that such services of the state were rendered to individuals as their human rights. The 'bearers of rights' (often divided, *de jure* or *de facto*, into the categories of functionaries, workers and ordinary citizens) had rights only in terms of the legal technique of dispensing necessary social benefits in accordance with the prevailing social doctrine and administrative or economic efficiency.

Those regimes in the Third World which were autocratic had similar attitudes to peace and an even more cynical stance regarding human rights. If one removes development from the triad of prime values discussed by the United Nations, it becomes obvious that, for many radicals in that area, peace and human rights have been, not secondary, but non-existent concerns.[5]

This 'hidden reality' was not readily visible in the international fora and was inadequately represented in mainstream journals. The debate has always been among those who generally accepted peace and human rights as values, or pretended to do so, but disagreed about their content, precedence and feasibility. Explicit or implicit acceptance of human rights and peace as values has recently been put to a severe test in the disturbed areas of the former Communist bloc. The renaissance of nationalism, now heavily influenced by the intellectual and political methodology of 'really existing socialism', lessened most inhibitions and returned to respectability political parties and authors openly rejecting peace if it conflicted with nation building or the national interest and, for similar reasons, disfiguring the idea of human rights beyond recognition. Under such terms, the paramount right is the right to self-determination in its state-creating form; in its shadow, only persons belonging to the ethnic nation can claim rights, and they have to wait until the final goal of fullest sovereignty and security (purity) is attained.[6] In such areas, many participants in the public discourse and political campaigns, even in learned journals, unabashedly discard peace (even in its rudimentary form of absence of deadly conflicts) as a value, and even deride it as cowardly and effeminate.[7] The very idea of human rights can be openly called into question, generally as subversive for the new (and now better) national state: after the creation of the latter, duties to the nation, manifested in its state, become more important than rights. In this view, no right can exist without the corresponding duty towards the community (state).[8]

The preceding sentences are sufficient to indicate that the debate on the relationship between peace and human rights is now being conducted in a quasi pre-Second World War atmosphere: total rejection of peace and human rights as values has again become a politically and intellectually legitimate stance. Those who deal with human rights and peace have sometimes to return to square one and to face politically and intellectually powerful opponents who do not believe that, at least in their case and the case of their nation or movement, peace or human rights are necessary or desirable. If neither of them is desired, the relationship between peace and human rights becomes a pointless topic: a discussion of the relationship and interaction of peace and human rights is meaningful only for those who recognize both values, irrespective of the order of importance and priority, or who accept at least one of these value clusters.

Values as Rights

The 'Right to Human Rights'

The proposition that certain accepted values shall be expressed in terms of individual rights, necessary for the attainment or protection of the relevant good (value), is at the origin of human rights thinking, especially in legal theory. For example, according to international human rights instruments, the best protected value is human dignity; within it, it is not human life (since capital punishment is permissible under certain conditions and killing in international conflict is legitimate under certain conditions) but the physical integrity of the person. For certain reasons, which will not be studied here, there is consensus that any attempt to encroach on the organic system of the human body is unacceptable. This is then expressed in the form of a set of human rights and concomitant prohibitions, such as the banning of torture and cruel, inhuman and degrading treatment and punishment. If not expressed in terms of rights, the value of human physical integrity would still be present, morally supported and socially accepted, but it would not be promoted to the higher degree of legal security and enforceability. Hence the attraction of transforming values into rights and hence the tendency to claim all good things as human rights.

If regarded in this light, the value cluster of 'human rights' reveals itself as a set of instrumental values, values which lead to or secure deeper, substantive values. To be sure, the very idea of human rights, meaning that every human being is by nature endowed with a certain set of inherent rights, which are not granted by the state and cannot be removed by it, is a value in itself, especially if compared with the pre-human rights era, when this idea was virtually unknown.[9] In this sense human rights as a value appear in the United Nations Charter, without indication of their content, save for the reference to equality of human beings ('without distinction as to race, sex, language, or religion').[10]

Unless some human rights pre-existed in customary international law, the process of transforming the Charter provisions into a coherent set of rights and freedoms which would be universally respected and observed was in fact a matter of agreeing on the values to be protected. The first list, contained in the Universal Declaration of Human Rights, owed much to tradition, to the proclamations, declarations, constitutions and laws of various nations, established in the preceding century and a half. This traditional set was believed to represent human rights, which the United Nations as a war coalition of states defended against the Axis powers and was determined to impose universally. Additions to that catalogue, mainly in the area of economic, social and cultural rights, were fewer and reflected the socialist tradition, officially represented by socialist states but strongly present in the late 1940s in the West. There was a broad consensus among the drafters and in the UN General Assembly on those received values so that the dilemmas about deciding on new values to be elevated to rights were not prominent.[11]

In the next step after the adoption of the Universal Declaration, the elaboration of an international legally binding treaty on human rights, it became clear that the consensus had not been perfect and that the debate on many values and their importance had to be reopened. The worsening international climate of the Cold War and the joining of the debate by the newly independent former colonies made the drafting of what, in the end, became two general human rights treaties, the International Covenant on Civil and Political Rights and the International Covenant on Economic, Social and Cultural Rights, a long, perilous and cumbersome procedure lasting from 1948 to 1966. In the realm of civil and political rights, some values had to be discarded (for example, private property in Article 17 of the Declaration), some were cast in doubt (such as the right to citizenship and international movement (Articles 13, 14 and 15 of the Declaration). The whole category of economic, social and cultural rights was envisaged in less stringent terms. It was set aside in a separate treaty, the International Covenant on Economic, Social and Cultural Rights, with a number of Western states not intending to ratify it at the time.[12]

The only significant enrichment of the traditional catalogue of human rights came in the form of the right of peoples to self-determination, which was transformed from a legitimate value (political principle) to a collective right, placed at the beginning of both covenants.

The true drive to recognize as rights values which had hitherto not been perceived as rights in such a way began only later and has been loosely connected with the efforts to list and recognize the solidarity rights of the 'third generation'.[13] A growing number of values were listed as candidates for promotion to rights, among them development, environment, food, communication and peace.[14] The development of human rights will certainly be a dynamic and endless process: not only will the recognized rights be refined, enriched and broadened, but new rights will be added to the list as soon as there is agreement that a value is of signal importance and that it can be properly expressed and protected as a human right.

The Collective Right to Peace

The statement that there is a right to peace means that this right is already included in the catalogue of human rights or, rhetorically, that it must be immediately included in it. This right was solemnly proclaimed by the UN General Assembly in the Declaration on the Right of Peoples to Peace on 12 November 1984:

> The General Assembly,
> Recognizing that the maintenance of a peaceful life for peoples is the sacred duty of each State,
> 1. Solemnly proclaims that the people of our planet have a sacred right to peace;
> 2. Solemnly declares that the preservation of the right of peoples to peace and the promotion of its implementation constitute a fundamental obligation of each State.[15]

There is a considerable literature on the right to peace, mostly from the pre-1989 era.[16] Advocates of this right do not find much legal support in the 1984 Declaration and the circumstances under which it was passed by the General Assembly. It was adopted hastily, without having been studied by a committee. There were no votes against it but many abstentions, with many delegations conspicuously absent from the room (92 for; 0 against; 34 abstentions).

Of more immediate legal concern was the absence in the text of a clearly stated nature and difference between the bearer and the beneficiary of the obligation to the right of 'all peoples of our planet' to peace. The former appears the singular 'each State', having a 'sacred duty' (5th preambular paragraph) and 'fundamental obligation' (para. 2) and, in the plural: 'all States and international organizations', to whom the appeal is addressed 'to do their utmost to assist in implementing' this right 'through the adoption of appropriate measures at both the national and international level' (para. 4).

As to the (bearer) subject of the right, the Declaration purports to proclaim a collective right, similar to the right of peoples to self-determination. However, on closer examination, it is a doubly collective right, the right of peoples in the plural, the right of the whole of mankind, the collective right of the population of the world. Reference to the planet and the consistent use of the plural indicates that it was conceived as a right which could be claimed, not by one people, but by all peoples.

The impression is that, again unlike the right to self-determination, there was no imaginable way that peoples demanding the right to peace could organize in order to act as true beneficiaries, except as states assembled in international organizations or, admittedly, in a super-organization of non-governmental organizations of peoples. The latter is difficult to imagine if the right of self-determination obtains, its goal being the establishment of states 'possessed of a government representing the whole people belonging to the territory'.[17] The subject of the right, the totality of living human beings, thus has the right vis-à-vis the community of states and each single member thereof.

The drafters' insecurity as to the legal nature of the right to peace was reflected in the wording: in paragraph 1 of the Declaration, this right was not a right of peoples *tout court*, but a 'sacred right', and there was no reference to enforcement, not even to the mechanisms linked to the traditional prohibition of the use of force in international relations (Chapter VII of the UN Charter).

The timing of the proposal, its author (socialist Mongolia), its vague, floral, political language ('peoples of our planet', 'sacred duty', 'sacred right') indicated that the Declaration was a propaganda effort on the part of the USSR in one of its traditional moves to support pacifists abroad. The support which came from Third World governments was generally due to their disposition to side with all suggestions to add to the list of collective rights of the third generation. The dictatorial regimes among them were on this side for an additional reason: ill-defined rights of the 'people' easily became the rights of the state, which the regime controlled, symbolized and represented in the international community: the regime then became the comfortable bearer of an entitlement towards all other states and international organizations. Power holders appeared then to act in favour of human rights whilst denying them to individuals in their jurisdiction, at least while the collective (state) rights were not attained.[18] It should be remembered that the late 1970s and the early 1980s were not an easy time for democracy at the national level. On the other hand, it was difficult to vote against the Declaration, which exhorted governments to act for peace and, vague and toothless as it was, contained no threat to anyone.

The Declaration was criticized as a simple but superfluous reiteration of the prohibition of force in international relations. Such a restatement would have some meaning if the rephrasing went the other way around: namely, from right to prohibition, which is not unusual in the field of human rights. Thus, for example, the right to legality is translated into the prohibition of retroactive legislation in criminal matters, the right to personal freedom into the prohibition of arbitrary arrest, and so on. Even if the existence of a prohibition is taken to imply a right, the Declaration is poor indeed: it neither includes a definition of peace, a mention of aggression or a reference to humanitarian law, nor addresses the related right to life.[19] Finally, the right to peace is conceived only as a collective right, without any consideration of its possible meaning in terms of the individual.[20]

More sophisticated and sincere proponents of the right to peace have not relied on the Declaration but regard this right to be an expression of the recognition of peace as a supreme international value, coupled with an insistence on accompanying preconditions for peace. But then it becomes a figure of speech: 'Designing procedures for peaceful articulation and negotiation of [...] conflicts could be the best contribution that the right to peace could make.'[21]

This is effective and attractive rhetoric, but not a statement of law. As with many attempts to secure and attain some important values, it essentially relies on the magic of bringing a value closer and making it stronger by declaring it a right. Apart from being legally problematic, it is not clear how this change of label from value to right can help the attainment and preservation of peace.

The Use of Individual Rights to Further Peace

Whereas the collective right to peace, as described above, has little meaning and relevance, attention should be given to the frequently neglected individual rights, which repose on peace as a value or can be used to maintain peace, prevent armed conflict or refuse personal involvement therein. They include rights and freedoms enabling individuals to act against violent methods of solving international and internal conflicts and to control decision makers who are in a position to involve society, deliberately or out of incompetence, in armed conflicts. The freedoms of movement, of expression and information, of peaceful assembly, of association, and the political rights to take part in the conduct of public affairs, as well as the rights to privacy and the protection of family and children come readily to mind.

The most conspicuous right directed against institutionalized violence and war is related to conscientious objection to military service. It is generally considered to be an emanation (correct interpretation) of the freedom of conscience,[22] although there are views that it is a part of a wider 'right to refuse', immanent to secularized societies.[23] It has been recognized in a number of countries with various explanations and justifications, following various procedures and with various effects, including consequences which could be interpreted as punitive, for example alternative unarmed national service of longer duration.[24]

For a long while there was no international agreement that the freedom of thought and conscience included the right to conscientious objection. On the other hand, it was not expressly excluded by international instruments. The wording of Article 8 (3.c.ii) of the International Covenant on Civil and Political Rights indicates that its drafters had been aware of the problem but seemed to leave it to the Contracting States to regulate matters relating to conscientious objection and to interpret Article 18, which deals with the freedom of thought, conscience and belief.

Initially, the Human Rights Committee, the body monitoring the implementation of this Covenant, also held the view that conscientious objection was not a recognized right but, in 1993, it adopted its General Comment on Article 18 which devotes a paragraph to conscientious objection. There the Committee expressed its belief 'that such a right can be derived from Article 18, inasmuch as the obligation to use lethal force may seriously conflict with the freedom of conscience and the right to manifest one's religion or belief'.[25] This is not a very strong statement; general comments of the Committee are a hybrid of its observations on state reports submitted to it and authoritative commentaries on the International Covenant on Civil and Political Rights. They cannot purport to be a binding interpretation of the Covenant.[26] Nevertheless, it can be taken that the general comment, coupled with obvious tendencies in individual states to recognize conscientious objection, clearly shows that there is growing consensus that individuals can practise their refusal to take part in preparations for armed conflict as a matter of their right.

However, there is strong resistance to widening the circle of people entitled to refuse to get involved in armed conflict against their will. The Convention on the Rights of the Child, adopted on 20 November 1989, allows States Parties to recruit for military service all persons above the age of 15 (Article 38(3)). It only appeals to them to 'take all feasible measures that persons who have not attained the age of fifteen years do not take a direct part in hostilities' (Article 38(2)). Besides condoning the involvement of children in armed conflict, such provisions are objectionable in another respect: few minors (and persons below the age of 18 are minors in most states) are likely, under present circumstances, to succeed in making a case that they object to military service for reasons of conviction and conscience. Furthermore, minors as a rule have no right to vote, so that they are called to implement decisions to resort to armed force which they have never been able to influence.[27]

Conversely, human rights can be exercised in such a manner as to endanger peace. In the present international human rights regime, it is up to states to restrict the exercise of rights, if it affects certain interests and under certain conditions. However, the grounds for permissible restrictions in existing human rights treaties, universal and regional, do not show that restrictions are envisaged as means to protect peace. Rather, they point in the opposite direction, that of primarily protecting the interests of the nation-state. Thus, under the European Convention for the Protection of Human Rights and Fundamental Freedoms, the freedom of expression can be restricted by law, if the restriction is necessary in a democratic society in the interests of national security, territorial integrity or public safety, for the prevention of disorder and crime, health and morals, of the reputation and rights of others, for preventing the disclosure of information received in confidence, or for maintaining the authority and impartiality of the judiciary (Article 10(2)). Such a collection of grounds appears to offer more protection to the military and patriotic establishment, with its insistence on secrecy, territorial integrity and its glory and reputation, than to interests of peace and peace activists, who can be easily blamed for acting contrary to national interest.

Accusations of abuse of human rights can be countered by claiming that some rights are inherently restricted to protect certain fundamental values. The theory of inherent limitations was supported by some courts, but such a doctrine has been criticized as giving too much power to the interpreters.[28] Article 20 of the International Covenant on Civil and Political Rights expressly prohibits propaganda for war and advocacy of national, racial or religious hatred. The position of this article in the Covenant indicates that it limits the freedoms of manifestation of thought and conscience and of expression. While the prohibition of incitement to hatred has been widely accepted, the prohibition of propaganda of war is resisted as a vague limitation of the freedom of expression, relying as it does on the uncertain notions of 'propaganda' and 'war'. A number of states have entered reservations and interpretative declarations to eliminate or restrict the application of the relevant Article 20(1).[29]

Peace and Human Rights: Causal Links

If accepted as values, peace and human rights can be studied in their causal relationship. The discussion is no longer about whether they are accepted and desirable values, and which of them is to be ranked higher (a ranking which is, in any case, difficult to accept in matters of value and culture), but how they influence one another. Questions to be raised in this context relate to the mutual influence of respect for human rights and peace, and vice versa.

Human Rights as a Precondition for Peace

Elementary peace (absence of armed conflict) was internationally recognized as a universal value earlier than human rights. The twentieth-century version of classical international law and the post-First World War generation of international organizations rested on the assumption that the international community was entitled to act against states which violated the prohibition of aggression or, at least, engaged in irregular and messy wars, but not against those which violated the human rights of their subjects.[30] International peace was not an internal affair of the state but human rights were, until very recently.

It is natural that traditional diplomatic thinking has been committed to the proposition that respect for human rights is conducive to peace. One clearly recognized value needed another one as a prerequisite, not only because of the inertia of the diplomatic mind: this line of reasoning was also the best way for advocates of human rights to 'sell' the need to guarantee the respect and protection of human rights to the sceptical realists controlling the process of the restructuring of the world order after the Second World War.

One does not have to go far for examples of this reasoning. According to Article 55 of the UN Charter, 'universal respect for, and the observance of, human rights and fundamental freedoms' is instrumental in 'the creation of conditions of stability and well-being which are necessary for *peaceful* and friendly relations among nations'.[31] In its Preamble, the Universal Declaration of Human Rights lists, in the first place and before reasons related to justice, dignity and worth of the human being, the conviction of the General Assembly that 'recognition of the inherent dignity and the equal and inalienable rights of all members of the human family is the foundation of freedom, justice and *peace* in the world'.[32] Similar wording appears in the identical first paragraphs of the Preamble of the two International Covenants on Human Rights.

The same thinking was in the foundations of the efforts of the Conference (now Organization) on Security and Co-operation in

Europe (CSCE). In the Helsinki Final Act of 1 August 1975: 'the Participating States recognize the universal significance of human rights and fundamental freedoms, respect for which is an essential factor for *peace*, justice and well-being necessary to ensure the development of friendly relations and co-operation among themselves as among all states'.[33] In this view, observance of human rights is prophylactic; it allegedly helps prevent armed conflict and preserve peace. As demonstrated above, it is a widely shared view in international, governmental and non-governmental organizations. The strength of this belief has served a very useful purpose in the strengthening of the international protection of human rights.[34] In order to examine the empirical validity of this proposition, one has to look at some of its components.

Apparently, the strongest impetus to such thinking, especially in the United Nations, came from the experience preceding the Second World War. The aggressors in this worldwide armed conflict were states with official ideologies of disdain for ideas of individualism and humanism, renowned for their disrespect for human rights and guilty of the resulting massive violations thereof. Hence it was inferred that oppression at home leads to proneness to use violent methods in the furtherance of perceived national interests. In other words, societies without human rights are a danger to international peace.

There are, however, historical examples which point the other way. Oppressive regimes sometimes shun involvement in international conflict for fear of internal destabilization: as, for example, with Franco's Spain. Stalin's USSR, at the height of internal terror, purges and show trials, tried desperately to avoid international conflict until 1941, only to become a dubious member of the pro-democracy and pro-human rights coalition in 1945.

Democracies respecting human rights of their own citizens have been known frequently to resort to war (France and the United Kingdom in the times of colonialism, the United States in its 'colonialist' episodes against Spain, Israel and so on). It was observed, however, that democracies seldom went to war one against another.[35]

Systematic empirical research also appears inconclusive. The results which purport to prove that 'libertarian' societies are less prone to international violence have immediately been challenged by other authors, mainly on the basis of the elusive operationalization of the concepts of 'free' societies and 'international violence'.[36] It is very difficult to determine even today which states are democratic and have an excellent human rights record. It is much harder to do it in a historical perspective. Where do colonial wars belong? In terms of the nineteenth century, was the United Kingdom a democracy respecting human rights? If it was, were autochthnous pre-colonial

states in Africa democracies according to contemporary African standards? This probably explains why empirically oriented researchers
have avoided the study of democracy and respect for human rights
as factors influencing involvement in international armed conflicts.
There are, on the other hand, strong statements that human rights
and freedom do not influence one another, that 'freedom and conflict
are basically unrelated'.[37]

Another support for the hypothesis that absence of human rights
endangers peace is that consistent deprivation of human rights leads
to rebellion, which causes internal violence and may result in international conflict. This is also a traditional belief, originating in the
theory of tyrannicide and the right to rebel against oppression.[38] It
was also reflected in the Preamble of the Universal Declaration of
Human Rights: 'it is essential, if man is not compelled to have recourse, as a last resort, to rebellion against tyranny and oppression,
that human rights shall be protected by the rule of law'.

In the later practice of the United Nations, the right to rebel was
mainly associated with the right to self-determination of peoples.
General Assembly resolutions referred to 'man's basic right to fight
for the self-determination of his people under colonial and foreign
domination'[39] and stated: 'The struggle of peoples under colonial,
alien domination and racist regimes for the implementation of their
right to self-determination and independence is legitimate and in full
accordance with the principles of international law'.[40]

It will be noted that this shift in the United Nations towards the
violation of human rights, taken to be in some sense committed by
'aliens', also gives the clue to understanding how rebellion which
would normally cause only internal disturbances could result in damage to international peace: namely, it is implied that rebels are entitled
to international assistance or, at least, that foreign states providing
help are not violating international law. If freed from the excessive
attachment to the right to self-determination, this boils down to the
right of the international community to act against governments
grossly violating human rights or to assist the rebellious victims of
human rights violations. This is how international conflict can be
generated, even if there is no formal alien domination.[41]

In other words, human rights violations open the door to humanitarian intervention. Some of the worst repressive systems have finally
been crushed by foreign intervention or by defeat in international
conflict. The definitive fall of the regime of Idi Amin in Uganda after
the Tanzanian intervention is often quoted as one recent example,
although it was also triggered by border transgressions by Ugandan
troops.[42] The motives of the intervening countries have been much
too frequently mixed to allow their intervention to be treated as
genuinely humanitarian, but this does not concern us here. There is

some merit in the statement that human rights violations lead to foreign involvement and conflict, not by the aggressive policies of the oppressive government but by opening the way and creating legitimacy for foreign involvement.

This statement has been rephrased to mean that insistence on human rights endangers peace.[43] If absence of international conflict is taken to mean peace, then any foreign interference to prevent, monitor, condemn or sanction human rights violations in a country, which inevitably results in more or less vehement reactions from the government, will certainly bring the parties closer to conflict than cooperation. This is also true when more structured, internationalized and 'polite' intervention is undertaken. The record of the United Nations and its various human rights organs, including treaty bodies monitoring various human rights covenants and conventions, shows that individual states have been extremely reluctant to use any existing opportunity to initiate action in state-against-state complaints, and that action started by individuals and groups has been pursued by political organs with little enthusiasm and efficiency. The non-political Human Rights Committee, which has already been active for 17 years, has not received a single communication from a State Party to the International Covenant on Civil and Political Rights claiming that another State Party is not fulfilling its obligations under Article 41. The Commission on Human Rights has not completed any of its actions, however circumspect, originating in reports that in some countries there appears to be a consistent pattern of gross violations of human rights and fundamental freedoms:[44] 'Since adoption of the 1503 procedure, the Commission has neither exercised its power to undertake a thorough study nor sought the consent of a delinquent State for the creation of an investigating committee.'[45]

To be sure, the reasons for such timidity are not only fear of armed conflict, but include hesitancy to affect economic interests, to imperil ideologically close and otherwise friendly and strategically reliable governments, to weaken international alliances, and so on. Nevertheless, it remains true that most atrocious internal repression has been preferred to armed conflict, even when the offending governments were militarily weak, if there were other motives. In this respect, a sharp distinction is still made between internal and international peace, with the latter being the only one that matters.[46]

According to one line of reasoning, societies where human rights are respected and observed tend to live in internal peace, but this does not always apply to their proneness to violate international peace if they follow one interpretation of the nature of the nation-state: namely that, if there is consensus that the state serves exclusively and predominantly the interests of its population, then aggression and international use of force are more easily accepted if they happen abroad. Then the majority of citizens who believe they are free and respectful of democracy and human rights can support going to war for something which is perceived as good for the whole national community. Moreover, respect for human rights can be regarded as a purely national value. This has recently been loudly proclaimed in societies dominated by nationalist rhetoric: human rights and democracy are meant only for the members of one's own nation. They are almost irrelevant abroad, unless they are the rights of conational minorities there. Within the state, ethnically different (alien) citizens are then excluded because they are not a true part of the body politic and it is not their right to self-determination which is the origin of all individual rights.[47] Being a part of the superior nation elevates each of its biological members to a higher civic status than any member of another ethnic group. Nationalist majorities and their government initially promise to treat their worst conational political opponents better than the tamest member of a minority. Human rights and democracy are conceived and held feasible only within the closed national group. This explains how some of the best legal minds and staunchest opponents of ideological totalitarianism easily become apologists of national discrimination.

As shown by the practice of the fascist brand of nationalist populism and recent events in East and Central Europe, this promise cannot be kept for long. *Nestbeschmutzer*, 'cosmopolitans', 'mondialists' and other non-nationalists become traitors, together with those who for reasons of mercy and humanity sabotage the war effort. Referring to the French Revolution, Steven Lukes observes: 'The revolutionary slogan "la fraternité ou la mort" [fraternity or death] thus acquired a new and ominous meaning, promising violence first against non-brothers and then against false brothers.'[48]

Through their readiness to disregard violations of human rights committed against 'others', apparent democracy reveals itself as a sham and eventually results in denial of human rights to individual members of their own group.

Human Rights as a Component of Peace

The statement that human rights are a prerequisite of peace can have a weaker or a stronger form. It can be maintained that human rights are conducive to peace, but it can also be said that there is no peace without human rights. The latter statement can be interpreted as meaning that human rights are an indispensable condition for peace, which means that the separate value of peace cannot be attained without securing the separate value of human rights. However, the interpretation is also possible that peace cannot exist without human rights, where human rights are part of peace, where peace is defined by reference to human rights, and peace and human rights merge in one value cluster. Peace without human rights is then not only unlikely or even impossible: it is unthinkable.

This conclusion has been reached by those who refuse to accept the traditional concept of peace only as absence of armed conflict (negative peace) or even as a set of instrumental values, but believe that it can be defined by reference to substantive values. In other and simpler words, peace in this view is not only a state of certain inactivity, which is precious because war is worse; it is not only a situation where all actors can pursue their relative goals (no matter how acceptable they are) by other means. It is defined as a set of values, which give peace substance and meaning (positive peace).

Such reasoning runs parallel to the efforts of some peace researchers to redefine violence, and to include in that concept not only the actual exercise of violent methods but also the results of former violence and the permanent production of violent structures, both national and international (structural violence).[49] This leads to the necessity to describe the emanations of structural violence, which in reverse is the description of a state without structural violence; that is, peace. For peace researchers, positive values to be included in the concept of peace are integration, human fulfilment, freedom, social justice, and so on. If this is coupled with their individualistic, anthropocentric view of the world system,[50] it is obvious that what is meant is more or less the set of values otherwise covered by the concept of human rights.[51]

There was a similar potential in Marxism, with its concept of alienation (*Entfremdung*). This notion, originally borrowed from Hegel, covered various forms of historical loss of true human essence through economic and social organization, politics, religion and so on.[52] This resembles Johan Galtung's and others' comments on the inadequacy of the affirmation of individual somatic and mental potentials.[53] Unfortunately, recent Marxist writers were not interested in matters of legal theory, tethered as they were by the vulgar definition of law as 'the will of the ruling class'. Hence the paucity of Marxist philosophical and legal writings on human rights issues,[54] and the failure to explore the possibilities of disalienation through human rights.

In the official thinking of states and international governmental organizations, the belief that peace was equal to human rights was not present in its radical form, described above; it was reduced to expressing the view that peace without human rights (and other values, including, most frequently, development) was still peace, but insecure and inferior. The General Conference of UNESCO has been very fond of language indicating that 'peace cannot consist solely in the absence of armed conflict but implies principally a process of progress, justice and mutual respect among the peoples [...] A peace founded on injustice and violation of human rights cannot last and leads inevitably to violence.'[55]

In the late 1970s and early 1980s, this discourse was replaced by the primacy of peace, which is to be served by human rights, and eventually resulted in the Declaration on the Right of Peoples to Peace. Politically, this can be explained by the stronger presence in the majority of non-aligned states from the Third World of regimes disinclined towards individualism and the related interpretation of human rights, which brought them closer to the political East. The concept of peace returned to its negative international meaning, as absence of war among nations. In political reality, the security of states, which came to be identified with state (regime) security,[56] became the most important concern.

Although well intentioned, all attempts to identify peace and human rights reveal methodological weaknesses. The inclusion of various desirable values and goals stretches the concept of peace beyond recognition. The effort to transform peace from a set of modal values to a collection of substantive values has also been in vain. There is a new competition to include everything desirable in the package of peace, which reveals the same stratagem used with human rights: declaring something to be identical to peace (or an essential component thereof) brings that something within reach. In less sophisticated terms of agitation, this comes close to semantic tricks related to value-laden terms. If there is a 'good' word, attach it to a desired value or result. Peace is good: everything which is subsumed thereunder is also good. As witnessed by a number of resolutions of international organizations and governmental statements, terrorism is bad: everything which has been thought to merit condemnation or to be noxious has then been called terrorism.

Peace as a Precondition for Human Rights

Conversely, it can be asked whether peace leads to the respect and enjoyment of human rights, or whether the latter can be enjoyed without peace at all. In terms of general ideological and political currents, this causal link has been proposed later historically than the human rights-leading-to-peace hypothesis.

In the most important international human rights instruments, the respecting of human rights is not made dependent on the conditions of peace. Furthermore, the whole structure of humanitarian law or the set of humanitarian rules of the international law of armed conflict (war), which was codified before the law of human rights,[57] rested on the assumption that individual rights ought to be specially protected in armed conflict and in spite of war, which was a legitimate means of furthering national interests and solving international disputes (*ius ad bellum*). To be sure, all this was an implicit recognition of the intuitive reasoning that absence of peace (war), international and later internal, was a menace to the enjoyment of human rights. It is axiomatic that, during a situation which is characterized by violence, most of it legitimate, individual human rights are very likely to suffer. In all its manifestations, human rights law[58] attempts to limit the damage which armed conflict causes to the enjoyment of human rights.

Humanitarian law deals with the danger of war to the human rights of human beings on the other, enemy side. Although forced to recognize the legitimacy of many forms of denial of human rights of the combatants, such as the right to life and physical integrity, and of the civilian population, such as the freedom of movement, assembly and association, it nevertheless limits the methods of warfare and control of occupied territory to the historically acceptable range, absolutely prohibiting some human rights violations and declaring them to be criminal offences (grave breaches).

Human rights law during wartime is concerned with the effects of the use of violence within the state at war on the whole population. International instruments allow for restrictions of some rights for reasons of national security, even in peacetime. They tolerate restriction and derogation of rights 'in time of emergency which threatens the life of the nation',[59] which certainly includes the state of war. The only condition is that derogation does not have discriminatory effects. Nevertheless, some rights are absolutely protected and cannot be temporarily abolished. According to Article 4(2) of the International Covenant on Civil and Political Rights, the non-derogable rights are the right to life, the right to physical integrity (prohibition of torture and similar treatment or punishment), prohibition of slavery and servitude, prohibition of imprisonment for inability to fulfil a contractual obligation (imprisonment for debt), right to legality in criminal law (*nullum crimen, nulla poena sine lege*), right to be a person before law, and freedom of thought, conscience and religion. It is not easy to determine why exactly the rights enumerated were chosen to represent the very gist of the catalogue of human rights, even after the perusal of the *travaux préparatoires*.[60] The rationale was obviously similar to that underlying humanitarian law: no derogation shall be permitted if it is morally repellent and if it does not meaningfully contribute to the legitimate war effort.

There are other ways in which armed conflict adversely affects human rights, many of them not easy to grasp in legal terms. The non-state actors and factors which militate against human rights of others and which can even in time of peace be more prone to human rights violations than government agencies and agents now feel less inhibited by moral restraints and encouraged by the culture of war, which offers the opportunity for criminal elements to ennoble their deeds with putative patriotic motives.[61] War enthusiasm and war hysteria lessen popular support for human rights and, without it, institutions designed to protect human rights lose their independence and effectiveness.

There is no evidence that even exceptionally stable democracies, based on the rule of law and strong 'law habits', manage to preserve the full enjoyment of the human rights of their own population during armed conflict. War is harmful to human rights. Peace is one of the preconditions for the full enjoyment of human rights. This does not mean, however, that conceptually there are no human rights without peace.

Conclusions

Human rights and peace are separate clusters of modal (instrumental) values. They partly overlap, but are not identical. Subsuming human rights under peace, or peace under human rights, is methodologically wrong and does not serve any meaningful educational or political purpose. In a world of sovereign nation-states, respect for human rights does not unequivocally result in peace. Peace and human rights being separate sets of values, one of them can take precedence so that, in the case of gross violations of human rights, the risk of international conflict becomes acceptable. There is no doubt that absence of peace, either international or national, endangers the enjoyment of human rights, totally or partially.

The collective (peoples') right to peace, as advocated by the United Nations and formulated in the 1984 Declaration on the Right of Peoples to Live in Peace, does not have a clear legal meaning and cannot be translated into meaningful action. However, many individual rights can be exercised with the view of defending peace and preventing national and personal involvement in war.

Notes

1   According to the official interpretation of Marxist theory in the former socialist camp, the right to private property which is, as the right to the peaceful enjoyment of possessions, a recognized human right under the European Convention for the Protection of Human Rights and Fundamental Freedoms (Protocol No. 1), represents the main cause of social evils, so that its abolition appears as the supreme goal which will result in social happiness comparable to that which other advocates of human rights imagine as a result of the successful implementation of the whole catalogue of human rights. See Vladimir Kartashkin, 'The socialist countries and human rights', in Karel Vasak (ed.), *The International Dimension of Human Rights*, Paris, UNESCO, 1982, p.631.

2 Lukes Steven, 'Five fables about human rights', in Stephen Shute and Susan Hurley (eds), *On Human Rights. The Oxford Amnesty Lectures*, New York, Basic Books, 1993, pp.19–40.
3 Stephen Marks, 'The peace–human rights–development dialectic', *Bulletin of Peace Proposals* (Oslo), **XI**, (4), 1980, 339–40.
4 Maurice Merlo-Ponty, *Humanisme et terreur*, Paris, Gallimard, 1947.
5 Frantz Fanon, *The Wretched of the Earth*, Harmondsworth, Penguin, 1967. See also the preface by Jean-Paul Sartre, pp.7–26.
6 Juris Bojars, 'The citizenship and human (rights) regulations in the Republic of Latvia', *The Finnish Yearbook of International Law*, Vol. 3, 1992, p.331.
7 Letter of Ljubomir Tadic, a renowned former Marxist philosopher, to the Belgrade weekly *NIN*, 16 September 1994.
8 See, for example, Nedjeljko Kujundzic, 'Ukazanje fasizma u boljseviekoj ropotarnici' (The spectre of fascism in Bolshevik waste storage), *Vjesnik*, Zagreb, 19 October 1994, p.14.
9 The prevailing understanding of human rights in socialist theory, even in the late 1970s, was also very conservative and state-centred. In the words of a Soviet scholar with a high position in the United Nations Secretariat, 'The theory of natural law [...] is in principle invalid, since it destroys the link between human rights and their creators – states'. Neither does positivism help; according to the same writer, if a state has ratified a human rights treaty, 'the concrete realization and implementation of [...] rights falls within the domestic jurisdiction of each contracting State and may not be [...] the object of foreign intervention' (Youri Rechetov, 'International responsibility for violations of human rights', in Antonio Cassese (ed.), *UN Law. Fundamental Rights. Two Topics in International Law*, Alphen aan den Rijn, Sijthoff and Noordhoff, 1979, pp.237–8 and 240); 'Human rights constitute a part of the rights a State, two or more States, awards to the individuals, to a group of people (the nation, an ethnic minority, the staff of an enterprise), or even to the entire population. Today human rights are [...] desirable rights' (Adam Lopatka, 'The right to live in peace as a human right', *Bulletin of Peace Proposals*, **11**, (4), December 1980, p.362).
10 References to human rights are found in the Preamble and Articles 1, 13, 55, 56, 62, 68 and 76 of the Charter. Rechetov believes that the UN Charter 'does not impose on Member States concrete obligations concerning specific human rights and fundamental freedoms', but that 'concrete obligations to promote higher standards of living, full employment and conditions of economic and social progress and development, solutions of international economic, social, health and related problems, international cultural and educational co-operation [...] have to be considered as a part of positive international law and must be strictly observed by states' (op. cit., note 9, p.23).
11 John Humphrey, *Human Rights and the United Nations: A Great Adventure*, Dobbs Ferry, Oceana, 1984.
12 The United States of America, which ratified the 'ideologically' more acceptable International Covenant on Civil and Political Rights only after hesitation and long delays, and with a number of far-reaching reservations, still does not show any inclination to ratify the International Covenant on Economic, Social and Cultural Rights. (See UN Doc. CCPR/C/2, Rev. 4.)
13 See Karel Vasak, 'For the third generation of human rights: the rights of solidarity', inaugural lecture to the Tenth Study Session of the International Institute of Human Rights, Strasbourg, 2–27 July 1979; André Holleaux, 'Les lois de la "troisième génération" des droits de l'homme', *Revue française d'administration publique*, **15**, 1980, 45. For a critique, see Jack Donnelly, 'In search of the uni-

corn: the jurisprudence and politics of the right to development', *California Western International Law Journal*, **15**, 1985, 473–509.

14   Philip Alston, 'A third generation of solidarity rights: progressive development or obfuscation of international human rights law?', *Netherlands International Law Review*, **XXIX**, (3), 1982, 307 ff.

15   Resolution 39/11.

16   For example, the special issue of the *Bulletin of Peace Proposals*, **11**, (4), 1980; Vojin Dimitrijevic, 'The interrelationship between peace and human rights', in Manfred Nowak, Dorothea Steurer and Hannes Tretter (eds), *Fortschritt im Bewusstsein der Grund- und Menschenrechte* (Progress in the Spirit of Human Rights) *Festschrift fuer Felix Ermacora*, Kehl/Strasbourg/Arlington, N.P. Engel Verlag, 1988, pp.589–98; Christian Tomuschat, 'Recht auf Frieden' (Right to peace), *Europa-Archiv*, **40**, 1985, 271ff; Coleen E. Dawes, 'The right to peace', *The Australian Law Journal*, **60**, (2), 1986, 156–61; Katarina Tomasevski, 'The right to peace', *Current Research on Peace and Violence*, **3**, (1), 1982, 42–68. Tomasevski was one of the few authors who revisited the subject after 1989: 'The right to peace after the Cold War', *Peace Review* (Palo Alto), **3**, (3), Fall 1991, 14–22. See also Philip Alston, 'The legal basis of the right to peace, ibid., 23–7.

17   Declaration on Principles of International Law Concerning Friendly Relations and Co-operation among States in Accordance with the Charter of the United Nations, General Assembly resolution 2625 (XXV), 1970.

18   Jacques Nzouankeu, 'The African attitude to democracy', *International Social Science Journal*, **43**, 1991, 376–7.

19   See the General Comment 14 (23) of the Human Rights Committee on Article 6 of the International Covenant on Civil and Political Rights: 'It is evident that the designing, testing, manufacture, possession and deployment of nuclear weapons are among the greatest threats to the right to life which confront mankind today' (Doc. UN CCPR/C/21/Rev.1, 19 May 1989).

20   See the next section, 'The use of individual rights to further peace'.

21   Tomasevski, 'The right to peace after the Cold War', 1991 (op. cit., note 16), 22.

22   See Erhard Mock, *Gewissen and Gewissensfreiheit*, Berlin, Duncker and Humblot, 1983; B.P. Vermeulen, *De Vrijheid van Geweten. Een Fundamenteel Rechtsprobleem* (The freedom of conscience. A fundamental problem of law), Arnhem, Gouda Quint, 1989. For the work of international organizations, see 'Conscientious objection to military service', report prepared in pursuance of resolutions 14 (XXXIV) and 1982/30 of the Sub-Commission on Prevention of Discrimination and Protection of Minorities by Asbjorn Eide and Chama Mubanga-Chipoya. See Resolution 337 and Recommendation 478 of the Assembly of the Council of Europe, 26 January 1967.

23   See Martin Scheinin, 'The right to say "No"', *Archiv fuer Rechts- und Sozialphilosophie*, **75**, (3), 1989, 345–56.

24   See the Explanatory Report to the Recommendation No. R(87) of the Committee of Ministers of the Council of Europe, Doc. H (87) 3, 22 June 1987.

25   UN Doc. CCPR/C/21 Rev. 1/Add. 2, 1993; HRI/GEN/1/Rev. 1, 1994. For a survey of the relevant decisions of the Human Rights Committee and comments thereon, see Bahiyyih G. Tahzib, *Freedom of Religion or Belief. Ensuring Effective International Protection*, Dordrecht, Nijhoff, 1996, pp.249ff.

26   Manfred Nowak, *UNO-Pakt uber burgerliche und politische Rechte und Fakultativprotokoll. CCPR-Kommentar*, Kehl/Strasbourg/Arlington, N.P. Engel, 1989, pp.613–19.

27   Tomasevski, 1991 (op. cit., note 16), 19.

28   For the European Commission and the European Court of Human Rights, see P. van Dijk and G.J.H. van Hoof, *Theory and Practice of the European Convention on Human Rights*, 2nd edn, Deventer/Boston, Kluwer, 1990, pp.575–8.

29 Nowak (op. cit., note 26), pp.392–3.
30 Tom J. Farer and Felice Gaer, 'The UN and human rights: at the end of the beginning', in Adam Roberts and Benedict Kingsbury (eds), *United Nations, Divided World*, 2nd edn, Oxford, Clarendon Press, 1993, pp.240–44, and the literature quoted therein.
31 Emphasis added.
32 Emphasis added.
33 Declaration on Principles, VII, para. 5; emphasis added.
34 'We have human rights norms officially because of the view that they contribute to peace. And that, in itself is a debatable notion' (David P. Forsythe, *Human Rights and World Politics*, Lincoln/London, University of Nebraska Press, 1983, p.31).
35 M.W. Doyle, 'Kant, liberal legacy, and foreign affairs', *Philosophy and Public Affairs*, **12**, 1983, 205–35; Norberto Bobbio, *Il Futuro della Democrazia*, Turin, Einaudi, 1984, pp.31–9.
36 For a sample of the debate see R.J. Rummel, 'Libertarianism and international violence', *Journal of Conflict Resolution*, **27**, (1), 1983, 27–71; Jack E. Vincent, 'Freedom and international conflict: another look', *International Studies Quarterly*, **31**, (1), 1987, 103–12; R.J. Rummel, 'On Vincent's view of freedom and international conflict', *International Studies Quarterly*, **31**, (1), 1987, 113–17; Jack E. Vincent, 'On Rummel's omnipresent theory', *International Studies Quarterly*, **31**, (1), 1987, 125.
37 Vincent, 'On Rummel's omnipresent theory' (op. cit., note 36), 125. Vincent refers to data collected by the late Edward Azar at the University of Maryland.
38 C.A. Cohen, 'The right and duty of resistance', *Human Rights Journal*, **1**, (4), 1968, 491–516.
39 General Assembly resolution 2787 (XXVI), 6 December 1971, Article 2.
40 General Assembly resolution 3103 (XXVIII), 12 December 1973, Article 3.
41 To perceive a regime as 'alien' can be easier than imagined and is not only limited to colonial situations. In almost all states of the world there are groups and political movements which consider their governments as 'alien' in national or political terms. For the nationalist ideologists in multinational federations, the federal authorities appear 'alien'. For Yugoslavia, see generally Sabrina P. Ramet, *Nationalism and Federalism in Yugoslavia*, 2nd edn, Bloomington/Indianapolis, Indiana University Press, 1992. It is interesting to compare the views of Serb and Slovene writers, writers being the traditional agents of national 'awakening' in Central and Eastern Europe: Drinka Gojkovic, 'Trauma without Catharsis', *The Republic*, Belgrade, 7, (118), 1995, I–XXVI; 'Samostojna Slovenija' (Independent Slovenia), thematic issue of *Nova Revija*, Ljubljana, 9, March 1990, 241–632. The most radical wings of the 'new left' believed that most Western governments were surrogates of the United States or of some kind of capitalist centre. When brought before courts, they maintained that they were prisoners of war. See Conrad Detrez (ed.), *Zerschlagt die Wohlstandsinseln der Dritten Welt*, Reinbeck bei Hamburg, Rowohlt, 1971.
42 Forsythe (op. cit., note 34), p.28.
43 'Human rights breeds confrontation' (Stanley Hoffmann, 'The hell of good intentions', *Foreign Policy*, 29, (1), 1977, 8.
44 Economic and Social Council resolutions 1235 (XLI), 1967; 1503 (XLIV), 1970.
45 Farer and Gaer (op. cit., note 30), p.281; Thomas M. Franck, *Nation Against Nation*, New York/Oxford, Oxford University Press, 1985, pp.224–45.
46 Tomasevski, 'The right to peace', 1982 (op. cit., note 16), 47.
47 Bojars (op. cit., note 6), p.242.
48 Lukes (op. cit., note 2), p.37.
49 The most influential writer on positive peace, structural violence and related

concepts has been Johan Galtung, 'A structural theory of integration', *Journal of Peace Research* (Oslo), **5**, (4), 1968, 375–95; 'Violence, peace and peace research', *Journal of Peace Research*, **6**, (3), 1969, 167–91; 'Feudal systems, structural violence and structural theory of revolution', *Essays in Peace Research*, Copenhagen, Christian Ejlers, Vol. 3, 1970; 'A structural theory of imperialism', *Essays in Peace Research*, op. cit., Vol. 4, 1970. See also authors listed in Hanna Newcombe and Alan Newcombe, *Peace Research around the World*, Oakville (Ontario), 1969. For a critique, see A. Eide and M. Kjell, 'Note on Galtung's concept of violence', *Journal of Peace Research*, **8**, (1), 1971, 71; Kenneth E. Boulding, 'Twelve friendly quarrels with Johan Galtung', in Nils Petter Gleditch, Odvar Leine *et al.* (eds), *Johan Galtung: A Bibliography of His Scholarly and Popular Writings 1950–1980*, Oslo, Peace Research Institute, 1980, pp.7–26.

50   Modern nationalists, who are strangely attracted to Galtung, object to this approach as disregarding the nation and its state. See, for example, Dragan Simic, *Pozitivan mir. Shvatanja Johana Galtunga* (Positive peace. The views of Johan Galtung), Belgrade, Akademija nova, 1993, p.77.

51   Galtung, 'The next twenty-five years of peace research: tasks and prospects', *Essays in Peace Research* (op. cit., note 49), Vol. 6, 1980, p.103.

52   J. Israel, *L'Aliénation de Marx à la sociologie contemporaine*, Paris, Anthropos, 1972; Manuel Atienza, *Marx y los derechos humanos*, Madrid, Mezquita, 1982. For a recent reappraisal, see Slavoj Zizek, *The Sublime Object of Ideology*, London/New York, Verso, 1989.

53   'Violence, peace' (op. cit., note 49), 110–11.

54   See, however, Mihailo Markovic, 'Differing conceptions of human rights in Europe. Toward a resolution', *Philosophical Foundations of Human Rights*, Paris, UNESCO, 1986, pp.113–30; Jukka Paastela, 'Human rights in the writings of Marx and Engels', in Allan Rosas and Jan Helgesen (eds), *Human Rights in a Changing East–West Perspective*, London/New York, Pinter, 1990, pp.6–16. For a survey of the Soviet Marxist legal doctrine on human rights, see Antonio Cassese, *International Law in a Divided World*, Oxford, Clarendon, 1986, pp.300–302.

55   Resolution 18 C/11.1, 1974. The Director-General of UNESCO wrote in the same vein: 'Peace is more than simply a matter of refraining from war; there can be no lasting peace if individuals are deprived of their rights and liberties, if people are oppressed by other peoples, if populations are beset with poverty or suffering from malnutrition and sickness.' (Quoted by Marks (op. cit., note 3), 341.)

56   Vojin Dimitrijevic, *Pojam bezbednosti u medjunarodnim odnosima* (The concept of security in international relations), Belgrade, Savez udru'enja pravnika, 1973.

57   Henri Coursier, 'L'évolution du droit international humanitaire', *Recueil de Cours*, Academy of International Law, 1960, p.357; Yoram Dinstein, 'Human rights in armed conflict: international humanitarian law', in Theodor Meron (ed.), *Human Rights in International Law. Legal and Policy Issues*, Oxford, Clarendon, 1985, pp.345–68.

58   After all, human rights law and humanitarian law are the expression of the same idea, influenced by the particular plight of the beneficiaries of rights and the historical circumstances of codification. See also A.H. Robertson, *Human Rights as the Basis of International Humanitarian Law*, Lugano, International Institute of Humanitarian Law, 1971.

59   International Covenant on Civil and Political Rights, Article 4(1).

60   Marc J. Bossuyt, *Guide to the 'travaux préparatoires' of the International Covenant on Civil and Political Rights*, Dordrecht, Nijhoff, 1987.

61   Bogdan Denitch, *Ethnic Nationalism*, Minneapolis/London, University of Minnesota Press, 1994, pp.187–205.

Bibliography

Alston, Philip (1982), 'A third generation of solidarity rights: progressive development or obfuscation of international human rights law?', *Netherlands International Law Review*, **29**, (3), 307–22.

Bulletin of Peace Proposals (Oslo), 'Special Issue. The right to peace and development', **11**, (4), 1980.

Dimitrijevic, Vojin (1988), 'The interrelationship between peace and human rights and the possible right to peace', in Manfred Nowak, Dorothea Steurer and Hannes Tretter (eds), *Fortschritt im Bewusstsein der Grund- und Menschenrechte* (Progress in the Spirit of Human Rights), Festschrift fuer Felix Ermacora, Kehl/Strasbourg/Arlington, N.P. Engel Verlag.

Farer, Tom J. and Felice Gaer (1993), 'The UN and human rights: at the end of the beginning', in Adam Roberts and Benedict Kingsbury (eds), *United Nations, Divided World*, 2nd edn, Oxford, Clarendon Press.

Shute, Stephen and Susan Hurley (1993), *On Human Rights. The Oxford Amnesty Lectures*, New York, Basic Books.

Tomaševski, Katarina (1991), 'The right to peace after the Cold War', *Peace Review*, Palo Alto, **3**, (3), Fall, 14–22.

Tomuschat, Christian (1985), 'Recht auf Frieden' (Right to peace), *Europa-Archiv*, **40**, 271–8.

3 Democracy and Human Rights: Civil, Political, Economic, Social and Cultural

DAVID BEETHAM

Democracy and human rights have historically been regarded as distinct phenomena, occupying different areas of the political sphere: the one a matter of the organization of government, the other a question of individual rights and their defence. When we speak of democracy, we have learnt to think of institutional arrangements such as competitive elections, multi-partyism, the separation of powers, and so forth. These are essentially matters of constitutional order, and of the organization of public power. Human rights, on the other hand, take the individual as their point of reference, and seek to guarantee to individuals the minimum necessary conditions for pursuing a distinctively human life. Moreover, as the term 'human' implies, such rights have always been defined as universal in their scope, and subject to international definition and regulation, whereas the constitutional arrangements of government have traditionally been regarded as entirely an internal matter for the state concerned, since they comprise the essence of 'sovereignty'. These distinctions have been further reinforced by an academic division of labour which has assigned the study of democracy to political science, and of human rights to law and jurisprudence: two disciplines which, in the Anglo-Saxon world at least, have had very little connection with one another.[1]

Today this separation is no longer tenable, if indeed it ever was. The collapse of communist regimes under popular pressure has revealed democracy, along with human rights, to be a universal aspiration, rather than a merely localized form of government. And the record of human rights abuses under all kinds of dictatorship, whether of left or right, has shown that the type of political system within a country is far from irrelevant to the standard of human rights its citizens enjoy. Democracy and human rights, we now acknowledge, belong firmly together. However, the precise relationship between them is often mistakenly characterized, either as an empirical correlation or as a matter of complementarity, rather than as an organic unity.[2] Thus it is often said that democracy is the system of government 'most likely' to defend human rights, while on the other hand democracy itself is said to need 'supplementing' by human rights, as if these were something to be added on to democracy, or even as themselves *vulnerable* to democracy, if they are not independently guaranteed. Such characterizations of the relationship, while understandable, are nevertheless wrongly posed.

At the heart of this issue is the question of how we are to define democracy itself. The weakness of any purely institutional definition in terms, say, of multi-partyism, electoral competition, the separation of powers, and so on, is that it fails to specify what exactly it is about these institutions that makes them *democratic*, as opposed to 'liberal', 'pluralist', or any other term we choose to employ. If the answer is that these are institutions which all countries that we call 'democratic' happen to have, such an answer simply begs the question of why these countries should be called democratic in the first place. The only way to avoid a question begging circularity is to specify the underlying principles which these institutions embody, or help to realize, and in terms of which they can plausibly be characterized as democratic.

What are these principles? The core idea of democracy is that of popular rule or popular control over collective decision making. Its starting point is with the citizen rather than with the institutions of government. Its defining principles are that all citizens are entitled to a say in public affairs, both through the associations of civil society and through participation in government; and that this entitlement should be available on terms of equality to all. Control *by* citizens over their collective affairs, and equality *between* citizens in the exercise of that control, are the key democratic principles. Whereas in very small-scale and simple societies or associations that control can be exercised directly, by citizens taking part in collective decisions themselves, in large and complex societies their control can only be exercised indirectly: through the right to stand for public office, to elect key public officials by universal equal suffrage, to hold government accountable and to approve directly the terms of any constitutional change.[3]

Once we start with these underlying principles of popular control over collective affairs on terms of equal citizenship, we can proceed to a second-order question: what is needed to make these principles effective in the context of the modern state? Answering this further question takes us in two directions simultaneously. One direction is towards an elucidation of the institutional arrangements which have proved themselves over time as necessary to ensure effective popular control. Thus we have electoral competition between political parties offering alternative programmes for popular approval; a representative legislature acting on behalf of the electorate in holding the executive to account; an independent judiciary to ensure that all public officials act according to the laws approved by the legislature; independent media acting to scrutinize government and to voice public opinion; institutions for individual redress in the event of maladministration, such as the Ombudsman, and so on. All these institutions can be termed democratic to the extent that they contribute to the popular control of government. No doubt they could do so more effectively, and with greater equality between citizens and between different sections of society. In other words, they could be *more* democratic than they currently are. But what makes them democratic, when they are all implemented, is that they embody, and contribute to, these underlying principles.

A second direction in which we are taken is to consider what other rights citizens require if their basic democratic right of having a voice in public affairs is to be effective. Here at once the necessity of the civil and political part of the human rights agenda becomes evident. Without the freedoms of expression, of association, of assembly, of movement, people cannot effectively have a say, whether in the organizations of civil society or in matters of government policy. Such freedoms are not *private* rights, since they presuppose communication between citizens, and the existence of a public forum, or a variety of public fora, in which to do so. However, they can only be guaranteed as rights to individuals; and they require underpinning in turn by the right to individual liberty, to personal security and to due legal process.

At the heart of democracy thus lies the right of all citizens to a voice in public affairs and to exercise control over government, on terms of equality with other citizens. For this right to be effective requires, on the one hand, the kind of political institutions – elections, parties, legislatures and so on – with which we are familiar from the experience of the established democracies. On the other hand, it requires the guarantee of those human rights which we call civil and political, and which are inscribed in such conventions as the International Covenant on Civil and Political Rights and the European Convention on Human Rights. Both are needed to realize the basic principles of democracy. Thus the connection between democracy and human rights is an intrinsic rather than extrinsic one; human rights constitute a necessary part of democracy.

It follows that to define democracy in terms of a set of political institutions alone is to make a double error. First, it ignores the underlying principles which mark them as democratic, and against which their degree of democratization can be assessed. Second, it treats those institutions as all that is required for democracy, by overlooking the human rights which are also an intrinsic part of it. It is because they are an intrinsic part that democratization may be more effectively advanced in certain conditions under a campaign for human rights than through a campaign for democracy *per se*.[4]

Now it is well known for there to exist a possible tension in practice between the 'will of the people', as expressed through a particular parliamentary majority, and the defence of individual rights, as when the pressure of public opinion or of some national exigency leads to the limitation or suspension of basic freedoms. From the time of Tocqueville and J.S. Mill onwards, this has been characterized as the so-called 'tyranny of the majority'.[5] To guard against such pressure, individual rights have required special protection, whether through bills of rights, judicial review or special parliamentary procedures or majorities.[6] It would be wrong, however, to describe this tension as one between democracy and human rights, or democracy and liberty, as is often done; or to say that constitutional limitations upon a parliamentary majority are a restriction upon democracy itself. Following the argument developed above, it would be more accurate to describe such a conflict as one between a particular expression of popular opinion, on the one hand, and the conditions necessary to guarantee the continuing expression of that opinion, on the other; between a particular voice, and the conditions for exercising voice on a continuing basis. It follows that democracies have necessarily to be self-limiting or self-limited, if they are not to be self-contradictory, by undermining the rights through which popular control over government is secured; though any such limitation in turn requires popular consent to the basic constitutional arrangements through which it is secured.

The conclusion, then, is that human rights constitute an intrinsic part of democracy, because the guarantee of basic freedoms is a necessary condition for people's voice to be effective in public affairs, and for popular control over government to be secured. There is a still deeper level, however, at which democracy and human rights are connected, and that is in the assumptions about human nature on which their justification is founded. The philosophical justification for the human rights agenda is based on an identification of the needs and capacities common to all humans, whatever the differences between them.[7] In particular, the so-called 'liberty' rights – to personal freedom, to the freedoms of thought, conscience, movement and so on – presuppose a capacity for self-conscious and reasoned choice, or reflective and purposive agency, in matters affecting one's individual life.[8] Democratic rights presuppose the same capacity in matters affecting the common or collective life. The right to vote, or to stand for public office, assumes the capacity to take part in deliberation about the public as well as one's private interest. Both sets of rights, to individual and collective decision, are assumed together on reaching adulthood.

To be sure, collective decisions typically restrict the freedom of individual choice, and in this sense there is a tension between the collective and individual levels. It is part of the task of a rights agenda to define the limits to collective decision, just as it is the task of democratic debate to negotiate where, within these limits, the balance between the two should be struck. But underpinning both levels, of individual freedom and democratic voice and democratic accountability, is a common assumption about human capacities, and the same anti-paternalist argument, to the effect that there are no 'superiors' competent to decide for us what is for our own good, whether individual or collective, except insofar as we specifically, and within clearly defined limits, authorize them to do so.

So far the discussion has concentrated primarily on the definition of democracy, because of the way in which inadequate definitions can lead to a misrepresentation of the relation between democracy and human rights. However, there is a parallel inadequacy to be observed in the definition of human rights, whereby they come to be treated as coterminous with, and exhausted by, the civil and political rights agenda. The Western emphasis has always been in this direction, and it is one that has been reinforced rather than diminished by the end of the Cold War. Take any statement about human rights by a Western government and you will mostly find that it is civil and political rights that are meant. The reasons for the neglect of economic, social and cultural rights need not detain us here.[9] Suffice to say that any discussion of democracy and human rights which does not include them is only half done. Indeed, it is much less than half done, since the relation between democracy and economic, social and cultural rights is considerably more complex than the relation between democracy and political rights already considered.

To say that the two sets of rights are 'indivisible', and that democracy must therefore contain both, would be a very simple way of concluding this chapter without further discussion. Yet readers would be right to feel cheated, since the issues are much more complex than this. They are also much more *contested*, both academically and politically, than is the relation between democracy and the civil and political rights agenda. To help sort out this complexity, we shall separate economic and social from cultural rights, and discuss them in turn, since their respective relation to democracy raises rather different issues.

The Contribution of Economic and Social Rights to Democracy

Does democracy require the guarantee of economic and social rights for its citizens? Do economic and social rights in turn require democracy? Or is the relationship looser than one of 'requirement' in each case? At first sight, these questions look similar to other more familiar and exhaustively debated questions. Does democracy require economic development? Does economic development require democracy?[10] However, they are different in two respects.

First, economic development and the protection of economic rights are not the same thing. The latter may be made easier by the former, but we should note that the UN Committee on Economic, Social and Cultural Rights has repeatedly insisted that low levels of economic development do not absolve states from their obligations under the Covenant, which are binding upon signatories, 'whatever their level of development'.[11] Nor does it follow, on the other side, that economic development, measured quantitatively in terms of GDP per head of population, will of itself deliver economic and social rights, in the absence of the social structures, economic institutions and public policies appropriate to securing them. As the history of the 1970s and 1980s has abundantly demonstrated, high levels of economic growth are perfectly consistent with intensified economic inequality and substantial erosion of economic rights.[12] To be concerned with economic rights is to focus on the distribution of economic growth as well as its aggregate level: not so much to secure equality as to ensure a minimum for all.

Second, a concern with the distributional dimensions of economic development will also direct us to the distributional or qualitative aspects of democracy, as well as to the question of its survival against possible threats. Most of the literature on democracy and development is concerned with the simple alternatives: democracy or dictatorship; democracy or authoritarianism. Does economic development promote transition from the latter to the former or protect against reversal? Do democracies fare better than authoritarian systems in promoting economic development? Such questions assume that there is a clear demarcation to be drawn between democratic and non-democratic forms of rule, and that we can without difficulty assign countries to one type or the other. Yet the analysis of democracy suggests that democracy is a matter of degree, as well as of simple categorization. Its starting point with the citizen invites us to pay attention to the way its citizens experience it, as well as to the sustainability of its central institutions: to the quality of democracy, as well as its durability. Raising the question of the relation between economic and social rights and democracy requires us to attend to both aspects, not just the latter.

Let us therefore rephrase the original questions in comparative terms. How far, and in what respects, does democracy require the guarantee of economic and social rights? How far, and in what respects, do economic and social rights in turn depend upon democracy? We shall take each of these questions in turn.

The first question requires us to assess the consequences that follow for democracy from the denial of basic economic and social rights to any significant section of the population. In the first instance there are the *direct* consequences which follow for the citizens so denied, for their exercise of civil and political rights, and for their effective citizenship. Then there are the *indirect* consequences, for the rest of the population, and for the viability of democratic political institutions.

As to the exercise of civil and political rights or liberties, it is an important feature of philosophical discussions of liberty that the negative freedom from interference by others or by the state is acknowledged to be of little value if individuals lack the personal capacities or resources to make use of the freedoms in question; and that legally established rights will be largely formalistic if the means necessary to exercise them are beyond people's reach.[13] What value is the freedom of expression to me if I lack the means to communicate with other citizens? What value is there in the right to due process or the right to stand for elective office, if legal protection and public office, respectively, are accessible only to the wealthy? It is considerations such as these that justify a social agenda for democracy, going beyond the juridical defence of civil and political rights, and even the standard anti-discrimination requirements needed to protect particular sections of the population.

This issue can be rephrased as a question about how much economic inequality is compatible with the basic democratic principle of equal citizenship. It is clear that civil and political equality does not require complete economic levelling. But it becomes severely compromised if, on the one hand, the privileged can use their wealth or status, to purchase undue political influence; or if, on the other, the poor are so deprived that they are incapable of exercising any basic civil or political rights, and are effectively excluded from any common citizenship. The former, the problems posed by wealth to democracy, is best dealt with by restricting the political scope of wealth: by laws preventing concentrations of media ownership, limiting the amounts that can be spent on electoral campaigning, requiring disclosure of the sources of party funding or payments to elected representatives, and so on. The latter, the problems of *exclusion*, requires positive attention to the guarantee of economic and social rights.

The most fundamental condition for exercising our civil and political rights is that we should be alive to do so, and this requires both physical security and access to the necessities of life: to the means of subsistence, to shelter, clean water, sanitation and basic health care.[14] Without life we cannot pursue a distinctively *human* life, or exercise the rights and freedoms that are characteristic of it. To the list of basic economic rights mentioned above we should add the right to education. As has repeatedly been shown, education is necessary to the attainment of other economic rights.[15] Without knowledge about nutrition or health care, the guarantee of a basic income or sanitation will prove insufficient. Education further provides the skills necessary for employment or self-employment, which are the surest means to a basic income and to other economic rights. And education is necessary if we are to be able to exercise our civil and political rights effectively, or even to know what these are. Education is thus a key economic and political right, and one whose denial is especially damaging to the democratic principle of civil and political equality.

The example of education illustrates the essential interdependence between different human rights. Nowhere is this more evident than with the economic right which stands first in the International Covenant, and which has been most widely neglected in the developed world over the past two decades: the right to work.[16] Over this period the developed world has witnessed the paradoxical combination of large-scale unemployment with intensified workloads and extended hours of work for the employed: the erosion of the right *to* work as well as of rights *in* work. The right to work, whether as employed or as self-employed, is fundamental in two senses to other economic rights. It is in itself the surest means to guaranteeing a basic income directly for the employed. And without it, as in a context of widespread unemployment, the ability and willingness of those in work to fund social security for the unemployed is undermined. As William Beveridge, the architect of the British welfare system, argued back in the 1940s, the provisions of the welfare state are conditional upon full or near-full employment.[17] To give up on the latter, or to treat the level of employment as an unalterable fact of nature, is to acquiesce in the erosion of economic rights across the board: to health, housing, nutrition, as well as to basic income.[18]

There is a further aspect of the right to work which is particularly relevant to political rights and to equal citizenship. To be able to meet one's needs by one's own efforts, and in doing so to contribute to meeting the needs of others, is important to human self-respect. A condition of idleness, and of one-sided dependency on others for one's means of existence (as opposed to a mutual interdependency) leads to the erosion of self-worth, of self-confidence and of the skills necessary to the exercise of other rights. It is not only that being treated as an economically dispensable commodity is in itself inconsistent with a democratic conception of the citizen as a bearer of civil and political rights; the experience of the one also undermines the other. As has already been argued, both liberal and democratic political theory are premised on the assumption that people are capable of self-determination: that they possess the capacity and the confidence to take responsibility for their own lives, whether individually or collectively. A condition of long-term unemployment is hardly conducive to the development of such a capacity.[19]

So far the argument has been that the guarantee of economic and social rights is necessary to democracy in order to ensure a minimum equality of access to civil and political rights for all citizens. Any significant denial of the necessities of life, or of education, or of employment opportunities, involves a diminution of citizenship for those so denied, both in itself, and by impairing their capacity to engage in civil and public life on the same terms as others. Besides the direct effects, however, for those deprived, there are also the indirect effects of their deprivation to be considered upon the democratic rights and the quality or sustainability of democracy for all. Here we enter upon the terrain of the larger societal consequences of economic deprivation, which are both more delayed or remote, and also variable between different types of society.

In a highly urbanized society the cost of large-scale unemployment today, we may expect, is its cost not only to the unemployed, but also to the rest of society, through the loss of production and services, and through the reduced security that comes from an increase in crime against property and the person, especially drugs-related crime.[20] In rural societies and communities, the result of destitution through exclusion from access to land is an increase in migration to the cities, to swell the ranks of the urban dispossessed or, more rarely, organized rebellion and armed resistance. Whatever form it takes, the consequent insecurity will require an increase in the repressive forces required to contain it, and an intensification of more authoritarian forms of social control. Although the problem may appear to be contained by the ghettoization of the deprived and the construction of protected enclaves for the privileged, society at large cannot escape the wider effects upon the quality of its social and political life.

Such an account will typically be challenged by right-wing thinkers, who contest both the statistical link between increased unemployment and crimes against property and the person, and also the normative link between them, on the grounds that no amount of destitution can serve as a justification for crime. As to the first, the statistical link, the evidence is strongest in respect of the key group of young males. Urban male youth seems increasingly to be being socialized into a life of crime rather than a life of employment.[21] If so, it is a particularly myopic theory which can justify public spending on repressing the symptoms, but not on alleviating the underlying causes. As to whether there can ever be any justification for crimes against property, this depends on the view one takes about the implicit social contract which provides the moral foundation for government and for obedience to the law. Do those for whom society can offer no adequate means of livelihood, or prospect for such means in the future, owe any obligation to abide by its rules, especially its rules of property? If it is difficult to give a categorical answer to this question without more evidence about the context, we can at least conclude that the force of any moral foundation is considerably weakened by the existence of widespread and long-term unemployment or dispossession. And since democratic government is typically government that depends upon consent, it will itself be compromised where a significant section of society has to be ruled by coercion rather than on the basis of any moral or contractual relationship.

A further political consequence of substantial unemployment, dispossession or destitution is that it provides a fertile breeding ground for the politics of intolerance, and makes electorates vulnerable to mobilization behind populist leaders or parties, which transfer the odium for economic insecurity onto visible minorities, or onto the very existence of ethnic, racial, religious or linguistic diversity. In securely established democracies, such parties are unlikely to threaten the survival of the electoral process itself, though their presence may well exacerbate social divisions and intensify the processes of social exclusion. In insecure or recently established democracies, on the other hand, the existence of such parties may lead to the subversion of democratic institutions, either as a consequence of their electoral success or to prevent them from taking office. A recurrence of the triumph of inter-war Fascism may look improbable in the present era, but its history serves as a warning of the dangers to which newly established democracies are vulnerable in a context of widespread economic insecurity, especially where democracy-supportive leaders and parties have proved incapable of providing effective solutions, and democratic institutions themselves have become associated with economic failure.

At this point the argument that democracies must pay attention to the protection of economic and social rights is open to two kinds of objection. One kind is a more narrowly economic one, and asserts a possible incompatibility between an agenda for economic and social rights and other necessary economic goals: in respect of developing economies, the incompatibility is held to lie between economic rights and economic development, because of the transfer from investment to consumption involved in the former; in respect of developed ones, the contradiction is within economic rights themselves, between the demands of social protection and employment, through the burden welfare costs impose upon economic competitiveness. Any political consequences of an economic rights programme, so it is argued, will be irrelevant if such a programme is economically self-contradictory or unsustainable.

The extensive debates that have taken place on both questions suggest that the objection is far from conclusive. As regards developing economies, what counts as investment is here too narrowly conceived. There is no better investment that a country can make than in the health and education of its present and future workforce.[22] What is primarily at issue in a basic rights programme is not whether economic development takes place, but what kind of development, and how its benefits are distributed. In respect of developed economies, the debate is more about the level of welfare benefits than about their existence, and cannot be decided *a priori*. However, it should be recognized that the orthodox financial opinion which has inveighed most heavily against the 'burden' of social costs has hardly been noted for its robust defence of employment either, but has subordinated both to the interests of sound money, low inflation and high dividend payments. What is at issue again is the politics of distribution as much as the science of economics.

A second, more explicitly political, objection to a programme of basic economic and social rights is that it conflicts with the fundamental institutions of a free democratic society: the integrity of private property and the freedom of exchange. It conflicts with the first, so it is argued, through the use of compulsory taxation for redistributive purposes, and with the second through state regulation and the bureaucratization of welfare provision.[23] The culmination of both processes can be seen in the command economy, where democracy proved impossible because of the lack of any independent civil society with the capacity to challenge the state. Without private property, people lack the economic resources to sustain an alternative voice or maintain effective political opposition; without the freedom to exchange, they lack the networks of lateral social coordination that might reduce and constrain the hierarchical relations of state command. In short, central to democracy is an independent civil society, and central to civil society are the institutions of a free economy.[24]

To this objection it can be answered that the premise of the argument is certainly correct, but the conclusion does not follow. That is to say, the necessity of private property and freedom of exchange to civil society, and in turn to democracy, is now surely incontestable. However, a programme of basic economic and social rights requires not so much the elimination of these institutions as their necessary regulation and supplementation in the wider public interest. This need not necessitate an enormous bureaucratic apparatus of public welfare. Apart from any necessary provision of collective goods through the agency of public authority, most people prefer to have the opportunity to meet their own needs through their own efforts, whether through access to land for subsistence farming, through a fair price for the goods they produce or through a sufficient wage for the labour they supply. It is only in the event of their inability to provide for themselves that 'welfare' in a narrow sense becomes necessary.

The extreme neoliberal view that private property and the freedom of exchange constitute absolute and untouchable 'natural rights' overlooks the obvious fact that both are socially constructed and validated institutions, whose primary justification lies in their effectiveness in securing people's means of livelihood. It follows that their justifiable limitation – of accumulation and use in respect of property, and of freedom to exchange – must lie at the point of their failure to secure this end. Even such an archetypal liberal as John Locke acknowledged that a condition of legitimacy for the enclosure of private property (which entails a socially recognized and enforceable right of exclusion, and hence a *restriction* on liberty) was that 'enough and as good' should be left for others.[25] To put this in terms of a modern context, it is a legitimating condition for the social institution of private property rights that the basic means of livelihood be guaranteed to all.

A democratic society, then, requires both the institutions of private property and free exchange, *and* the guarantee of basic economic rights, if it is to be founded upon a general consent. Although at a superficial level these two requirements seem to be in conflict, at a deeper level the moral justifiability and social acceptability of the first depend upon the guarantee of the second. In the immediate aftermath of the collapse of the Soviet command economies, the immediate priority for democratization may have appeared to lie in the development of an autonomous civil society, and in the construction of free economic institutions. However, their subsequent history has shown the dangers of popular disillusionment with democracy where the free market logic is driven to the exclusion of basic economic rights. It is a similar story in those Third World countries where structural adjustment programmes imposed from outside have led to substantial reductions in social welfare. In such situations, it is not just the quality of democratic citizenship, but the legitimacy of democratic institutions themselves, that is at stake.

We can conclude that the failure to protect economic and social rights is damaging to democracy in a number of different ways. First, and most directly, it undermines the citizenship status of those whose rights are unprotected, and their capacity to exercise their civil and political rights along with others. Social or economic exclusion and political exclusion go hand in hand. Second, it diminishes the quality of public life for all, through the loss of security to property and person, and the correspondingly intensified organization of repression. Finally, it erodes the legitimacy of democratic institutions themselves, and makes them more vulnerable to subversion. Such effects can be expected to be the more pronounced, the deeper and more widespread the absence of economic and social rights.

It is of course possible to point to countries where the institutions of electoral democracy coexist with widespread destitution and impoverishment. In this sense the protection of basic economic and social rights could be argued to be not strictly a *necessary* condition for the survival of democracy. However, such electoral systems remain vulnerable in the ways outlined earlier. And it is a very attenuated conception of democracy which takes no account at all of the quality of the civil and political life of its citizens.

Democracy as a Condition for Economic and Social Rights

The significance of the protection of economic and social rights for democracy is only one side of the relationship. What about the significance of democracy for economic and social rights? Do economic and social rights require democracy? Or might they be better protected, as some have argued, under an authoritarian regime, so that there is a choice, or 'trade-off', to be made between social and economic rights on the one side and civil and political rights on the other? Civil and political rights may certainly require economic and social rights as their necessary complement, as already argued, but the latter might be attainable, or even better attainable, without the former. Since the end of the Cold War, this idea of a 'trade-off' between the two sets of rights has become generally discredited, and the arguments in favour of authoritarianism might therefore seem to have a merely historical interest.[26] However, it will be useful to examine them, if only the better to identify what it is about democracy that is relevant to the protection of economic and social rights, and within what limits.

Most discussions which compare the economic records of authoritarian and democratic regimes treat the former as an entirely undifferentiated category.[27] Yet it should be evident that the arguments on behalf of left-wing and right-wing forms of authoritarianism are markedly different, especially as far as economic rights are concerned; in other words, that left-wing and right-wing versions of the argument are not the same. This is so both in respect of the positive arguments for authoritarianism and with regard to the particular faults each finds with democracy.

The economic arguments that have been advanced in favour of right-wing or capitalist forms of authoritarianism have typically been arguments about economic growth or economic development, and only secondarily about economic and social rights. That is to say, insofar as economic rights have been considered at all, they have been seen as a consequence of economic development: first expand the cake, then concern ourselves with its distribution. As far as the expansion of the cake is concerned, this can be much more effectively achieved, so it is contended, by authoritarian regimes, which possess the key advantage over democratic ones of being able to insulate economic policy from the short-term vagaries of popular pressure. How precisely this benefits economic growth will depend upon the context, but it typically works economically by containing inflationary pressures, by facilitating a strict monetary policy and by allowing the transfer of resources from consumption to investment. The political means will include the containment or destruction of trade union power, the depression of social spending and social protection, and the limitation of claims upon the state from a variety of client groups, constituency interests or other bases of electoral support.[28]

Whatever the differences of context, the authoritarian argument seeks to present a contrast between democratic systems, on the one hand, which are continually vulnerable to being diverted from sound economic policies by the pressure of organized interests and electoral considerations, and authoritarian ones, on the other, which are able to act decisively in the long-term economic interests of society, precisely because the exclusion of the population from politics has insulated them from such pressures. If even at advanced stages of capitalist development there is an 'economic cost to democracy' arising from the pressures of the electoral cycle, how much more must this be true of developing economies.[29]

One thing should be immediately obvious about the argument just summarized. It is that authoritarian regimes of the right and their protagonists are self-confessedly not in the business of protecting economic and social rights; indeed, quite the reverse. It is the self-proclaimed virtue of such regimes that they *suppress* economic rights, and the political means for protecting them, in the interests of longer-term economic growth. Insofar as there is anything to be said in their favour, it can only be in terms of securing a platform for the protection of economic rights in the future, not in the present. In other words, authoritarian regimes of the right are economically as well as politically justifiable only as temporary, transitional or 'exceptional' regimes. Just as democracy has to be suppressed to make it safe for the future, so economic and social rights have to be suppressed to secure the basis for their future realization. There is a neat symmetry here between the political and the economic versions of the right-wing apologia for authoritarianism.

The economic version – expand the cake now so as to have more to distribute in the future – requires us to accept three different assumptions, each of which is questionable. The first is that the suppression of economic and social rights is necessary for economic growth. This has already been examined and found wanting, at least as a general thesis, without very careful specification of the precise aspects and levels of economic rights which might be shown to be in tension with the requirements of growth, at particular stages, and within given strategies, of economic development.

The second assumption is that the structures of economic inequality, and the public spending on the forces of repression, which are both reinforced under authoritarian regimes of the right, will readily yield to more socially progressive policies under a future democratic restoration. The characteristic legacy of such regimes to their successors is a pattern of economic and military interests which typically have to be appeased in order to pre-empt further political reaction. The neglect or suppression of economic rights, once established, is thus not easily reversed; the strategies for economic development, and the social interests supportive of these strategies, once consolidated, are not readily altered.

The third assumption is that authoritarian systems are actually better at delivering economic growth than democratic ones. Comparative evidence shows such a claim to be false, at least as a general proposition, rather than in respect of specific cases.[30] The reasons are not hard to find. In the absence of any systematic public accountability or legal sanction, there is nothing to deter authoritarian rulers from using state power for the private advantage of themselves and their immediate supporters rather than in the public interest. An economic theory which emphasizes self-interest as the dominant human motivation sits uneasily with the assumption of a disinterested pursuit of society's long-term economic development on the part of office holders, who are subject to no systematic sanction to ensure the alignment of their personal interests with the public good. By the same token, there is no reason to expect either that wealthy elites will use their burgeoning wealth for investment rather than conspicuous consumption, especially of imported consumer goods.

Given the implausibility of its assumptions, it is hardly surprising that the economic case for authoritarianism of the right is now thoroughly discredited. Of course, that discredit is also the product of the serious abuses of civil and political rights that can be laid at the door of such regimes. The point to be made here, however, is that there is simply no trade-off at all evident between the loss of civil and political rights, on the one side, and economic and social rights, on the other. The only trade-off – between present and future – is a highly unequal one. The pain in the present is guaranteed; the gain in the future is speculative and illusory. Few would freely opt for such a bargain.

In comparison with the right-wing argument, the case for a left-wing version of authoritarianism, although now also discredited, did for a period carry a certain plausibility, in that there was at least something to be 'traded off' for the absence of civil and political rights. Most socialist and communist regimes have had an explicit commitment to the protection of economic and social rights, and their records in respect of employment, basic income, housing, health care and education have usually been better than capitalist regimes at equivalent levels of economic development. It was precisely its record in these respects that made the Soviet Union attractive as a model of economic development for Third World countries.[31]

The left-wing critique of democracy, from an economic point of view, is here the obverse of the right's: not that popular pressures have too much influence on economic policy, but that they have too little. Democracy in capitalist societies, on this view, is no more than a *capitalist* democracy, in which public policy is subject to the economic and ideological influence of powerful financial interests, whatever the government in power, and economic rights for the many take second place to the requirements of profitability for the few. It is such considerations that have served to justify large-scale public ownership, the subordination of the media to political control and the elimination of competing parties which might campaign for the restoration of capitalist freedoms.

The collapse of communist systems in 1989 showed that this 'trade-off' was politically unsustainable, on both sides of the equation. The denial of civil and political rights proved increasingly unacceptable to educated populations; and the guarantee of basic economic rights could not compensate for chronic economic stagnation and consumer shortages. In any case we should question how secure these economic rights in fact ever were, in the light of the history of the two major communist powers, which included the mass starvations under forced collectivization and the Great Leap Forward, the forced labour camps, the dependence of employment on political acceptability, and so on. One-off sets of comparative statistics of health, literacy or life-expectancy rates do not record these massive denials of basic economic rights. Only in societies without a free press and public opinion could such abuses go either undetected or uncorrected.

Between them the negative records of both right and left forms of authoritarianism help construct the argument to be made positively for democracies in respect of economic and social rights.[32] This argument embraces two considerations: the first, that of openness and accountability; the second, the distribution of political power. In an open political system, economic policies have to be publicly justified; their consequences are accessible to independent scrutiny; alternatives can be openly canvassed; and the activities of public officials are a matter of record and, in principle, subject to accountability. This does not mean that the degree of openness is everywhere satisfactory, especially when the activities of private corporations are included, as well as those of government. But there is a world of difference between a political system that is not sufficiently open in practice and one that is closed on principle, or by government fiat.

Secondly, to the extent that democracies empower ordinary people through elections at local and national level, through systematic processes of consultation, through the self-organizing associations of civil society, to that extent will economic policy be responsive to their needs. Of course, that empowerment is often spasmodic in practice, and limited by the inbuilt bias of capitalist politics towards the economically privileged. But without any counterweight from popular forces, the demand for basic economic rights will go unattended. Moreover, as many studies of the delivery of basic rights and basic needs have shown, their effectiveness is directly proportionate to the extent to which the people involved are consulted about the manner of their delivery.

The systemic features of democracy, therefore, openness, accountability, the distribution of power, make it likely that democratic governments will pay attention to the protection of economic and social rights. However, what is likely is not thereby inevitable; the 'indivisibility' of the two sets of rights is not in practice altogether secure. As the UN Committee on Economic, Social and Cultural Rights emphasized in its submission to the World Conference on Human Rights (Vienna, 1993), 'there is no basis whatsoever to assume that the realization of economic, social and cultural rights will *necessarily* [emphasis added] result from the achievement of civil and political rights'.[33] In other words, democracy may be a necessary, but is not a sufficient, condition for the protection of economic and social rights. The reasons for this are not far to seek, though they differ somewhat in the democracies of the developed and the developing world.

In the developed democracies, the threat to economic and social rights comes from what J.K. Galbraith has termed the political culture of 'contentment'. Whereas the development of the welfare state occurred in a period when the vast majority saw the need for state protection from the insecurities of the capitalist market, and voted to support it, now the majority belong to the ranks of the 'contented', and can readily be convinced that spending on the deprived constitutes a threat to their contentment, and is in any case both ineffective and undeserved, since the deprived are largely responsible for their own condition. The deprived for their part are not only a minority, but a disorganized and disempowered one, who have no ready means of collective action and who often are not even registered to vote. 'It follows,' he concludes, 'that presidential and legislative action or, more seriously, inaction, however adverse and alienating the effect on the socially excluded homelessness, hunger, inadequate education, drug affliction, poverty in general – occurs under the broad sanction of democracy.'[34]

Whereas the problem in the developed democracies is that the majority may collude in the neglect of economic and social rights, the problem in the developing ones is that majorities may not have the power to make their voice effective, despite the formal institutions of multi-partyism, elected legislatures and so on. Here there are both external and internal factors at work. In countries subject to international debt repayment, economic policy will be largely dominated by the international financial institutions, and not effectively subject to domestic control. Internally, many of the same countries have only a weak tradition of public accountability, and electoral sanctions may be insufficient on their own to prevent state power from continuing to be used for the private enrichment of office holders and their clienteles. The combination of the state's external subordination and internal vulnerability may thus render the democratic principle of popular control over public policy largely impotent.[35]

It is a commonplace today that the triumph of democracy has coincided with democracy's internal malaise. This is not least because the collapse of the Soviet system has served to validate the international dominance of a neoliberal economic ideology, affecting developed and developing democracies alike, which accords low priority to economic rights and proclaims the impotence of government in the face of impoverishment and social deprivation. If economic and social rights cannot do without democracy, nevertheless their future depends as much on an effective challenge to this ideology as it does on the institutions of democracy themselves.

Cultural Rights and Democracy

The final set of issues to consider concerns the relation between democracy and cultural rights. Two different kinds of cultural right can be distinguished. One kind is the rights specified in the International Covenant on Economic, Social and Cultural Rights – to education (Articles 13 and 14) and to the benefits of scientific knowledge (Article 15) – which are rights of individuals to the means of personal development and of access to the universal culture of science.[36] As has already been argued, education constitutes a pivotal individual right, since it is necessary to the effective exercise of most other rights, both economic and political. Non-discriminatory access to education, therefore, is essential to the equal citizenship that lies at the heart of democracy.

A second kind of cultural right, however, is the right of groups to practise and reproduce their own distinctive culture. This right is included in the International Covenant on Civil and Political Rights (Article 27) as a right of minorities, but only tentatively, in negative terms:

> In those States in which ethnic, religious or linguistic minorities exist, persons belonging to such minorities shall not be denied the right, in community with other members of their group, to enjoy their own culture, to profess and practise their own religion, or to use their own language.[37]

By the time of the separate UN Declaration on the Rights of Persons Belonging to National or Ethnic, Religious and Linguistic Minorities in 1992, this right had come to be phrased more robustly, and 'national' had been added to the list of relevant minorities (Article 2):

> Persons belonging to national or ethnic, religious and linguistic minorities [...] have the right to enjoy their own culture, to profess and practise their own religion, and to use their own language, in private and in public, freely and without interference or any form of discrimination.[38]

In comparison with the first type of cultural right, it is characteristic of this second type of right that it is a right which belongs to groups or cultural communities, as well as to the individuals who comprise them; and that it acknowledges cultural particularity or distinctiveness, rather than universality. This is because the cultures of groups and communities are precisely specific and differentiated cultures, and their value to their members lies in what makes their form of life different or distinctive from that of others.

At first sight, the recognition of the right to difference might appear to be in contradiction with the universalist assumptions about human needs and capacities which underpin human rights, and with the principle of equality, or equal human dignity, that is essential to them. That would only be a superficial conclusion, however. The assumption underlying the right to cultural specificity or difference is that the need for a distinctive identity, which is accorded recognition and respect by others, is a *universal* human need, and that this need is fulfilled in part through group membership and through the reproduction of its distinctive way of life. Although this is to be acknowledged as a universal human need, if all are to enjoy it equally it has particularly to be protected for members of minorities, whose culture is likely to be vulnerable to erosion, suppression or discrimination at the hands of majorities, in a way in which a majority culture is not. Equality and difference are thus not contradictory but complementary principles, when understood here as the equal right to develop and express a distinctive identity and way of life along with others.

The issues raised by cultural rights have been among the most intensely debated issues of liberal political philosophy over the past two decades.[39] Philosophical 'communitarians', so-called, have insisted that the liberal conception of the freely choosing or autonomous individual is incoherent, because it abstracts individuals from the context of the cultural groups or communities within which their lives are carried on. It is these communities that provide the language of communication and the source of meaning, value and identity for their members. There can be no 'disembodied self', they argue, choosing life plans or conceptions of 'the good' in abstraction from a received cultural tradition and its own definitions of value. Insofar as individuality or individualism is possible, it is only within the context of a distinctive cultural tradition, whether through new interpretations of it, through opposition to it, or through the admixture of other cultural traditions. From this socially rooted conception of the person, and of individuality itself, it follows that states cannot be neutral about the well-being of the different cultures within their territory; and they can justifiably take measures to ensure their survival when under threat, even if this means treating their members differently in certain respects from other citizens. So Will Kymlika, for instance, writes:

> People are owed respect as citizens and as members of cultural communities. In many situations, the two are perfectly compatible, and in fact may coincide. But in culturally plural societies, differential citizenship rights may be needed to protect a cultural community from unwanted disintegration. If so, then the demands of citizenship and cultural membership pull in different directions.[40]

It is considerations such as these which lie behind the special protection accorded to indigenous peoples, minority languages, religious practices, and so on.

However, we also need to recognize the limits of any such argument, from a human rights point of view. If the justification for the protection of cultural communities derives from their value to the individuals who comprise them, then the interests of individuals also set limits to the range of cultural practices that such protection can be allowed to validate. If states should not be neutral about the well-being of cultural communities within their borders, neither should they be neutral about practices which violate basic human rights standards, such as preventing individuals from leaving the community; discriminating against women; campaigning for the denial of rights to members of other communities, or advocating supremacy over them; and so on. The appeal for the protection of distinctive cultural rights within a human rights framework cannot divorce itself from the wider standards of that framework. In Kymlika's terms, the context of a common citizenship is the larger context within which cultural difference has to be located.[41]

What implications do these considerations have for *democracy*? How do democratic processes in turn affect the cultural rights of minorities? It should be acknowledged straight away that the history of democratic thought from Rousseau onwards has tended to assume the existence of a relatively homogeneous population within the territory of the self-governing state, and has taken questions of national identity as settled rather than as the subject of disagreement. Rousseau himself took the principle of homogeneity to an extreme, whereas most other theorists have recognized the existence of significant differences of opinion and interest between different sections of the population as not only a fact of life, but as desirable for democratic diversity. Yet this diversity has only been seen to be sustainable against a background of a common or settled national identity.[42]

This background assumption has been necessary for two central aspects of modern democracies. The first is the mobilization of a mass electorate in the competition for political power, with numbers counting as the decisive criterion for access to office. The divisiveness of this process has only been tolerable to the extent that questions of fundamental political identity have not been brought into play in the competition for power, and that the national question has been resolved. The second is the procedure of majoritarianism as the method for resolving contested issues. This procedure can only be justified, and minority acquiescence in the outcome only expected, according to a principle of reciprocity: the minority will have their chance to be part of a winning majority in the future, and will expect acquiescence from the losers in their turn. But this principle of reciprocity presumes that the questions to be decided are matters of opinion and interest, which are changeable according to changing circumstances, rather than of basic identity, which are not, or at least to nothing like the same extent.[43]

Both these familiar democratic procedures become problematic, therefore, in the context of multicultural and multinational societies, which are the norm in the modern world. Where party competition coincides with the lines of cultural division, rather than cuts across them, the struggle for power is waged as an exclusive and particularistic one, in the interests of the specific community, how-

ever large, rather than of the society as a whole. Whether intention-
ally or not, it becomes a struggle about who constitutes the nation,
and who is to be privileged within it, as much as about policies *for*
the nation. In such circumstances the majoritarian procedure, which
requires minorities to accept the majority verdict and its consequences
for policy, loses its justification, since the minority is a permanent
one, and the principle of reciprocity cannot apply. The emergence of
this lacuna in democratic legitimacy is of course most serious in
recently established states, whose nationhood is still underdevel-
oped. Yet, as the history of Western Europe over the past decades
demonstrates, it can occur in any multicultural or multinational society, given the salience of the politics of identity, and the ease with
which voters can be mobilized behind it.

The problematic character of these familiar democratic processes
of inter-party competition and majoritarianism suggests that any
legal guarantee for the cultural rights of minorities will be insufficient on its own to protect their cultural identity or to ensure
recognition and respect for it, without a guaranteed share in public
office and political power. Without a due share in political power,
what confidence can members of a minority have that their cultural
rights will be protected, or their material needs and distinctive circumstances be attended to, or that they will be accorded recognition
and respect by the majority community?

It is considerations such as these that have led to the development
in a number of democracies of procedures designed to qualify the
majoritarian, 'winner-take-all', character of party competition. Which
procedures are appropriate depends largely on the context, especially on whether the relevant minorities are territorially concentrated
or dispersed. Where they are concentrated, forms of regional autonomy may work by giving the minority a majority in its own
region, albeit at the cost of constructing new minorities in turn. Other
procedures may involve the requirement of electoral majorities which
transcend ethnic or regional support, or protected quotas, either directly or through the way constituency boundaries are drawn. Or
there may be protected legislation, which requires special majorities
to enact, or the approval of specified communities. Then there is the
power-sharing executive, and rotation for leading offices of state
between different communities. Below them, there are quotas and
other affirmative action programmes for government employment of
all kinds. All these measures can be seen as different forms of power
sharing, whether territorial, electoral, legislative or administrative,
which guarantee to members of minorities their due place in the
polity.[44]

What incentive is there for majorities to accept such a limitation on
their supremacy? It is primarily a negative one, of the consequences

that may follow if the demands of minorities for recognition are not attended to. These are the by now familiar consequences of secessionist movements, urban terrorism and outright civil war. From the denial of cultural rights, the infringement of basic civil and political rights can be expected to follow, first for the minority community, and then for the majority itself.

It is also a question of right, and not merely of anticipated consequences. Basic questions to do with the construction of the political nation and the relation between its communities are not ones to be decided by majority vote, but only through dialogue and consensus. Majoritarianism can only come into play once there is agreement about who constitutes the people among whom majorities are to count as binding, and within what limits. Rousseau put the matter succinctly, although multicultural societies were far from his mind, when he wrote that, logically prior to any act of government or operation of constitutional procedures, a people had first to constitute itself as a people, and to do so by mutual agreement:

> This act is the true foundation of society. Indeed, if there were no prior convention, where would be the obligation on the minority to submit to the choice of the majority? [...] The law of majority voting is itself something established by convention, and presupposes unanimity, on one occasion at least.[45]

Theoretically, Rousseau is perfectly correct, though his assumptions about a founding convention are ahistorical. The boundaries of most states were rarely fixed originally by the agreement of their populations, but rather by a mixture of force, dynastic or imperial convenience, and historical or geographical accident. Even if they had been, the balance of their populations is continually shifting, with new waves of immigration, differential birth rates between their respective communities and long-term cultural changes at work. What this suggests is that the idea of a unanimous founding assembly has to be reconstituted as a forum for continuing dialogue and consensus formation between the different cultural communities, about issues affecting the political nation and their respective needs and place within it. Whether this forum is an informal one, with moral and persuasive influence over a legislative assembly, or formalized as a second chamber with legal powers over constitutional issues, must be a matter to be determined according to local circumstances.

The issue of cultural rights, therefore, raises questions that go to the heart of our understanding of democracy itself. The received conception, with its familiar procedures, has treated citizens as simply the undifferentiated bearers of rights, and not also as members of particular communities; it has regarded national allegiance as monopolistic rather than multiple; it has seen political parties as competitors for support, not as bearers of identity; and it has assumed that minorities could be future majorities, not consigned to a permanently second-class status. The increasing prevalence of culturally plural societies requires us to revise these conceptions and the procedures appropriate to them: not to replace equality of citizenship, but so that it can be realized more effectively.

Conclusion: Democracy and Human Rights

The relation between democracy and human rights is a complex one, but one that can be simply summarized. The complexity derives from the enormous variation in the content of human rights themselves. Indeed, one criticism that may be made of this chapter, is that it has not been sensitive enough to that variation. Within the broad threefold classification, however, of civil and political, economic and social, and cultural rights, we can distinguish a somewhat different relationship in which each stands to democracy. Civil and political rights constitute an *integral part* of democracy. Democracy without them would be a contradiction in terms, since the absence of freedoms of speech, of association, of assembly, of movement, or of guaranteed security of the person and due process, would make elections a facade and render any popular control over government impossible. Economic and social rights can best be described as standing in a relation of *mutual dependency* with democracy. The widespread absence of such rights compromises civil and political equality, the quality of public life and the long-term viability of democratic institutions themselves; democracy, on the other hand, constitutes a necessary if not sufficient condition for the protection of economic and social rights. The defence of cultural rights, finally, in the context of multicultural societies, requires a *re-evaluated conception* of democracy and its procedures, if equality of citizenship is to be realized and the political nation is not to be broken apart. Democracy in the modern age, in sum, has to be understood not only as political democracy, but also as social democracy and as a committedly pluralist democracy as well.

Notes

1   This academic separation is discussed more fully in the introductory chapter 'Human rights in the study of politics', of D. Beetham (ed.), *Politics and Human Rights*, Oxford, Blackwell, 1995, pp.1–9.
2   The practice of treating the relation between democratic institutions and civil

and political freedoms, or alternatively the avoidance of human rights abuses, as a matter of statistical correlation, is well established in the literature of political science. See, for example, K.A. Bollen, 'Issues in the comparative measurement of political democracy', *American Sociological Review*, **45**, 1980, 370–90; T.R. Gurr, 'The political origins of state violence and terror: a theoretical analysis', in M. Stohl and G.A. Lopez (eds), *Government Violence and Repression: an Agenda for Research*, New York, Greenwood, pp.47–71; C. Henderson, 'Conditions affecting the use of political repression', *Journal of Conflict Resolution*, **35**, 1991, 120–42.

3   For a fuller discussion of these definitional questions, see 'Key principles and indices for a democratic audit', in D. Beetham (ed.), *Defining and Measuring Democracy*, London, Sage Publications, 1994, pp.25–43.

4   F. Panizza, 'Human rights in the processes of transition and consolidation of democracy in Latin America', in Beetham (ed.), *Politics and Human Rights* (op. cit., note 1), pp.171–91.

5   J.S. Mill, *On Liberty*, London, Dent, Everyman edition, 1964, p.68.

6   For a recent survey of such measures, and of debates about them, see J. Elster, 'Majority rule and individual rights', in S. Shute and S. Hurley (eds), *On Human Rights*, New York, Basic Books, 1993, pp.175–216.

7   S.M. Okin, 'Liberty and welfare: some issues in human rights theory', in J.R. Pennock and J.W. Chapman (eds), *Human Rights*, New York, New York University Press, 1981, pp.230–56; M. Freeman, 'The philosophical foundations of human rights', *Human Rights Quarterly*, **16**, 1994, 491–514.

8   For human rights as the 'necessary conditions for agency', see A. Gewirth, *Human Rights*, Chicago, University of Chicago Press, 1982, ch. 1; R. Plant, *Modern Political Thought*, Oxford, Blackwell, 1991, ch. 5.

9   These are discussed in 'What future for economic and social rights?', in Beetham (ed.), *Politics and Human Rights* (op. cit., note 1), pp.42–61.

10 For the most recent and thoroughgoing analysis of the first of these questions, see A. Hadenius, *Democracy and Development*, Cambridge, Cambridge University Press, 1992; for an overview of the second, see J. Healey and M. Robinson, *Democracy, Governance and Economic Policy*, London, Overseas Development Institute 1992, chs 6–7.

11 UN Doc. E/C 4/1987/17, principle 25; UN Doc. E/C 12/1990/8, pp.41 and 86.

12 UNDP, *Human Development Report, 1992*, New York, Oxford University Press, 1992. For the conjunction of economic growth with increasing inequality in the UK, see Rowntree Foundation, *Inquiry into Income and Wealth*, 2 vols, York, Joseph Rowntree Foundation, 1995; Commission on Social Justice, *Social Justice*, London, Vintage, 1994, ch. 1.

13 See the discussion in Plant (op. cit., note 8), chs 6–7.

14 H. Shue, *Basic Rights*, Princeton, Princeton University Press, 1980, ch. 1; Okin, 'Liberty and welfare: some issues in human rights theory', in Pennock and Chapman (op. cit., note 7).

15 F. Stewart, 'Basic needs strategies, human rights and the right to development', *Human Rights Quarterly*, **11**, 1989, 347–74, esp. p.355; P. Streeten, *First Things First: Meeting Basic Needs in Developing Countries*, New York, Oxford University Press for World Bank, 1981, esp. pp.134–8.

16 Article 6 of the International Covenant on Economic, Social and Cultural Rights, see I. Brownlie (ed.), *Basic Documents on Human Rights*, 3rd edn, Oxford, Oxford University Press, 1992, p.116.

17 W.H. Beveridge, *Full Employment in a Free Society*, London, Allen and Unwin, 1944.

18 Commission on Social Justice (op. cit., note 12), chs 1 and 5.

19 The demoralizing effect of unemployment is particularly stressed in Beveridge's

Report. For contemporary studies, see P.B. Warr, *Work, Unemployment and Mental Health*, Oxford, Clarendon Press, 1987; M. White, *Against Unemployment*, London, Policy Studies Institute, 1991, chs 2–4.

20　A. Glyn and D. Miliband (eds), *Paying for Inequality: the Economic Cost of Social Justice*, London, Rivers Oram/IPPR, 1994.

21　See the chapter by John Hagan on crime in Glyn and Miliband (op. cit., note 20), pp.80–99; for a graphic account of the effects of youth unemployment in a typical inner city, see F.F. Ridley, 'View from a disaster area: unemployed youth in Merseyside', in B. Crick (ed.), *Unemployment*, London, Methuen, 1981.

22　N. Hicks, 'Growth versus basic needs: is there a tradeoff?', *World Development*, 7, 1979, 985–94; Streeten (op. cit., note 15), ch 4. See also the successive volumes of the yearly UNDP, *Human Development Report*, 1990 onwards.

23　The classic statement of this objection is to be found in R. Nozick, *Anarchy, State and Utopia*, New York, Basic Books, 1974.

24　M. Friedman, *Capitalism and Freedom*, Chicago, University of Chicago Press, 1962; C.E. Lindblom, *Politics and Markets*, New Haven, Yale University Press, 1977; E. Gellner, *Conditions of Liberty*, London, Hamish Hamilton, 1994.

25　J. Locke, *Two Treatises of Government*, P. Laslett, (ed.), Cambridge, Cambridge University Press, p.291. For private property as a restriction on liberty, see the chapter 'Freedom, justice and capitalism' in G.A. Cohen, *History, Labour and Freedom*, Oxford, Clarendon Press, 1988, pp.286–304.

26　Actually, refutations of the idea of such a 'trade-off' go back much further. See, for example, R.E. Goodin, 'The development rights trade-off: some unwarranted economic and political assumptions', *Universal Human Rights*, 1, 1979, 31–42; R. Howard, 'The full-belly thesis: should economic rights take priority over civil and political rights?', *Human Rights Quarterly*, 5, 1987, 467–90.

27　See the surveys by L. Sirowy and A. Inkeles, 'The effects of democracy on economic growth and inequality: a review', *Studies in Comparative International Development*, 25, 1990, 126–57, reprinted in A. Inkeles (ed.), *On Measuring Democracy*, New Brunswick/London, Transaction Publishers, 1991, pp.125–56; M. Olson, 'Autocracy, democracy and prosperity', in R.J. Zeckhauser (ed.), *Strategy and Choice*, Cambridge, MA, MIT Press, 1991, pp.131–57; J. Healey and M. Robinson, *Democracy, Governance and Economic Policy*, London, Overseas Development Institute, 1992, ch. 6; A. Przeworski and F. Limongi, 'Political regimes and economic growth', *Journal of Economic Perspectives*, 7, (3), 1993, 51–69.

28　Sirowy and Inkeles (op. cit., note 27), 129–31; Przeworski and Limongi (op. cit., note 27), pp.54–7.

29　S. Brittan, 'The economic contradictions of democracy', *British Journal of Political Science*, 5, 1975, 128–59; and *Economic Consequences of Democracy*, London, Wildwood House, 1977.

30　Healey and Robinson (op. cit., note 27), pp.103–112; Sirowy and Inkeles (op. cit., note 27), 135–42.

31　The evidence is reviewed in L. Doyal and I. Gough, *A Theory of Human Need*, Basingstoke, Macmillan Education, 1991, pp.283–7.

32　Howard (op. cit., note 26), 471–8.

33　UN Doc. E/C 12/1992/2, pp.82–3.

34　J.K. Galbraith, *The Culture of Contentment*, London, Sinclair-Stevenson, 1992, p.151.

35　See the literature reviewed in D. Beetham, 'Conditions for democratic consolidation', *Review of African Political Economy*, 60, 1994, 157–72.

36　I. Brownlie (ed.), *Basic Documents on Human Rights*, 3rd edn, Oxford, Clarendon Press, pp.118–20.

37　Brownlie (op. cit., note 36), p.134.

38　UN Doc. 32 I.L.M. 915 (1993).

39 For useful contributions to, and summaries of, the debates, see W. Kymlika, *Liberalism, Community and Culture*, New York, Oxford University Press, 1989; D. Miller and M. Walzer (eds), *Pluralism, Justice and Equality*, Oxford, Oxford University Press, 1995; S. Mulhall and A. Swift, *Liberals and Communitarians*, Oxford, Blackwell, 1992; C. Taylor and A. Gutman, *Multiculturalism*, Princeton, Princeton University Press, 1994.
40 Kymlika (op. cit., note 39), pp.151–2.
41 A similar conclusion, though from rather different premises, is reached by Bhikhu Parekh in his 'Cultural diversity and liberal democracy', in Beetham (ed.), *Defining and Measuring Democracy* (op. cit., note 3), pp.199–221. For a feminist treatment of issues of group difference, see I.M. Young, *Justice and the Politics of Difference*, Princeton, Princeton University Press, 1990.
42 J.S. Mill took it as axiomatic that 'free institutions are next to impossible in a country made up of different nationalities' (J.S. Mill, *On Representative Government*, London, Dent, Everyman edn, 1964, p.361).
43 M. Freeman, 'Are there collective human rights?', in Beetham (ed.), *Politics and Human Rights* (op. cit., note 1), pp.26–41.
44 Many of these measures have been theorized under the concept of 'consociational democracy', and in the contrast between 'consensus' and 'majoritarian' forms of government; see A. Lijphart, *Democracy in Plural Societies: A Comparative Exploration*, New Haven, Yale University Press, 1977; and *Democracie*New Haven, Yale University Press, 1984.
45 J.-J. Rousseau, *The Social Contract*, London, Dent, Everyman edn, 1963, bk 1, ch. v.

4 The Development of the Right to Development

UPENDRA BAXI

The Adoption of the Declaration on the Right to Development

A landmark in the enunciation of new human rights occurred when, on 4 December 1986, the General Assembly adopted the Declaration on the Right to Development.[1] The right to development had been in gestation since at least 1981, when the Commission on Human Rights established a working group of 15 governmental experts which had also received very substantial inputs from non-governmental organizations.[2] As P. Alston says, of all the various new rights which have been proposed, the right to development has attracted the greatest scholarly and diplomatic attention.[3] However, the task was hardly finished with the adoption of the Declaration. On the agenda of the states and peoples of the world there still remains the major task of finding concrete ways and means to develop the right to development.

This task was only inaugurated by the Declaration because consensus among states on the nature and scope of the right to development is necessarily abstract. Consensus offers a rich variety of starting points, nationally, regionally and internationally, for a new quest for human rights. Already the General Assembly has expressed the desire that governments, specialized agencies of the United Nations and non-governmental organizations comment on the text of the Declaration, including practical proposals and ideas which could contribute substantively to the further enhancement and implementation of the Declaration.[4] All this suggests that the right to development is to be taken seriously and summons all of us to 'stand up and be counted'. For cynicism and indifference, always the well-cultivated enemies of human rights, certainly have a potential for converting this precious Declaration into a lifeless text.

The Core Conceptions

The Preamble to the Declaration indicates that it is a lineal descend-ant of the Universal Declaration of Human Rights, the two International Covenants and all other subsequent enunciations of human rights, such as those on the prevention of racial discrimina-tion, maintenance of peace or self-determination. The conception of the right to development embraces the following crucial notions:

- the right of peoples to self-determination, meaning the right to determine freely their political status and to pursue their eco-nomic, social and cultural development;
- their right to full and complete sovereignty over all their wealth and natural resources;
- elimination of massive and flagrant violations of the human rights of peoples and individuals;[5]
- all human rights and fundamental freedoms are indivisible and interdependent, and equal attention should be paid to the promotion and protection of all rights, civil political, economic, social and cultural. Promotion of certain human rights and fundamental freedoms cannot justify the denial of other hu-man rights and fundamental freedoms;
- international peace and security are essential elements for the realization of the right to development;
- the human person is the central subject of the development process and development policy should therefore make the human being the main participant and beneficiary of develop-ment;
- equality of opportunity for development is a prerogative both of nations and of individuals who make up nations and, hence, resources released through disarmament should be devoted to the economic and social development and well-being of all peoples and, in particular, those of the developing countries;
- efforts at the international level to promote and protect human rights and fundamental freedoms should be accompanied by efforts to establish a new international economic order.

When the right to development is declared an inalienable human right, we must recall that it is so proclaimed in the light of the foregoing value premises. The right to development is, in effect, the right of all human persons everywhere, and of humanity as a whole, to realize their potential. For the first time in recent history, we move from conception of rights as resources for individuals against state power to the conception of human rights as species rights as well.[6] And therefore it is natural that rights should apply not just to states but to international organizations as well, whose major historical role is to enunciate the new future of humankind through the reconstruction of a human person whose loyalties are global or planetary. Transcendence from state sovereignty, which concerns mapping new trajectories for an alternative human future, can only be achieved by retooling the notions of human rights and fundamental freedoms. It is for this reason that the Preamble lays particular stress on the centrality of the human person.

Underlying the Declaration and animating all its formulations is a central duty of all human beings, the performance of which alone justifies their having the inalienable right to development. This cardinal duty is to work towards a world order which is free of massive and flagrant violations of human rights and fundamental freedoms and to contribute to human survival and peace. The Declaration on the Right to Development is, furthermore, an explicit charter of duties for human beings everywhere to struggle to create and maintain conditions where authentic human, social and civilizational development is possible. Further concretization of this duty is an ineluctable aspect of the development of the right to development.

Towards Participation and Responsibility

The *leitmotiv* of the Declaration is that the human person is the central subject of development and therefore an active participant and beneficiary of the right to development: states have the right and duty to formulate appropriate national development policies that aim at the constant improvement of the well-being of the entire population and of all individuals (Article 2(3)), but the performance of this duty requires solicitude regarding active, free and meaningful participation of all individuals.

In other words, appropriate development stands identified with participatory development. The kind of development in which a few people take all developmental decisions, through the idiom of paternalism (whether of the old liberal variety or of its newer and sinister form reflected in scientific or technological paternalism), loses its legitimacy through the notions of appropriate development. Development policies which treat people as objects of development and not as subjects are clearly not appropriate. Human rights as conceived by the Declaration are not merely liberties which individuals may exercise at their will. They now betoken a responsibility to participate in development decisions, at both the national and international levels.

This right is accompanied by a responsibility on all human beings for development. That responsibility requires respect for human rights and fundamental freedoms as well as duties to promote and protect an appropriate political, social and economic order for development. A whole new ethic is reinforced when Article 9(2) further declares:

> Nothing in the present Declaration shall be construed as being contrary to the purposes and principles of the United Nations, or as implying that any State, group or person has a right to engage in any activity or to perform any act aimed at the violation of the rights set forth in the Universal Declaration of Human Rights and in the International Covenants on Human Rights.

The parameters of participation are thus clearly indicated by Article 2. So is its immanent logic which consists, in the felicitous words of J.R. Lucas, in 'the abandonment of the [...] one-dimensional concept of the public interest of which the Government is the best judge'.[7] But this repudiation is not enough. If multidimensional processes of determination concerning development are to be initiated and institutionalized, participation has to be conceptualized as the diffusion of public power and authority. What is known as decentralization of power is usually inhibited by the notion that it entails decentring of power. This, of course, is not so. After all, some centres of power will finally and formally have to adopt, announce and administer public decisions.

The right to participation may take both reactive and proactive forms. In its reactive form, participation consists in the collective articulation of the response to development policies. In its proactive form, participation invokes the responsibility of the people in the initiation of the articulation of development policies. In the first form, governments propose and citizens respond; in the second, citizens propose and governments respond. In both forms, participatory rights assume a logic of collaboration for development. The final aim of participatory endeavours is to identify and strive towards the goals of appropriate development, and this requires the creation and maintenance of spaces for dialogue in civil society and state structures. This, in turn, entails a vigorous tolerance of dissent on the part of individuals, groups and states.

The rights to freedom of speech and expression, and of the mass media, have therefore to be recognized as prerequisites of the right to participation. Repression of these rights negates participatory rights at their very source. At the same time, the underlying ethic of participation forbids the crime of silence in the face of massive and flagrant violations of human rights, at home and abroad, on the part of individuals and groups. Strange though it may seem to some, at a purely analytical level, freedom of speech and expression entails a human rights responsibility for the articulation of issues of public policy.

The notion that the right to speak also includes the right not to speak is fatal to the logic of participatory rights, except in circumstances where the right to silence is an aspect of human rights, as in the case of the right not to incriminate oneself.

Similarly, the right to participation imposes duties going beyond the traditional duties of forbearance or non-interference with the rights to freedom of the press, expression and speech. The duties are now expanded. First, the right to participation entails a duty not to criminalize speech; except in the rarest of rare situations, speaking, writing and other forms of communication should not be offences punishable by criminal law. Second, the right to free speech must entail a duty to hear, listen and respond. Neither reactive nor proactive forms of the right to participation hold any prospect of impact without the postulation of such a duty. Third, the right to freedom of speech and expression, as a participatory right, must extend effectively not just to individuals but to collectivities. Freedom of speech and expression should also extend to the right of association and activities congenial to associations, provided they respect the parameters of Article 2 of the Declaration. Fourth, the rights to speech must entail fair access to the institutionalized media of expression (whether state-owned or corporate), especially the mass media which alone can make participation in developmental decisions and policies meaningful. Fifth, participatory rights require access to relevant information in languages (both 'natural' and 'artificial', that is the specialized languages of sciences, including social sciences, and technologies). Privatization of information and secrecy defeat, at the very outset, the purposes of participatory rights. Sixth, participatory rights entail costs to governments, groups and individuals. The costs are those of time, money, effort and related resources. National-level planning must conceptualize this problem of costs of participation and provide for their just distribution.

Participation, above all, is participation in decision making. All these, and many more, aspects of participation as a human right need further thought and action if we are at all to develop the right to development.[8]

Popular Participation

The Declaration refers to the duties of states, in Article 8(2), 'to encourage … popular participation in all spheres as an important factor in development and in the full realization of all human rights'.

In a sense, popular participation is an aspect of the right to participation assured by the Declaration as a whole. As Article 9(1) declares, all aspects of the right to development are indivisible and interdependent. At the same time, there is merit in addressing the right to popular participation as a discrete, though related, aspect of the right to development. If we attend closely to the formulation in Article 8(2), we find that popular participation applies to all spheres and not just to developmental decisions. It would not be too far wrong to assume that what is intended by this provision is a reference to popular participation in governance. The article declares, in effect, that governance must be based on the consent of the governed. The means and modes of articulation of the consent of the governed have varied in human history but, as we read the Declaration as a whole, it is clear that its conception of appropriate development is impossible and even inconceivable to attain without the security of the principle of the consent of the governed.

Whatever its specific structuring may be, popular participation in governance entails some recourse to elective processes for public offices. These may also entail the rights of referendum and recall. Integrity of elective processes also forms a vital aspect of the right to popular participation, as does the idea that constitutions may be adopted and amended through the processes of popular participation because constitutions provide the very title to legitimate governance.

The right to popular participation, of course, extends further to suggest that legal and extralegal repression of acts of participation in all spheres of life is suspect at the bar of the right to development. Justification of such repression is, indeed, problematic, especially when it is urged in furtherance of participation and development rights. Criminal and penal policies must respect rights to popular participation.

The agenda of the development of the right to development thus extends to a close scrutiny of national legal systems in their structuring of electoral processes and of criminal and preventive legislation, including law enforcement policies and personnel which, in turn, structure legal and extralegal repression. A critical review of the theory and practice of legislation is thus urgently called for. Fortunately, as regards the former, a number of international guidelines exist, especially following the valuable work of the UN Committee on Prevention of Crime and Treatment of Offenders.

SLAPPS: Corporate Governance and Public/Popular Participation

A yet more pressing issue on the agenda of development of the right to development, in this era of headlong and heedless globalization, relates to ways devised by national and transnational corporate capital to impose regimes of silence on activists seeking to implement the values enshrined in the Declaration.

A crucial question, of course, is whether the Declaration extends to non-state actors. There is ample scope for its being read as so extending. The dominant ideology of globalization, expressed through structural adjustment programmes, ordains that markets or the economy are a better vehicle of development than the polity or the state. Assuming this to be the case, there is no reason why the right of peoples regarded as subjects and not objects cannot be extended to non-state entities, directing development under the auspices of globalization processes. At a more technical level of analysis concerning the issue whether non-state entities are subjects of international law, one might at least be able to say that they can be construed as objects of international law, without necessarily exposing the endangered species of positivistic international lawyers or publicists to any further risk!

Even if this latter aspect may still be said to be problematical, it needs some re-examination in the light of existing international human rights law and jurisprudence. A brief excursus on SLAPPS will, perhaps, show why. SLAPPS stands for 'Strategic Lawsuits Against Public Participation'. The term, invented by G. Pring and P. Cannan,[9] represents use of national law to 'sue' activists or people into silence. The strategy involves the use of existing legal structures and processes, especially by multinational/transnational corporations, to instigate very heavy libel suits against active citizens' groups, regardless of whether they violate the First Amendment type of human rights.[10] The processes of SLAPPS tend to impose onerous costs on relatively resourceless activist groups in the South: resourceless in the market sense of staying power to face the might or the wrath of legal processes and structures. Although there have been instances of 'reverse' SLAPPing by some activist groups, present studies show that SLAPPS indicates the tendency of global capital to thwart the nascent right of peoples to regard themselves as subjects of development.

The Declaration orients state legal systems towards a programme of law reform which would prevent unconscious excesses of corporate rights militating. If they do (and I believe this to be the case) under positive international law, there will, of course, be scope for enforcing the responsibility necessarily associated with rights of popular/public participation. However, these responsibilities of social activists have only to be identified as demonstrably reckless and malicious to be deprived of all sense of serving the logic of participatory rights enunciated in the Declaration.

In other words, the development of the right to development ought not to burden social activists disproportionately, except in situations (in common law terms) where malice *de jure* and *de facto* is demonstrably proved. The taming of SLAPPS is thus justified, given the incomparable levels of resources commanded by global capital which until now make it 'convenient' for Ken Saro Wiwa to be executed. Any activist, worthy of the name knows the power of global capital to organize even judicial murders, when extrajudicial ones tend to be relatively inefficient in terms of market rationality. That the latter remain the more favoured strategies of global capital does not detract from the organized prowess of the former.

If participatory rights are to prefigure a new human future, or even a new human rights future, the emergent phenomenon of SLAPPS (a close cousin of SAPS: Structural Adjustment Programmes) invites a thoroughgoing regime of discipline and punishment. The Declaration must be so read, if it is not to be regarded as nothing more than a scrap of paper.

Removal of Obstacles to Development

Article 6(3) calls on states to take steps to eliminate obstacles to development resulting from the failure to observe civil and political rights, as well as economic, social and cultural rights. The nature and the context of these rights are crystallized in the International Covenants and the various related human rights instruments adopted under the auspices of the United Nations.

The notion of obstacles to human rights and fundamental freedoms is a momentous innovation. States are charged with a duty to remove these obstacles. Clearly, this assumes that the state itself will observe rights and freedoms, as otherwise it would itself constitute an obstacle to be removed by the people. When a particular state structure or operation becomes an obstacle arising from a violation of human rights and fundamental freedoms, the right to development must indicate, if we read the Declaration as a whole, two component rights: the human right to reform state structures and processes and the human right to transform them where necessary. It would be too much to read the right to rebellion or revolution into any human rights codification. The foregoing two component rights fall far short of the right to revolution and it is this feature which seems to have commended itself to the community of states when it adopted the Declaration with such an overwhelming majority at the General Assembly.

But obstacles to development also arise within civil society. It is here that much work awaits us, particularly in the developing societies, though by no means only there. Some deep-seated tendencies towards violation of the rights of indigenous ethnic groups, other traditionally disadvantaged social groups and women operate in civil society. When the state and the law assume a relatively just profile, the requisite militancy in action against these forms of violation is difficult to achieve. In this area, the violators of rights are not so much agents of state power as holders of social status and economic power. The idea of obstacles to rights and the call for their removal is fascinating in that it draws our attention to the hydra-headed monster of human rights violation which resides not just in states but in human collectivities inscribed in the very order which constitutes society.

What strategies should be adopted to empower the disadvantaged in any endeavour to end violation of their rights and freedoms by social collectivities is an exceedingly important question, the answer to which is sometimes a danger to the wider struggle for the achievement of human rights. Certainly, empowerment strategies must not be such as to deprive the adversary social groups of their rights; this is clearly prohibited by the Declaration as a whole. Nor could they be such, either for the depressed groups or the hegemonic ones which deny them the structure of opportunities provided by the participatory rights, even when the latter tend to overprotect the numerical and vocal majorities against minorities. If the historically disadvantaged groups have to be empowered to fight unconscionable domination, repression and exploitation within the framework of the Declaration, considerable innovative thought and action are required, especially in terms of avoiding what Professor C. Ake has recently termed, though in an altogether different context, the democratization of disempowerment.[11]

This is linked with the problem of revisiting the idea that progress in the achievement of human rights is marked by incremental disempowerment of the state in relation to individuals and groups. Reduction and elimination of socially and culturally secure despotic domination by certain groups over others, however, require suitable strategies of empowering the state, without at the same time creating a new Leviathan. This remains the most formidable challenge to human rights thought and theory, where a large number of cognitive and epistemic obstacles also need to be overcome!

Article 8(1) of the Declaration does refer to carrying out, obviously in a participative manner, economic and social reforms, with a view to eradicating all social injustices. This formulation, read with Article 6(3), now at least helps us to identify obstacles to human rights as a form of social injustice. But removal of injustices has to be itself a just process. And herein lies the new problematic of the development of the right to development.

Women and the Right to Development

From a feminist point of view, the Declaration may seem somewhat unsatisfactory. Only Article 6(1) and Article 8(1) specifically refer to women. The former reinforces the well-accepted prohibition of discrimination based on sex, and the latter, importantly, prescribes that effective measures should be undertaken to ensure that women have an active role in the development process. It must be conceded that these formulations, put together, do not fully respond to the emerging feminist critiques of rights, state and society. The Declaration does not embody many of the implications of the feminist maxim: the personal is political. There is growing feminist consensus over the value of women's autonomy of the self, the right over their own bodies and reproductive rights. The Declaration, at most, addresses the issues of non-discrimination; in this it does not move beyond women's rights (in a man's world) to the rights of women (in a human world).

Perhaps the phrase 'active role' to be ensured for women in development may be made into a verbal vessel into which the feminist mood, method and message may be poured. But the feminist task here is difficult, since formulations of human rights still continue to occur within the hegemonic patriarchal tradition, as the regressive text of the draft Platform for Action for the Fourth World Conference on Women (Beijing, 1995) so poignantly demonstrates, perhaps redeemed in the final text by concerted NGO efforts. The task of the feminist contribution to the development of the right to development is, on the one hand, to enrich the consensus already codified in the Declaration and, on the other, to transform to a feminist mould, against all odds, the enunciation of the component rights of the right to development.

Juridical Critique

In a curious reversal of roles, while states have subscribed without many qualms to the Declaration, publicists and jurists have raised a plethora of difficulties and interrogations. Some critiques are basically 'Declaration-friendly'. Others question, and even deny, at both the legal and the ethical levels, the coherence and justification of the Declaration. Put together, juridical critiques raise the following issues.

- What ought to be a legitimate mode of production of new human rights in the United Nations system?
- Can we speak at all of collective rights of states or peoples as human rights?

- Given the distinction between 'rights' and 'righteousness', the so-called 'right to development' cannot be a legal right, even of individuals; nor can it be a moral right.

The right to development is an accomplished juridical fact of human rights law and jurisprudence. In order to ensure that its legitimacy is not jeopardized, or its further development thwarted by critiques, primarily emanating from North America, it is necessary to examine the salient issues.

Mode of Creation of New Human Rights

How new rights should be created is undoubtedly an important question related to but going beyond the context of the Declaration on the Right to Development. O. Schachter[12] has already suggested that conformity with minimum procedural standards is an essential requirement for legitimating international decisions. Pursuing this theme, P. Alston has powerfully argued against the magical mode of production of new human rights, and suggested a model of procedural and substantive steps. Necromancy occurs

> when bodies at lower level in the international hierarchy than the General Assembly have tended to proclaim new rights without adequate consideration of basis, let alone advisability or implications, for such action and without leaving the [General] Assembly with an adequate opportunity to determine whether or not the giving of the imprimatur is warranted.[13]

The elaborate procedure Alston proposes is designed to reinforce the declaratory authority of the General Assembly which depends on the maintenance of its: 'credibility as a responsible and discerning arbiter and as a weather vane of the state of world public and governmental opinion'.[14] These are, undoubtedly, important considerations, especially at the present juncture of free-market structuring processes of 'globalization'. The production of new human rights, indeed, may further the paradigm (of what we have called) trade-related human rights. The oft-mentioned example of this trend is the proposal of the World Tourism Organization to recognize tourism as a basic individual and collective human need and therefore as the right!

At the same time, the realization of latent or unrecognized human rights and the normativeness of strict criteria and procedures may impede their progress towards explicit enunciation and universal recognition. The list of such latent human rights may be small, but its significance may well be of global importance.

Additionally, any overrationalized perspective of the production of rights seems to be based on notions of rationality and legitimacy which are themselves questionable. For one thing, the emphasis on reason over emotion reincarnates patriarchy. As A. Baier has reminded us, in so many respects Hume is a better guru than Kant. Baier stressed not merely frivolous factors such as historical chance and human fancy and what they select as salient, but also our capacity for sympathy, that is 'our ability to recognise and share sympathetically the reaction of others to … [the] system of rights, to communicate feelings and understand what our fellows are feeling and so to realise what resentment and satisfaction the present social scheme generates.[15] On this view, human rights signify progress in moral sentiments. The perils and promise of human rights production ought to be grasped through a creative mix of reason and emotion, and even political passion, especially in the content of the unfolding of latent human rights. Any serious ethical understanding of human rights as signifiers of progress in moral sentiments ought also to facilitate the struggle against the globalization-induced promotion of trade-related human rights at the expense of basic human rights. And, by definition, such a concept would also enhance struggles to preserve people's security, peace, productivity and denuclearization – the congeries of human-rights-in-the-making. Male visions of rationality and legitimacy ought surely to be informed by an alternative, and not merely supplemental, model of human rights creation.

Are People's Rights Human Rights?

It has recently been vociferously argued that not only does the Declaration mix up individual human rights and collective (people's) rights which are different and should be kept distinct but, since people as collective rights holders are not physical persons, they require an institutional person to exercise their rights. The most plausible 'person' to exercise such people's rights is, unfortunately, the state. This represents a radical reconceptualization of human rights – and an especially dangerous one.[16] It is dangerous because all human rights are held primarily against the state and the

> danger here is that the State is […] placed in a position to use its human rights to deny the individual human rights while still plausibly claiming to be pursuing human rights. 'Human rights' are thus transformed into but another mechanism of political tyranny and oppression.[17]

Moreover, the very idea of a human right held by the state is incoherent and the very term 'human rights' of states involves a logical contradiction.[18]

The Declaration, carefully read, does not provide any notion of human rights of states; rather, it forcefully articulates human rights responsibilities of states, acting within their jurisdiction as well as in the international arena.[19] The fact that a handful of publicists derive from the Declaration a notion of the human rights of states is in itself too insignificant a factor to constitute criticism of the right to development. Nor does the fact that some states (notably Colombia, Togo and the Federal Republic of Yugoslavia) referred to the human rights of states in the discussions leading to the Declaration now militate against its final text. Thus this line of attack is, essentially, an exercise in the slaying of straw men!

What is dangerous is not the existence or enunciation of the peoples' right to development (or the declaration-in-the-making of the human rights of indigenous peoples) but the obtuseness of moral philosophers. It is indeed perverse to say that the Declaration on the Right to Development may facilitate political tyranny or social oppression, neither of which needs to don the mask of the right to development. And it can be safely said that the modern development of human rights law and jurisprudence does not acknowledge sovereignty (or domestic jurisdiction) as a shield for flagrant violations of human rights. Nor, furthermore, is it possible to read into the Declaration a whole configuration of elements legitimating violations of rights.

The notion that peoples are not entities in international law adheres to a classical premise which constructs only states as primary, or pre-eminent, subjects. But the increasing participation of non-governmental organizations (now termed 'international civil society') in the making of international law at the Rio, Vienna, Copenhagen, Cairo, Beijing and Istanbul Summit Conferences simply cannot be denied. Nor may the impact of women's movements throughout the world, which have sculpted the obligations of states in ways which radically reconfigure the very notion of human rights through the Convention on Elimination of Discrimination Against Women. The Declaration in many ways consummates this tendency and it is indeed logically possible only because nation-states, as well as the society of states as a whole, stand designated as bearers of obligations.

The point that state formations have their own distinctive ends, and that they may seek to pursue these in ways which frustrate rather than fulfil the Declaration's assurances of rights, makes historically valid sense. But to say that a state may not ever personify people's rights, even when in contradiction to its own distinctive interests or ends, is far from being grounded in reality.[20] For example (and these are very complex illustrations), the struggle by many states of the South against the legitimacy and legality of the conditionalities to developmental assistance by the international financial institutions or the struggle against certain aspects of General Agreement on Tariffs and Trade/World Tourism Organization (GATT/WTO) reformulations do, indeed, present states as potentially examples of personified peoples. States may be seen to personify other people's human rights, as an aspect of the internationalization of a human rights culture, as in the case of India's assistance to the people's liberation struggle in former East Pakistan, or Vietnamese leadership in finally overthrowing the Khmer Rouge regimes in Cambodia. Of course, such personifications remain contentious, especially when undertaken by Third World states.

Modern history shows that the superpower humanitarian interventions reek of barely disguised national interest and hegemonic considerations. The basic point, however, is this: conceding that sovereign states are never enterprising in the redressing of human rights abroad (and more often than not are bystanders or accomplices in perversions of power elsewhere), there exist examples of 'altruistic' state behaviour where it makes overall, non-hegemonic sense to speak of states as, even if momentarily, authentically personifying the people's right to development.

This leaves us with a rather familiar problem, overall, in the field of the creation of human rights; that is, if people have collective human rights, how do they enforce these outside the juridical personification of people by the state entity to which they owe allegiance? In a sense, this is a problem with all sorts of collective rights (whether of indigenous peoples, migrant workers or diasporic minority groups). But the sphere of acknowledgment or enunciation of human rights is distinct from, though related to, the sphere of the realization and fulfilment of rights. It is only when rights are brought into existence that the issue of effective implementation comes into being. Undoubtedly, there exist substantial problems in the realization of the right to development, but that constitutes no justifiable reason to denounce the acts of enunciation.

Neither a Legal nor a Moral Right Thou shalt be!

It has been maintained that, in the absence of a broad, almost universal consensus concerning a derived right to development, it cannot be accepted as a part of customary international law and that such a consensus does not exist. Even when one might legitimately speak of an international legal regime of development, one may not derive from it any right to development.[21]

This kind of nihilism, of course, does not deny the variety of sources or lineages constituting a substantial body of principles from which the right to development may be said to have been derived, but it contests the logic of such a derivation.[22] A detailed rebuttal must remain the task of another study, but one or two instances of such nihilism must be emphasized here.

For example, it has been strenuously argued that a substantially broader right to development cannot be derived from the right to self-determination, recognized by the two International Covenants. Neither, it is said, implies a right to live in a developing society or a right to be developed; both imply simply a right to pursue development.[23] Such bizarre readings of the two Covenants are as rare as they are outrageous. The Covenants certainly create individual and group rights, and an integrated approach to both the Covenants enables a reading consistent with derivation of the right to development from those texts;[24] and, indeed, Article 6(3) of the Declaration summoning all states to eliminate obstacles to development due to a failure to observe the obligations of the two International Covenants reinforces this reasoning.

Another example of this type of nihilism is furnished by the way Article 28 of the Universal Declaration of Human Rights is construed. That Article assures everyone's right 'to a social and international order in which the rights and freedoms set forth in this Declaration can be fully realized'. It is argued that the right to development cannot be derived from this provision because development suggests process or result, while 'order' refers to 'structure'. Article 28 is

> most plausibly interpreted as prohibiting structures that deny the opportunities or resources for the realization of civil, political, economic or cultural human rights. To get a right to development out of this would require showing that development is impossible or positively denied by current national or international structures. Clearly such an argument is [...] most contentious.[25]

Contentious or not, the massive attempt at standard setting in terms of human rights is sufficient to show that the structures of power, nationally and globally, are not simply and conducive to development. Even a momentary and rudimentary glance at the evolution of women's rights or the right to environment, for example, would lead to this inevitable conclusion. It is not necessary here to go further into the problematic stipulative definitions offered to elucidate notions of 'processes' and 'structures'.

Is the moral case for right to development largely baseless, as the nihilists would have us believe? Surely, it is trite to say that not all moral 'oughts' are grounded in or give rise to rights, and that one does not have a right to everything that is or would be right for one to possess.[26] But does this imply or entail any widespread confusion in the enunciation of the right to development? Why righteousness does not at times give rise to moral rights is a question which nihilists neither pose nor answer. For them, the distinction between righteousness and moral rights constitutes a kind of species-barrier. If there is a case for cogent argumentation for this position, a moral right to development can never be brought to existence, as this would create distinct moral obligations on states individually and collectively. This case is clearly not made by nihilists.

Conclusion: Avoidance of Non-proliferation

What holds good for nuclear weapons is bad for human rights. Non-proliferation should be the operative norm for nuclear weapons; proliferation should be the *grundnorm* for the right to development. The next step in the struggle for the development of the right to development is the proliferation of whole constellations of component rights. On the notions and nature of these component rights, we may not arrive at global consensus without a prolonged struggle. And one aspect of the struggle must be waged everywhere at the national level: the discourse on the right to development has to be initiated at all levels of policy making and activism.[27] The easy-minded cynicism towards the right to development has to be displaced, its practical uses demonstrated, its scope concretized through praxis.

More than any other authoritative enunciation of a vision of human rights, the Declaration on the Right to Development seeks to move beyond the traditional approaches to human rights and to structure respect for every person's right to be human amidst growing concerns about the next millennium and the future(s) it may hold for human rights. Above all, this aspect should continually engage our imagination and action.

Notes

1   Resolution 41/128 of 4 December 1986.
2   NGO Document (1981).
3   Philip Alston, 'Making space for human rights: the case of the right to development', *Harvard Human Rights Yearbook*, 1, (1), 1998.
4   See United Nations General Assembly resolution 43/160.
5   Described as violations arising from: 'colonialism, neocolonialism, apartheid, all forms of racism and racial discrimination, foreign domination and occupation, aggression [...] and threats of war' (see the Preamble to the Declaration). Widening of this category in ways which describe violations of human rights practice at non-state or societal levels would be an important task for the future. This also appears in Article 5 of the Declaration.

6   K. Marx, *Collected Works of Marx and Engels*, 1, Progress Publishers, Moscow, 1975, 164.
7   J.R. Lucas, *Democracy and Participation*, London, Pelican Books, 1976, 243.
8   Perhaps the most sustained articulation of 'participation' has occurred, unsurprisingly, in the context of environment protection: see para 23.2, Agenda 21; Principle 10, the Rio Declaration; Article 4.1, the Climate Change Convention; Article 16, OECD Council Recommendation Concerning ... Accidents, Involving Hazardous Substances; ILO Convention 141 (the Rural Workers). The listing here is not exhaustive; see paragraphs 123–39, *Report of the Expert Group Meeting on Identification of Principles of International Law for Sustainable Development* Geneva, September 1995.
9   George W. Pring and Penelope Cannan, 'Strategic lawsuits against public participation', *Bridgeport Law Review*, 12, 1992, 931–62.
10 For a detailed narrative, see Andrew Rowell, *Green Backlash: Global Subversion of the Environmental Movement*, London, Routledge, 1996, 179–81, 247–9, 279–81, 336–8.
11 Claude Ake, 'The democratization of disempowerment in Africa', in J. Hippler (ed.), *The Democratization of Disempowerment: The Problem of Democracy in the Third World*, London, Pluto Press, 1995, 70.
12 Oscar Schachter, 'The crisis of legitimation in the United Nations', *Nordic Journal of International Law: Acta Scandanavia Juris Gentium*, 50, 1981, 3–4.
13 Philip Alston, 'Conjuring up new human rights', *American Journal of International Law*, 78, 1984, 608.
14 Ibid., 609.
15 Annette C. Baier, *A Progress of Sentiments: Reflection on Hume's Treatise*, Cambridge, MA, Harvard University Press, 1991, 55–6.
16 Jack Donnelly, 'In search of the unicorn: the jurisprudence and politics of the right to development', *California Western International Law Journal*, 15, 1985, 499.
17 Ibid., 499–500.
18 Ibid., 499.
19 See especially Article 4(2) of the Declaration stating the duty of all states, individually and collectively to 'formulate international development policies with a view to facilitating the full realization of the right to development'. Also see Article 7 casting similar obligations on states to 'promote the establishment, maintenance and strengthening of international peace and security'.
20 It is noteworthy that in federal state formations the discourse on states' rights is not devoid of human rights coherence.
21 See Donnelly (1985, 487 and 489).
22 For a comprehensive listing of sources acknowledging the right to development, see the United Nations Secretary-General's Report, UN Doc. E/CN.6/1336 (1979).
23 See Donnelly (1985, 484).
24 Rolf Kunnemann, 'A coherent approach to human rights', *Human Rights Quarterly*, 17, 1995, 332–42.
25 See Donnelly (1985, 487–8).
26 Ibid., 490.
27 In New Zealand, the Report of the Waitangi Tribunal on the Muriwheuna Fishing Claim (June 1988) has taken full account of the right to development in interpreting the treaty with the Maoris (see, for example, p.234); see also the judicial recognition accorded to the right to development in *Simon* v. *The Queen* (1985) 24 *DLR* (4th), pp.390 and 402. Parallel developments have been reported from Pakistan. And the Interim Draft Constitution of the Republic of South Africa, now finally certified by the Constitutional Court of South Africa, seems suffused with the values explicated in the Declaration.

Bibliography

Ake, Claude (1995), 'The democratization of disempowerment in Africa', in J. Hippler (ed.)., *The Democratization of Disempowerment: The Problem of Democracy in the Third World*, London, Pluto Press.

Alston, Philip (1984), 'Conjuring up new human rights', *American Journal of International Law*, **78**.

Alston, Philip (1988), 'Making space for human rights: the case of the right to development', *Harvard Human Rights Yearbook*, **1**, (1).

Baier, Annette C. (1991), *A Progress of Sentiments: Reflection on Hume's Treatise*, Cambridge, MA, Harvard University Press.

Baxi, Upendra (1983), 'The new international economic order, basic needs and rights: notes towards development of the right to development', *Indian Journal of International Law*, **23**.

Baxi, Upendra (1987), 'From human rights to the right to be human: some heresies', in U. Baxi (ed.), *The Rights to be Human*, New Delhi, Lance Publication.

Baxi, Upendra (1994a), *Inhuman Wrongs and Human Rights*, New Delhi, Har-Anand, pp.1–7.

Baxi, Upendra (1994b), *Mambrino's Helmet? Human Rights for a Changing World*, Delhi, Har-Anand.

Baxi, Upendra (1995), 'Summit of hope in the depths of despair? Social development as a human right', mimeo, March.

Donnelly, Jack (1985), 'In search of the unicorn: the jurisprudence and politics of the right to development', *California Western International Law Journal*, **15**.

Kunnemann, Rolf (1995), 'A coherent approach to human rights', *Human Rights Quarterly*, **17**, 332–42.

Lucas, J.R. (1976), *Democracy and Participation*, London, Pelican Books.

Marx, K. (1975), *Collected Works of Marx and Engels*, Vol. 1, Moscow, Progress Publishers.

NGO (1981), Document prepared by the International Commission for the UN Working Group of Governmental Experts, E/CN.4/AC34/WP.10 of 16 November.

Pring, George W. and Penelope Cannan (1992), 'Strategic lawsuits against public participation', *Bridgeport Law Review*, **12**, 931–62.

Rowell, Andrew (1996), *Green Backlash: Global Subversion of the Environmental Movement*, London, Routledge.

Schachter, Oscar (1981), 'The crisis of legitimation in the United Nations', *Nordic Journal of International Law: Acta Scandanavia Juris Gentium*, **50**.

5 Human Rights and the Environment

ANTONIO AUGUSTO CANÇADO
TRINDADE

Introduction

Modern international life has been deeply marked and transformed by current endeavours to meet the needs and fulfil the requirements of protection of the human person and of the environment. Such endeavours have been encouraged by the widespread recognition that protection of human beings and the environment reflects common superior values and constitutes a common concern of mankind. The affinities between the systems of protection in the two domains of human rights and the environment are *per se* deserving of close attention, being further called for by the injustice perpetrated by the grave and persisting inequalities of the conditions of life among human beings and among nations; such injustice is further reflected in, and aggravated by, environmental degradation. It can hardly be doubted that human rights protection and environmental protection thus represent two major and universal challenges of our time.

The parallelisms in the evolutions of these two domains of protection remain a very topical subject, insufficiently explored to date. A general overview of the matter is bound to encompass a wide variety of aspects and concerns pertaining to the present state of the two domains of protection and the ways and means resorted to in order to secure their expansion and enhancement in the years which conduct us into the new century. For the purpose of examination of this novel topic, we shall develop four lines of consideration: first, the identification of affinities in the parallel evolutions of human rights protection and of environmental protection; second, the identification of the wide dimension of the fundamental right to life, added to the right to health, at the basis of the *ratio legis* of international human rights law and of environmental law; third, the question of the implementation of the right to a healthy environment, with its various implications, and the jurisprudential beginnings on the matter; fourth, the relevance of the right of democratic participation. The present subject is undergoing a constant and rapid evolution, which is deserving of permanent attention and research, conducive to a better understanding of the proper sense of the expansion and enhancement of the two domains of protection, of the human person and the environment.

The Growth of Human Rights Protection and of Environmental Protection: from Internationalization to Globalization

The Internationalization of Human Rights Protection and of Environmental Protection

The parallel evolutions of human rights protection and environmental protection disclose some affinities which should not pass unnoticed. They both witness, and precipitate, the gradual erosion of the so-called 'domestic jurisdiction' of states. The treatment by the state of its own nationals becomes a matter of international concern. Conservation of the environment and control of pollution become likewise a matter of international concern. There occurs a process of internationalization of both human rights protection and environmental protection, the former beginning with the 1948 Universal Declaration of Human Rights, the latter – years later – with the 1972 Stockholm Declaration on the Human Environment.

With regard to human rights protection, 18 years after the adoption of the 1948 Universal Declaration the International Bill of Human Rights was completed with the adoption of the two UN International Covenants, on Civil and Political (and [first] Optional Protocol), and on Economic, Social and Cultural Rights (1966), respectively. The normative corpus of international human rights law is today a vast one, comprising a multiplicity of treaties and instruments, at both global and regional levels, with varying ambits of application and covering the protection of human rights of various kinds and in distinct domains of human activity.

As for environmental protection, the years following the Stockholm Declaration likewise witnessed a multiplicity of international instruments on the matter, also at both global and regional levels. It is estimated that nowadays there are more than 300 multilateral treaties and around 900 bilateral treaties providing for the protection and conservation of the biosphere, to which over 200 texts from international organizations can be added.[1] The considerable growth of international regulation in the present domain has, by and large, followed a sectoral approach, leading to the celebration of conventions addressing certain sectors or areas, or concrete situations (for example, oceans, continental waters, atmosphere, wild life). In sum, international regulation in the domain of environmental protection has taken place in the form of responses to specific challenges.

The same appears to have been the case in the field of human rights protection, where we witness a multiplicity of international instruments: parallel to general human rights treaties (such as the two UN Covenants on Human Rights and the three regional – European, American and African – Conventions, followed in 1994 by the Arab Charter on Human Rights), there are conventions addressing concrete situations (for example, prevention of discrimination, prevention and punishment of torture and ill-treatment), specific human conditions (for example, refugee status, nationality and statelessness) and certain groups in special need of protection (for example, workers' rights, women's rights, protection of the child, protection of the elderly, protection of the disadvantaged). In sum, human rights instruments have grown, at normative and procedural levels, likewise as *responses* to violations of human rights of various kinds.

This being so, it is not surprising that certain gaps may appear as awareness grows of the increasing needs of protection. An example of such a gap in the field of human rights protection can be found at the present time, for example, in the protection to be extended to certain vulnerable groups, in particular indigenous populations. Another example of such a gap, which in the area of environmental protection persisted until the 1992 UN Conference on Environment and Development, could be found in the needed enhancement of international regulation on climate change and protection of the atmosphere.

A significant task for the near future – if not for the present – will consist precisely in ensuring the proper coordination of multiple instruments which have been adopted in the last decades, at global and regional levels, pursuant to the 'sectoral' approach (see above), in the domains of human rights protection[2] as well as environmental protection. Beyond the internationalization of the two domains of protection following the pattern referred to above, it was soon realized that in each of them there existed an interrelatedness among the distinct sectors which were the object of regulation.

The Globalization of Human Rights Protection and of Environmental Protection

The awareness of this interrelatedness has contributed decisively to the evolution, in recent years, from the internationalization to the globalization of human rights protection and environmental protection. As far as human rights protection is concerned, two decades after the adoption of the 1948 Universal Declaration of Human Rights, the first World Conference on Human Rights, held in Tehran in 1968, in a global reassessment of the matter, proclaimed the indivisibility of all human rights (civil and political, as well as economic, social and cultural rights). This was followed by the landmark resolution 32/130, adopted by the UN General Assembly in 1977, acknowledging that human rights questions were to be examined from a globalist perspective, and drawing attention to the priority to be accorded to the search for solutions to massive and flagrant violations of human rights.[3] Three decades after the adoption of the 1948 Universal Declaration, the UN General Assembly, bearing in mind the fundamental changes undergone by international society – decolonization, capacity for massive destruction, population growth, environmental conditions and energy consumption, amongst others – endeavoured to go beyond the old categorizations of rights and to proceed to a needed global analysis of existing problems in the field of human rights.

Such a new global outlook and conception of the indivisibility of human rights contributed to drawing closer attention in particular to the rights pertaining to human collectivities and the measures of their implementation. The matter was taken up again by General Assembly resolutions 39/145, of 1984, and 41/117, of 1986, which reiterated the interrelatedness of all human rights, whereby the protection of one category of rights should not exempt states from safeguarding the other rights. Thus human rights instruments aimed at the protection of certain categories of rights, or of certain rights in given situations, or of rights of certain groups in special need of protection, are to be properly approached on the understanding that they are complementary to general human rights treaties. Multiple human rights instruments reinforce each other, enhance the degree of the protection due and disclose an overwhelming identity of purpose.

As heralded by the UN Charter itself and the 1948 Universal Declaration, the observance of human rights worldwide constitutes a common concern of mankind. The interrelatedness of all human rights – civil and political, and economic, social and cultural – is today widely acknowledged pursuant to a global or universal approach. More recently, such an approach has found expression in the Vienna Declaration and Programme of Action, adopted by the second World Conference on Human Rights, held in June 1993. The Vienna Conference urged the 'universal ratification' by states of human rights treaties by the end of the century, the incorporation of the human rights dimension in all programmes and activities of the UN system, the coordination and greater efficacy of coexisting mechanisms of protection, the adoption of national measures of implementation and the strengthening of democratic institutions directly engaged in securing the rule of law and the full observance of human rights.

The reasserting by the 1993 Vienna Conference of the universality of human rights and the current endeavours to secure in practice the indivisibility of all human rights, with special attention to those in greater need of protection – the socially excluded and the poorer and more vulnerable segments of the population – point in the right direction. They further indicate that, after many years of struggle, the principles of the international law of human rights seem at last to have reached the very bases of national societies.[4]

In the domain of environmental protection, the presence, despite the 'sectoral' regulation, of 'transversal' issues and rules contributed to the globalist approach. It was reckoned that, more and more often, certain activities and products (for example, toxic or dangerous substances and wastes, ionizing radiations and radioactive wastes) may cause harmful effects in any environment; in fact, the problem of dangerous substances is present in the whole of 'sectoral' regulation, which points to globalization.[5] As early as 1974, two years after the adoption of the Stockholm Declaration, the UN Charter on Economic Rights and Duties of States warned that the protection and preservation of the environment for present and future generations were the responsibility of all states (Article 30), and in 1980 the UN General Assembly proclaimed the historical responsibility of states for the preservation of nature on behalf of present and future generations.

While, in the past, states tended to regard the regulation of pollution by sectors as a national or local issue, more recently they gradually realized that some environmental problems and concerns were essentially global in scope.[6] In its resolution 44/228, of 1989, whereby it decided to convene a UN Conference on Environment and Development in 1992, the UN General Assembly recognized that the global character of environmental problems required action at all levels (global, regional and national), involving the commitment and participation of all countries; the resolution further affirmed that the protection and enhancement of the environment were major issues which affected the well-being of peoples, and singled out, as one of the environmental issues of major concern, the 'protection of human health conditions and improvement of the quality of life' (para. 12(i)).

The global character of environmental issues is reflected in the question of conservation of biological diversity; it is further illustrated, in particular, by the problems linked to atmospheric pollution (such as depletion of the ozone layer and global climate change). These problems, initially thought of as being essentially local, were to reveal their marked global character.[7] The threat of damage to many nations resulting from global warming, for example, is a major problem, the cause of which could hardly be traceable to a single state or group of states, thus calling for a new approach on the basis of strategies of prevention and adaptation and considerable international cooperation.[8] Thus the UN General Assembly, by resolution 43/53 of 1988, recognized that climate change was a common concern of mankind, and determined that action should be taken promptly to deal with it within a global framework.

Subsequently, in pursuance of a globalist approach, climate change was recognized as a 'common concern of mankind' by the 1992 Convention on the matter. The same occurred with the 1992 Convention on Biological Diversity, both of them pursuing a universal approach, and expressly referring, in their respective preambles, to the fundamental and urgent aim of eradication of poverty.

Agenda 21, adopted by UNCED in Rio de Janeiro in 1992, expressly refers (Chapters 3, 6 and 7) to vulnerable groups (exemplified by the urban and rural poor, indigenous populations, children, women, the elderly, the homeless, the terminally ill and the disabled), in a way reminiscent of parallel references found in the domain of human rights. The central preoccupation is with the satisfaction of basic human needs (Chapters 4, 6 and 7), such as food, health preservation, adequate housing and education. Significantly, *Agenda 21* makes express reference to two instruments of human rights – the Universal Declaration of 1948 and the UN Covenant on Economic, Social and Cultural Rights – in approaching the right to adequate housing, warning that, despite its formulation in those two instruments, it was estimated that today at least one billion people do not have access to adequate or safe housing, and if such a problem were to persist, this total could dramatically increase by the turn of the century (Chapter 7).

For its part, the 1993 Vienna Declaration and Programme of Action, adopted by the second World Conference on Human Rights, contains a cross-reference to the objectives on global action for women regarding sustainable and equitable development set forth in *Agenda 21* (Chapter 24) and the Rio Declaration adopted by UNCED. The Vienna Declaration calls for concerted endeavours in favour of economic, social and cultural rights, singling out 'the rights of everyone to a standard of living adequate for their health and well-being, including food and medical care, housing and the necessary social services'; it condemns continuing violations of and obstacles to the full enjoyment of human rights in various parts of the world, *inter alia*, 'poverty, hunger and other denials of economic, social and cultural rights' (Part I, paras 30–31). In sum, recent trends in environmental protection as well as in human rights protection disclose a clear and progressive passage from internationalization towards globalization, stressing the relevance of the right of participation (see below).

The Globalization of Protection and erga omnes *Obligations*

The globalization of human rights protection and of environmental protection can also be attested from a distinct approach, namely, that of the emergence of *erga omnes* obligations and the consequent decline and gradual abandonment of reciprocity. In the field of human rights protection, reciprocity is overcome and overwhelmed by the notion of collective guarantee and considerations of *ordre public*. Hence the specificity of human rights treaties. Traces of this new philosophy are also found in international humanitarian law: pursuant to common Article 1 of the 1949 Geneva Conventions, Contracting Parties are bound 'to respect and to ensure respect' for the four Conventions 'in all circumstances', that is, irrespective of considerations of reciprocity. Provisions with analogous effects can be found in human rights treaties (for example, UN International Covenant on Civil and Political Rights, Article 2; European Convention on Human Rights, Article 1; American Convention on Human Rights, Article 1). These humanitarian instruments have transcended the purely interstate level in search of a higher degree of protection of the human person so as to ensure the safeguard of common superior interests protected by them. Hence the universal character of the system of protection of international humanitarian law which creates for states obligations *erga omnes*.

The evolution of environmental protection likewise bears witness to the emergence of obligations of an objective character without reciprocal advantages for states. The 1972 Stockholm Declaration on the Human Environment expressly refers to the 'common good of mankind' (Principle 18). Rules on the protection of the environment are adopted, and obligations to that effect are undertaken, in the common superior interest of mankind. This has been expressly acknowledged in some treaties in the field of the environment (for example, preambles of the 1971 Treaty on the Prohibition of the Emplacement of Nuclear Weapons and Other Weapons of Mass Destruction on the Sea-Bed and the Ocean Floor and in the Subsoil Thereof; the 1972 Convention on the Prohibition of the Development, Production and Stockpiling of Bacteriological (Biological) and Toxin Weapons and on Their Destruction; the 1977 Convention on the Prohibition of Military or Any Other Hostile Use of Environmental Modification Techniques; the 1972 Convention on the Prevention of Marine Pollution by Dumping of Wastes and Other Matter; the 1974 Convention for the Prevention of Marine Pollution from Land-Based Sources; the 1972 Convention for the Prevention of Marine Pollution by Dumping from Ships and Aircraft; the 1972 UNESCO Convention for the Protection of the World Cultural and Natural Heritage). It is also implicit in references to 'human health' in some environmental law treaties (for example, the 1985 Vienna Convention for the Protection of the Ozone Layer, preamble and Article 2; the 1987 Montreal Protocol on Substances that Deplete the Ozone Layer, preamble; Article 1 of the three marine pollution conventions quoted above).

The evolution from internationalization to globalization of environmental protection can also be detected in its spatial dimension. In the beginnings of international environmental regulation, attention was turned to environmental protection in zones under the competence of states of the territorial type. Thus one spoke of control of trans-boundary or trans-frontier pollution (a terminology reminiscent of that employed in the OECD), with an underlying emphasis on the relations between neighbouring countries or on contacts or conflicts between state sovereignties. Soon it became evident that, to face wider threats to the environment – as in marine pollution and atmospheric pollution (acid rain, depletion of the ozone layer, global warming) – it was necessary to consider also principles applicable *urbi et orbi*, on a global scale, not only in zones where state interests were immediately affected (trans-boundary pollution), but also in other areas where state interests appeared not so visibly affected (for example, protection of the atmosphere and of the marine environment).

In this common international law of the environment, principles of a global character are to apply to the territory of states, irrespective of any trans-boundary or trans-frontier effect, and are to govern zones which are not under any national territorial competence.[9] In this connection the Brundtland Commission, reporting to the UN General Assembly in 1987, dedicated a whole chapter to the management, in the 'common interest', of the so-called 'global commons', that is, those zones falling outside or beyond national jurisdictions.[10] In sum, we have witnessed the gradual evolution from a trans-boundary or 'trans-territorial' perspective into a global approach to the preservation of the environment (and the action in favour of resources of the common heritage of mankind).[11]

That international law is no longer exclusively state-oriented can be seen from reiterated references to 'mankind', not only in doctrinal writings,[12] but also and significantly in various international instruments, possibly pointing towards an international law of mankind, pursuing preservation of the environment and sustainable development on behalf of present and future generations. Thus the notion of a cultural heritage of mankind can be found in the UNESCO Conventions for the Protection of Cultural Property in the Event of Armed Conflict (1954) and for the Protection of the World Cultural and Natural Heritage (1974). The legal principle of the common heritage of mankind has found expression in the realms of the law of the sea (1982 UN Convention on the Law of the Sea, Part XI, especially

Articles 136–45 and 311(6); 1970 UN Declaration of Principles Governing the Sea-Bed and Ocean Floor, and the Subsoil Thereof, Beyond the Limits of National Jurisdiction) and of the law of outer space (1979 Treaty Governing the Activities of States on the Moon and Other Celestial Bodies, Article 11; and cf. 1967 Treaty on Principles Governing the Activities of States in the Exploration and Use of Outer Space, Including the Moon and Other Celestial Bodies, Article I).[13] This calls for a reconsideration of the basic postulates of international law bearing in mind the superior common interest of mankind.

Despite semantic variations in international instruments on environmental protection when referring to mankind, a common denominator of them all appears to be the common interest of mankind. There seems to be occurring lately an evolution from the notion of a common heritage of mankind (as emerged in the contexts of the law of the sea and space law) to that of a common concern of mankind. The latter has been the object of consideration by the United Nations Environment Programme (UNEP) Group of Legal Experts, which convened in Malta on 13–15 December 1990, in order to examine the implications of the concept of the 'common concern of mankind' in relation to global environmental issues.[14]

This newly proposed concept is inspired by considerations of international *ordre public*. It appears as a derivative of the earlier 'common heritage' approach, meant to shift emphasis from the sharing of benefits from exploitation of environmental wealth to fair or equitable sharing of burdens in environmental protection, and the necessary concerted actions to that effect with social and temporal dimensions.[15] It could hardly be doubted, as UNEP itself has acknowledged, that environmental protection is 'decisively linked' to the 'human rights issue',[16] to the very fulfilment of the fundamental right to life in its wide dimension (see below).

Resort to the very notion of mankind or humankind immediately brings to the fore, or places the whole discussion within, the human rights framework – and this should be properly emphasized: it should not be left implicit or neglected as allegedly redundant. Just as law, or the rule of law itself, does not operate in a vacuum, mankind or humankind is neither a social nor a legal abstraction: it is composed of human collectivities, of all human beings of flesh and bone, living in human societies. If it is conceded that rights and obligations are bound to flow from the concept of the common concern of mankind, we will then be led to consider as a manifestation or even a materialization of this latter the right to a healthy environment. Within the ambit of the law of mankind, the common concern of the humankind finds expression in the exercise of the recognized right to a healthy environment, in all its dimensions (individual, group, social or collective and intergenerational: see below), just as mankind is not a social or legal abstraction and is formed by a multitude of human beings living in societies and extended in time. The human rights framework is ineluctably present in the consideration of the system of protection of the human environment in all its aspects; we are here ultimately confronted by the crucial question of survival of the humankind, with the assertion, in the face of threats to the human environment, of the fundamental human right to live.

Just as a couple of decades ago there were questions which were 'withdrawn' from the domestic jurisdiction of states to become matters of international concern (essentially, in cases pertaining to human rights protection and self-determination of peoples),[17] there are nowadays global issues (such as climate change) which are being presented as the common concern of mankind. Here, again, the contribution of human rights protection and environmental protection heralds the end of reciprocity and the emergence of *erga omnes* obligations. The prohibition of the invocation of reciprocity as an excuse for non-compliance of *erga omnes* obligations is confirmed in unequivocal terms by the 1969 Vienna Convention on the Law of Treaties: in providing for the conditions in which a breach of a treaty may bring about its suspension or termination, the Vienna Convention (Article 60(5)) expressly excepts 'provisions relating to the protection of the human person contained in treaties of a humanitarian character'. This provision enters a domain of international law, the law of treaties, traditionally so markedly infiltrated by the voluntarism of states, and constitutes a clause of safeguard or defence of human beings.

The overcoming of reciprocity in human rights protection and in environmental protection (global issues) has taken place in the constant search for an expansion of the ambit of protection (for the safeguard of an increasingly wide circle of beneficiaries, human beings and, ultimately, mankind), for the achievement of a higher degree of the protection due, and for the gradual strengthening of the mechanisms of supervision, in the defence of common superior interests.

Further Affinities in the Evolution of Human Rights Protection and of Environmental Protection

Protection of the Human Person and Environmental Protection: Mutual Concerns

Just as concern for human rights protection can be found in the realm of international environmental law (Preamble and Principle 1 of the 1972 Stockholm Declaration on the Human Environment; Preamble and Principles 6 and 23 of the 1982 World Charter for Nature; Principles 1 and 20 proposed by the World Commission on Environment and Development in its 1987 report), concern for environmental protection can also be found in the express recognition of the right to a healthy environment in two human rights instruments, namely, the 1988 Additional Protocol to the American Convention on Human Rights in the Area of Economic, Social and Cultural Rights (Article 11) and the 1981 African Charter on Human and Peoples' Rights (Article 24); in the former, it is recognized as a right of 'everyone' (paragraph 1), to be protected by the States Parties (paragraph 2), whereas in the latter it is acknowledged as a peoples' right.

Likewise, concern for the protection of the environment can nowadays be found in the realm of international humanitarian law, namely, Articles 35(3) and 55 of the 1977 Additional Protocol I to the 1949 Geneva Conventions (prohibition of methods or means of warfare severely damaging the environment), added to the 1977 UN Convention on the Prohibition of Military or Any Other Hostile Use of Environmental Modification Techniques, and to the 1982 World Charter for Nature (paragraphs 5 and 20), among other provisions. Similarly, recent developments in international refugee law are worthy of attention, such as the possible assimilation of victims of environmental disasters to protected (displaced) persons under refugee law (for example, the 1984 Cartagena Declaration on Refugees, recommending for use in Central America an expanded concept of refugee, followed by the recent 1994 San José Declaration on Refugees and Displaced Persons[18]).

Furthermore, the protection of vulnerable groups[19] (for example, indigenous populations, ethnic and religious and linguistic minorities, mentally and physically handicapped persons) appears today at the confluence of international human rights law and international environmental law; concern for the protection of vulnerable groups can nowadays be found in international instruments and initiatives pertaining both to human rights protection and to environmental protection, where the issue has been approached on the basis of both human and environmental considerations.[20]

Present-day human rights protection and environmental protection thus display mutual concerns. A reflection of this lies, for example, in the outlook of the 1992 Rio Declaration on Environment and Development, adopted by the UN Conference on Environment and Development (UNCED): it places human beings at the centre of concerns for sustainable development, whereas the 1993 Vienna Declaration and Programme of Action, adopted by the second World Conference on Human Rights, for its part, addresses *inter alia* sustainable development in relation to distinct aspects of international human rights law.

Incidence of the Temporal Dimension in Environmental Protection and in Human Rights Protection

In the recent developments of human rights protection and environmental protection, another affinity between them, which has not been sufficiently examined to date, lies in the incidence of the temporal dimension in both domains. The temporal dimension, so noticeable in the field of environmental protection, is likewise present in other domains of international law (for example, law of treaties, peaceful settlement of international disputes, international economic law, law of the sea, law of outer space and state succession). The notion of time and the element of foreseeability inhere in legal science as such. The predominantly preventive character of the normative corpus on environmental protection, stressed time and time again, is also present in the field of human rights protection. Its incidence can be detected at distinct stages or levels, starting with the *travaux préparatoires*, the underlying conceptions and the adopted texts of human rights instruments (for example, the three conventions – the Inter-American, the UN and the European – against torture, of an essentially preventive character; the 1948 Convention against Genocide, the 1973 Convention against Apartheid, besides international instruments addressing the prevention of discrimination of distinct kinds). The temporal dimension is also present in international refugee law (for example, the elements for the very definition of 'refugee' under the 1951 Convention and the 1967 Protocol on the Status of Refugees, namely, the well-founded fear of persecution, the threats or risks of persecutions, besides in practice the UN 'early warning' efforts for prevention or forecasting of refugee flows).

Secondly, the incidence of the temporal dimension can also be detected in the 'evolutionary' interpretation of human rights treaties, which has ensured that they remain living instruments: a dynamic process of evolution of international human rights law through interpretation has been occurring.[21] And thirdly, also in respect of the application of human rights treaties, the practice of international supervisory organs (for example, at global level, that of the Human Rights Committee under the Covenant on Civil and Political Rights and its [first] Optional Protocol) affords illustrations of the temporal dimension in human rights protection. Thus the *jurisprudence constante* of the European Commission and Court of Human Rights under the European Convention on Human Rights has in recent years upheld, in numerous cases, the notion of potential or prospective victims, that is, victims claiming a valid potential personal interest under the Convention, thus enhancing the condition of individual applicants.[22] Likewise, the Inter-American Court of Human Rights, in its judgments of 1988 in two of the three *Honduran* cases where it found a breach of the American Convention (*Velasquez Rodriguez* and *Godinez Cruz* cases), stressed the states' duty of due diligence to prevent violations of protected human rights.[23]

In fact, the incidence of the temporal dimension can be detected not only in the interpretation and application of norms pertaining to guaranteed rights but also in the conditions of their exercise (as in public emergencies); it can further be detected in the protection, not only of civil and political rights, but also – and perhaps here it is more pronounced – of economic, social and cultural rights (for example, right to education, right to cultural integrity), or else of the right to development and the right to a healthy environment, extending in time. Manifestations of the temporal dimension become quite concrete, in particular precisely in the field of human rights protection, where they do not appear as soft law. Here, more clearly than in other chapters or fields of international law, the evolving jurisprudence (for example, on the notion of potential victims or on the duty of prevention of violations of human rights) may serve as inspiration for environmental protection also.

The Right to Life and the Right to Health on the Basis of the *Ratio Legis* of International Human Rights Law and Environmental Law

The Fundamental Right to Life in its Wide Dimension

The right to life is nowadays universally acknowledged as a basic or fundamental human right, the enjoyment of which is a 'necessary condition of the enjoyment of all other human rights'.[24] As indicated by the Inter-American Court of Human Rights in its Advisory Opinion on *Restrictions to the Death Penalty* (1983), the human right to life encompasses a 'substantive principle' whereby every human being has an inalienable right to have his life respected, and a 'procedural principle' whereby no human being shall be arbitrarily deprived of his life.[25] The Human Rights Committee, operating under the UN Covenant on Civil and Political Rights, has stressed that the human right to life in its wide dimension, as the 'supreme right of the human being', requires positive measures on the part of states.[26] The Inter-American Commission on Human Rights has likewise drawn attention to the binding character of the right to life and warned against 'the arbitrary deprivation of life'.[27]

Under international human rights instruments, the assertion of the inherent right to life of every human being is accompanied by an assertion of the legal protection of that basic human right and of the negative obligation not to deprive arbitrarily of life (for example, UN Covenant on Civil and Political Rights, Article 6(1); European

Convention on Human Rights, Article 2; American Convention on Human Rights, Article 4(1); African Charter on Human and Peoples' Rights, Article 4).[28] But this negative obligation is accompanied by the positive obligation to take all appropriate measures to protect and preserve human life. This has been acknowledged by the European Commission of Human Rights, whose case law has evolved to the point of holding (*Association X v. United Kingdom*, 1978) that Article 2 of the European Convention on Human Rights also imposed on states a wider and positive obligation to take adequate measures to protect life.[29]

Taken in its wide and proper dimension, the fundamental right to life comprises the right of every human being not to be deprived of his life (right to life) and the right of every human being to have the appropriate means of subsistence and a decent standard of life (preservation of life, right of living). As has been rightly pointed out, 'the former belongs to the area of civil and political rights, the latter to that of economic, social and cultural rights'.[30] The fundamental right to life, thus properly understood, affords an eloquent illustration of the indivisibility and interrelatedness of all human rights.[31] In fact, some members of the Human Rights Committee have expressed the view that Article 6 of the UN Covenant on Civil and Political Rights requires the state 'to take positive measures to ensure the right to life'.[32]

During the drafting of the 1948 Universal Declaration of Human Rights, attempts were made to make its Article 3, which proclaims the right to life, more precise.[33] A number of issues were the subject of discussion in the drafting of corresponding provisions on the right to life of human rights treaties,[34] but it is the views and decisions more recently rendered by international supervisory organs that have gradually given more precision to the right to life as enshrined in the respective human rights treaties (see above). Even those who insist on regarding the right to life strictly as a civil right[35] cannot fail to admit that, ultimately, without an adequate standard of living (as recognized, for example, in Articles 11–12 of the UN International Covenant on Economic, Social and Cultural Rights, following Article 25(1) of the 1948 Universal Declaration), the right to life could not possibly be realized in its full sense[36] (for example, in its close relationships with the right to health and medical care, the right to food and the right to housing).[37] Thus both the UN General Assembly (resolution 37/189A, of 1982) and the UN Commission on Human Rights (resolutions 1982/7, of 1982, and 1983/43, of 1983) have unequivocally taken the firm view that all individuals and all peoples have an inherent right to life, and that the safeguarding of this foremost right is an essential condition for the enjoyment of the entire range of civil and political rights, as well as economic, social and cultural rights.[38]

Two points are deserving of particular emphasis here. First, it has not passed unnoticed that the provision of the UN Covenant on Civil and Political Rights on the fundamental and inherent right to life (Article 6(1)) is 'the only Article of the Covenant where the inherence of a right is expressly referred to'.[39] Secondly, the United Nations has formed its conviction that not only all individuals but also all peoples have an inherent right to life (see above). This brings to the fore the safeguard of the right to life of all persons as well as human collectivities, with special attention to the requirements of survival (as a component of the right to life) of vulnerable groups (for example, the dispossessed and deprived, disabled or handicapped persons, children and the elderly, ethnic minorities, indigenous populations and migrant workers – see above).[40]

From this perspective, the right to a healthy environment and the right to peace appear as extensions or corollaries of the right to life. The fundamental character of the right to life renders narrow approaches to it inadequate nowadays; under the right to life, in its modern and proper sense, not only is protection against any arbitrary deprivation of life upheld, but states are under the duty 'to pursue policies which are designed to ensure access to the means of survival'[41] for all individuals and all peoples. To this effect, states are under the obligation to avoid serious environmental hazards or risks to life, and to set in motion 'monitoring and early warning systems' to detect such serious environmental hazards or risks and 'urgent action systems' to deal with such threats.[42]

In the same line, in the first European Conference on the Environment and Human Rights (Strasbourg, 1979), the point was made that mankind needed to protect itself against its own threats to the environment, in particular when those threats had negative repercussions on the conditions of existence: life itself, physical and mental health, and the well-being of present and future generations.[43] In a way, it was further pointed out, it was the right to life itself, in its wide dimension, which entailed the necessary recognition of the right to a healthy environment; this latter appears as the right to living conditions assuring physical and mental health – life itself – and the social well-being of present and future generations.[44] The right to a healthy environment, moreover, discloses a wide temporal dimension: as, in environmental matters, certain threats to the environment produce effects on human life and health only in the long run, the recognition of the right to a healthy environment should admit a 'wide notion of threats'.[45] The necessary wider characterization of attempts or threats against the rights to life, to health and to a healthy environment, in turn, calls for a higher degree of their protection.[46] The use of the expression 'the right *to* live' (rather than 'right *to* life'), as found in the 1989 Hague Declaration on the Atmosphere (paragraphs 1 and 5), seems well in line with the understanding that the right to life entails negative as well as positive obligations as to preservation of human life (see above). The Institut de Droit International, while drafting its Resolution on Transboundary Air Pollution (session of Cairo, 1987), was careful to include therein provisions referring to the protection of life and human health.[47]

In fact, both the Inter-American Commission on Human Rights[48] and the UN General Assembly[49] have been attentive to the need to address the requirements of survival as a component of the right to life. In this connection, in its general comment 14(23), of 1985, the Human Rights Committee, after recalling its earlier general comment 6(16), of 1982, both on the right to life under Article 6 of the Covenant on Civil and Political Rights, related the current proliferation of weapons of mass destruction to 'the supreme duty of States to prevent wars'. The Committee characterized that danger as one of the 'greatest threats to the right to life which confronts mankind today', which created 'a climate of suspicion and fear between States, which is in itself antagonistic to the promotion of universal respect for and observance of human rights' in accordance with the UN Charter and the UN International Covenants on Human Rights.[50] The Committee, accordingly, 'in the interest of mankind', called upon all states, whether parties to the Covenant or not, 'to take urgent steps, unilaterally and by agreement, to rid the world of this menace'.[51]

In sum, the basic right to life, encompassing the right of living, entails negative as well as positive obligations in favour of the preservation of human life. Its enjoyment is a precondition of the enjoyment of other human rights. It belongs at once to the realm of civil and political rights and to that of economic, social and cultural rights, thus illustrating the indivisibility of all human rights. It establishes a 'link' between the domains of international human rights law and environmental law. It inheres in all individuals and all peoples, with special application to the requirements of survival. It has as extensions or corollaries the right to a healthy environment and the right to peace (and disarmament). It is closely related, in its wide dimension, to the right to development as a human right (the right to live with fulfilment of basic human needs). And it lies at the root of the ultimate *ratio legis* of the domains of international human rights law and environmental law, addressing the protection and survival of the human person and mankind.

The Right to Health as the First Step towards the Right to a Healthy Environment

Like the right to life (right of living, above), the right to health entails negative as well as positive obligations. In fact, the right to health is inextricably interwoven with the right to life itself and the exercise of freedom. The right to health implies the *negative* obligation not to practise any act which can endanger one's health, thus linking this basic right to the right to physical and mental integrity and to the prohibition of torture and of cruel, inhuman or degrading treatment (as recognized and provided for in the UN Covenant on Civil and Political Rights, Article 7; the European Convention on Human Rights, Article 3; the American Convention on Human Rights, Articles 4 and 5). But this duty of abstention (so crucial, for example, in the treatment of detainees and prisoners) is accompanied by the positive obligation to take all appropriate measures to protect and preserve human health (including measures of prevention of diseases).

Such a positive obligation (as recognized and provided for in, for example, the UN Covenant on Economic, Social and Cultural Rights, Article 12, and the European Social Charter, Article 11, besides WHO and ILO resolutions on specific aspects), linking the right to life to the right to an adequate standard of life,[52] discloses the fact that the right to health, in its proper and wide dimension, partakes of the nature of, at one and the same time, an individual and a social right. Belonging, like the right to life, to the realm of basic or fundamental rights, the right to health is an individual right, in that it requires the protection of the physical and mental integrity of the individual and his dignity; and it is also a social right, in that it imposes on the state and society the collective responsibility for the protection of the health of the citizenry and the prevention and treatment of diseases.[53] The right to health, thus properly understood, affords, like the right to life, a vivid illustration of the indivisibility and interrelatedness of all human rights.

The right to health in its 'positive' aspect (see above) found expression, at the global level, in Article 12 of the UN Covenant on Economic, Social and Cultural Rights; that provision, in laying down the guidelines for the implementation of the right to health, singled out, *inter alia*, Article 12.2(b), 'the improvement of all aspects of environmental and industrial hygiene'. The way thereby seemed paved for the future recognition of the right to a healthy environment (see below). This point was the subject of attention at the 1978 Colloquy of the Hague Academy of International Law on 'The Right to Health as a Human Right', where the issue of the human right to environmental salubrity was raised. On that occasion, the warning was voiced that the degradation of the environment now constitutes a collective threat to human health; the necessary assertion or proclamation of the human right to environmental salubrity as the 'supreme guarantee' of the right to health was further advocated also in the interests of the collectivity, bearing in mind its importance to the fundamental right to life itself.[54]

The protection of the whole of the biosphere as such entails 'indirectly but necessarily' the protection of human beings, insofar as the object of environmental law and hence of the right to a healthy environment is to protect them by securing to them an adequate *modus vivendi*.[55] The right to a healthy environment 'completes' other recognized human rights also from another point of view: it contributes to the establishment of more egalitarian conditions of living and to the implementation of other human rights.[56]

The interrelatedness between environmental protection and the safeguarding of the right to health is clearly evidenced in the implementation of Article 11 (on the right to protection of health) of the 1961 European Social Charter. The Committee of Independent Experts, operating under the Charter, has been attentive, in the consideration of national reports, to measures taken at the domestic level, pursuant to Article 11 of the Charter, to prevent, reduce or control pollution,[57] so as to remove causes of ill-health (Article 11(1)).[58] The collection, *Case Law on the European Social Charter*, contains other pertinent indications.[59] The Committee of Independent Experts has, for example, expressed the opinion that states bound by Article 11 of the Charter should be considered as fulfilling their obligations in that respect if they provide evidence of the existence of a medical and health system comprising, *inter alia*, 'general measures aimed in particular at the prevention of air and water pollution, protection from radioactive substances, noise abatement, the food control, environmental hygiene, and the control of alcoholism and drugs'.[60]

An attempt has in fact been made, on the European continent, to extend the protection of the rights to life and health so as to include well-being, under the aegis of the European Convention on Human Rights itself: prior to the convening of the 1973 European Ministerial Conference on Environment, a Draft Protocol to the European Convention on Human Rights to that effect was prepared by H. Steiger. The Draft Protocol, containing two Articles, provided for the protection of life and health as encompassing well-being (Article 1(1)) and admitted limitations on the right to a healthy environment (Article 1(2)); it further provided for the protection of individuals against the acts of other private persons (Article 2(1) and (2)). This point (*Drittwirkung*), though giving rise to much debate and controversy, has been touched upon by the European Commission of Human Rights, which, in its 1979 report on the *Young, James* and *Webster* cases, admitted that the European Convention contained provisions that not only protect the individual against the state, but also oblige the state to protect the individual against acts by others.[61] Although Steiger's proposed Draft Protocol, purporting to place under the machinery of implementation of the European Convention the provisions referred to above (Articles 1 and 2), was not at the time accepted by Member States, it remains the sole existing proposal on the matter (insofar as the European Convention system is concerned) and its underlying ideas deserve today further and closer consideration[62] (see below). Although the question remains an open one, there has been express recognition of the right to a healthy environment in more recent human rights instruments, as we have already seen.

The Question of the Implementation of the Right to a Healthy Environment

The Issue of Justiciability

It can hardly be doubted that the appropriate formulation of a right may facilitate its implementation. But, given that certain concepts escape any scientific definition, it becomes necessary to relate them to a given context for the sake of normative precision and effective implementation (*mise en œuvre*); thus, for example, the term 'environment' may be taken to cover anything from the immediate physical *milieu* surrounding the individual concerned to the whole of the biosphere, and it may thus be necessary to add qualifications to the term.[63] In the implementation of any right, one can hardly make abstraction of the context in which it is invoked and applied: relating it to the context becomes necessary for its vindication in the *cas d'espèce*.[64]

This applies to all rights, including the right to a healthy environment, which admittedly presents a greater challenge when one comes to implementation. International human rights law counts largely on means of implementation other than the purely judicial one;[65] besides recourse to such judicial organs as the European and the Inter-American Courts of Human Rights, there occurs most often resort to various other means – non-judicial – of implementation of guaranteed human rights (for example, friendly settlement, conciliation or fact finding).[66]

Formal justiciability or enforceability is by no means a definitive criterion for ascertaining the existence of a right under international human rights law. The fact that many recognized human rights have not yet achieved a level of elaboration such as to render them justiciable does not mean that those rights simply do not exist: enforceability is not to be confounded with the existence itself of a right.[67] Attention must be focused on the nature of obligations; it is certain that, for example, some of the obligations under the UN Covenant on Economic, Social and Cultural Rights [for example, the basic provisions of Articles 2 and 11] were elaborated in such a way that they 'cannot easily be made justiciable (manageable by third-party judicial settlement). Nevertheless, the obligations exist and can in no way be neglected'.[68]

To summarize, as far as the issue of justiciability is concerned, we must assume that there are rights which simply cannot be properly vindicated before a tribunal by their active subjects (*titulaires*). In the specific case of the right to a healthy environment, however, if this latter is interpreted, not as the (virtually impracticable) right to an ideal environment, but rather as the right to the conservation – that is, protection and improvement – of the environment, it can then be implemented, as is pertinently pointed out by Kiss, like any other individual right. It is then taken as a 'procedural' right, the right to a due process before a competent organ, and thus assimilated to any other right guaranteed to individuals and groups of individuals. This right entails, as corollaries, the right of the individual concerned to be informed of projects and decisions which could threaten the environment (the protection of which counting on preventive measures) and the right of the individual concerned to participate in the taking of decisions which may affect the environment (active sharing of responsibilities in the management of the interests of the whole collectivity).[69] To such rights to information and to participation one can add the right to available and effective domestic remedies. And it should not be overlooked in this connection that some economic and social rights were made enforceable in domestic law once their component parts were 'formulated in a sufficiently precise and detailed manner'.[70]

Focusing on the *subjects* of the right to a healthy environment, we see first that it has an individual dimension, as it can be implemented, as just indicated, like other human rights. But the beneficiaries of the right to a healthy environment are not only individuals, but also groups, associations, human collectivities and, indeed, the whole of mankind. Hence it has a collective dimension as well. The right to a healthy environment, like the right to development,[71] discloses an individual and a collective dimension at the same time. If the subject is an individual or a private group, the legal relationship is exhausted in the relation between the individual (or group of individuals) and the state; but if we have in mind mankind as a whole, the legal relationship is not exhausted in that relation. This is probably why the distinction between individual and collective dimensions is often resorted to.

If we focus on implementation, it is conceded that all rights, whether 'individual' or 'collective', are exercised in a societal context, all having a 'social' dimension in that sense, since their vindication requires the intervention, in varying degrees, of public authority for them to be exercised. There is, however, yet another approach which can shed some light on the problem at issue: to focus on the object of protection. Taking as such an object a common good like the human environment, not only are we thereby provided with objective criteria to approach the subject, but also we can better grasp the proper meaning of 'collective' rights.

Such rights pertain simultaneously to each member as well as to all members of a given human collectivity, the object of protection being the same, a common good (*bien commun*) such as the human environment, so that the observance of those rights benefits at the same time each member and all members of the human collectivity, and the violation of those rights affects or harms at the same time each member and all members of the human collectivity at issue. This reflects the essence of 'collective' rights, such as the right to a healthy environment insofar as the object of protection is concerned. The multifaceted nature of the right to a healthy environment thus becomes clearer: the right to a healthy environment has an individual and a collective dimension, being at the same time an 'individual' and a 'collective' right, insofar as its subjects or beneficiaries are concerned. Its 'social' dimension becomes manifest insofar as its implementation is concerned (given the complexity of the legal relations involved). And it clearly appears in its 'collective' dimension insofar as the object of protection is concerned (a *bien commun*, the human environment).

This matter has not been sufficiently studied to date, and considerable in-depth reflection and research are required to clarify the issues surrounding the implementation of the right to a healthy environment and the very conceptual universe in which it rests. Insofar as the subjects of the relationships involved are concerned, one has moved from the individuals and groups to the whole of mankind, and in this wide range of *titulaires* one has also spoken of generational rights (rights of future generations[72] – see above). Insofar as the methods of protection are concerned, it still has to be carefully explored to what extent the mechanisms of protection evolved under international human rights law (essentially, the petitioning, the reporting and the fact-finding systems)[73] can be utilized also in the realm of environmental protection.

It seems that the experience accumulated in this respect over the last decades in human rights protection can, if properly assessed, be of assistance to the development of methods of environmental protection. Some inspiration can indeed be derived from the experience of application of mechanisms of international implementation of human rights for the improvement of international implementation of instruments on environmental protection.[74] It has been suggested, for example, that UN international environmental organs could be given 'powers similar to those' of the UN Committee on Economic, Social and Cultural Rights to study and comment on reports submitted by states, given the affinities between the right to a healthy environment and economic and social rights.[75] Such acknowledgments are quite understood and beneficial to environmental protection, given the fact that human rights protection antedates it in time and the experience with the implementation of the latter can be of use and value to the implementation of the former.

In the fields of human rights protection and environmental protection there occur variations in the obligations (some norms being susceptible of direct applicability, others appearing rather programmatic in nature); attention ought thus to be turned to the *nature* of the obligations. An important issue, in this connection, is that of the *erga omnes* protection of certain guaranteed rights, which raises the issue of third-party applicability of conventional provisions. This issue, called *Drittwirkung* in German legal literature, has incidence in the domains of both human rights protection and environmental protection.[76] The right to a healthy environment, it may be argued, is opposable to third parties (including private individuals),[77] *Drittwirkung* amounts to the situation whereby everyone is a beneficiary of that right and everyone has duties vis-à-vis the whole community.[78]

The right of everyone to a healthy environment, entailing duties incumbent upon everyone, has been the object of special attention lately. In 1989, the UN Sub-Commission on Prevention of Discrimination and Protection of Minorities adopted a decision (n.1989/108) to undertake a study of environmental issues in their relation to human rights. Already in the preliminary report of 1991, its designated special rapporteur (F.Z. Ksentini) regarded the right to the environment as a 'right of solidarity', besides being a 'right of "prevention" of ecological risks' and a 'right to the "conservation" of nature'.[79] On 16 May 1994, a group of experts on the matter convened at the United Nations Office in Geneva,[80] at the invitation of the Sierra Club Legal Defense Fund, on behalf of the Sub-Commission's special rapporteur, and drafted the first-ever Declaration of Principles on Human Rights and the Environment. The Draft Declaration, composed of a preamble and five parts (with a total of 27 paragraphs), comprehensively addresses the links between human rights and the environment, and demonstrates that human rights and environmental principles embody the right of everyone to a secure, healthy and ecologically sound environment.

Part I of the Draft Declaration acknowledges the interdependence and indivisibility of human rights, an ecologically sound environment, sustainable development and peace (paragraph 1). It adds that the right to a secure, healthy and ecologically sound environment, and other human rights, including civil, cultural, economic, political and social rights, are universal, interdependent and indivisible (paragraph 2, and preamble). Part II is attentive to the fact, acknowledged also in the preamble, that human rights violations lead to environmental degradation and environmental degradation leads to human rights violations. Part III spells out the rights to information, to education, to express opinions, to participation, to free and peaceful association and to effective remedies and redress, in the present context. Part IV covers the duty of everyone to protect and preserve the environment, and the duty of all states to respect and ensure the right to a secure, healthy and ecologically sound environment and, accordingly, the duty to adopt the administrative, legislative and other measures necessary to implement effectively the rights provided for in this Draft Declaration (paragraph 22). Part V devotes special attention to vulnerable persons and groups (paragraph 25).[81]

The Absence of Restrictions in the Expansion of Human Rights Protection and Environmental Protection (and their Effects upon Each Other)

The gradual recognition of 'new' human rights, such as the right to a healthy environment, cannot possibly have the effect of lowering the degree of protection accorded to existing rights. The emergence of 'new' human rights cannot possibly undermine the protection extended to pre-existing rights. That would simply go against the course of historical evolution of the process of expansion of international human rights law, which has consistently pointed towards the enlargement, improvement and strengthening of the degree and extent of protection of recognized rights. In sum, the only permissible limits to the exercise of recognized rights are those expressly provided for under human rights treaties themselves (in whichever form, namely, as limitations or restrictions, or as exceptions, or as derogations, or as reservations); such limits are to be restrictively interpreted, always bearing in mind the accomplishment of the object and purpose of those treaties.

The emergence of 'new' rights is followed by their 'adaptation' to the corpus of existing rights and their means of implementation; what may at first sight appear as restrictions on pre-existing rights are in reality no more than necessary adjustments entailed by the 'new' rights.[82] Given the continuing expansion of international human rights law and the multiplicity of coexisting rights, it may well happen that, in given circumstances, 'priorities may have to be set and limited resources devoted to fulfilling one right which is at more risk or more significant in the circumstances than another'.[83] And this does not mean that the other rights are restricted, contradicted or ignored; there is a balance between the various recognized rights, set by the human rights treaties and instruments themselves.[84]

A key role is reserved here for the international supervisory organs themselves. This issue of the balancing rights may arise with regard, not only to such 'new' rights as the right to a healthy environment, but also to any other right (reconciling the right to freedom of expression and the right to privacy, the freedoms of association and of movement, the right to property and certain social rights, to give but a few examples).[85] Furthermore, the recognition of such 'new' rights as the right to a healthy environment can only have the effect, not of restricting, but rather of complementing, enriching and enhancing pre-existing rights (the right to work, the freedom of movement, the right to education, the right to participation and the right to information, among others).[86] Last but not least, it should not pass unnoticed that rights which are at the basis of the *ratio legis* of both environmental protection and human rights protection – such as the right to life – are asserted by human rights treaties[87] as non-derogable: they admit no restrictions whatsoever, they are truly fundamental rights. As for the other recognized rights, in the 'balancing' between them dictated by circumstances, 'new' rights such as the right to a healthy environment have emerged ultimately to enhance rather than to restrict them, in the same way as they enhance the fundamental non-derogable rights.

The Protection of the Right to a Healthy Environment in its Jurisprudential Beginnings

The protection of the right to a healthy environment is of course not confined to its formulation in such international human rights instruments as the 1981 African Charter on Human and Peoples' Rights (Article 24) and the 1988 Additional Protocol to the American Convention on Human Rights in the Area of Economic, Social and Cultural Rights (Article 11). International supervisory organs operating under other human rights treaties, at both global and regional levels, have displayed sensitiveness to the issue, and have given in recent years indications of what may amount to jurisprudential beginnings of the protection of the right to a healthy environment.

Thus, at the global level, for example, the case linking human rights protection and environmental protection was decided by the Human Rights Committee (under the UN Covenant on Civil and Political Rights). The applicant argued, also on behalf of 129 residents of the Canadian town of Port Hope (Ontario), that the dumping of nuclear wastes nearby generated widespread pollution with threats (excessive radioactivity) to their health and to the life of 'present and future generations of Port Hope'. In its decision of 27 October 1982, the Human Rights Committee found that the complainant could submit the communication also on behalf of the other residents of Port Hope who authorized her to do so; the reference to 'future generations', the Committee added, was an expression of concern putting the matter at issue in the right perspective.[88] Although the Committee ended up dismissing the application for non-exhaustion of local remedies, its acceptance of the *jus standi* of the complainant (acting also on behalf of the 129 residents of Port Hope concerned) and its recognition of the importance of the issue also for 'future generations' were significant, bearing witness to the interrelationship of human rights protection and environmental protection, especially when fundamental rights, such as the rights to life and to health, are at stake.[89]

At the regional level, there have been decisions of the European Commission and Court of Human Rights dealing with environmental issues (in particular, noise pollution near airports) under Article 8 of the European Convention on Human Rights (right to privacy) and Article 1 of Protocol I to the Convention (right to peaceful enjoyment of one's possessions) (for example, *Arrondelle* v. *United Kingdom*, 1980; *Zimmermann* v. *Switzerland*, 1983; *Baggs* v. *United Kingdom*, 1985; *Powell and Rayner* v. *United Kingdom*, 1990; *X* v. *France*, the so-called '*Nuclear Power Plant*' case, 1990). It has been argued that Article 8 of the Convention can also cover potential environmental effects, if the consequences for the environment are grave and irreparable, affecting the privacy of individuals and their quality of life, and constituting a threat of loss of life.[90] In fact, in the *G. and E. (Lapps)* v. *Norway* case (1983), the applicants invoked the right to respect for their particular life style (Lapp minority) under Article 8 of the Convention, in connection with the consequences (partial flooding) of the building of a hydroelectric plant in the valley where they were born. Although the Commission found the application inadmissible in the circumstances of the case, it nevertheless admitted that such a threat to the environment could constitute an interference in the privacy of the members of a minority, who could thus invoke the right to respect for their private life.[91]

The European Court of Human Rights, for its part, in *Fredin* v. *Sweden* (1991), balanced the individual interest (of peaceful enjoyment of possessions, under Article 1 of Protocol I to the Convention) with the general interest or 'legitimate purpose' of environmental protection.[92] Likewise, six years earlier, in *Herrick* v. *United Kingdom*, the European Commission had also balanced the individual interest of the owner of a house with the general interest of protecting the values of leisure in rural areas (thus safeguarding the rights of others), achieving a balance in favour of the environment.[93] More recently, in *López Ostra* v. *Spain* (1994), the European Court held that there had been a breach of Article 8 of the European Convention on account of nuisance and pollution caused by a plant nearby, for over three years, which led the applicant to move house. The court considered that the respondent state did not succeed in striking a 'fair balance' between the interest of the town's economic well-being (that of having a waste-treatment plant) and the applicant's 'effective enjoyment of her right to respect for her home and her private and family life'.[94]

In the inter-American human rights system, the taking of measures of preservation of health and well-being figured among the recommendations of the Inter-American Commission on Human Rights in the cases of the *Aché-Guayakí Indians in Paraguay* (1977) and of the *Yanomami Indians in Brazil* (1985),[95] paving the way for further elaboration in the near future on the interrelationship between human rights protection and environmental protection. In sum, the pioneering decisions referred to above, at both global and regional levels, indicate that, apart from the recognition of that interrelationship between the two domains of protection (of human rights and the environment), the protection of the right to a healthy environment, via pre-existing rights, counts nowadays on doctrinal as well as jurisprudential grounds.

The Paramount Importance of the Right of Democratic Participation

The normative advances in human rights protection and environmental protection disclose the paramount importance of the exercise of the right of participation, both at domestic and international levels, including participation in the process of creation of the norms of protection. Public participation in this context is no longer a mere theoretical possibility: it has become a reality, even at the international level, as demonstrated by public participation, particularly of non-governmental organizations, in the preparatory work of the Convention on the Rights of the Child (1989), in the field of human rights protection, and of the Protocol (of 1991) on Environmental Protection to the Antarctica Treaty, in the realm of environmental protection.

Public participation in the environmental decision-making process finds expression, for example, in the World Charter for Nature of 1982 (paragraph 23). UNEP's Review of the Montevideo Programme for the Development and Periodic Review of Environmental Law (1981–91) reserves a special place for the role of public participation in this domain. The 1992 Rio Declaration on Environment and Development, adopted by UNCED, devotes particular attention to the right of participation (in environmental management and in the promotion of sustainable development – Principles 20–22), the exercise of which is the subject of detailed treatment by *Agenda 21* (Chapters 23–7, 29–32 and 38), also adopted by UNCED. *Agenda 21* is attentive to the promotion of education and public awareness (Chapter 36) as one of the means of its implementation. In turning to the pressing problems of today and the challenges of the forthcoming century, *Agenda 21* supports the 'broadest public participation' (Chapter 1).

Likewise, in human rights protection, the role of public participation is recognized as of capital importance, for example, in the implementation of the right to development as a human right, as indicated in the preparatory studies of the 1986 UN Declaration on the Right to Development.[96] The assertion of the right to development by the 1992 Rio Declaration (of UNCED), and the 1993 Vienna Declaration and Programme of Action, followed by the UN General Assembly decision 48/141 of December 1993 (on the creation of the post of UN High Commissioner for Human Rights), has contributed decisively to its crystallization and insertion into the realm of positive international human rights law. The 1993 Vienna Declaration and Programme of Action, adopted by the Second World Conference on Human Rights, addresses the issue of the strengthening of democratic institutions, in particular those concerned with the independent administration of justice (part I, paragraph 27); the concern with securing free and full democratic participation for everyone permeates several passages of the Vienna Declaration and Programme of Action.

Agenda 21, as well as the Vienna Declaration and Programme of Action, contains passages ranging from meeting basic human needs to fostering people's empowerment in all domains of human activity (see above). The exercise of such 'new' rights as the right to a healthy environment and the right to development, as well as other rights, presupposes a free and responsible society where information is accessible to everyone, so as to enable effective democratic participation, counting also on the right to effective remedies. Participating democracy is a significant element of approximation between human rights protection and environmental protection, engaging the responsibility of everybody (states as well as individuals and their associations) in the sense of the 1982 World Charter for Nature and the 1986 UN Declaration on the Right to Development.[97]

Democratic practices are not, however, to be confined within national borders: they are to be followed also at international level. The interrelationship between human rights, democracy and development (making human beings the central subject of the latter) was the focus of attention in the 1993 World Conference on Human Rights. Recent developments on the European and American continents reveal that the preservation and strengthening of democracy nowadays constitute a subject of legitimate international concern.[98] Democratic practices are to prevail also at international level, reaching international financial agencies as well, in assuming responsibility to prevent economic recession and unemployment and their negative impact upon human rights and consequent implications for the environment as a whole. This aspect did not pass unnoticed in the debates of the 1990 UN Global Consultation on the Right to Development as a Human Right. Three years later, the Vienna Declaration called upon the international community 'to make all efforts to help alleviate the external debt burden of developing countries' (paragraph 12). And, more recently, the 1995 World Summit for Social Development addressed the core issues of eradication of poverty (and expansion of productive employment) as well as enhancement of social integration (in particular of the more disadvantaged groups).

The strengthening of the systems of human rights protection and environmental protection is to be accompanied by non-formal and non-institutionalized promotion and protection of human rights and the environment in civil society; to public participation and the democratic processes is reserved an important function in the strengthening of civil society itself.[99] The ultimate aim is the creation of a culture of observance of human rights as well as conservation of the environment.

Conclusions

The expansion of the international normative corpus of human rights and the environment has been motivated by the needs of protection, in the face of new threats and situations of non-observance or violation of human rights, and of deterioration of the environment, to require responses or reparation and regulation. To the contemporary global approach to human rights and the environment corresponds a global or integral protection. The rights to information and of democratic participation are of key importance here, as is the underlying idea of *solidarity*: it is certainly on the basis of solidarity, rather than sovereignty, that states, individually so vulnerable, are bound to contain nuclear armament, to combat the hunger and poverty of most of their populations, to resist epidemics, to recover from natural disasters and to benefit from the transfer of technology and international communications.

Environmental protection and human rights protection are today, and will certainly remain in the forthcoming years, in the forefront of contemporary international law. These two domains of protection, in making abstraction of the classical jurisdictional and spatial (territorial) solutions of public international law, urge us to rethink the very foundations and principles of the latter, thus contributing to its revitalization. Only thus will it be possible to promote its adaptation to new realities and to secure its capacity to face new problems. The protection of the human person and of the environment requires an enrichment of the conceptual legal universe, starting with an in-depth analysis and development of such notions as those of the common concern of mankind, of *jus cogens* and *erga omnes* obligations, of fulfilment of basic human needs, of common but differentiated responsibilities, of sustainable human development, of intergenerational equity and rights of future generations, of entitlements (in the contexts of the right to development as a human right, and of the rights of peoples) and of equitable global partnership.

Even the process of formation and evolution of the normative corpus of the domains of protection of human rights and the environment, marked by a new global awareness, benefits today from the contribution of a multiplicity of new actors (groups, associations, non-governmental organizations, opinion makers, scientists) in interaction at the international level. That contribution renders the law-making process, besides partly non-institutionalized, at the same time more dynamic and complex. The degree of intensified participation of that multiplicity of new actors at international level is bound to mark the establishment of new conceptual–normative foundations of regimes of protection of fundamental and universal values in modern international law.

It can hardly be doubted that, at least, the links between human rights protection and environmental protection are clearly established nowadays. They represent two major challenges of our time and constitute a legitimate common concern of the whole of mankind. Pursuant to the decisions taken at the 1992 UN Conference on Environment and Development (UNCED, Rio de Janeiro) and the 1993 World Conference on Human Rights (Vienna), it is to be expected that a system of continuous monitoring (comprising also preventive measures) of respect for human rights and the environment at both national and international levels will become consolidated in the period leading up to the beginning of the new century. The unequivocal recognition by UNCED and the Vienna Conference of the legitimacy of the concern of the whole international community with, respectively, environmental protection and human rights protection, by everyone and everywhere, constitutes one of the main legacies of those two world conferences, which will certainly accelerate the construction of a universal culture of observance of human rights and the environment.

Notes

1   Reference can further be made to domestic legislation on the matter in virtually all states: it is estimated that domestic legislative instruments today reach a total of 30 000. See A.C. Kiss, *Droit international de l'environnement*, Paris, Pédone, 1989, p.46.

2   See A.A. Cançado Trindade, 'Co-existence and Co-ordination of Mechanisms of International Protection of Human Rights (at Global and Regional Levels)', *Recueil des cours de l'Académie de droit international de La Haye*, **202**, 1987, 21–435.

3   Th. Van Boven, 'United Nations Policies and Strategies: Global Perspective?', in *Human Rights: Thirty Years after the Universal Declaration* B.G. Ramcharan (ed.), The Hague, Nijhoff, 1979, pp.88–9 and 89–91.

4   For an account, see A.A. Cançado Trindade, 'Memória da Conferência Mundial de Direitos Humanos (Viena, 1993)', 87/90 *Boletim da Sociedade Brasileira de Direito Internacional*, 1993, 9–57.

5   Kiss (op. cit., note 1), pp.46,. 93, 106, 204, 275–6.

6   R.W. Hahn and K.R. Richards, 'The Internationalization of Environmental Regulation', *Harvard International Law Journal*, **30**, 1989, 421, 423, 444–5.

7   Kiss (op. cit., note 1), p.212.

8   V.P. Nanda, 'Global Warming and International Environmental Law – A Preliminary Inquiry', *Harvard International Law Journal*, **30**, 1989, 380–85.

9   Kiss (op. cit., note 1), pp.67–8, 70–72, 93; L.A. Teclaff, 'The impact of environmental concern on the development of international law', in, L.A. Teclaff and A.E. Utton (eds), *International Environmental Law*, New York, Praeger, 1974, p.251; Ian Brownlie, 'A Survey of International Customary Rules Environmental Protection', in *International Environmental Law*, p.5.

10 World Commission on Environment and Development, *Our Common Future*, Oxford, Oxford University Press, 1987, ch. 10, pp.261–89.

11 P.M. Dupuy, 'Bilan de recherches de la section de langue française du Centre d'Etude et de Recherche de l'Académie', *La pollution transfrontière et le droit international* – 1985, La Haye, Sijhoff/Académie de Droit International, 1986.

12 See, for example, C.W. Jenks, *The Common Law of Mankind*, London, Stevens, 1958; R.J. Dupuy, *La communauté internationale entre le mythe et l'histoire*, Paris, Economica/UNESCO, 1986, pp.11–182.

13 N.J. Schrijver, 'Permanent sovereignty over natural resources versus the common heritage of mankind: complementary or contradictory principles of international economic law?', in P. De Waart, P. Peters and E. Denters (eds), *International Law and Development*, Dordrecht, Nijhoff/Kluwer, 1988, pp.95–6, 98, 101.

14 UNEP, *The Meeting of the Group of Legal Experts to Examine the Concept of the Common Concern of Mankind in Relation to Global Environmental Issues* (Malta, UNEP, 1990); D.J. Attard (ed.), *Report on the Proceedings of the Meeting* (co-rapporteurs, A.A. Cançado Trindade and D.J. Attard), Malta/Nairobi, UNEP, 1991, pp.24–5.

15 On this last point, see UNEP/Executive Director and Secretariat, 'Note to the Group of Legal Experts to Examine the Implications of the "Common Concern of Mankind" Concept on Global Environmental Issues', Malta Meeting, 13–15 December 1990, document UNEP/ELIU/WG.1/1/2, pp.1–2, para. 4, pp.4–5, paras 8–9 (mimeographed, internal circulation).

16 Ibid., p.14, para. 22.

17 A.A. Cançado Trindade, 'The domestic jurisdiction of states in the practice of the United Nations and regional organizations', *International and Comparative Law Quarterly*, **25**, 1976, 723, 731, 737, 742, 761–2, 765. On the rationale of the rule of exhaustion of local remedies in the international protection of human rights, see A.A. Cançado Trindade, *The Application of the Rule of Exhaustion of Local Remedies in International Law*, Cambridge, Cambridge University Press, 1983.

18 See *Diez Años de la Declaración de Cartagena sobre Refugiados – Memoria del Coloquio Internacional*, San José, ACNUR/IIDH/Gob. Costa Rica, 1995.

19 The necessity of group protection is becoming clearer in the cultural and lin-

guistic fields; see J.J. Lador-Lederer, *International Group Protection*, Leyden, Sijthoff, 1968, pp.19, 25; see also pp.13, 15–17, 23–4, 30.

20 See A.A. Cançado Trindade, *Direitos Humanos e Meio Ambiente – Paralelo dos Sistemas de Proteção Internacional*, Porto Alegre, S.A. Fabris Ed., 1993, pp.89–112; E. Ward, *Indigenous Peoples between Human Rights and Environmental Protection* (based on an Empirical Study of Greenland), Copenhagen, Danish Centre for Human Rights, 1994, pp.9–148.

21 Cançado Trindade, 'Co-existence and Co-ordination' (op. cit., note 2), 91–112.

22 Ibid., 243–99.

23 A.A. Cançado Trindade, 'The contribution of international human rights law to environmental protection, with special reference to global environmental change', in E. Brown Weiss (ed.), *Environmental Change and International Law* Tokyo, United Nations University Press, 1993, pp.244–312.

24 F. Przetacznik, 'The Right to Life as a Basic Human Right', *Revue des droits de l'homme/Human Rights Journal*, 9, 1976, 589, 603.

25 I.A. Court HR, Advisory Opinion OC-3/83, of 8 September 1983, Series A, Note 3, pp.53 and 59.

26 J.G.C. Van Aggelen, *Le rôle des organisations internationales dans la protection du droit à la vie*, Brussels, Story-Scientia, 1986, pp.23, 38.

27 See resolution 3/87, on case no. 9647 (concerning the United States), in OAS, *Annual Report of the Inter-American Commission on Human Rights – 1986–1987*, pp.170, 172–3.

28 Th. Desch, 'The Concept and Dimensions of the Right to Life (As Defined in International Standards and in International and Comparative Jurisprudence)', *Österreichische Zeitschrift für Öffentliches Recht und Völkerrecht*, 36, 1985, 86, 99.

29 See Van Aggelen (op. cit., note 26), p.32.

30 Przetacznik (op. cit., note 24), 603; see also 586.

31 On the right to life bearing witness to the indivisibility of all human rights, see W.P. Gormley, 'The Right to a Safe and Decent Environment', *Indian Journal of International Law*, 20, 1988, 23–4.

32 Desch (op. cit., note 28), 101.

33 See H. Kanger, *Human Rights in the UN Declaration*, Uppsala/Stockholm, Almqvist and Wiksell, 1984, pp.81–2.

34 On the legislative history of Article 6 of the UN Covenant on Civil and Political Rights, see B.G. Ramcharan, 'The Drafting History of Article 6 of the International Covenant on Civil and Political Rights', in B.G. Ramcharan (ed.), *The Right to Life in International Law*, Dordrecht, Nijhoff/Kluwer, 1985, pp.42–56; on the legislative history of Article 2 of the European Convention on Human Rights, see B.G. Ramcharan, 'The Drafting History of Article 2 of the European Convention on Human Rights', in ibid., pp.57–61; and on the legislative history of Article 4 (and antecedents) of the American Convention on Human Rights, see J. Colon-Collazo, 'A Legislative History of the Right to Life in the Inter-American Legal System', in ibid., pp.33–41.

35 See, to this effect, the analysis by Y. Dinstein, 'The Right to Life, Physical Integrity and Liberty', in L. Henkin (ed.), *The International Bill of Rights*, New York, Columbia University Press, 1981, pp.114–37.

36 Th. Van Boven, *People Matter – Views on International Human Rights Policy*, Amsterdam, Meulenhoff, 1982, p.77.

37 On this latter, see S. Leckie, 'The UN Committee on Economic, Social and Cultural Rights and the Right to Adequate Housing: Towards an Appropriate Approach', *Human Rights Quarterly*, 11, 1989, 522–60.

38 B.G. Ramcharan, 'The Right to Life', *Netherlands International Law Review*, 30, 1983, 301.

39 Ibid., 316.

40   Ibid., 305–6; Van Boven (op. cit., note 36), pp.179, 181–3.

41   Ramcharam (op. cit., note 38), 302–3, 308–10.

42   Ibid., 304, 329; B.G. Ramcharan, 'The concept and dimensions of the right to life', in B.G. Ramcharan (ed.), *The Right to Life in International Law*, Dordrecht, Nijhoff/Kluwer, 1985, pp.1–32.

43   P. Kromarek, 'Le droit à un environnement équilibré et sain, considéré comme un droit de l'homme: sa mise-en-oeuvre nationale, européenne et internationale', *Ière Conférence européenne sur l'environnement et les droits de l'homme*, Strasbourg, Institute for European Environmental Policy, 1979, pp.2–3, 31, 34 (mimeographed, restricted circulation).

44   Ibid., pp.5, 12–13.

45   Ibid., pp.21, 43.

46   For examples of those threats, see J.T.B. Tripp, 'The UNEP Montreal Protocol: industrialized and developing countries sharing the responsibility for protecting the stratospheric ozone layer', *New York University Journal of International Law and Politics*, **20**, 1988, 734; Ch.B. Davidson, 'The Montreal Protocol: The first step toward protecting the global ozone layer', ibid., 807–9.

47   See preamble and Articles 10(2) and 11; text in *Annuaire de l'Institut de Droit International*, **62**, 1987, 204, 207–8, 211.

48   See Comisión Interamericana de Derechos Humanos, *Diez Años de Actividades – 1971–1981*, Washington DC, OAS General Secretariat, 1982, pp.321, 329–30, 338–9.

49   Ramcharan (op. cit., note 38), p.303.

50   UN, *Report of the Human Rights Committee, G.A.O.R.*, 40th Session (1985), suppl. Note 40 (A/40/40), p.162.

51   Ibid.

52   As proclaimed by the 1948 Universal Declaration of Human Rights, Article 25(1). On the 'negative' and 'positive' aspects of the right to health, see M. Bothe, 'Les concepts fondamentaux du droit à la santé: le point de vue juridique', *Le Droit à la santé en tant que droit de l'homme – Colloque 1978* (Académie de Droit International de la Haye), The Hague, Sijthoff, 1979; Scalabrino-Spadea, 'Le droit à la santé – Inventaire de normes et principes de droit international', *Le Médecin face aux droits de l'homme*, Padua, Cedam, 1990.

53   R. Roemer, 'El Derecho a la Atención de la Salud', in H.L. Fuenzalida-Puelma and S.S. Connor (eds), *El Derecho a la Salud en las Américas*, Washington, OPAS, Publ. no. 509, p.16. See also the report of the I International Conference on Health and Human Rights, in *Health and Human Rights – Quarterly*, 1995, **2**, 129–51.

54   Dupuy, 'Le droit à la santé et la protection de l'environnement', *Le Droit à la santé* (op. cit., note 52), pp. 351, 406, 409–10, 412.

55   A. Ch. Kiss, 'Le droit à la qualité de l'environnement: un droit de l'homme?', in N. Duplé (ed.), *Le Droit à la qualité de l'environnement: un droit en devenir, un droit à définir*, Vieux-Montréal (Quebec), Editions Québec/Amérique, 1988, pp.69–70.

56   Ibid., p.71.

57   See, for example, Council of Europe/European Social Charter, *Committee of Independent Experts – Conclusions IX-2*, Strasbourg, C.E., 1986, p.71; ibid., *Conclusions XI-1*, Strasbourg, C.E., 1989, p.119.

58   See, for example, ibid., *Conclusions IX-2*, pp.71–2; *Conclusions XI-1*, p.118.

59   Council of Europe/European Social Charter, *Case Law on the European Social Charter Supplement*, Strasbourg, C.E., 1982, pp.37, 105.

60   Ibid., p.104. On the protection of health vis-à-vis the environment under Article 11 of the European Social Charter, see further: Council of Europe doc. 6030, of 22.3.1989, p.9; Conseil de l'Europe/Charte Sociale Européenne, *Comité d'Experts Indépendants – Conclusions X-2*, Strasbourg, C.E., 1988, pp.111–12; Coun-

cil of Europe/European Social Charter, *Committee of Independent Experts – Conclusions X-1*, Strasbourg, C.E., 1987, p.108.

61 J.P. Jacqué, 'La protection du droit à l'environnement au niveau européen ou régional', in P. Kromarek (ed.), *Environnement et droits de l'homme*, Paris, UNESCO, 1987, pp.72–75. On Steiger's proposed Draft Protocol, see W.P. Gormley, *Human Rights and Environment: The Need for International Co-operation*, Leyden, Sijthoff, 1976, pp.90–95; Dupuy (op. cit., note 54), pp.408–13.

62 Gormley (op. cit., note 61), pp.112–13; Jacqué (op. cit., note 61), pp.73, 75–6; Dupuy (op. cit., note 54), pp.412–13. For the complete text of Steiger's 1973 proposed Draft Protocol, see Working Group for Environmental Law (Bonn – rapporteur, H. Steiger), 'The Right to a Humane Environment/Das Recht auf eine menschenwürdige Umwelt', *Beiträge zur Umweltgestaltung* (Heft A 13), Berlin, Erich Schmidt Verlag, 1973, pp.27–54.

63 A. Ch. Kiss, 'La mise-en-œuvre du droit à l'environnement: problématique et moyens', *II Conférence européenne sur l'environnement et les droits de l'homme*, Salzburg, Institute for European Environmental Policy, 1980, p.4 (mimeographed, restricted circulation).

64 Ibid., p.5.

65 K. Vasak, 'Pour les droits de l'homme de la troisième génération: les droits de solidarité', *Résumés des Cours de l'Institut International des Droits de l'Homme* (X Session d'Enseignement, 1979), Strasbourg, IIDH, 1979, p.6 (mimeographed); Ph. Alston, 'Making space for new human rights: the case of the right to development', *Harvard Human Rights Yearbook*, 1, 1988, 33, 35, 38.

66 For a study of the operation of international mechanisms of human rights protection, see Cançado Trindade, 'Co-existence and Co-ordination' (op. cit., note 2), 21–435.

67 A. Eide, 'Realization of Social and Economic Rights and the Minimum Threshold Approach', *Human Rights Law Journal*, 10, 1989, 36, 38.

68 Ibid., 41.

69 Kiss, 'Le droit à la qualité de l'environnement' (op. cit., note 55), pp.69–87. See also Kromarek, 'Le droit à un environnement équilibré et sain' (op. cit., note 43), p.15. On the remedies (in domestic comparative law) for the exercise of the right of information and the right of participation, see L.P. Suetens, 'La protection du droit à l'information et du droit de participation: les recours', *II Conférence européenne sur l'environnement et les droits de l'homme*, Salzburg, Institute for European Environmental Policy, 1980, pp.1–13 (mimeographed, restricted circulation); and, on private recourses for environmental harm (in domestic comparative law), see S.C. McCaffrey and R.E. Lutz (eds), *Environmental Pollution and Individual Rights: An International Symposium*, Deventer, Kluwer, 1978, pp.xvii–xxiii, 3–162.

70 Eide (op. cit., note 67), 36.

71 As to this latter, see A.A. Cançado Trindade, 'Environment and Development: Formulation and Implementation of the Right to Development as a Human Right', *Asian Yearbook of International Law*, 3, 1994, 15–45.

72 See E. Brown Weiss, *In Fairness to Future Generations: International Law, Common Patrimony and Intergenerational Equity*, Tokyo/Dobbs Ferry NY, UNU/Transnational Publications, 1989.

73 On their functioning and coordination, see Cançado Trindade, 'Co-existence and Co-ordination' (op. cit., note 2), 13–435.

74 Cançado Trindade, 'The contribution of international human rights law to environmental protection' (op. cit., note 23), pp.244–312. See also *Conclusion of the Siena Forum on International Law of the Environment* (April 1990), p.8, para. 23 (mimeographed, restricted circulation).

75 L.A. Teclaff, 'The impact of environmental concern on the development of

international law', in L.A. Teclaf and A.E. Utton (eds), *International Environmental Law*, New York, Praeger, 1975, p.252.

76   For a study, see A.A. Cançado Trindade, 'Environmental protection and the absence of restrictions on human rights', in K.E. Mahoney and P. Mahoney (eds), *Human Rights in the Twenty-First Century: A Global Challenge*, Dordrecht, Nijhoff, 1993, pp.561–93.

77   Kromarek, 'Le droit à un environnement équilibré et sain' (op. cit., note 43), p.38.

78   Kiss, 'Le droit à la qualité de l'environnement' (op. cit., note 55), pp. 80, 83; Kiss, 'La mise-en-oeuvre' (op. cit., note 63), see pp.6, 8–9.

79   UN doc. E/CN.4/Sub.2/1991/8, of 2.8.1991, pp.1–33.

80   The group of experts was composed of J. Cameron (London), A.A. Cançado Trindade (Brasilia), D.J.A. Goldberg (Glasgow), M. Ibarra (Geneva), A.Ch. Kiss (Strasbourg), M. Kothari (New Delhi), F.Z. Ksentini (Vienna), Y. Lador (Geneva), D.C. McDonald (Minneapolis), M. Raman (Penang), D. Shelton (Budapest), A. Simpson (Sydney), M. Tebourbi (Strasbourg) and T. Thamage (Athlone, South Africa). The meeting of the group of experts was also attended by members of the Sierra Club Legal Defense Fund.

81   The full text of the *1994 Draft Declaration of Principles on Human Rights and the Environment* has been published in leaflet form by the Sierra Club Legal Defense Fund, and is reproduced in A.A. Cançado Trindade (ed.), *Derechos Humanos, Desarrollo Sustentable y Medio Ambiente/Human Rights, Sustainable Development and Environment*, 2nd edn, San José, Costa Rica, IIDH/BID, 1995, Annex XIV, pp. 379–83.

82   M. Ali Mekouar, 'Le droit à l'environnement dans ses rapports avec les autres droits de l'homme', in P. Kromarek (ed.), *Environnement et droits de l'homme*, Paris, UNESCO, 1987, pp.94–6; F. Doré, 'Conséquences des exigences d'un environnement équilibré et sain sur la définition, la portée et les limitations des différents droits de l'homme – Rapport introductif', *I Conférence européenne sur l'environnement et les droits de l'homme*, Strasbourg, Institute for European Environmental Policy, 1979, pp.3–5, 7–12, 14 (mimeographed, restricted circulation); see also F. Doré (Interventions) ibid., pp.25–7, 37–8.

83   J. Crawford, 'The Rights of Peoples: Some Conclusions', J. Crawford (ed.), *The Rights of Peoples*, Oxford, Clarendon Press, 1988, p.167.

84   Ibid., pp.167–8.

85   See ibid., p.168.

86   Mekouar (op. cit., note 82), pp.96–100, 103–4.

87   For example, UN Covenant on Civil and Political Rights, Article 4(2); European Convention on Human Rights, Article 15(2); American Convention on Human Rights, Article 27.

88   International Covenant on Civil and Political Rights, *Selected Decisions of the Human Rights Committee under the Optional Protocol*, Vol. 2, New York, United Nations, 1990, Doc. CCPR/C/OP/2, pp.20–22.

89   For a review of the emerging case law on the issue, see Cançado Trindade, *Direitos Humanos e Meio-Ambiente* (op. cit., note 20), pp.151–5.

90   S. Weber, 'Environmental information and the European Convention on Human Rights', *Human Rights Law Journal*, 12, 1991, 177–85, esp. 181–2; see also, on the matter, M. Déjeant-Pons, 'L'insertion du droit de l'homme à l'environnement dans les systèmes régionaux de protection des droits de l'homme', *Revue universelle des droits de l'homme*, 3, 1991, 469–70; M. Prieur, *Droit de l'environnement*, 2nd edn, Paris, Dalloz, 1991, p.133; P.W. Birnie and A.E. Boyle, *International Law and the Environment*, Oxford, Clarendon Press, 1994 (reprint), pp.192–3; A.Ch. Kiss and D. Shelton, *International Environmental Law*, New York/London, Transnational Publishers/Graham and Trotman, 1991,

pp.28–31; M. Prieur, 'Le droit à l'environnement et les citoyens: la participation', *Conferência Internacional: A Garantia do Direito ao Ambiente*, Lisbon, Associação Portuguesa para o Direito do Ambiente/Fund. C. Gulbenkian, 1988, pp.183–210.

91 Applications 9278/81 and 9415/81 (joined), *G. and E. (Lapps) versus Norway* case (1983), in European Commission of Human Rights, *Decisions and Reports*, Vol. 35, Strasbourg, 1984, pp.35–8, esp. 36.

92 Paragraphs 55 and 48 of the judgment, text in *Human Rights Law Journal* **12**, 1991, note 3, 97–8; see generally 93–100.

93 Weber, 'Environmental information' (op. cit., note 90), 177–85.

94 European Court of Human Rights, *Case of López Ostra versus Spain*, judgment of 9 December 1994, Strasbourg, C.E., p.17; see also pp. 11, 15, 20.

95 Inter-American Commission on Human Rights, *Ten Years of Activities 1971–1981*, Washington, DC, OAS General Secretariat, 1982, pp.151–2; OAS, *Annual Report of the Inter-American Commission on Human Rights 1984–1985*, pp.24–34; see also S.H. Davis, *Land Rights and Indigenous Peoples – The Role of the Inter-American Commission on Human Rights*, Cambridge, MA, Cultural Survival Inc., 1988, pp.7–15.

96 See N.U./Conseil Économique et Social, *La participation populaire sous ses diverses formes en tant que facteur important du développement et de la réalisation integrale de tous les droits de l'homme*, doc. E/CN.4/1985/10, of 31.12.1985, pp.1–39; UN/ECOSOC, *Question of the Realization in All Countries of the Economic, Social and Cultural Rights [...] and Study of Special Problems which the Developing Countries Face in their Efforts to Achieve these Human Rights*, doc. E/CN.4/1334, of 2.1.1979, pp.118–29; and doc. E/CN.4/1488, of 31.12.1981, pp.5–123.

97 A. Kiss and A.A. Cançado Trindade, 'Two major challenges of our time: human rights and the environment', in A.A. Cançado Trindade (ed.), *Human Rights, Sustainable Development and Environment/Derechos Humanos, Desarrollo Sustentable y Medio Ambiente*, 2nd edn, San José, Costa Rica, IIDH/BID, 1995, pp.287–90.

98 See A.A. Cançado Trindade, 'Democracia y Derechos Humanos: Desarrollos Recientes, con Atención Especial al Continente Americano', in *Federico Mayor Amicorum Liber – Solidarité, Égalité, Liberté*, Vol. I, Brussels, Bruylant, 1995, pp.371–90; James Crawford, *Democracy in International Law* (Inaugural Lecture, 5 March 1993), Cambridge, Cambridge University Press, 1994, pp.1–43.

99 See in general, for example, A.M. Micou and B. Lindsnaes (eds), *The Role of Voluntary Organisations in Emerging Democracies*, Copenhagen, Danish Centre for Human Rights/IIE, 1993, pp.13–188.

Bibliography

Birnie, P.W. and A.E. Boyle (1994), *International Law and the Environment*, Oxford, Clarendon Press (reprint).

Brown Weiss, E. (1989), *In Fairness to Future Generations: International Law, Common Patrimony and Intergenerational Equity*, Tokyo/Dobbs Ferry NY, UNU Press/Transnational Publications.

Cançado Trindade, A.A. (1987), 'Co-existence and co-ordination of mechanisms of international protection of human rights (at global and regional levels)', *Recueil des Cours de l'Académie de droit international de la Haye*, **202**.

Cançado Trindade, A.A. 1993), 'Environmental protection and the absence of restrictions on human rights', in K.E. Mahoney and P. Mahoney (eds), *Human Rights in the Twenty-First Century: A Global Challenge*, Dordrecht, Nijhoff, pp.561–93.

Cançado Trindade, A.A. (1993), 'The contribution of international human rights law to environmental protection, with special reference to global environmental change', in E. Brown Weiss (ed.), *Environmental Change and International Law*, Tokyo, UNU Press.

Cançado Trindade, A.A. (1994), 'Environment and development: formulation and implementation of the right to development as a human right', *Asian Yearbook of International Law*, 3.

Cançado Trindade, A.A. (ed.) (1995), *Derechos Humanos, Desarrollo Sustentable y Medio Ambiente* (Human Rights, Sustainable Development and Environment), 2nd edn, San José, Costa Rica, IIDH/BID.

Cançado Trindade, A.A. (1995), 'Democracia y Derechos Humanos: Desarrollos Recientes, con Atención Especial al Continente Americano', *Federico Mayor Amicorum Liber – Solidarité, Égalité, Liberté*, Vol. I, Brussels, Bruylant.

Cançado Trindade, A.A. and D.J. Attard (1991), 'The implications of the common concern of mankind's concept on global environmental issues', in T. Iwama (ed.), *Policies and Laws on Global Warming: International and Comparative Analysis*, Tokyo, Environmental Research Center.

Davidson, Ch.B. (1988), 'The Montreal Protocol: the first step toward protecting the global ozone layer', *New York University Journal of International Law and Politics*, **20**.

Eide, A. (1989), 'Realization of social and economic rights and the minimun threshold approach', *Human Rights Law Journal*, **10**.

Gormley, W.P. (1988), 'The right to a safe and decent environment', *Indian Journal of International Law*, **20**.

Kiss, A.Ch. (1988), 'Le droit à la qualité de l'environnement: un droit de l'homme?', in N. Duplé (ed.), *Le droit à la qualité de l'environnement: un droit en devenir, un droit à définir*, Vieux-Montréal, Quebec, Editions Québec/Amérique.

Kiss, A.Ch. (1989), *Droit international de l'environnement*, Paris, Pédone.

Kiss, A.Ch. and A.A. Cançado Trindade (1995), 'Two major challenges of our time: human rights and the environment', in A.A. Cançado Trindade (ed.), *Derechos Humanos, Desarrollo Sustentable y Medio Ambiente* (Human Rights, Sustainable Development and the Environment), 2nd edn, San José, Costa Rica, IIDH/BID.

Kiss, A.Ch. and D. Shelton (1991), *International Environmental Law*, New York/London, Transnational Publications/Graham and Trotman.

Kromarek, P. (ed.) (1987), *Environnement et droits de l'homme*, Paris, UNESCO.

Nanda, V.P. (1989), 'Global warming and international environmental law – a preliminary inquiry', *Harvard International Law Journal*, **30**.

Prieur, M. (1991), *Droit de l'environnement*, 2nd edn, Paris, Dalloz.

Ramcharan, B.G. (1985), *The Right to Life in International Law*, Dordrecht, Nijhoff/Kluwer.

Schrijver, N.J. (1988), 'Permanent sovereignty over natural resources versus the common heritage of mankind: complementary or contradictory principles of international economic law?', in P. De Waart, P. Peters and E. Denters (eds), *International Law and Development*, Dordrecht, Nijhoff/Kluwer.

Teclaff, L.A. and A.E. Utton (1974), *International Environmental Law*, New York, Praeger.

Tripp, J.T.B. (1988), 'The UNEP Montreal Protocol: industrialized and developing countries sharing the responsibility for protecting the stratospheric ozone layer', *New York University Journal of International Law and Politics*, **20**.

UNEP (1991), *Review of the Montevideo Programme for the Development and Periodic Review of Environmental Law 1981–1991*, Nairobi, UNEP.

UNEP (1991), *The Meeting of the Group of Legal Experts to Examine the Concept of the Common Concern of Mankind in Relation to Global Environmental Issues* (Malta, 1990) ed. D.J. Attard, Malta/Nairobi, UNEP.

Van Boven, Th. (1982), *People Matter – Views on International Human Rights Policy*, Amsterdam, Meulenhoff.

Ward, E. (1994), *Indigenous Peoples between Human Rights and Environmental Protection* (based on an empirical study of Greenland), Copenhagen, Danish Centre for Human Rights.

World Commission on Environment and Development (1987), *Our Common Future*, Oxford, University Press.

PART II
OBSTACLES

6 Human Rights and Extreme Poverty

LOUIS-EDMOND PETTITI and PATRICE MEYER-BISCH

By dint of concentrating on gaining recognition for first one category of rights and then another, have we not lost sight of the very raison d'être and ultimate purpose of all rights, namely, the inalienable dignity of each human being? Without this oversight, what explanation or excuse can there be for the fact that our societies tolerate the abandonment of some of their members to a devastating destitution far beyond ordinary insecurity and poverty without those societies mobilizing all their forces to eliminate it? (Joseph Wrésinski, 1989, p.229)

Poverty Does Not Exist

Poverty as a Crime

Though one is dismayed to find that so little attention has been paid to poverty and extreme poverty in the logic of human rights, the explanation for this is unhappily simple: a poor person hardly exists and can only lay claim, modestly, to 'poor' rights. We have gradually become accustomed to consider the poor person as 'having exhausted his entitlements'.[1] As for the extremely poor, they do not exist at all; at best they may benefit from charity. Even the help they receive is in most cases an additional token of exclusion from a society that makes them feel guilty. The public authorities ignore them so long as they cannot convict them of some criminal offence. Many adolescents come to the view that people only begin to take an interest in their person when the police suspect them of an offence. Who can stand in judgment over someone who was once denied any form of civil identity as an abandoned child, a child of the streets?

When the subject of law is not ignored, he or she is denied. If a person plucks up the courage to lay claim to a right, to ask for assistance, he or she must first of all submit to ceaseless questioning about their private lives and to constant accusations that are all the more unbearable in that their needs are a matter of life and death. When such persons demand a place to live, they must prove they have no weak points, otherwise they will find themselves accused of bearing responsibility for the deprivation of their own rights,[2] as if they had to justify their own miserable existence. If they wish to show that their child has been hurt, they must first of all prove that they were not the ones who hit it. For them, the burden of proof is always reversed: it is much easier like that, as it means that society will not need to face up to the gap in its arrangements. In violent reaction to the economic and social difficulties of the very poor, society arrogates to itself the right to deprive them of custody of their children. Since such people fail to exercise their responsibilities, they are stripped of every right, every sign of individual identity. Thus do we conceal the gap. There lies the root of the contradiction and the root of our shame.

'In short, we are afraid that the excluded might get themselves included – and in so doing change the rules. We are afraid that they might even exist in their own right and not just as the mirror image of social assistance, social administration or social policy.'[3] It is essential that the excluded, though they might be offered help, remain excluded so that the system can be maintained. The excluded do not form a class, as they do not possess their own culture; they form a mass. It is possible to go even further along this reductionist path by speaking of an *underclass* characterized by a pattern of behaviour including refusal to work, abnormal sexuality, a weakened sense of family, dependence on welfare, various forms of drug abuse, and so forth. Such descriptions, widely used in the United States of America, are criticized in many quarters[4] since they take the outcome (behaviour of the excluded person) for the cause and tend to inculpate such individuals, or at least to make them responsible for their own exclusion. Such a discriminatory and moralizing judgment, which maintains inequality, is at the opposite extreme from a culture of human rights in which every person is a subject of law and is entitled to have that status restored when caught up in various forms of insecurity.

The poor show up the weaknesses and inconsistencies of our democratic system. Unrecognized and underrated, they furnish living proof of the general disregard for indivisible human dignity. That is the reason for the lack of interest in and consideration for the poorest segment of the population, a point noted by the special rapporteur, Leandro Despouy.[5] The conclusions of a study on the representation of poor people show that such representation is impossible

because the social status of those it is intended to represent is precisely zero: neither class, nor corps, nor group, nor social movement
nor people. They are socially nothing and that, when all is said and
done, might well be the socio-political definition of poverty [...] Having no existence of their own but existing merely by reference to
something else (in this case society), they are of no interest. Is it
possible to represent a mirror?[6]

Recognizing and taking account of this exclusion implies a fundamental criticism of the underlying rationale of our system and not
just a criticism of its inadequacies in a world replete with violations
of every kind that exceed our capacity to respond. The wealthy can
afford to cast doubt on the excessively abstract conceptions of universality. But people whose rights are radically denied and those
who join with them to reclaim such rights discover every day that
the concept of universality is the most concrete of battle lines. The
poor are denied the universal application of human rights in at least
two ways.

Poverty is increasing everywhere   Poverty and extreme poverty are not
peripheral phenomena confined to the South or to the outskirts of
wealthy areas; they are universal.[7] True, the phenomenon occurs on a
more massive scale in the least developed countries and in countries
undergoing rapid structural transformation, but it has equally serious consequences for the victims in rich countries. Indeed, poverty is
increasing everywhere: increasing wealth is accompanied by increasing poverty and there is no point in preaching about the egoism of
economic systems or the Establishment because everything proceeds
as if no-one today had the least idea of how to develop otherwise. We
are cruelly short of know-how because our know-how is fragmented.

Poverty renders all human rights inoperative   The violation of the right
to a reasonable standard of living entails the violation of all the other
human rights, since their observance is quite simply made materially
and structurally impossible. Poverty aggravates discrimination since
it particularly affects women,[8] the elderly and the disabled. Moreover, the very poor are in most cases unable even to discover their
rights. And this 'violation' not only affects individuals, through and
within their precarious day-to-day existence, but it entraps their entire social world over several generations in a spiral from which it is
virtually impossible to escape. Who will rid us of the suspicion that,
as far as the majority of the well-to-do are concerned, poor people
should not beget children?[9]

It must be said that our legal system is made even more powerless
by the fact that social rights are regarded as 'programmed rights'.

That is to say that their observance in practical terms is in fact left to the discretion of the political and economic authorities. The poor are victims of an institutional conservatism in the very field of human rights which permits distinctions to be made between the most fundamental rights – civil and social rights – owing to the simple fact that we have not yet managed to find a correct positive form for all human rights. The most important moral imperative is therefore to give serious attention to the indivisibility of human rights and to incorporate it into our legal and political systems.

The Downward Spiral of Insecurity

It is impossible for us to respond to the demands of the poor because our social systems are fragmented. The failure to recognize the idea of indivisibility is systematically reflected in administrative divisions. Let us call this pattern the 'exclusion system'. It possesses an institutional dimension (bureaucratic divisions of responsibility) but also a theoretical one (non-communication between areas of knowledge, in particular lack of interdisciplinarity). The poor are the victims of but also the witnesses to this system. In other words, they can show us a good number of specific ways of re-establishing links between what should not be separated in order to bring the human person as the subject of law back to the centre of things.

Poverty is undoubtedly a general phenomenon, a social relation which as such is subject to law,[10] and whose overall logic needs to be understood. However, both the analysis of poverty and the strategies to fight it require a distinction to be made between poverty and extreme poverty.[11] Poverty is a situation of insecurity, whereas extreme poverty is a spiral of different kinds of insecurity, with each kind aggravating the effects of the others in a circular process that hems the individual in completely.[12] The distinction is therefore not just a question of degree, it is structural. Extreme poverty lies in a no-man's-land where people are abandoned by exclusion systems and where the different authorities do not know how to work together. The purpose of the right to a decent standard of living is to provide a minimum guarantee, not against each and every form of insecurity but against their combination. This very particular area of society, or rather, no-man's-land, makes the person in extreme poverty a precious witness of a very special kind. It is also essential to analyse the timescale:

> If the problem of exclusion is exploding, if it is outstripping the possibilities of treatment and conceptualization in terms of inequality – that is to say that it is no longer possible merely to measure the extent of inequalities and decide which ones will be considered, if not as

being just, at least as being tolerable and perhaps even functional – is not this because exclusion persists, that is to say that it reproduces itself?[13]

The thresholds of poverty are not just quantitative, they are systemic, they are the points at which the systems malfunction.

If society manages, as the first and most important step, to rehabilitate the poor as authors and actors by listening to and treating them as partners then the latter will become most useful agents for social peace and common dignity. Adopting the practical idealism of the human rights tradition and drawing upon the experience of organizations working with the extremely poor, we take as our starting point the clear principle that a person in extreme poverty is not primarily someone to whom something must be given but someone from whom we should receive something. That person alone can be the author of his or her rights and the co-author and co-protagonist of the strategies for putting those rights into practice. That person alone can teach us the unity and dynamics of our human rights.

The Poorest of the Poor, Heralds of the Indivisibility of Human Rights

The task has theoretical implications, though it is evident that progress is needed in the use of existing instruments and in the building of new legal bulwarks, as we shall show below; there must above all be considerable and decisive progress in our understanding of the forms of social interdependence. For that, we need first of all to learn all the lessons from the 'objection' of the poor. This is not new; human rights have always advanced in this way, by learning from victims. 'Unfortunately, people rapidly forget what they owe in this way to the poorest of the *poor* from age to age. Today they appear in particular to have forgotten that they owe to them a conception of man as born equal, free and essential to the lives of others.'[14]

Objection on Grounds of Poverty

Objection on grounds of poverty must be regarded as equivalent to objection on grounds of conscience: both constitute absolute criteria of democratic legitimacy. A society in which the majority consents to exclusion loses its legitimacy as it does when it fails to respect the right of a person to express what he or she considers a matter of conscience. In both cases the fundamental denial of the right of that individual reveals a basic flaw in the construction founded on majority law. Majority law becomes essentially tyrannical – the law of numbers – when it fails to respect the universality of human rights, especially in regard to the weakest. The majority is not the arbiter of human dignity, but is required to recognize the means of its protection.

Even more directly, objection on grounds of poverty is a form of conscientious objection, since maintaining people in a situation of extreme poverty amounts to denying them what is legitimately theirs and the opportunity to assume the responsibilities pertaining to their own consciences, such as looking after their children, seeking work or living genuine relationships. The poor person sinks deeper and deeper into institutional and moral alienation. Thus we find that economic and social rights are no less individual than civil rights. Our systems of exclusion have led us to mistake their weaknesses for rational distinctions. It is administrative action that assimilates individual subjects of law to planning categories, turning them into the targets of welfare or control measures. We have no reason to postpone efforts to make social rights, at long last, subject to due process of law and to adapt our legal cultures to the indivisibility and universality of human rights.

There has been a shift from the object to the subject. In fact, it is the object of economic, social and cultural rights that is common and belongs to the economic logic of the various systems, but the subject of human rights is always the same, the human person, alone or together, who is there, physically, with the various aspects of his or her dignity. And so we need to pause a while to analyse the *objective* indivisibility of human rights.

The Indivisibility of the Object of Rights

The indivisibility of the object of rights may be understood first of all through the spiral of violations, the vicious circle of insecurity. The violation of each human right undermines respect for all the others. Denial of the right to housing leads to a formal and practical incapacity not only to enjoy the majority of civil rights but also, at the very least, to look for work, to send one's children to school and to experience harmonious family relations. A homeless person repels others and a homeless family is even more a subject of reproach. Indeed, the very presence of the extremely poor is an assault on society, which responds by other forms of violence, particularly measures of placement, classification or confinement. Violence takes root, leading inexorably to physical exclusion and to the development of a moral straitjacket. Such exclusion is reinforced by arbitrary discrimination between the categories of human rights.

And yet objectivity is now accessible. The negation of indivisibility (the dividing up of human rights) leads to the perversion of the entire relation in law (subject–object–obligor (person by whom the obligation is owed)) which constitutes each human right.

> The very existence of the extremely poor in all continents demonstrates that according civil liberties and political rights without giving the concrete means of assuming those rights may be worse than refusing them. ... To find oneself automatically allotted a minimum income and some sort of a job or accommodation without being in a position to give one's opinion, to choose, to negotiate or to refuse, is once again to be reduced to second class citizenship.'[15]

To concede the substance of a right without respecting the complex and indivisible nature of its object is to deny the subject by making him or her subservient to the obligor. In consequence, those concerned are kept dependent and their chances of taking action for themselves and for others are further decreased. This reinforces the conservatism of those who think that too much is already being done, that the poor are responsible for their own shipwreck, or simply that the problem is insoluble.

In reality, the resources are available, and much more abundant than is generally believed; but if the poor and their associations are not recognized as being the authors and actors of their own rights, we are depriving ourselves of their human and cultural capital. The indivisibility of rights is at once the indivisibility of their object and the indivisibility of their subject which, in both cases, is human dignity.[16] It is not a roof over one's head, food or the assistance of a lawyer appointed by the court that constitutes the object of a human right but the possibility of living in dignity, keeping body and soul together while upholding one's values, defending the dignity of one's fundamental rights and the related rights of other people. Dignity is the real object of each human right, which can therefore be interpreted only in the light of all the other rights. The principle of indivisibility requires us to advance from an approach based on the mere cataloguing of rights to the idea of a system, that is to say an approach that would highlight and exploit relations of interdependence.

Introduction to International Texts

A General Inadequacy

The relevant articles of the Universal Declaration and Covenants of the United Nations which indirectly refer to protection from poverty are of little significance. The regional Conventions in Europe or America steer clear of the problem. Only the Charter drawn up by the Organization of African Unity, Chapter II of which is devoted to duties, appeals directly for solidarity.

A comparison of these texts is instructive. They were drawn up with different ends in view and for different regions of the world in response to the same suffering; but not one was truly designed to deal with the problem of poverty, as if contemporary society refused to recognize that dimension, as if it were capable only of devising piecemeal measures with no close links to specific rights. All the human rights are concerned, some of them more directly.[17] The analysis of poverty presupposes a transverse approach to civil rights and social rights. Non-recognition of the indivisibility of human rights boils down to the acceptance of exclusion. A turning point came with the declaration on the right to development, and then again with the Copenhagen summit, to be discussed in the next section. But although we find approaches to poverty that are more satisfactory because they are more integrated, there is still no question of positive rights.

The concept of equal opportunity has not been truly incorporated into international documents. To achieve such equality, the first stage must be to recognize more rights for the disadvantaged so as to enable them to reach the first level of their enjoyment. Recognition must be given as a matter of priority to *the right to rights*.

The very existence of the subject of law being in reality contested, the existing instruments have little effective impact and the role of non-governmental organizations in their implementation and criticism is, and needs to be, preponderant.

Legal Obstacles: the Case of Europe

The importance of the rights recognized in legal instruments, especially the rights of the very poor, is diminished by the fact that such covenants and charters do not include coercive elements and thus make it impossible to sanction states. The implementation of the European Convention, which allows individual appeal, offers remedies and guarantees beneficiaries their fundamental rights, with the possibility of asking the courts to uphold such rights. Could this be extended to social rights?

Case law in Europe   The first appeals (*Von Volsem*, Belgium) were declared inadmissible, possibly through lack of specific factors and because the originality of such appeals led the Commission to act with prudence. The *Buckley* appeal came before the European Court at the end of 1995.

The problem of poverty was posed by the interpretation of the European Convention on Human Rights, in particular because of the economic policy of overconsumption and legislation on contracts that left too much power to financial decision makers in relation to a body of consumers unskilled in detecting the traps in contracts. European states have waited too long to enact laws to reduce the risks arising from the freedom of contract and to introduce clauses and time limits that afford consumers a minimum of protection. This has led to households getting too deeply into debt and, among such households, the most disadvantaged have been the main victims.[18] The European Court, by emphasizing the positive obligation of states to promote human rights, is indirectly inviting them to remedy the omissions in their legislation of their own accord. With the growing case law of the Convention's institutions, there is hope for a positive application that other regional instruments might also adopt by taking over in appropriate form the machinery of individual complaint.

The European Court of Human Rights has sought, in the field of its competence but by active, open-ended interpretation, to provide some protection for social rights. The extensive interpretation of Article 3 of the European Convention on Human Rights may be explained by the profound changes in social relationships: since 1950, the widening gap between rich and poor has become a form of discrimination as serious as that on ethnic grounds. It is in the light of this general reflection that the outcome of application to the Court referring to Articles 3, 8, 11 and 14 of the Convention together or separately must be re-examined. The decisions of the Court in the cases of *Airey* and *Articon* open the way to recognition of the right to a right.[19]

In the report submitted to the seventh International Colloquy of the Council of Europe in Copenhagen,[20] the Commission speaks of treatment that is 'grossly humiliating in the eyes of other people' or which 'lowers the rank, position or reputation of the person concerned in the eyes of others or in his own eyes'.[21] The Court has also taken account of the possibility of a person being humiliated 'in his own eyes' (*Tyrer* v. *United Kingdom*).[22] The Commission emphasized that the concept does not necessarily require a physical or corporal element. In a judgment of 15 December 1977 relating to a case of transsexuality, it referred to 'humiliation and social discredit'.[23] These forms of words are clearly applicable to situations of severe poverty. The European Court has further stated that the prohibition in Article 3 is absolute and applies 'irrespective of the victim's conduct' (*Ireland* v. *United Kingdom*).[24]

The European Court had to take a decision in the so-called 'vagrancy' case (Belgium, *de Wilde*). Later, it showed its support for the social defence school of thought (*Vanderbrugen–Weeks*). In the *de Wilde* case, the definition manifestly corresponds to the description of a situation of extreme poverty, which is confirmed by the context of the case. The Court used the term 'hardship' when it decided that the fact of reporting voluntarily to the police with a view to confinement does not exclude the possibility that a deprivation of freedom may have occurred. For Fiérens, 'as things stand at present, respect for privacy is practically a hollow formula when applied to the seriously underprivileged'.[25]

The Court decided that, although the main purpose of Article 8 was to protect the individual against arbitrary interference by the public authorities, it did not simply compel the state to abstain from such interference. To such a negative undertaking may be added positive obligations inherent in an effective respect for private or family life. Indeed, the measures adopted may be designed to secure respect for private life even in the sphere of the relations of individuals between themselves (case of *X* v. *Netherlands*).

> The evolving nature of the European Convention on Human Rights now comes into the story. It raises questions about the Convention's capacity to defend the very poor; it appears to need to be supplemented by certain economic and social rights; it will possibly conduct a regular evaluation of the benefits drawn from it by the people most affected by severe poverty.

But the question raised by Father Joseph Wrésinski is How can we invent a way of making the very poorest people partners of the Convention?

Nicholas Valticos, referring to the work of the Council of Europe on poverty and the proposals addressed to it by ATD-Fourth World, observed: 'It is self-evident that, in order to combat poverty, a series of short-, medium- and long-term measures of different types has to be contemplated which, taken as a whole, ought to be the target of a co-ordinated action.'[26]

Projects for reform   Several of the measures that should be included in a programme to combat poverty are related to rights already covered in a more general way by the Social Charter.[27] That Charter, however, is well known for the weakness of its supervisory machinery, which is based exclusively on governmental reports. The 'relaunch mechanism' of the Social Charter provides for two types of reform.

First is the *reform of the supervisory machinery*. The protocol provides for a procedure of collective complaint empowering non-governmental organizations (NGOs) and both sides of industry to submit reports on collective situations to a committee of independent experts. This new procedure will have the advantage of being based not only on existing measures (such as the French RMI or minimum integration income) but also on their effectiveness. At the same time, it will make it possible to apply articles of the Charter in combination, as is done at the Court, instead of simply examining the articles one after the other on the basis of governmental reports.

The second is the *draft of the revised Social Charter*. The wording proposed by ATD-Fourth World and Valticos for insertion into a protocol to the Charter has on the whole been incorporated into Article 30, entitled 'The right to protection against poverty and social exclusion', of the revised European Social Charter:

> With a view to ensuring the effective exercise of the right to protection against poverty, the Parties undertake:
> (a) to take measures within the framework of an overall and co-ordinated approach to promote the effective access of persons who live or risk living in a situation of social exclusion or poverty, as well as their families, to, in particular, employment, housing, training, education, culture and social and medical assistance;
> (b) to review these measures with a view to their adaptation if necessary.

What is new in this article is the obligation for states to adopt a global and coordinated approach,[28] which should make for better use of the existing provisions of the Charter. The type of complaints that would then be useful would be those with a sufficiently 'comprehensive' character to permit an examination as to whether the programmes, general measures and policies to combat poverty are satisfactory.

However, in our view, the most useful and effective approach would not be an annex to the Social Charter but the incorporation of the Social Charter into the European Convention on Human Rights in order to ensure that social rights are directly justiciable.

In conclusion, such a development should take account of two concepts applied by the institutions of the European Convention: (1) the negative obligation for states not to interfere in private and family life and the positive obligation to promote the necessary provisions to guarantee the right to a right; and (2) the 'vertical' dimension of the Convention (that is, individual or group appeal against the state). To this must be added the 'horizontal' dimension, that is the application of the Convention to protect victims against groups or 'lobbies' that infringe fundamental rights.

Copenhagen: a New Impetus

An Integrated Approach

Taking the path opened up by the 1986 Declaration on the right to development, the Copenhagen Declaration on Social Development of 12 March 1995 has the advantage of presenting sustainable development in a context that is centred on people and at the same time requires the integration of various areas of policy. Thus the fight against poverty, which is defined as having priority, is approached with the necessary unity in order to 'integrate economic, cultural and social policies so that they become mutually supportive, and acknowledge the interdependence of public and private spheres of activity'.[29] While stressing basic values which, as is normal in intergovernmental texts, are enumerated one after the other redundantly (human dignity, human rights, equality, respect and so on), the Declaration constantly recreates respect for the values inherent in the various social and cultural systems and respect for the independence of members of society.

For example, when the signatories declare that they 'recognize the family as the basic unit of society, and acknowledge that [it] plays a key role in social development', they immediately go on to state that 'as such it should be strengthened, with attention to the rights, capabilities and responsibilities of its members. In different cultural, political and social systems various forms of family exist' (section B, sub-paragraph (h)). Under the pressure of reality, a governmental and administrative approach is thus abandoned in favour of concerted action between the various public and civil parties involved. Not only does the Declaration insist that 'participation by the people concerned is an integral part of such programmes' (Commitment 2, h), which should have become obvious a long time ago, but it appears to take into consideration the logical implications of such participation by affirming that due account must be taken 'of the informal sector in our employment development strategies with a view to increasing its contribution to the eradication of poverty … and to strengthening its linkages with the formal economy' (Commitment 3, h). When one realizes the capacity of poor people to create bonds of solidarity and also the capacity of the informal economy, this remark turns out to be important. The administrative authority must listen and adapt.

There are two fundamental assumptions underpinning this reconstruction: economic development and social development are interdependent, and so are peace and development. On them are built the 10 commitments of the heads of state and government present in Copenhagen. These include commitments 'to the goal of eradicating poverty'; 'to promoting social integration by fostering societies that are stable, safe and just'; 'to achieving equality and equity between women and men'; 'to accelerating the economic, social and human resource development of Africa and the least-developed countries'; and 'to ensuring that ... structural adjustment programmes ... include social development goals'.

Social development is also a matter for the United Nations system as a whole since there exists a principle of solidarity that can only be made effective at the international level. Numerous institutions, such as the United Nations Development Programme (UNDP), the International Labour Organization (ILO) and the United Nations Educational, Scientific and Cultural Organization (UNESCO) have taken steps that are beginning to have an impact.

There remain some ambiguities, particularly the reference to basic needs, which are much vaguer than human rights as standards and indicators of social development, as we shall show. Similarly, the governmental approach inherent in this type of declaration is still very much present. When the states commit themselves to 'creating an economic, political, social, cultural and legal environment that will enable people to achieve social development' (Commitment 1), we cannot give it much credence, owing to the weakness of states.[30] States are guarantors of rights, but are not the most important actors of social development. An analysis of the subsidiary role of public authorities remains to be done in the whole field of human rights. However, the unconditional defence of the poorest people at both the national and international levels is indeed the business of states. The eighth Commitment, on the need to include social goals in structural adjustment policies, will, if it becomes effective, have a considerable impact in this respect.[31]

The Issue of a Social Clause

The International Labour Organization, while carefully avoiding the idea of a 'social clause' that had been raised in Europe as a condition for the freeing of exchanges, demands respect for its own conventions which condemn child labour and forced labour, and guarantee the freedom to organize, collective negotiation and non-discrimination. The precision of this demand will give rise to delicate negotiations with certain Third World states on whose territory such rights are far from being respected and concerning ILO's role in 'monitoring' the commitments.

The idea of a social clause is not new; it is part of the history and tradition of ILO which, in the preamble to its constitution (1919), states: 'The failure of any nation to adopt human conditions of labour is an obstacle in the way of other nations which desire to improve the conditions in their own countries.' Similarly, the Havana Charter of 1948, which has never been ratified, stipulates that states should recognize that unfair working conditions, particularly in the production of goods for export, create difficulties in international trade. Consequently, each state should take all appropriate and feasible steps to eliminate such conditions on its territory. The social clause is based on a foundation of minimum universally applicable standards, the human rights defended by ILO in its field of competence together with a reminder of their indivisibility.

The novelty at the world summits is the growing contribution of NGOs. These organizations have insisted on a social clause. They have advocated the inclusion of 'social development contracts' to back up the efforts of governments that affirm their determination to respect strictly the ILO conventions on workers' rights.

Another proposal has been the introduction of a tax on short-term international financial transactions, advocated by the Nobel Prize winner for economics, James Tobin. He observed that a minute percentage would free considerable resources but would be very difficult to obtain, as he had no illusions where financial transactions were concerned. In fact, only Canada and Sweden are in favour of the 'Tobin tax'. For those states, poverty and exclusion are not inevitable.

At the opening of the Copenhagen Summit, Boutros Boutros-Ghali invited the international community to reflect on a 'new planet-wide pact of solidarity'. To that end one must combine the efforts of states but also rethink all bonds of solidarity and the general responsibility of society in regard to human rights.

Interdependence of the Approaches to Implementation

Basic Needs or Human Rights

No-one can draw up a list of basic needs that, if satisfied, would absolve us of our direct responsibility. 'To judge from what these people teach us, the very poor pay the price in the form of additional humiliation, dependence and disdainful attitude for the rights granted to them in bits and pieces.'[32] The reasoning based on the needs misses the point, partly because it is founded on an enumeration and partly because it fails to consider the relation at the level of rights and in particular its cultural dimension. We also find a certain vagueness in the Copenhagen Declaration which, after reaffirming the rights (paragraph 29, Commitment 1(f) and (n)), refers to 'basic needs' (Commitment 2(e)). In legal theory, a vital element in the fight against extreme poverty is still missing: the clear definition of an inviolable core of human rights. Any strategy for implementation needs to incorporate a carefully worded reminder of the difference in approach between needs and rights.

Ignorance of the relations at the level of rights   The object of a right and the object of a need are different: the object of a need is conceived as a benefit or a service that can be considered in isolation, while the object of a right is a relation based on a system of rules. In the case of a human right, universal human dignity is at stake in the relation: it is a subject and object of law and also an obligor, since every person is an obligor of human rights. A list of basic needs may serve as partial indicators, but never as the justification for a policy, since such needs do not cover the whole field of the relation in rights based on universality.

Ignorance of the cultural dimension   Moreover, the theory of basic needs leaves the impression that there exists a minimum of vital requirements regardless of cultural and individual differences. This conception disregards the various freedoms. Many women and men in extreme poverty consider the right to recognition of their identity, including the cultural dimension of that identity, as being just as urgent as their most immediate social and economic rights. This is because they know that only when their cultural rights are taken into account will their other rights be treated as rights and not as needs. These cultural rights are all rights to identity: recognition of membership of a community, freedom to engage in activities expressing that identity (in particular to express themselves in their own language), rights of access to the natural and cultural heritage and, especially, the right to be initiators of and partners in policies that concern them.

Only the rich are able to think that culture is a secondary need coming after the satisfaction of basic needs. That is not the logic of human rights. Nor is it the experience of poor people. The International Movement ATD-Fourth World sets up libraries and universities in shantytowns and encourages the poorest families to feast their eyes on classical paintings in museums. For the wealthy, that appears of secondary importance, but for poor people it is a matter of priority: they see their dignity recognized because their freedoms can find expression. They are actors and authors of their lives and their needs are recognized as legitimate expressions of their dignity. The rich perceive cultural rights as rights to be different, whereas the poor place more emphasis on the rights entitling them to be like other people, understood not as being uniform but as enjoying the same dignity.

Though they testify to the indivisibility of human rights, poor people bear witness more particularly to the fundamental dimension of cultural rights. In this role, they show us how cultural rights, with their multiple linkages, must be given substance in ways that bear little resemblance to a series of administrative measures.

Investment in Extreme Poverty

Many jurists and moralists find the idea of using the language of economists repugnant, since to them it always smacks of utilitarianism. Yet it is hard to see how one could fight against poverty without resorting to economic arguments. Poor people possess and constitute a capital that is extremely precious for society as a whole; that is the paradoxical conclusion we must acknowledge.[33]

The World Conference on Education for All, held at Jomtien, Thailand from 5 to 9 March 1990, attached great importance to basic education. Poor people cannot wait until states have made or are willing to make the necessary resources available: 'All of society has a contribution to make, recognizing that time, energy and funding directed to basic education are perhaps the most profound investment in people and in the future of a country which can be made.'[34] Paradoxically, the logic of political economy facilitates the dignified treatment of poor people since it enables us to consider them as partners in a relationship of exchange. The harm springs from the fact that, all too often, we perceive only the monetary aspects of economics, in which case the poor person simply represents a hole in the budget. But an economic agent is also a social and cultural asset. In other words, he or she represents a potential or an asset for development that it is important not to neglect. *Respecting a person means first of all admitting that he or she is able to give something.* This is a matter of human rights and good economics, a matter of economic ethics.

The Logic of Thresholds

To make sure that this ethic becomes more than just an ideal, it is essential to define the thresholds needed for the existence of a human being or community. Defining a threshold means giving objective force to an obligation and re-establishing a minimum level of dignity on the basis of which a person can become a subject of law. Such a measure is not only descriptive but also progressive. It is not a question of asking theoretical questions about the minimum necessary for survival, in terms of basic needs, but of defining under what conditions a person is able not only to subsist but also to be recognized as an active participant in a social system.

The danger of the dynamic approach might be its relativism. Though it is true that housing in India and in Canada do not have the same material standard, a dynamic definition should lead to material indicators in each economic and social system. Thus an approach consisting of introducing minimum legal entitlements to water, electricity, food and health care, to be guaranteed unconditionally and protected from seizure, is essential.

But there is another problem. How can we make sure that the beneficiaries of these guaranteed minima do not come to see themselves as permanent welfare cases? Here, again, we should get rid of the administrative way of thinking in terms of 'benefits' and replace it with the economic logic of exchange. Without going into this subject in detail, we shall simply say that poor people *have a right to give*: a right to expect that the society which gives to them should expect something in return. It would appear that two new approaches – not mutually exclusive – are currently under consideration.

The welfare approach   This is the traditional approach and consists of offering the person on welfare odd jobs. The deficiencies of this approach are well known, in particular the lack of self-esteem derived from odd jobs. But there is no reason for not inventing more serious types of work. Who could deny the immensity of needs in areas such as the environment and the rehabilitation of housing and, indeed, the need for social actors among the victims of extreme poverty? Again, the vital condition is to consider the person concerned as capable of undertaking a job worth doing in his or her eyes. The poor person then ceases to be on the receiving end of a placement measure but is given assistance in the real sense: that is to say, applying the notion of subsidiarity. The public authority or the mutual aid organization takes action only in a subsidiary capacity to help the person rehabilitate himself or herself as a social and economic actor. What is expected in return is not primarily the product of some odd job that has been done but an effort involving initiative, research and creativity, however humble it may be.

Universal income benefit   The second approach is more radically economic, in a very liberal sense. The introduction of a universal income benefit means enabling each individual to become an economic agent and hence a social agent. It is 'primary social income distributed on egalitarian principles without conditions. It is truly the income of the citizen.'[35] This new approach is a direct challenge to a society that looks askance at the idea of people receiving a wage without working for it. No matter. It has the advantage of taking into account the real cost of poverty and proposing a viable solution. Lastly, and above all, it gives the beneficiaries freedom to choose what they buy with that money. However, the drawbacks are real. At the global level, to begin with, the liberal society risks cutting its losses and paying no further attention to those whom the market has marginalized, thus confirming trends towards two-track development. The fight against extreme poverty will continue, but perhaps at the cost of strengthening the vicious circle constituted by poverty. As for the beneficiaries, we might well find society losing interest in their social problems because a minimal solution has been found for their economic problems. If, as seems likely, the allowance does not provide them with the human resources to fight against alcoholism and every form of social exclusion, they may well find themselves in a worse position than before, in debt to society and therefore delinquents.

Legislative Reform

Legislative reform in favour of severely disadvantaged populations would require a programme law such as the one prepared by Joseph Wrésinski for the French Economic and Social Council. Such a law to establish a global policy aimed at preventing all forms of insecurity and eliminating severe poverty must fix objectives, link rights and duties coherently, define responsibilities, provide the necessary resources and create guarantees in the form of obligations. It would provide the possibility for families and individuals who are excluded and destitute, as well as those who have joined such people to organize their defence, and enable them to lodge a complaint for non-application of the law.

The constituents of a programme law, whose purpose is to rehabilitate the poor person as a subject of law, are a web of reforms which has nothing in common with a catalogue of welfare measures; they amount to treating the poor as the authors and actors of the reforms concerning them.

The Purpose of Rights to be Introduced

Our guide is the principle of indivisibility. With regard to application, this means that each inviolable right can be claimed independently of the others; otherwise, violations would combine like the different forms of insecurity. The right to basic services (water, gas, electricity and so on), the right to vote with or without a fixed abode, the schooling of children whether or not their parents are legally resident, with economic assistance being provided, are rights *without conditions attached*. This is the price that must be paid if the subject of law is to exist and exercise his or her own responsibilities instead of remaining a burden in the vicious circle of assistance. It is quite clear that such measures benefit society more than they cost it, since they concentrate efforts on the sources of what will later become the most serious problems.

If the social and economic linkages between the different forms of insecurity are to be broken, high priority must also be given to cultural rights. Poor people have a fundamental right to culture, not just to sharing in the benefits of culture but to joining the communities that create culture. Joseph Wrésinksi (1995) shows us that cultural action in an environment of poverty must be based on three lines of thrust. First is *access to culture*, making it possible to realize the other rights: 'To be master of a right is to become part of a historical process and share responsibility for it.' It is only when poverty-stricken families can grasp the history of the family combat for the right to housing that they are able to absorb what is at stake and the various strategies. For them, this right is no longer the satisfaction of a need but the right to exist with dignity, which is the condition for the exercise of the other rights and responsibilities. The life history of a poor person is discontinuous; it precludes planning or the imposition of any coherent pattern and is dominated by the necessity of dealing with the most urgent things first – and such situations often extend over several generations of non-history. This temporal incoherence makes it impossible to understand or control anything. The poor have a right to history, for it is one of the most important avenues to integration and is an absolute condition for the capacity to plan ahead.

Second is *the creation of places where the most disadvantaged can express themselves*. 'In order that this history may be read and understood, the International Movement ATD-Fourth World has established people's universities', as meeting-places for the underprivileged and other citizens where this history can be written and thus given recognition. The point is not that the poor should be considered as a separate group of people, a cultural community in need of its own means of expression as such. Given the variety of their origins, all they have in common is their experience of exclusion, an experience which they want to express and share. The aim, however, is to escape from such exclusion and rejoin communities that are based on an experience of integration. All the same, it is in these universities that the poor can experience, not a negative community of the excluded, but a community of resistance, testing their common dignity in dialogue and projects.

The third thrust is *towards a universal culture*. To achieve the objectives mentioned above, the poor need to have access to the heritage (works of art, books and techniques) and means of expression. A 'cultural hub' established in the heart of a shantytown is not an act of charity:

it is the focus of commitment for the whole society [...] To set in place, recognize and finance such actions is a sign that the society wishes to offer the best of itself to the poorest of all. It is a sign of its belief that the Fourth World may in turn offer the best of itself. This best of oneself, when it is shared, is the true response to the human question of exclusion.[36]

That is where the difficulty lies: recognizing the rights of poor people means at the same time admitting that our society does not give culture and cultural rights their proper place, at the centre of things.

Partnership between All Obligors

If poor people are to be themselves co-authors and co-obligors of their rights, this implies demolishing not only the separations between administrative departments but also the barriers between associations and public authorities. In other words, it implies a different culture of power.

The necessary condition to prevent administrative departments from continuing indefinitely to pass the buck from one to the other is the recognition of inviolable rights. All such departments are jointly and severally bound by those rights. Whereas it is at present in their interest to off-load their responsibilities, this tendency should logically be reversed; where an inviolable obligation is recognized it is in their interest to work together in order not to bear the full burden on their own.

Each authority has its fields of competence. Local and regional authorities should correct the dysfunctions in their own treatment of people and enable associations and any individuals willing to do so to conduct their own projects. They should also resist clientelism and discriminatory pressures, particularly in questions of housing, accept supervision by the state in its role of guarantor of domestic law and universal right and encourage the birth of a caring economy by supporting attempts to meet as yet unsatisfied needs.

Associations, regarded as partners and not as trade unions always demanding more, enable the public authorities to invest the community's redistributed income where it will be of greatest use, in accordance with flexible and coherent strategies based primarily on rehabilitation. This means that the public authority agrees to act in accordance with a culture of subsidiarity: the role of the administration is not to distribute assistance to the most impoverished but to support, without taking control over it, a movement for the rehabilitation of persons and communities.

What must be understood, as the recent *Report of the World Commission on Culture and Development* clearly demonstrates, is that development is based to a large extent on cultural rights. The ideals of UNESCO are in keeping with this task, provided that care is taken to give priority to the poorest people of all of the Organization's programmes, primarily for ethical reasons but also because such a priority follows on from a proper understanding of the development process.

Notes

1 See Imbert (1989, para.16).
2 'This failure leads to the treatment of homelessness as a kind of deviancy, something that happens as a result of individuals violating or straying from accepted social norms. Thus, instead of homelessness being seen as the result of a social process which involves a deep sense of alienation that is *often accompanied by* such symptoms as psychiatric problems and undue reliance on drugs and alcohol, such symptoms are viewed as the *causes* of homelessness' (CDPS, 1993, p.44).
3 See (Balibar, 1992, p.201).
4 See (Katz, 1993).
5 'The fact that persons living in extreme poverty do not appear in the statistics is not attributable solely to technical difficulties; it reflects, above all, the lack of interest and consideration from which they suffer, as a result of which they do not yet enjoy the fundamental right to be included correctly in censuses' (Despouy, 1995, para. 30). The analysis is taken further in paragraphs 63 to 70 of the Final Report (1996). 'Various sources estimate the number of persons living in poverty at more than one billion and, according to the Secretariat's Department of Economic and Social Development, of those persons the proportion living in extreme poverty amounts to about 60 per cent, or 20 per cent of the world population according to the Commission on Science and Technology for Development' (Despouy, 1995, para.24). (See also document E/CN.16/1995/2.)
6 Marc-Henri Soulet, 'Rapport de synthèse', in Caillaux and Join-Lambert *et al.* (1991, pp.252–3).
7 The special rapporteur refers to General Assembly resolutions 46/121 of 17 December 1991, 47/134 of 18 December 1992 and 49/179 of 23 December 1994, and to WHO's *World Health Report 1995*.
8 Declaration of Copenhagen, para. 16(g).
9 'Do not the daily lives of children in the Fourth World force us to ask ourselves this question, since our attitudes and our responses can sometimes give the impression that, for us, if we were pushed, such children should not come into the world?' (Wrésinski, 1989, p.231).
10 See Fierens (1992, p.3).
11 In stating this, we follow the recommendations of the special rapporteur, referring to the Declaration and Programme of Action of the Social Summit of Copenhagen: 'All studies concerning poverty distinguish an extreme category within poverty' (Despouy, 1995, para.22).
12 Cf. Decision of the French Economic and Social Council in its report, *Grande pauvreté et précarité économique et sociale* of 11 February 1987 (quoted in Wrésinski, 1989, p.226): 'Situations of great poverty are produced by a spiral of different kinds of insecurity which affect various facets of daily life, persist and jeopardize the chances of reassuming responsibilities and regaining rights

independently in the foreseeable future.' Part of this definition is borrowed and refined in Annex III to the Final Report (Despouy, 1996).

13 See Balibar (1992, pp.203–4).

14 See Wrésinski (1989, p.222). The list of grievances drawn up by ATD-Fourth World in 'Un peuple parle' expressed the indivisibility and interdependence of human rights in a way that no university research or political programme had done hitherto. 'Without education, without a roof and without resources, what good are civil and political rights? What is the point in being free to do what one does not have the means to do?'

15 See Wrésinski (1989, p.228).

16 The divisions of the subject strike the individual in their own being and in their relations with other people. J. Wrésinski (1989, p.222) thus shows how the various forms of indivisibility pertaining to the poor are linked together. He speaks of 'a conception of an indivisible human being who for that reason has indivisible responsibilities and rights. But also of a person indissociable from others, a member of an indivisible humanity in which the poorest people must be able to play their part in the common mission'. On the various forms of indivisibility in regard to object and subject, see Meyer-Bisch (1992).

17 The rapporteur proposed 'to examine, but not exhaustively' (Despouy, 1996, paras 122–74): the rights to a decent standard of living, to housing, to education, to work, to health, to protection of the family, to privacy, to recognition as a person before the law and to be registered, to life and physical integrity, to justice and to take part in political affairs and in social and cultural life.

18 In France, the Neïertz Law of 1990 brought to light this aspect of a phenomenon that had been causing havoc for some 20 years without any intervention by the public authorities.

19 The Commission and the Court considered that such access should be effective, which made it necessary to have a system of legal aid (judgments, *Airey* and *Artico*) for the disadvantaged.

20 June 1990. Report by J. Fiérens to the Commission on 'Equality and non-discrimination'. For the European Court, statement by Louis Pettiti to the seventh International Colloquy on the European Convention on Human Rights, Council of Europe, Oslo, 1990.

21 In regard to the same cases, see the report of the Commission of 14 December 1973, cited by Cohen-Jonathan (1989, p.291, para. 47).

22 Judgment of 25 April 1978, Series A, No. 26, para. 32.

23 *Mrs X ...* v. *Federal Republic of Germany*, Decision of 14 December 1977, cited by Cohen-Jonathan (1989, p.292, note 53). See Sudre (1984). The case law on freedom of expression also provides a basis for guaranteeing privacy. The press may oppose intervention by the authorities against 'privacy' and against the forms of scorn that stigmatize the poor, marginals and the excluded.

24 Judgment of 29 April 1976, Series A, No. 25, para. 163.

25 'The award of social security benefits or non-contributory social assistance is more often than not conditional on inquiries concerning the composition of the household and means tests. These inquiries are additional to those carried out, where appropriate, in the context of child welfare schemes or criminal prosecutions.' Poor people are more likely to be put on file than other citizens.

26 Cf. Report by N. Valticos to the Seventh International Colloquy of the Council of Europe, Oslo, 1990, p.5; also report by ATD-Fourth World to the Seventh International Colloquy of the Council of Europe, Oslo, 1990; report by J. Wrésinski to the Economic and Social Council, 1987, JO 22 February 1987.

27 Article 1 on the right to work, Article 4 on the right to fair remuneration, Article 10 on the right to vocational training, Article 11 on the right to the

protection of health, Article 12 on the right to social and medical assistance, Article 14 on the right to benefit from social welfare services, and so on.

28 Mention should also be made of Article 31 on the right to housing. Cf. on this subject the paper by R. Brillat of the Council of Europe's Directorate of Human Rights, presented at a Colloquy on 'Extreme Poverty and Human Rights in Europe: defending significant causes', ATD-Fourth World, 1995, Pierrelaye.

29 United Nations (1995a, section B on Principles and goals, sub-paragraph (d)).

30 The wording used in the 'principles and goals' is extremely ambiguous: 'We acknowledge that it is the primary responsibility of States to attain these goals. We also acknowledge that these goals cannot be achieved by States alone' (para. 27). We should be delighted that, in a liberal climate, states acknowledge their responsibilities. But the list of partners given includes the international community, then intergovernmental organizations and in last place all actors of civil society; that is, the people themselves. Were the state to claim all the responsibility, it would act inadequately. It is the one with the biggest responsibility, but not the one with the most competence. It is the leading guarantor but not the leading actor.

31 'We commit ourselves to ensuring that when structural adjustment programmes are agreed to they include social development goals, in particular eradicating poverty, promoting full and productive employment, and enhancing social integration' (Commitment 8).

32 See Wrésinski (1989, p.229).

33 The World Summit 1995 on Social Development is clear: 'We affirm that, in both economic and social terms, the most productive policies and investments are those that empower people to maximize their capacities, resources and opportunities' (annex 1, para. 7). A long time before this, J. Wrésinski (1989, p.225) had made the point clearly: 'Great poverty, by causing the failure of human rights, represents an unbearable wastage of intelligence, inventiveness, hope and love. It is the wasting of an inestimable capital of men, women and children who are left on the sidelines of the law, the administration, the community and democracy itself'.

34 World Declaration on Education for All, Jomtien, Article 9 (Mobilizing resources).

35 See Ferry (1995).

36 See Wrésinski (1995, p.16).

Bibliography

Balibar, E. (1992), *Les Frontières de la démocratie*, Paris, La Découverte/essais.

Bonafe-Schmitt, J.B. (1992), *La Médiation, une justice douce*, Paris, Alternatives Sociales.

Caillaux, J.-C. and L. Join-Lambert et al. (1991), *Démocratie et pauvreté. Du quatrième ordre au quart monde*, Paris, Editions Quart Monde/Albin Michel.

CDPS – Steering Committee on Social Policy (1993), *Homelessness*, Strasbourg, Council of Europe.

Cohen-Jonathan, G. (1989), *La Convention européenne des droits de l'homme*, Paris, Economica.

Council of Europe (1992), 'Towards Justice Accessible to All: Legal Aid Machinery and Certain Local Initiatives as seen by Families Affected by Severe Poverty', Strasbourg, Council of Europe, Directorate of Human Rights. Document H(92)2.

Despouy, L. (1995), *The Realization of Economic, Social and Cultural Rights* (Second Interim Report on Human Rights and Extreme Poverty), United Nations

Economic and Social Council, document E/CN.4/Sub.2/1995/15 (original: French/English).

Despouy, L. (1996), *The Realization of Economic, Social and Cultural Rights* (Final Report on Human Rights and Extreme Poverty), United Nations Economic and Social Council, document E/CN.4/Sub.2/1996/13 (original: English/Spanish/French).

Ferry, J.M. (1995), *L'Allocation universelle. Pour un revenu de citoyenneté*, Paris, Cerf.

Fiérens, J. (1992), *Droit et pauvreté. Droits de l'homme, sécurité sociale, aide sociale*, Brussels, Bruylant.

Imbert, P.H. (1989), 'Droits des pauvres, pauvre(s) droit(s)', *Revue du droit public et de la science politique en France et à l'étranger*, **3**, 739–66.

Katz, M.B. (1993), *The Underclass Debate*, Princeton, Princeton University Press.

Labbens, J. (1965), *La Condition sous-prolétarienne, héritage du passé*, Paris, Editions Science et Service.

Meyer-Bisch, P. (1992), *Le Corps des droits de l'homme. L'indivisibilité comme principe d'interprétation et de mise en œuvre des droits de l'homme*, Fribourg, Editions universitaires.

Meyer-Bisch, P. (ed.) (1995), *Culture of Democracy: A Challenge for Schools*, Paris, UNESCO.

Oyen, E. (ed.) (1996), *Poverty. A Global Review. Handbook on International Poverty Research*, Oslo/Paris, Scandinavian University Press/UNESCO.

Pettiti, L.-E. (1991), Pauvreté et Convention européenne des droits de l'homme, *Droit social*.

Six, J.-F. (1990), *Le Temps des médiateurs*, Paris, Le Seuil.

Sudre, M. (1984), *Notion de peines et traitements inhumains dans la jurisprudence européenne en droits de l'homme*, Paris, R.G.D.I.P.

United Nations (1995a), *Report of the World Summit for Social Development* (Copenhagen, 6–12 March 1995), document A/CONF.166/9 (preliminary version of the report dated 19 April 1995; original: English/French/Spanish).

United Nations (1995b), *Report of the Seminar on Extreme Poverty and the Denial of Human Rights* (Commission on Human Rights, 51st session, document E/CN.4/1995/101; original: English/French/Spanish).

Vandamme, F. (1995), 'La Charte européenne et la lutte contre la pauvreté', *Droit en Quart Monde*, **8**, October.

Vos Van Steenwijk, A. de (1977), *Le Quart Monde, pierre de touche de la démocratie européenne*, Paris, Editions Science et Service.

World Health Organization (1995), *World Health Report 1995*, Geneva, WHO.

Wrésinski, J. (1989), 'Les plus pauvres, révélateurs de l'indivisibilité des droits de l'homme', *Les Droits de l'homme en question*, Livre blanc de la Commission nationale consultative des droits de l'homme, Paris, La Documentation française.

Wrésinski, J. (1995), 'Quart Monde et culture', *Se relier: une culture en ouvrage. Quart Monde*, **156**, December, 8–16; reprinted from the volume *Culture et pauvretés*, Paris, La Documentation française, 1988.

7 Discrimination, Xenophobia and Racism

RÜDIGER WOLFRUM

Introduction

Racism, xenophobia and discrimination are historically recognized phenomena of human behaviour. They are of an almost universal nature and have emerged in widely diverse places ranging from Asia to Africa and from Europe to the Americas, and at many times throughout recorded history. Early patterns of prejudice based upon colour or origin reveal that racially or xenophobically motivated discrimination existed long before the emergence of modern racism. Early documentation exists in that regard. For example, King Maximilian I, designated Emperor of the Holy Roman Empire, found it necessary to lay down in his order for the conduct of the *Reichstag* (Imperial Diet) of 1495 in Worms that any mistreatment of Jews was prohibited, and foreigners, in spite of their different appearance and customs, were to be treated with tolerance and respect. Grotius[1] and Pufendorf[2] argued against racism and xenophobia. In the eighteenth century, Blackstone summarized the state of international law and common law concerning foreigners: 'great tenderness is shown by our laws [...] with regard to the admission of strangers who come spontaneously. For so long as a nation continues at peace with ours, and they themselves behave peacefully, they are under the King's protection'.[3]

To be able to counter racism and xenophobia effectively, with a view to their abolition, it is necessary to fathom the historical factors and processes which have contributed to the emergence of racist or xenophobic ideas, policies or practices. Reference in this respect has often been made to events which are indicative of the existence of racist policies or attitudes such as slavery and the slave trade,[4] economic exploitation, white settlement, colonial conquest, imperialism, genocide practices against populations because of their religion or ethnic origin, economic-motivated migration and religious conflicts. However, it is necessary to look into the causes or motivations which lead to racism or xenophobia. These may be, for example, economic[5] or political factors,[6] the fear that one's (presumed) cultural identity has been endangered[7] by the immigration[8] of considerable numbers of aliens, the rejection of everyone who is allegedly not identical and with whom communication seems to be more difficult. The latter motivation is very often at the root of xenophobic tendencies. In this context, Article 1 of the 1966 Declaration on the Principles of International Cultural Co-operation should be mentioned. It proclaims that each culture has a dignity and value which must be respected and preserved. It further stresses that all peoples have the right and the duty to develop their culture and that, in their rich variety and diversity and in the reciprocal influences they exert on one another, all cultures form part of the common heritage of all mankind.[9]

The first step for racist or xenophobic attitudes may be the singling out of a given group of a population or of its members as being different. Such identification may be initiated by the majority – or even the minority – of a given population or the members of the respective group themselves.[10] This process as such cannot yet be regarded as being negative as long as it does not lead to racist or xenophobic attitudes. If the process is upheld by the members of a given group themselves, such a process may even be vital for the self-identification of such a group.[11]

Motivations or assumptions which are to be qualified as 'racist' have been identified in the Declaration on Race and Racial Prejudice adopted by the General Conference of UNESCO at its 20th session on 27 November 1978.[12] Its Article 2 reads:

(1)   Any theory which involves the claim that racial or ethnic groups are inherently superior or inferior, thus implying that some would be entitled to dominate or eliminate others, presumed to be inferior, or which bases value judgements on racial differentiation, has not scientific foundation and is contrary to the moral and ethical principles of humanity.
(2)   Racism includes racist ideologies, prejudged attitudes, discriminatory behaviour, structural arrangements and institutionalized practices resulting in racial inequality as well as fallacious notions that discriminatory relations between groups are morally and scientifically justifiable [...]

In fact, racism, racial discrimination and xenophobia deny or at least do not respect the fact that all human beings, although they may be different in appearance, language, life style or in religious belief, may have undergone a particular historical development or may appear different for other reasons, and belong to a single species and that aspects such as appearance, language, origin and so on cannot justify any discriminatory treatment, be it intended or *de facto*.

The present legal order of most states expressly recognizes that individuals are entitled to equality of treatment before the law.[13] Not all of them, however, state specifically that no distinction, restriction, exclusion or preference may be based on race, colour, ethnic origin, language, religion and so on. National legislation distinguishes in most states between citizens and non-citizens. In most states, the latter are excluded from the enjoyment of political rights, such as the right to participate in elections and to stand for election. As far as civil, economic, social and cultural rights are concerned, attempts have been made at the international level to define approximately the status of citizens and non-citizens.[14] However, recognizing in the legal order the equality of human beings does not necessarily guarantee the equal treatment of everyone and the non-existence of discrimination. For that reason, many states have established specific institutions for the enforcement of such principles and/or for the promotion of racial tolerance. Such efforts deserve further international endorsement.

All national policies designed to abolish racial discrimination are to a high degree influenced by or even based upon instruments and policies adopted at the international level. Only three years after the creation of the United Nations, the General Assembly adopted the Universal Declaration of Human Rights,[15] Article 1 of which states that 'all human beings are born equal in dignity and rights'. It is further stated in Article 2 that everyone is entitled to the rights enumerated in the Universal Declaration 'without discrimination of any kind, such as race, colour, sex, language, religion, political or other opinion, national or social origin, property, birth or other status'. Several international conventions further elaborate upon and implement the principles enshrined in the Universal Declaration: for example, the International Convention on the Elimination of All Forms of Racial Discrimination,[16] the UNESCO Convention against Discrimination in Education[17] and the International Labour Organization (ILO) Convention (No. 111) Concerning Discrimination in Respect of Employment and Occupation.[18]

In spite of the attempts which have been made to abolish policies and practices reflecting xenophobia and racist motivations and to counter theories endorsing these practices, such policies and practices are still in existence or even gaining ground, or taking new forms, or both. A serious new form of racism is so-called 'ethnic cleansing'.

Because manifestations of racism and xenophobia are again gaining ground, the international community has renewed its efforts to combat racism, racial discrimination, xenophobia and related forms of intolerance. The World Conference on Human Rights (Vienna, 1993) called for the elimination of racism and racial discrimination as a primary objective for the international community.[19] The General Assembly of the United Nations proclaimed the Third Decade to Combat Racism and Racial Discrimination from 1993 to 2003,[20] and has adopted a programme to achieve measurable results in reducing and eliminating discrimination through specific national and international action.[21] The UN Commission on Human Rights decided to appoint for a three-year period a special rapporteur on contemporary forms of racism, racial discrimination and xenophobia and related intolerance.[22] Subsequently, the Commission made the mandate of the special rapporteur more explicit by requesting him to examine incidents of contemporary forms of racism, racial discrimination, any form of discrimination against Blacks, Arabs and Muslims, xenophobia, negrophobia, anti-Semitism and related intolerance.[23] The reason for this action was the 'growing magnitude of the phenomena of racism, racial discrimination, xenophobia and related intolerance in segments of many societies and their consequences for migrant workers'. Finally, the UN Sub-Commission on Prevention of Discrimination and Protection of Minorities has suggested that a world conference against racism, racial and ethnic discrimination, xenophobia and other contemporary forms of intolerance be convened.[24]

Efforts Undertaken at the International Level to Combat Racial Discrimination and Xenophobia

Overview

Although the Charter of the United Nations does not contain a catalogue on human rights and fundamental freedoms, and instead entrusts the General Assembly with the task of promoting the development of respective instruments, it already formulates the rule of non-discrimination as a directly binding principle.[25] This indicates that the United Nations was established to build a new international legal order based, not only on the sovereign equality of every state, large or small, but also on the equality and dignity of every human being. Thus the elimination of racial discrimination has become the common concern of humankind as a whole.[26]

The prohibition of racial discrimination as enshrined in the Charter of the United Nations constitutes a directly applicable norm which does not require further implementation. In its Advisory Opinion on the Legal Consequences for States of the Continued Presence of South Africa in Namibia (South West Africa),[27] the International Court of Justice recognized the direct applicability of that prohibition. Its violation constituted a flagrant violation of the principles and purposes of the Charter.[28] In prohibiting discrimination, the Charter expressly mentions only four criteria which must not be used as an excuse for different treatment, that is race, sex, language and religion.[29] These criteria were considerably enlarged by the Universal Declaration on Human Rights in 1948, which adds 'colour, political or other opinions, national or social origin, property, birth or other status' to the catalogue. The two International Covenants on Human Rights of 1966,[30] as well as several other regional human rights instruments, have copied this catalogue verbatim. The African Charter on Human and Peoples' Rights, for example, prohibits mass expulsions aimed at national, racial, ethnic or religious groups.

The United Nations as well as other international organizations have adopted numerous instruments to combat racial discrimination, xenophobia or particular aspects thereof. Such instruments either prohibit racist activities or xenophobia undertaken by states or individuals in general or in such fields as education or employment, or strive for the protection of certain groups. In any event, all international agreements which aim at abolishing racial discrimination in any form whatsoever oblige States Parties to take the required action. Thus the implementation of the international prohibition of racial discrimination is an obligation of states; the performance of such an obligation, however, is under international monitoring and control.

One of the first instruments of protection against the most serious effect of racist policies was the Convention on the Prevention and Punishment of the Crime of Genocide.[31] This Convention attempts to protect the basic right of any group, namely its right to existence. It defines as a crime under international law any act aimed at destroying a national, ethnic, racial or religious group as such.[32] The International Convention on the Suppression and Punishment of the Crime of Apartheid[33] followed an identical approach, since it declared that apartheid is a crime against humanity and that inhuman acts resulting from the policies and practices of apartheid, and similar policies and practices of racial segregation and discrimination, were crimes violating the principles of international law.[34]

Among instruments dealing with the protection of particularly disadvantaged groups are the two Conventions of the ILO concerning Indigenous and Tribal Populations or Peoples. Both include provisions recognizing the rights of indigenous populations to the preservation of their institutions and traditions, as well as their languages and land rights. The rights and interests of indigenous people have, not so far, played a dominant role in the programmes of the United Nations to abolish racial discrimination, although the efforts in that respect are increasing.[35] Furthermore, the International Convention against Apartheid in Sports[36] fell into this category. Several instruments exist for the protection of migrant workers, which is another vulnerable group requiring protection against xenophobia-motivated discrimination. They are the ILO Migration for Employment Convention (No. 97) of 1949, the ILO Convention (No. 143) concerning Migrations in Abusive Conditions and the Promotion of Equality of Opportunity and Treatment of Migrant Workers of 1975,[37] and the UN International Convention on the Protection of the Rights of All Migrant Workers and Members of their Families of 1990.[38] These conventions attempt to protect migrant workers in regard to employment and to labour conditions. The UN Convention is more far-reaching, since it attempts to protect migrant workers and their families in the enjoyment of human rights without discrimination. According to its Article 7, States Parties undertake to respect and to ensure to all migrant workers and members of their families, within their territory or jurisdiction, the rights provided for in the Convention without distinction of any kind, for example as to sex, race, colour, language, religion or conviction, or national, ethnic or social origin.

The ILO Convention (No. 111) Concerning Discrimination in Respect of Employment and Occupation[39] and the UNESCO Convention against Discrimination in Education[40] attempt to protect against discrimination in specific fields where members of vulnerable groups frequently face discrimination and need particular protection.

The most general approach concerning the abolition of racial discrimination has been taken by the International Covenant on Civil and Political Rights as well as the International Covenant on Economic, Social and Cultural Rights and, in particular, the International Convention on the Elimination of All Forms of Racial Discrimination.[41]

The International Convention on the Elimination of All Forms of Racial Discrimination

The elaboration of the Convention was preceded by resolutions of the General Assembly of the United Nations as well as of other UN bodies. With Resolution 1510 (XV) of 12 December 1960, the General Assembly condemned all manifestations and practices of racial, religious and national hatred in the political, economic, social, educational and cultural spheres of life of society as violations of the UN Charter and the Universal Declaration of Human Rights. Similar resolutions were adopted by the Sub-Commission on Prevention of Discrimination and Protection of Minorities, the Commission on Human Rights and the Economic and Social Council.[42] Several studies were undertaken on this issue in order to elaborate and to define the basis of a solution. These actions were mainly the consequence of anti-Semitic incidents in Europe in the 1960s.

The action within the United Nations finally culminated in the adoption of the Declaration on the Elimination of All Forms of Racial Discrimination.[43] The Declaration reflected the results of previous studies and reiterated the legal foundation of the prohibition of racial discrimination. Paragraph 5 of the Preamble, for example, emphasizes that 'any doctrine of racial differentiation or superiority is false, morally condemnable, socially unjust and dangerous, and that there is no justification for racial discrimination either in theory or practice'. The Declaration further refers to the UN Charter as the foundation for the prohibition of racial discrimination. The main feature of the Convention already found its expression in the Declaration, namely that States Parties should not only abstain from any discriminatory act but are under an obligation to prevent them from occurring in public and private life. The Declaration, however, did not yet disclose how the compliance of the States Parties with these obligations was to be controlled.

The International Convention on the Elimination of All Forms of Racial Discrimination describes 'racial discrimination' as

> any distinction, exclusion, restriction or reference based on race, colour, descent, or national or ethnic origin which has the purpose or effect of nullifying or impairing the recognition, enjoyment or exercise on an equal footing of human rights and fundamental freedoms in the political, economic, social, cultural or any other field of public life.[44]

The definition combines several criteria: 'race and colour' are physical criteria, 'descent' denotes the social origin, and 'national or ethnic origin' has certain linguistic, cultural or historic connotations.[45] The Committee on the Elimination of Racial Discrimination (CERD) in this context has also referred to religious differences, pointing out that religion may, in a historical development, serve as one integration factor for the formation and preservation of particular population entities.[46] What is important in this definition is the fact that it does not attempt to define race according to physical elements alone, but includes subjective and social elements as well. This is reflected in the practice of CERD,[47] whereas States Parties occasionally understand it as referring to physical differences only.[48]

The Convention identifies four actions or omissions as being potentially discriminatory, namely distinction, exclusion, restriction and preference. This is the case, however, only if such action or omission is racially motivated, if it has racial purpose or has such an effect, and if it impairs the recognition, enjoyment or exercise of human rights and freedoms as referred to in Article 5 of the Convention.[49] What is most important is that the Convention prohibits not only actions or omissions undertaken with a racial motivation or which serve a corresponding purpose, but also those which have such an effect.

CERD has stressed this point in a General Recommendation.[50] As far as preferential treatment is concerned, such treatment may be permitted, albeit for a limited period, if undertaken solely for the purpose of 'securing adequate advancement of certain racial or ethnic groups or individuals requiring such protection as may be necessary in order to ensure such groups or individuals equal enjoyment or exercise of human rights and fundamental freedoms'.[51] This provision is supplemented by Article 2, paragraph 2, of the Convention according to which States Parties are under an obligation to take special and concrete measures to ensure the adequate development and protection of certain racial groups in social, economic, cultural and other fields. Both provisions are designed to ensure that particular racial groups enjoy the same social, economic and other standards enjoyed by the rest of the population of a given State Party.

This is an objective not yet achieved in many countries, even though it is of a limited nature: it does not oblige States Parties to undertake positive measures to ensure the preservation of the cultural identity of such groups, as is required – to a moderate extent – under Article 27 of the International Covenant on Civil and Political Rights.[52] In that respect, the UNESCO Convention against Discrimination in Education and, in particular, the ILO Convention (No. 169) Concerning Indigenous and Tribal Peoples in Independent Countries are more far-reaching.

Although the definition is a broad one, it is not open-ended. As specified in Article 1, paragraph 2, the Convention does not apply to distinctions, exclusions, restrictions or preferences made between citizens and non-citizens; nor, by virtue of Article 1, paragraph 3, does it affect legal provisions concerning nationality, citizenship or naturalization as long as such provisions do not discriminate against any particular nationality.[53] In assessing these provisions, account has to be taken of the time when the Convention was drafted. Since then efforts have been made at the international level to approximate the status of foreigners to the one of citizens as far as economic, social, cultural and civil rights are concerned.[54] The Committee has dealt with this issue in its General Recommendation XX (48) of 8 March 1996. Its relevant provision (paragraph 2) reads:

> Whenever a State imposes a restriction upon one of the rights listed in article 5 of the Convention which applies ostensibly to all within its jurisdiction, it must ensure that neither in purpose nor effect is the restriction incompatible with article 1 of the Convention as an integral part of international human rights standards. To ascertain whether

this is the case, the Committee is obliged to inquire further to make sure that any such restriction does not entail racial discrimination.

The issue has frequently been highlighted by the General Assembly of the United Nations.[55]

The Convention is designed to abolish racial discrimination in all fields of public life. The meaning of this reference was discussed controversially in the Committee. Although designed to remove from the scope of the Convention discrimination within private relations, the Committee, rightly, proceeded from a limiting interpretation of that clause. According to it, States Parties cannot escape the prohibition of Article 1, paragraph 1, of the Convention by privatizing issues (such as schools) which have to be, by their very nature, open to the public.[56] This is endorsed by the wording of Article 5(f) of the Convention, which indicates that the clause is used in a broader meaning, including the access to places, institutions or events which under normal circumstances are open for everyone. In further specifying this overall objective, Article 2 provides generally that States Parties condemn racial discrimination and are under an obligation to pursue a policy of eliminating racial discrimination and to promote understanding among all races. The actions to be taken are defined in detail in Articles 2 and 5 of the Convention.

The relationship between these two articles is not quite clear. Article 2 and the opening paragraph of Article 5 establish the fundamental obligation of States Parties, Article 2 further describes the actions to be or not to be taken by States Parties. Finally, Article 5 of the Convention refers to the rights whose enjoyment must not be endangered or curtailed through racial discrimination.[57] However, States Parties' obligations go further than protecting the rights referred to under Article 5 against racial discrimination. States Parties are under an obligation to abolish the roots of racial discrimination undertaken by state agents, private persons or organizations. In that respect, the approach taken by the Convention is more comprehensive than that of other international instruments protecting the enjoyment of certain rights against racial discrimination. Thus the General Assembly for example:

1. Declares once again that all forms of racism and racial discrimination, whether in their institutionalized form or resulting from official doctrines of racial superiority or exclusivity, such as ethnic cleansing, are among the most serious violations of human rights in the contemporary world and must be combated by all available means ...
4. Urges all Governments to take all necessary measures to combat new forms of racism, in particular by adapting constantly the means provided to combat them, especially in the legislative, administrative, educational and information fields.[58]

The comprehensive nature of the approach to be undertaken under the Convention becomes even clearer in resolutions of the Commission on Human Rights which, in its resolution 1997/73, stated:

> Conscious of the fundamental difference between, on the one hand, racism and racial discrimination as an institutionalized governmental policy or resulting from official doctrines of racial superiority or exclusivity and, on the other hand, other manifestations of racism, racial discrimination, xenophobia and related intolerance taking place in segments of many societies and perpetrated by individuals or groups, some of which are directed against migrant workers and their families ...[59]

The Convention establishes negative as well as positive obligations[60] of States Parties. According to Article 2, paragraph 1(a) of the Convention, States Parties undertake to engage in no act or practice contrary to the general obligation of the Convention. This obligation is supplemented by the one in Article 5. Another negative obligation is contained in Article 2, paragraph 1(b), according to which States Parties undertake not to support racial protagonists or organizations. These negative obligations are addressed against the States Parties and cover all activities in territories under their jurisdiction. All state agents at the federal, national, state or local levels have to act in conformity with this obligation. This includes state agents acting in autonomous entities or entities which are state-controlled. Finally, States Parties are under an obligation not to sponsor, defend or support racial discrimination. Whereas the two previous obligations prohibit discriminatory actions undertaken by a state, the latter refers to a duty of the state to lend its support to private persons or organizations. This obligation is a supplement to the former, although supporting discriminatory acts or private persons or organizations already amounts to discriminatory behaviour of the state in question.

The Convention establishes a variety of positive State Party obligations. Among the most far-reaching is the obligation, in accordance with Article 2, paragraph 1(c), to review governmental, national and local policies as well as the whole legal order, with a view to amending, nullifying or rescinding those policies or laws having the effect of creating or perpetuating racial discrimination. As indicated earlier, States Parties have, not only abolished discriminatory provisions but have incorporated into the legal system guarantees for the protection of equality before the law or even provisions explicitly prohibiting racial discrimination. This does not yet constitute a guarantee that racial discrimination has been abolished effectively – practices may still exist which, although not necessarily racially motivated, may result in *de facto* racial discrimination or may perpetuate the marginalization of a certain part of the population. For example, literacy tests as a precondition for the participation in elections or for certain licences will, in practice, affect an already disadvantaged group of the population more significantly than others.

To verify whether States Parties have lived up to this obligation, it is necessary to establish – as is done by the CERD – whether all groups in a given state have an equal opportunity to participate in the economic, social and cultural advantages or if some groups are left in a marginalized position. This, however, requires a thorough analysis of the living conditions in a given state, rather than only an assessment of its legal order and, in particular, its Constitution. Indications of a situation where racially discriminatory practices may still exist are, amongst others, differences in life expectancy, a disproportionately high percentage of unemployment, delinquency and illiteracy, unequal access to higher education and inferior infrastructure of regions predominantly inhabited by a particular ethnic group.[61]

Article 3 of the Convention, in particular, addresses racial segregation and apartheid. States are under an obligation to prevent, prohibit and eradicate all practices of this nature in territories under their jurisdiction. Although apartheid may be a phenomenon of the past, segregation – undertaken by private persons or private institutions – is not. States Parties have to become increasingly alert to new forms of ghetto building which may lead to ethnic tensions or xenophobia.[62]

The obligations of States Parties mentioned so far are supplemented by Article 6 of the Convention. Accordingly, States Parties have to provide for effective remedies against any act of racial discrimination undertaken by state agents, private persons or organizations. They also have to provide victims of racial discrimination with the opportunity of seeking just and adequate compensation.

Further, according to Article 2, paragraph 1(d), States Parties are under an obligation to prohibit and to bring to an end, by all means, including legislation as required by circumstances, racial discrimination by any person, group or organization. This obligation is closely connected to the one of Article 4 which calls for the penalization of the dissemination of ideas based on racial superiority or hatred or by racist organizations. Article 2, paragraph 1(d) and Article 4 work on different levels, thus reflecting the critical nature of the activity involved. However, in both cases, States Parties are under an obligation to act and take preventive action. It cannot be argued that no racial discrimination exists and that therefore no legal or other measures are required.

To comply with Article 2, paragraph 1(d), States Parties have to take measures to ensure that nobody is discriminated against by private persons or organizations to the extent that he or she may be jeopardized in the enjoyment of rights as referred to in Article 5, in particular sub-paragraph (f).[63] Article 4 imposes upon States Parties an obligation to penalize the dissemination of ideas based on racial superiority or hatred, incitement to racial discrimination, as well as acts of violence or incitement to such acts. Racist organizations or respective propaganda activities must be declared illegal and the participation in such organizations or activities penalized. Such penalization necessarily limits the freedom of expression as well as the freedom of association. The Convention recognizes this by indicating that such penalization is to be undertaken 'with due regard to the principles embodied in the Universal Declaration of Human Rights'.[64] This is to be understood as a reference to the limitation clauses of Articles 29 and 30 of the Universal Declaration of Human Rights which, in the case where human rights guarantees collide, provide for a mutual accommodation.

In practice, many States Parties are reluctant to implement fully Article 4 of the Convention. This is to be regretted. The fight against racist theories or organizations based thereupon – as also mentioned in the UNESCO Declaration on Race and Racial Prejudice – is one of the more promising means of reaching the roots of racism and racial discrimination.[65]

Finally, each State Party is obliged to encourage integrationist and multiracial organizations and movements (Article 2, paragraph 1(d)) and to undertake measures in the field of teaching and education with a view to combating prejudices which lead to racial discrimination. Although this preventive approach is promising, States Parties so far have given no indication that these obligations have been implemented on a systematic basis.

Conclusion

International efforts against racism, racial discrimination, xenophobia and other related forms of intolerance have so far not been successful. Although the struggle against apartheid has led to a positive result, new forms of racism, racial discrimination and ethnic prejudice or prosecution have emerged. The international bodies engaged in the struggle against all these forms of intolerance, and violence based thereon, in particular the CERD, should nevertheless continue and even increase their efforts.

Only through these efforts may a public awareness be created, with the conviction within the world community that the above-mentioned forms of intolerance and violence are intolerable violations of human dignity and constitute an international crime. Renewed efforts should be undertaken, in particular by UNESCO, to fight against racism as well as racial discrimination, xenophobia and other prejudices at the level of education and teaching.

Notes

1   *De iure belle ac pacis,* 1720, Lib. II, Cap. 5, no. XXIV.2.
2   *De iure naturae et gentium,* Vol. I, reprint 1934, p.247.
3   *Commentaries on the Law of England,* 1765, Vol. I, p.261.
4   See *Human Rights: Political, Historical, Economic, Social and Cultural Factors Contributing to Racism, Racial Discrimination and Apartheid,* UN Centre for Human Rights, Geneva, 1991, p. 6. It has been argued that slavery and racism seemed to become equally cause and effect. It was in the search for the justification of slavery that the proponents developed the idea of race and the supposed superiority of one race over another; see also *Le Racisme devant la science,* Paris, UNESCO, 1973; Taguieff (1989, p.357).
5   The view has been expressed that social and economic well-being and tolerance of other people or of people regarded as different were interdependent (*Human Rights,* op. cit., note 4), p.8.
6   Reference was made in this regard to nationalism, which may be combined with a superiority complex or a policy striving for domination; see *Human Rights* (op. cit., note 4), p.6. In this respect the elaboration and teaching of racist theories may have an initiating or aggravating effect, or both. See Banton (1987).
7   According to Taguieff (op. cit., note 4), p.362, neoracism no longer presupposes dogmatism and plain inequality in the relation between races, but corresponds to 'racist theorizing based on the postulate of the irreducibility, incompatibility or incommunicability, or total separation of cultures, mental structures, morals or community traditions'. This is not quite correct. Even now theories that posit a biological (or genetic) justification for racial inequality remain in vogue; see Herrnstein and Murray (1994) for an example.
8   One has to differentiate between different forms of immigrants – refugees in the meaning of Article 1 of the Convention relating to the Status of Refugees, 1950, and Article I of the Protocol relating to the Status of Refugees, 1966 – people forced to leave their country of origin for different reasons, migrant workers and students as well as others leaving their country of origin temporarily for reasons of training and education. The failure of national law to distinguish appropriately between these groups may also lead to racist feelings or xenophobia.
9   Text in *Human Rights: A Compilation of International Instruments,* Geneva, United Nations, 1994, Vol. I, p.595.
10 This has been emphasized by Partsch (1995, p.1005); according to Banton (1996, p.201), separation may become a cause of racial disadvantage.
11 The Declaration on Race and Racial Prejudice, adopted by the General Conference of UNESCO on 27 November 1978 (see *Human Rights: A Compilation of International Instruments,* p.132, op. cit., note 9), emphasizes the need to protect the identity and the full development of groups. The Declaration affirms the right to be different and the right to cultural identity; it prohibits forced assimilation and stresses the need of affirmative action for disadvantaged or discriminated groups. See also Lerner (1991, pp.16ff).
12 Declaration on Race and Racial Prejudice: see note 11; see also *Le Racisme devant la science* (op. cit., note 4).
13 See *Human Rights: Second Decade to Combat Racism and Racial Discrimination, Global Compilation of National Legislation Against Racial Discrimination,* New York, United Nations, 1991, p.7; European Parliament (1991).
14 See the Declaration on the Human Rights of Individuals Who Are Not Nationals of the Country in Which They Live, General Assembly res. 40/144, 13 December 1985.

15   General Assembly res. 217 A (III), 10 December 1948.
16   Text in *Human Rights: A Compilation* (op. cit., note 9), p.66.
17   Ibid., p.101.
18   Ibid., p.96.
19   A/Conf. 157/24 (Part I), ch. III.
20   A/res. 48/91 20 December 1993.
21   General Assembly res. 49/146, 7 February 1995, Annex. The proclamation of
     the First Decade for Action to Combat Racism and Racial Discrimination coin-
     cided with the twenty-fifth anniversary (1973) of the Universal Declaration on
     Human Rights (General Assembly res. 2919 (XVII) of 15 November 1972). In
     launching the First Decade, the General Assembly defined the goals concern-
     ing the promotion of human rights and fundamental freedoms for all, without
     distinction of any kind on grounds of race, colour, descent or national or ethnic
     origin, especially by eradication of racial prejudice, racism and racial discrimi-
     nation. In resolution 38/14, the General Assembly approved the Programme of
     Action for the Second Decade.
22   Res. 1993/20, 2 March 1993.
23   Commission on Human Rights, res. 1994/64, 9 March 1994; see also report of
     the special rapporteur, E/CN.4/1995/78, para. 3. In his report A/49/677 to the
     General Assembly, the special rapporteur defined the terms of his mandate as
     follows: 'Racism is a product of human history, a persistent phenomenon that
     recurs in different forms as societies develop, economically and socially and
     even scientifically and technologically, and in international relations. In its
     specific sense, racism denotes a theory, which purports to be scientific, but is in
     reality pseudo-scientific, of the immutable natural (or biological) inequality of
     human races, which leads to contempt, hatred, exclusion and persecution or
     even extermination' (pp.6, 7). Defining 'racial discrimination', the special rap-
     porteur refers to Article 1 of the International Convention on the Elimination of
     All Forms of Racial Discrimination: 'Xenophobia is defined as a rejection of
     outsiders [...]. Xenophobia is fed by such theories and movements as "national
     preference", "ethnic cleansing", by exclusions and by a desire on the part of
     communities to turn inward and reserve society's benefits in order to share
     them with people of the same culture or the same level of development' (pp. 8,
     9); 'Negrophobia is the fear and rejection of Blacks [...] The African slave trade
     and colonization have helped to forge racial stereotypes' (p.9); 'anti-Semitism
     [...] can be considered to be one of the root causes of racial and religious
     hatred' (p.10).
24   Recommendation 1994/2.
25   The International Court of Justice has stated: 'To establish [...] and to enforce
     distinctions, exclusions, restrictions and limitations exclusively based on
     grounds of race, colour, descent or national or ethnic origin which constitute a
     denial of fundamental human rights is a flagrant violation of the purposes and
     principles of the Charter (Opinion on the presence of South Africa in Namibia',
     ICJ Reports, 1971, para. 131.
26   Report of Asbjorn Eide on 'Elimination of racial discrimination: measures to
     combat racism and racial discrimination and the role of the Sub-Commission',
     UN Doc. E/CN.4/Sub.2/1989/8, p.2.
27   *ICJ Reports,* 1971, p. 16.
28   Partsch, 'Racial discrimination' (op. cit., note 10), p.1003.
29   In Article 1, para. 3; Article 13, para. 2(b); Article 55, subpara. c; and Article 76,
     subpara. c.
30   Article 2, para. 2, of the International Covenant on Economic, Social and Cul-
     tural Rights and Article 2, para. 1, of the International Covenant on Civil and

Political Rights, texts in: *Human Rights* (op. cit., note 9), pp.8 and 20, respectively.
31 *Human Rights* (op. cit., note 9), Vol. II, p.673.
32 As to the Convention, see J.L. Kunz (1949, pp.738–46); L.R. Beres (1988, pp.271–9); also M.Ch. Bassiouni, 'Introduction to the Genocide Convention', ibid., pp.281–6.
33 Text in *Human Rights* (op. cit., note 9), p.80.
34 Apartheid has been defined by the Convention as a series of acts 'committed for the purpose of establishing and maintaining domination by one racial group of persons over any other racial group of persons and systematically oppressing them' (Article II); Jost Delbrück defines apartheid as 'a special type of discrimination and separation of peoples or groups of individuals along racial lines' (Delbrück, 1992, p.192).
35 See Eide (note 26), p.64: 'The current manifestations of racial discrimination affecting indigenous peoples and their individual members is the result of a long, historical process of conquest, penetration and marginalization. A two-fold process has been at work: a gradual destruction of the material conditions necessary for indigenous peoples to continue their own form of life and to maintain their own language and culture; simultaneously, members of indigenous peoples have often been met with attitudes and behaviour by members of the dominant group of exclusion and negative distinction when they seek to participate in the social and economic activities of the dominant society.'
36 Text in *Human Rights* (op. cit., note 9), p.87.
37 Also of relevance in this respect are the ILO Recommendation concerning Migration for Employment (No. 86) and the Recommendation concerning Migrant Workers (No. 151).
38 As of 31 March 1997, this Convention had still not entered into force. Text in *Human Rights* (op. cit., note 9), p.554.
39 See note 18.
40 See note 17.
41 Text in *Human Rights* (op. cit., note 9), p.66; as to the legislative history of the Convention, see Lerner (1980, pp.1ff); Schwelb (1966, pp.996ff); Ténékidès (1980, pp.269–487); Banton (1996, pp.74ff).
42 For details, see Lerner (1991, p.46); Banton (1996, 51ff).
43 General Assembly res. 1904 (XVIII), 20 November 1963.
44 Article 1; for an interpretation of this Article, see Meron (1986, p.11).
45 See Partsch (op. cit., note 10).
46 The exclusion of religion as a distinguishing factor, referred to in the Universal Declaration, was done with a view to not involving CERD in the Israel–Arab dispute; see in this respect Schwelb (1966, p.996); Partsch (1995, p.1006); and, Lerner (1991, p.46).
47 In its General Recommendation VIII (1990), it was stated that the way in which individuals are identified as being members of a particular group should be based upon self-identification (UN Doc. HRI/GEN/Rev.1, 65); see Lerner (1980, p.25) on the legislative history of Article 1; as to the functioning of CERD in general, see Partsch (1992, pp.339–68).
48 See, for example, the report of El Salvador.
49 See Schwelb (1966, p.1001).
50 General Recommendation XIV on Article 1, para. 1, of the Convention, 1993, UN Doc. HRI/GEN/Rev.1, p.67.
51 Article 1, para. 4, of the Convention.
52 See Tomuschat (1983, pp.949–79); Wolfrum (1993, pp. 163 ff).
53 See International Convention on the Protection of the Rights of All Migrant Workers and Members of Their Families (see note 38); Declaration on the

Human Rights of Individuals Who Are Not Nationals of the Country in Which They Live, General Assembly res. 40/144 of 13 December 1985. The two International Covenants (note 30) distinguish between citizens and non-citizens only with respect to political rights (to take part in the conduct of public affairs, to vote and to be elected, to have access to public service): Article 25, International Covenant on Civil and Political Rights.

54　Most States Parties report on the situation of foreigners, and CERD deals with their treatment. This is done on the basis of the understanding that, although the Convention does not exclude distinctions between citizens and non-citizens, it prohibits at least the discriminatory treatment of foreigners compared to others.

55　See, for example, A/RES/51/81 of 12 December 1996.

56　See Banton (1996, p.195).

57　See Partsch (1979, 193–250).

58　See A/RES/49/146 of 7 February 1995.

59　Equal resolution of the General Assembly: A/RES/51/79 of 25 February 1979.

60　This classification is used by Lerner (1991, pp.50ff).

61　For further details, see Banton (1996, pp.195ff).

62　See, in particular, Banton (1996, pp.203ff).

63　The right of access to any place or service intended for use by the general public, such as transport, hotels, restaurants, cafes, theatres and parks. The scope of this provision is controversial; see Meron (1985, 283–318).

64　See Ingles (1983); Partsch (1977, pp.119–38); Partsch (1992, pp.359ff) with further references; Wolfrum (1990, pp.515–25).

65　See also Banton (1996, pp.202ff).

Bibliography

Banton, Michael (1987), *Racial Theories*, New York, Cambridge University Press.

Bassiouni, M.Ch. (1988), 'Introduction to the Genocide Convention', *International Criminal Law: Crimes*, New York, Dobbs Ferry.

Beres, L.R. (1988), 'Genocide and genocide-like crimes', in M.Ch. Bassiouni (ed.), *International Criminal Law: Crimes*, New York, Dobbs Ferry.

Delbrück, Jost (1992), 'Apartheid', in R. Bernhardt (ed.), *Encyclopedia of International Law*, Vol. I.

European Parliament (1991), *Report of the Commission of Enquiry on Racism and Xenophobia*, Brussels.

Grotius, H. de (1720), *De iure belle ac pacis*, Lib. II, Cap. 5, No. XXIV.2.

Herrnstein, Richard J. and Charles Murray (1994), *The Bell Curve*, New York, Free Press.

Human Rights: A Compilation of International Instruments, Vol. I, Geneva, United Nations, 1994.

Human Rights: Political, Historical, Economic, Social and Cultural Factors Contributing to Racism, Racial Discrimination and Apartheid, Geneva, UN Centre for Human Rights, 1991.

Human Rights: Second Decade to Combat Racism and Racial Discrimination, Global Compilation of National Legislation Against Racial Discrimination, New York, United Nations, 1991.

Kunz, J.L. (1949), 'The United Nations Convention on Genocide', *American Journal of International Law*, **43**.

Le Racisme devant la science, Paris, UNESCO, 1973.

Lerner, Natan (1980), *The UN Convention on the Elimination of All Forms of Racial Discrimination*, 2nd edn, Dordrecht, Kluwer Academic.
Lerner, Natan (1991), *Group Rights and Discrimination in International Law*, Dordrecht, Kluwer Academic.
Meron, T. (1985), 'The meaning and reach of the International Convention on the Elimination of All Forms of Racial Discrimination', *American Journal of International Law*, 79.
Meron, T. (1986), *Human Rights Law-Making in the United Nations*, Oxford, Oxford University Press.
Partsch, Karl Josef (1977), 'Die Strafbarkeit der Rassendiskriminierung nach dem Internationalen Abkommen und die Verwirklichung der Verpflichtung in internationalen Strafrechtsordnungen', *German Yearbook of International Law*, 20.
Partsch, Karl Josef (1979), 'Elimination of racial discrimination in the enjoyment of civil and political rights', *Texas International Law Journal*, 14.
Partsch, Karl Josef (1992), 'The Committee on the Elimination of Racial Discrimination', in P. Alston (ed.), *The United Nations and Human Rights: A Critical Appraisal*, Oxford, Oxford University Press.
Partsch, Karl Josef (1995), 'Racial discrimination', in R. Wolfrum (ed.), *United Nations: Law, Policies and Practice*, Dordrecht, Martinus Nijhoff.
Schwelb, Egon (1966), 'The International Convention on the Elimination of All Forms of Racial Discrimination', *International Comparative Law Quarterly*, 15.
Taguieff, Pierre-André (1989), 'L'évolution contemporaine de l'idéologie raciste: de l'inégalité biologique à l'absolutisation de la différence culturelle', *Rapport de la Commission nationale consultative des droits de l'homme*.
Ténékidès, G. (1980), 'L'action des Nations Unies contre la discrimination raciale', *Recueil de Cours*, Academy of International Law, Dordrecht/Boston/London, Martinus Nijhoff, 168.
Tomuschat, Christian (1983), 'Protection of Minorities under Article 27 of the International Covenant on Civil and Political Rights', Festschrift für Hermann Mosler, Berlin.
Wolfrum, Rüdiger (1990), 'Das Verbot der Rassendiskriminierung im Spannungsfeld zwischen dem Schutz individueller Freiheitsrechte und der Verpflichtung des einzelnen im Allgemeininteresse', *Festschrift für Peter Schneider*, Frankfurt.
Wolfrum, Rüdiger (1993), 'The emergence of "new minorities" as a result of migration', in C. Brölman, R. Lefeber and M. Zieck (eds), *Peoples and Minorities in International Law*, Dordrecht, Martinus Nijhoff.

8 Human Rights and Tolerance

CLAUDIO ZANGHI

The Reawakening of Manifestations of Intolerance

In the last decade, and particularly in recent years, we have witnessed an increasing development of manifestations of intolerance on different levels. In Europe, we find that, added to the existing difficulties connected with immigration in the 1960s and afterwards, the ethnic incompatibilities which for decades had been controlled by a rigid communist regime have now exploded with particular force following the collapse of the USSR and of the totalitarian regimes of the countries of Central and Eastern Europe.

On the African continent, ethnic and tribal tensions have become more acute, leading to civil war in Somalia, Rwanda, Burundi and elsewhere, and have often culminated in acts of genocide of a particularly violent and atrocious nature. Furthermore, in many Islamic countries, not excluding other religious contexts, the expansion and the radicalization of religious integralism lead to manifestations of violent intolerance which recall episodes from the sixteenth and seventeenth centuries.

Notwithstanding the contemporaneity of the events, the causes which are at the origin of the above manifestations are certainly numerous and differ one from the other, but this is not the place or the time for in-depth sociological research which may provide an answer to the problem. The bitter realization is that, from whichever point of view reality is observed, it prompts a consideration which is also a conclusion pertinent to all of these events: there has been a new awareness within the whole of humanity of the growth of intolerance towards that which is 'different'; this is displayed in a multiplicity of attitudes on the part of individuals, of groups and of governments. Amongst these attitudes, racism, ethnocentricsm, anti-Semitism, nationalism, xenophobia, religious antagonism, sexism and so on are well known.

All this gives relevance to the need to proclaim and spread tolerance as an element of paramount importance for establishing civilization, democracy and the respect of human rights in an adequate manner. Such a need has already been felt by the United Nations which, with General Assembly resolutions 48/126 of 30 December 1993 and 49/213 of 23 December 1994, proclaimed 1995 the 'UN Year of tolerance'. The UNESCO General Conference, with resolutions 26C/5.6 of 2 November 1991 and 27C/5.14 of 15 November 1993, was the first to promote and encourage the United Nations' initiative, followed by the Council of Europe and numerous recommendations of the Parliamentary Assembly, as well as the recommendations, resolutions and declarations of the Council of Ministers. In particular, amongst these can be seen the Declaration on Intolerance of 14 May 1981 and the Declaration and Plan for Action in the Fight Against Racism, Xenophobia and Intolerance of 8–9 November 1993, which also set up a European Commission against Racism and Intolerance.

The relevance of the problem and the seriousness of its manifestations therefore justify a re-examination in an attempt to re-elaborate the concept of 'tolerance', together with its implications and its limits, not only in its historical and philosophical interpretation but also in the context of current reality. In such a perspective it also seems opportune to evaluate the relationship between tolerance and human rights in the light of international texts in force and of the initiatives undertaken and foreseen.

Historical Development of the Concept of Tolerance

From the Classical World to the Age of Enlightenment

Historically, the concept of tolerance was developed at the beginning of the modern age, but it had a few significant antecedents in the Old World from which modern authors not infrequently draw inspiration. Amongst these antecedents one should first of all highlight the critique which the sophists made against the concept of civilization and its traditional distinction between Greeks and Barbarians. Antifonte proclaimed the principle of natural equality between all men and Ippia went further by professing a cosmopolitical ideal which implied the recognition of the legitimacy of customs and beliefs for all peoples. It is significant that Ippia should have dealt in particular with studies which today would be defined as ethnographic, a topic which, to a certain extent, has resurfaced since the birth of Greek philosophical culture. Protagoras observed that what seems right and moral to one population appears unjust and immoral to another, from which are derived a variety of laws and customs and the impossibility of establishing a criterion valid for all men.

In the Roman world the persecution of religious dissenters was often politically motivated because of the connection established between the recognition of the divinity of the Emperor and that of his political authority. The dissenters often defended themselves with an argument which was to be used in the modern age to support tolerance: religious dissent does not imply either moral corruption or political antagonism; one can be the loyal subject of a political authority, even without sharing its religious ideas.

The grafting of Christian thought onto such a line of classical thought led to contradictory results because, on the one hand, Christianity confirmed and widened the concept of equality between all men as sons of the same God the Creator whilst, on the other, it rejected all religious traditions different from its own, showing in the matter (analogously to the other great monotheistic religion – Islam) a strong tendency to intolerance which not infrequently expressed itself in cruel persecutions and organized wars. It is from this intimate contrast that the modern concept of tolerance is born.

It is usual to find in Marsilio Da Padova a precursor of the political theory of tolerance. He sustained that the Holy Scripture invites one to teach, demonstrate and convince, not to force and punish because, since conscience is free, any faith violently imposed does not give benefits for spiritual salvation; this thesis had already been postulated by the first Christians and was to be taken up again with strong conviction by Spinoza.[1] The problem was systematically and extensively dealt with afterwards in literature when it developed in the form of religious tolerance.

Until the Reformation, one almost never dared to claim religious tolerance although, on the other hand, dissent never reached the proportions of the sixteenth and seventeenth centuries. The Reformation brought about a proliferation of religious confessions and created a situation in which the problem of tolerance and intolerance presented itself with great urgency as a political one. Almost every sovereign found himself having to come to terms with numerous political communities which subjected themselves to him politically but dissented on religious issues. The thesis summed up in the principle *cuius regio eius religio* revealed itself only too soon to be untenable. The persecuted communities and many independent thinkers claimed religious tolerance by using arguments which were afterwards repeatedly taken up again and are still used today in other contexts.[2]

In correlation with the religious problem, the advance of a 'humanist' culture and the diffusion of a 'humanitarian' sensibility constituted a series of factors from which emerged, during Human-

ism and the Renaissance, the first expressions of the principle of
tolerance. Significant examples are the project of Pico della Mirandola
for a universal agreement between all the main religious and philosophical beliefs; Campanella's defence of 'natural' religiousness,
common to all men regardless of supernatural revelations; the distinction after Bruno between common religious beliefs and philosophy,
with the request to recognize for the philosopher total freedom of
thought even in the theological sphere; the explicit recognition of
what was afterwards to be called the principle of tolerance by Thomas More who, in the imaginary state of Utopia, advocates that all
religions and all faiths be freely admitted.

*The Foundations of Religious Tolerance in the Writings of Seventeenth and
Eighteenth-century Philosophers*

However, the theoretician of the modern principle of tolerance is
Locke. From his early writings on tolerance (1661–2) to the *First
Letter on Tolerance* (1689), Locke formulated those criteria which still
today are considered fundamental and of current relevance in the
issue of freedom of thought and of cult. They may be summed up as
follows: speculative and religious opinions do not concern the state
and must therefore benefit from unlimited tolerance, as long as their
manifestation does not damage the economic and moral interests of
society; religious censures must not reflect in any way on civil rights;
the state is a society of men constituted to preserve and promote
common good: every issue regarding 'the soul' is outside the bounds
of its institutional duties and does not fall under its sovereignty.

The issue most thoroughly developed by Locke is, however, the
relativistic one: in the religious field, only subjective conviction is
possible, not a certainty comparable to the one obtained in the sciences. This is proved by the fact that contrasting opinions are sustained
by the same number of arguments. The truth, in the name of which
dissent is pursued, is always somebody's truth; the evidence put
forth by the claimant to prove that truth manifests itself to him
cannot but be subjective. Just as it is not possible to demonstrate the
absolute truth of one's own beliefs, so one is not authorized to consider as error opinions different from one's own.

In Bayle's more radical approach, the affirmation of the rights of
conscience leaves behind the distinction between the realm of the
state and that of individuals, because it tends to dissociate freedom
of conscience from normative references to which it could be subjected.[3] For Bayle, what is essential in tolerance is the affirmation of a
'moral' conscience separable from belief or from religious conscience;
consequently tolerance, differing from what was sustained by Locke,
must be extended to atheists as well.

The double inspiration then finds in Voltaire the clearest and most fulfilled expression of Enlightenment. From the *Treaty on Tolerance* (1783), written on the occasion of the conviction of the Protestant Jean Calais, to the various editions of the *Philosophical Dictionary*, Voltaire's work is entirely devoted to fighting fanaticism and to affirming the principles of religious freedom and political/ideological tolerance.

Thus through Spinoza, Locke, Voltaire, Hume, Rousseau and the other major figures of the School of Enlightenment, European thought found the tradition of liberal/democratic ethos taking root, its cardinal point being religious, political and cultural tolerance. It obtained, through the more thorough historical and ethnological knowledge which characterized the eighteenth century, further grounds for confirmation and it was also accepted by the Catholic Church in Leon XIII's encyclical, with many restrictions and as a lesser evil.

It is undeniable that a complete implementation of the principle of tolerance is incompatible with religious dogmatism which, professing the certainty of truth received through grace, imposes truth and falsity and the division between chosen and reprobate men, between believers and infidels. However, the most recent developments in the thought of the Catholic Church contained in the declarations of the Vatican II Council and in the encyclicals of John XXIII and Paul VI explicitly address the principle of tolerance, since in recognizing and lauding the natural dignity of a human person, which is not lost even in the presence of error, it confirms once again that the search for truth is a voluntary act of conscience over which civil authority has no power of intervention.

Religious Tolerance and Political Tolerance

Not all the argumentations cited extended, in the intention of their authors, to tolerance of dissident political opinions, which was explicitly excluded by the greater part of the believers in religious tolerance. Tolerance of political opinions is a claim of eighteenth-century liberalism, one of whose typical promoters was J.S. Mill.[4] We also owe to Mill the extension of the concept of tolerance from political authority to 'public opinion' and the interpretation of persecution, not only as legal repression, but also as social pressure against the dissident.

The structure of argumentation in favour of political tolerance is more or less the same in all cases: the believers in tolerance will sustain that repression is in itself bad (ethical argument); or that it is futile because it sets itself against unessential differences; or that it violates the rights of individual conscience by forcing choices which regard only those who make them; or that it is counterproductive for those who put it into practice (political argument); or that it is founded on an unsustainable dogmatism (relativist argument); and in all cases it will be specified that the opinions and behaviour which tolerance strives for do not necessarily imply deleterious consequences.

Reintroduction of Tolerance in the Twentieth Century

After the First World War, the concept of tolerance was introduced by the Society of Nations, in particular through the system of protection of minorities. Successively, the outbreak of the Second World War and the persecutions by the Nazis, Soviets and others erased from memory the respect for the individual and for human dignity, until the new order instituted by the Conference of San Francisco and, specifically, the Universal Declaration on Human Rights (1948).

It was in this context that the United Nations specified the characteristics of a peaceful world order. It has become apparent that a great deal of inter-community strife instigated by intolerance is due to the fact that populations insist on their right to administer for themselves their own political and economic issues. As the Universal Declaration emphasizes, violence can ensue from the repression of democratic aspirations, as well as from intolerance.

After the end of the Cold War, world society set its hopes on the advent of an epoch of peace. But these hopes have been badly tried by the eruption of regional conflicts and hostilities between peoples who have divided nations and radically changed the world political order established some 50 years ago. The entire planet has become the stage for ethnic conflicts and religious hostilities between groups. Many long-forgotten conflicts now hold the world's attention. Deep hatreds, some of which had been hidden thanks to the reconciliation which had allowed different ethnic groups to cooperate and coexist peacefully, have come to the surface, have been articulated in the mass media, in conferences and so on, and have often given vent to armed conflicts.

These conflicts, together with the problem of poverty which has accelerated the level of immigration, have increased the number of refugees asking for asylum and of immigrants looking for work in countries and in communities which were previously monocultural. Often unforeseen, multiculturalism has appeared on the scene as a social factor; it has permeated several communities and has made its influence felt.

Beyond these phenomena, particular attention should be paid to the unstable political situation in Central and Eastern Europe after the fall of the Soviet bloc. Even here the animosities of the different ethnic groups have come to the surface; there is also a reawakening of racist and xenophobic attitudes in some European countries, mainly in the multi-ethnic areas and, in particular, against Arabs, Turks and other ethnic minorities. In these cases, prejudice and intolerance, without any adequate basis, form an opinion against others, provoking emotional and irrational reactions.

The Modern Meaning of the Notion of Tolerance

Elements for a Definition of Tolerance

The attempts to define tolerance have been numerous. Apart from its lexical origins from the Latin *tolero*, without doubt the semantic history of the concept which the term strives to express follows the above-mentioned historical events. Numerous analyses have been carried out to evaluate the exact meaning of the expression in the different geographical and cultural/philosophical areas.

Differing from what has been observed in European civilizations, in Asia tolerance refers to a personal virtue and has few sociopolitical implications.[5] Differences correlated to culture, to historical context and to social evolution have been found even in different languages.[6]

Apart from its implications in the philosophical, religious and political spheres, the situation of origin which the concept evokes implies in any case a situation of diversity and of distinction. In the absence of differences, tolerance has no reason to exist; it is inevitably accompanied by a plurality of ideas, of behaviours and often by a conflict as well. In such a situation, to 'tolerate', to be 'tolerant' or to have 'tolerance' towards what is different evokes the readiness to accept, even with difficulty. It is thus an attitude which allows one to accept in others a way of thinking or of acting which is different from one's own. In this elementary sense, tolerance implies the erroneous conviction that there is a truth, one's own, and that one may accept what is different, and so wrong in principle, as long as one does not go beyond certain limits.

In another sense, tolerance also means 'non-interference', and may therefore be understood as 'permissiveness'. In the *Oxford Dictionary*, 'tolerance' is presented in terms of permissiveness. Even in the *Larousse* the term *tolérer* is defined as 'to accept with indulgence, to tacitly allow'. However, one must be careful because the term to 'allow' presupposes, on the contrary, forbidding, and consequently becomes an unacceptable interpretation because an individual does not have the power to allow or to forbid. The permissive facet may be only coincidental with tolerance and not an element of the latter.

Variability and Limits of Tolerance

In its simplest and most fundamental form, tolerance consists in recognizing the right of others to be respected as persons and for their identities. The modern political and social values from which international norms have arisen in the field of human rights were first of all formulated in an appeal for tolerance as an essential condition to maintain social order. Western political thinkers demonstrated the necessity of tolerance for a society which could no longer tolerate intolerance and the wars of religion of the sixteenth and seventeenth centuries. The recognition that tolerance was a fundamental factor for peace between nations was an important element in the historical evolution which led to the first declarations on human rights in the modern age, ultimately crowned by the Universal Declaration.

If tolerance does not admit an absolute truth or a 'revealed' truth, nevertheless it does not identify with indifference, which is the negation of every positive social relation. Tolerance cannot be understood as indiscriminate acceptance, because it tends to admit the diversities and differences based in any case on a general principle directed towards protecting the ideals of freedom, justice, human dignity and peace.

At times one is tempted to tolerate, but in the negative sense of a total lack of interest in what happens in other social contexts, as long as the behaviour in question remains confined there. This is false tolerance, for which the 'right to be different' has also been constructed,[7] and which immediately changes into manifest intolerance when the behaviour virtually tolerated encroaches on the boundaries of the society which justifies it.

Tolerance is not indifference, it is not a lack of interest in the different, determined by a society's vision of closure towards others, as though their behaviour were insulated – a vision which today is definitely anti-historical – but confrontation, dialogue which envisages a global society in which the whole of humanity is involved.

Common Parameters of Tolerance

One can thus perceive the need for a common parameter, for a limit which cannot be breached, grafted onto the concept of tolerance. The very same authors of the sixteenth and seventeenth centuries recognized the need to set limits to tolerance by identifying them in the sphere of social order. One must therefore speak, not about fixed, preconstituted and unchangeable rules, but of rules which inevitably vary according to the evolution of society.

The variability of tolerance may, however, reach the paradox of allowing intolerance for behaviour which does not conform to the essential limits required by respect for social order. The paradox becomes apparent when one merely brings close together the principle of tolerance and that of freedom. If the practice of freedom impinges on that of another, it is no longer freedom but free arbitrariness! As an analogy, if one were to tolerate, without any limit, all types of behaviour, even those which destroy social order and coexistence itself, this type of tolerance would lead to total chaos.

The notion of limits which can or must be set for what is different becomes difficult to put into practice when one deems it opportune or necessary to reach a solution through an adequate judicial regulation. As already observed by the Sophists of ancient Greece, what is acceptable for one society may not be for another, and vice versa. On numerous occasions an attempt has been made to identify a minimum common denominator which may be valid in all places and at all times; but it is certainly very difficult to set the limit between what is licit and what is illicit in a variety of behaviours dictated by presumed needs of specific cultures, religions and societies.

There is no doubt that the so-called 'Western world' finds repugnant specific practices dictated by well-known religious doctrines, for example those which prevent blood transfusions when it is known that this refusal will lead to death for the individual, or those which cause serious sexual mutilations to female children. But what could be the objective reason, valid both in the West and in the East, in the North as well as in the South, what could be the limit which cannot be breached, the *noyaux dur* of human rights of which one always feels the need? The answer may be found in the very norms of universally accepted human rights.

The rights to life, to physical integrity, to equality between human beings, and so on certainly constitute absolute values to which exceptions may not be made. It is therefore sufficient to invoke the right to life of the subject who is in need of a blood transfusion in order to consider as objectively illicit and therefore unacceptable a religious rule which, by preventing aid from being given, places itself in opposition to the right to life. Furthermore, it is sufficient to invoke the right to a girl's physical integrity to deem the mutilations imposed by certain societies as unacceptable.

By citing the same universal human rights it is possible to find objective limits not determined by religious, cultural or sectoral needs, to identify the often cited *noyaux dur* and to identify those behaviours which cannot and should not be tolerated. As has been mentioned, the limits of tolerance vary according to sociohistorical conditions. The evolution can easily be shown in every social context. The legal principles which organize a modern democratic society must set its limits by interpreting the supreme good: justice. The legislator's responsibility lies in deciding what is against society; the risk is that he may be induced to decide under pressure from groups, from particular interests or from other situations.

In addition to variability, which essentially refers to the social group in its complexity, it is also possible to verify a different degree of tolerance at an individual level determined by cultural and environmental factors. According to this research, tolerance varies in direct relation to different education levels, to the region and the city where one resides and, inversely, according to the number of immigrants present in one's area of residence; it is also influenced by sex and by type of work.[8]

The above definitions demonstrate differences which are dear to pluralism, but each of them in any case captures the fundamental essence of respecting the rights of others; there is in the word 'tolerance' the intuition of unity, the interdependence of humanity; unity and interdependence which the age of ecology has taught us to understand as including the human species and the whole of the planetary system. So, notwithstanding differences, there are common elements for a notion of tolerance which constitute a common basis for founding a practice. In particular, everybody agrees in recognizing that tolerance is a necessity not only for civil society but also for the survival of humanity:

> il convient tout d'abord de constater que, si la notion de tolérance est controversée, la pratique de la tolérance ne l'est pas. Dans le préambule de la Charte des Nations Unies, il s'agit en effet de pratiquer la tolérance aux fins de maintenir la paix, la justice, le respect des droits de l'homme et de favoriser le progrès social. La tolérance ne peut se manifester sous la forme la plus active que dans un cadre où sont respectées la dignité humaine et les libertés publiques.[9]

The difficulty in giving a thorough unitary definition of the concept is essentially due to the variability of the same and to the multiplicity of its implications. As has already happened in other cases, for example the difficulty in reaching a correct definition of the concept of 'minority', this does not prevent one from quoting its principle in order to establish a culture and therefore a practice of tolerance, based on the feeling of freedom from prejudice and dogmas and on the recognition that there is no culture, nation, religion and so on which has total control over knowledge and truth and that tolerance entails respect for the rights and freedom of others, recognition and acceptance of individual differences. Furthermore, one should learn to know others and to communicate with them, to appreciate cultural differences, maintaining an open mind towards different thoughts and ideas and towards other visions of life, all of which arise out of curiosity and interest rather than from rejection.

From the notion of tolerance intended in the rather negative sense of forced acceptance, of putting up with that which is different, a positive attitude has thus been reached which must evolve in coexistence, collaboration and respect for others. 'Cette tolérance n'est pas une vertu passive car elle a ses racines dans un amour actif et elle tend à se transformer et à devenir un effort positif pour assurer la liberté et la paix à tous.'[10]

We cannot limit ourselves to societies which tolerate more and more but accept less and less. For a practice of tolerance, one needs to promote interlocution, dialogue and comprehension. Of course they are difficult policies because they imply the need to discuss once again one's own convictions whenever one comes into contact with different ideas and behaviour. Rather than dispensing us, they encourage us to proclaim and promote them.

Tolerance in International Instruments

Tolerance in Instruments Adopted by the United Nations

The concept of tolerance was confirmed once again after the Second World War in relation to the manifestations of intolerance which had to be eliminated. The spirit of tolerance is therefore summoned in the acts of international organizations as a precondition and corollary of the new philosophy of human rights founded on equality between men, already enunciated in the declaration of the allied states (the United Nations) of 1942: 'All men are born free and equal in dignity and rights [...] they must act towards one another with a feeling of brotherhood.'

In the Preamble to the Charter of the United Nations, adopted in San Francisco in 1945, it is affirmed that 'the peoples of the United Nations [...] practice tolerance and live together in peace'. The fundamental text of the new culture of human rights, the Universal Declaration of Human Rights of 1948 in its Article 26, paragraph 2, states: 'It shall promote understanding, tolerance and friendship among all nations, racial or religious groups.'[11]

The very same demand for an attitude of tolerance, for peaceful coexistence between peoples, groups and individuals, is therefore reaffirmed in a series of texts adopted in subsequent years by the United Nations, amongst which are the Declaration of the Rights of the Child of 1959, in whose context (Principle 7) he 'shall be brought up in a spirit of understanding, tolerance, friendship among peoples', the UNESCO Convention Against Discrimination in Education of 1960; Resolution 1904 (XVIII) of 1963 in which, at Article 8, the promotion of 'tolerance and friendship among nations and racial groups' is confirmed; the Declaration for the Elimination of All Forms of Racial Discrimination of 1963, the subsequent Convention of 1965, as well as the specific one on Discrimination Against Women of 1979; and the Declaration on the Promoting Among Youth of the Ideals of Peace, Mutual Respect and Understanding Between Peoples, of 1965.

When, with the adoption of the International Covenants on Human Rights of 1966, the United Nations managed to translate into conventional norms the principles expounded in the Universal Declaration of 1948, similar formulae to proclaim and promote tolerance appeared in Article 13 of the International Covenant on Economic, Social and Cultural Rights 'promoting understanding, tolerance and friendship among all nations' and, implicitly, in Article 20 of the International Covenant on Civil and Political Rights.

In this period, the appearance of new manifestations of intolerance was the basis of numerous recommendations and resolutions adopted by the UN General Assembly – as well as in Europe, as will be shown – explicitly directed at condemning and fighting intolerance in its different forms; these resolutions include General Assembly resolution 2331 (XXII) of 1967 against racism and other totalitarian ideologies and practices based on incitement to hatred, prejudice and intolerance; ECOSOC resolution 1235 (XLII) of 1967; and General Assembly resolutions 2438 (XXIII) of 1968, 2839 (XXVI) of 1971 and the Declaration of Principles concerning Friendly Relations of 1970 in which it is recalled that 'the peoples of the United Nations are determined to practice tolerance'.

Within the same family of the United Nations and specifically within UNESCO, one may recall the Recommendation concerning Education for International Understanding, Cooperation and Peace and Education relating to Human Rights and Fundamental Freedoms of 1974, and the Declaration on Race and Racial Prejudice of 1978. Already in the early years of UNESCO, numerous resolutions of the General Conference had denounced and condemned racial prejudices and discriminations: 5C/Res.3.26 (1950); 8C/Res.IV.1.1.423 (1954); 11C/Res.1.531 (1960).[12]

In the activity of the UN dedicated to the specific topic of intolerance in more recent times, the fundamental document is certainly the Declaration on the Elimination of All Forms of Intolerance and Discrimination Based on Religion or Belief of 25 November 1981, Res.36/55. Similar needs are taken up again in the Convention on the Rights of the Child of 1989 in whose Article 19(d) reference is made to the 'spirit of understanding, peace and tolerance', and in the Declaration on the Rights of Persons Belonging to National or Ethnic, Religious and Linguistic Minorities of 1992.

Knowing that the promotion of tolerance may develop only through an adequate education, the UN World Conference on Human Rights, which took place in Vienna in June 1993, concluded with the adoption of the Vienna Declaration and Programme of Action, in which education for tolerance is explicitly mentioned (para. 33). The same educational needs are taken up again by UNESCO in the World Plan of Action on Education for Human Rights and Democracy adopted by the International Congress on Education for Human Rights and Democracy held in Montreal in March 1993, in which it is held that 'education for human rights and democracy is itself a human right'.[13]

With General Assembly resolution 48/121 of 1993, the United Nations again took up the principles expressed by the Vienna Conference and with resolution 49/189 of 23 December 1994 instituted a Decade for Human Rights Education. Finally, with resolutions 48/126 of 20 December 1993 and 49/213 of 23 December 1994, the United Nations Year for Tolerance (1995) was promulgated.

Tolerance in Instruments Adopted by Regional Organizations

Even in the context of regional organizations, one has witnessed a parallel development of initiatives in the field of tolerance. The Council of Europe has paid particular attention to the matter. In the context of the initiatives of the Parliamentary Assembly, one notes firstly resolution 743 of 1980, 'on the need to combat resurgent fascist propaganda and its racist aspects'. Amongst others, one may recall recommendation 1089 of 1988 on xenophobic attitudes and movements in Member State countries with regard to migrant workers, recommendation 1034 of 1986 on the improvement in Europe of mutual understanding between ethnic communities; recommendation 1089 of 1988 on improving community relations; recommendation 1202 of 1993 on religious tolerance in a democratic society and recommendation 1222 of 1993 on the fight against racism, xenophobia and intolerance.[14]

Amongst the proceedings of the Council of Ministers of the Council of Europe the most significant is certainly the Declaration on intolerance – a threat to democracy, of 1981. Amongst other texts are resolution (68)30 on measures to be taken against incitement to national and religious hatred; the Declaration on freedom of expression and information of 29 April 1982; recommendation R(84)18 on the training of teachers for an education on intercultural comprehension especially in the immigration context; recommendation R(85)2 relative to judicial protection against sex-based discrimination; the Declaration on equality between men and women of 16 November 1988; and recommendation R(92)12 on inter-community relations.[15]

The Council of Europe Declaration of Vienna of 9 December 1993 invites the Heads of State and of Government of the member countries 'to launch an urgent appeal to European peoples, groups and citizens, and young people in particular, that they resolutely engage in combating all forms of intolerance and that they actively participate in the construction of a European society based on common values, characterized by democracy, tolerance and solidarity'.

In a wider European context, that of the Conference on Security and Co-operation in Europe (CSCE), which today has become OSCE, even in the Final Act of Helsinki (1975) there is mention of 'social tolerance' and, in the proceedings of the reunions of Geneva of 1991, a reference to 'tolerance and respect for different cultures'. Finally, in the document of Helsinki (1992), *Challenge and Change*, six whole paragraphs are dedicated to 'Tolerance and non-discrimination'.[16]

In other regional contexts, similar references can be found in the Inter-American Convention on Human Rights and in the more recent African Charter on Human and Peoples' Rights where one reads: 'Every individual shall have the duty to respect and consider his fellow being without discrimination, and to maintain relations aimed at promoting, safeguarding and reinforcing mutual respect and tolerance.'

Separate mention should be made of the Declaration of Cairo on human rights in Islam (1990), in the Preamble of which one can read that human rights 'are considered an integral part of the Islamic religion' and Islam is defined as a 'religion of unspoiled nature' (Article 10) in the sense of 'compulsion [...] in order to convert a man to another religion or to atheism'. In the same text, it is also specified that all rights and freedoms contained within it 'are subject to the Islamic Sharia' (Article 24). It is understandable how such statements are in open conflict with the principles deduced from a correct interpretation of the notion of tolerance, since the times of the proclamation of religious tolerance, and even more so in the modern world.[17]

Tolerance in the Context of Non-discrimination, of the Protection of Minorities and of Immigrants

As has been already mentioned, international texts on human rights mention the need to promote tolerance with the principal objective of fighting all forms of intolerance. The most obvious of these manifestations is the one which materializes in discriminatory actions and behaviour (for reasons of sex, language, religion, ethnicity and so on) and it is therefore in conformity with such needs that certain acts and dispositions be directly aimed at eliminating all forms of discrimination.

It is well known that the development of international action aimed at the promotion and the protection of human rights, initially focused on individual rights, then embracing the collective rights of groups and peoples. It is in such a context that the topic was already an object of consideration and codification at the time of the League of Nations, with regard to the protection of minorities, and was taken up again in the context of the United Nations and in Europe.

The UN Declaration on the Rights of Persons Belonging to National or Ethnic, Religious and Linguistic Minorities of 18 December 1992, the Declaration of Vienna of the Council of Europe of 9 October 1993 and the Framework Convention for the Protection of National Minorities adopted by the Council of Europe on 1 February 1995 explicitly condemn the manifestations of intolerance against them and promote the institution of an attitude of tolerance. So, in Appendix II of the Declaration of Vienna of 9 October 1993, the Heads of State and of Government of the Member Countries of the Council of Europe, convinced that 'ces phénomènes d'intolérance menacent les societés democratiques' condemn 'le racisme sous toutes ses formes, la xénophobie, l'antisémitisme ainsi que l'intolérance et toute les formes de discrimination religieuse' and make an appeal for 'la construction d'une societé européenne démocratique tolérante et solidaire sur la base de valeurs communs'.

The Convention on Minorities of 1 February 1955 calls, from the very Preamble, for 'l'épanouissement d'une Europe tolérante' and commits the Contracting Parties 'à promouvoir l'esprit de tolérance et le dialogue interculturel ainsi qu'à prendre les mesures efficaces pour favoriser le respect et la compréhension mutuels et la coopération entre toutes les personnes vivant sur leur territoire' (Article 6, paragraph 1), while, in the context of national legislation, committing them to adopting 'les mesures adéquates pour ... promouvoir la tolérance' (Article 9, paragraph 4).

Finally, another group which has attracted the attention and the action of international organizations in the field of human rights is constituted by the immigrants. The growth of immigration, which has been the springboard for manifestations of intolerance and xenophobia arising in Europe, has determined the adoption of certain texts specifically aimed at the protection of immigrants and at the development of multicultural relations.[18]

For a Culture of Tolerance and Respect for Human Rights

The need to proclaim, promote and spread an attitude of tolerance amongst individuals, groups, societies and nations has always been felt. This is even more the case today, ever since respect for human rights was imposed in modern society.

The attempt has been made to show how a general attitude of tolerance, whatever the definition of the multiplicity of contents attributed to it, is an element of paramount importance for all democratic societies and an essential precondition for the respecting of human rights.

In the modern structure of states and of international society, founded on the need for a judicial regulation of human behaviour for the establishment of a 'constitutional state' at all levels of organized society, tolerance, which essentially materializes in attitudes and in individual consciences, meets real difficulties in introducing itself into national and international legal systems.

Law can discipline the individual's action by defining what is licit or illicit, it can determine the individual's choices in the field of action, it can – in the last analysis – prevent him from demonstrating with deeds, words or writings his thoughts, his philosophical, religious and political beliefs and so on, but it certainly cannot influence thought and conscience as long as these remain within the ego of the individual and manifest themselves through external actions.

It is coherent, therefore, and at the same time necessary, if one wishes to intervene with legal instruments to promote tolerance, to act first of all on external manifestations by prohibiting and pursuing those which appear to be incompatible with the requirements of tolerance. A so-called 'negative' action is the first field in which the law can act to remove the obstacles to achieving tolerance, by forbidding antagonistic behaviours in order to abolish them, so that a favourable mood for the establishment and growth of a feeling of tolerance may be brought about, since tolerance, by its very nature, cannot be imposed by judicial norms.

It is in this sense that all the initiatives of the international community with regard to national legislation, which have codified in numerous judicial texts the illegality of different, multiple manifestations of intolerance,[19] as well as those which, operating in a positive sense, have formulated the rights of individuals or of particular groups aimed at full equality between men, represent the only type of real intervention which national and international law may use to contribute towards the establishment of a general feeling, of a diffused attitude of tolerance.

Evaluating the multiplicity and variety of texts adopted, it is certain that much has been done, but it is also evident that the mission cannot be said to be fulfilled. On the one hand, it is necessary to act because international texts do not – as unfortunately often happens in the field of human rights – remain written documents but become concretely operative. On the other hand, and especially at the national level, it is necessary not to 'slacken one's vigilance' against the appearance of new manifestations of intolerance in order to intervene quickly with adequate legal instruments.

As has already been anticipated, laws can forbid the manifestations of intolerance which may be made punishable. It can thus remove obstacles but is, by itself, incapable of changing attitudes on tolerance. Of course, the solemn statements on tolerance, democracy, respect for human rights and so on can multiply at all levels, but all this is insufficient to obtain a positive result.

In this context, all further interventions can be effective only through an adequate educational programme aimed at training individual consciences in favour of tolerance and respect for others. The recent initiatives of certain international organisms, in particular the UN, UNESCO and the Council of Europe,[20] seem to provide an answer to these needs by developing of education for human rights, laying particular emphasis on youth, with a view to building the foundations for a better future.

Notes

1 *Tractatus theologico-politicus* (1670, Chapter XX).
2 Polemical debates followed, involving the Italian refugees, amongst whom was the Sienese Bernardino Ochino (1487–1564), culminating in the publication, under the pseudonym of Martinus Bellius, of *De haeretics an sint persequendi et omnino quomodo sit cum eis agendum, Luteri et Brentii, aliorumquemultorum tum veterum tum recentiorum sententiae* (1554), written by the Savoyard humanist Sebastiano Castellione, with the collaboration of Cecilio Secondo Curione.
3 P. Bayle, 'Nouvelles lettres de l'auteur de la critique générale du calvinisme', *Œuvres diverses; Dictionnaire historique et critique* (1695–7); *Pensées diverses sur la comète*, Paris, 1984.
4 *On Freedom*, 1859.
5 Wang-sang Han, 'The issues of tolerance as an element of peaceful unification of the Korean peninsula', *Democracy and Tolerance*, Proceedings of the International Conference, Seoul, Republic of Korea, 27–9 September 1994, Paris/Seoul, UNESCO/Korean National Commission for UNESCO, p.xv.
6 In the use of the English language, evidence has been found of a specific problem related to the terms 'tolerance' and 'toleration' (Kathinka Evers, 'On the nature of tolerance', *Democracy and Tolerance* (op. cit., note 5), p.3) and it has also been suggested that the term 'toleration' be used as it is closer to the current Western interpretation (Dummet, 'La tolérance aujourd'hui', *Analyses philosophiques*, Working Document for the XIXth World Congress of Philosophy in Moscow, UNESCO, 1993 p.17). Personally, I do not feel I have the competence to participate in the linguistic debate and I limit myself to using the term 'tolerance' simply because it is more widespread.
7 J. Boisson, *Actes du Colloque sur les droits de l'homme des étrangers en Europe*, Strasbourg, Council of Europe, 1985, p.314; P.H. Imbert, ibid., p.335.
8 Wang-sang Han, 'The issue of tolerance' (op. cit., note 5), p.xviii.
9 Doc. UNESCO 278/25, Proclamation of the Year of the United Nations on Tolerance and Declaration on Tolerance.
10 'L'intolérance, une serieuse menace pour la paix', Message of John Paul II, in G. Filibek, *Les Droits de l'homme dans l'enseignement de l'Eglise, de Jean XXII à Jean Paul II*, Vatican City, 1992, p.351. In the same volume there are numerous other texts on religious freedom, the Encyclical *Dignitatis humanae* and the Declaration of the Second Vatican Council of 7 December 1965, *Nostra Aetate*.

11 E.-I. A. Daes, *Freedom of the individual under law, an analysis of article 29 of the Universal Declaration on Human Rights*, New York, 1990.
12 J. Symonides, 'Prohibition of advocacy of hatred, prejudice and intolerance in the United Nations instruments', *Democracy and Tolerance* (op. cit., note 5), p.79.
13 Doc. UNESCO SHS-93/CONF.402/LD.2.
14 European Commission Against Racism and Intolerance, Recommendations adopted by the Parliamentary Assembly, Secretariat Memorandum, Strasbourg, March 1995; Espersen, 'Rapport sur la lutte contre le racisme, la xénophobie, et l'intolérance', Parliamentary Assembly, 16 September 1993, Doc. 6915.
15 European Commission against Racism and Intolerance, Recommendations adopted by the Committee of Ministers, Secretariat Memorandum, March 1995; Work of the Council of Europe connected with the work of the European Commission against Racism and Intolerance, Doc. CRI(94)4; 'Activités dans les domaines de la lutte contre le racisme et l'intolérance', Doc. CRI(95)10.
16 F. Margiotta Broglio, 'Law and tolerance', *Democracy and Tolerance* (op. cit., note 5), p.24.
17 Ibid.
18 Amongst the numerous texts of the Council of Europe one may recall, as regards the Committee of Ministers: resolution (74)15, resolution (76)17 and recommendation R(84)18; for the Parliamentary Assembly: recommendation 968 of 1983 'on xenophobic attitudes and movements in Member State countries with regard to migrant workers', recommendation 1082 of 1988 'on the right of permanent residence for migrant workers', recommendation 1125 of 1990 'on the new immigration countries'; recommendation 1154 of 1991 'on North African migrants in Europe'; recommendation 1187 of 1992 'on relations between immigrants and trade unions'; recommendation 1203 of 1993 'on Gypsies in Europe'; recommendation 1206 of 1993 'on the integration of migrants and community relations'; and recommendation 1211 of 1993 'on clandestine migrations: traffickers and employers of clandestine migrants'. For full research on the conditions of foreigners in Europe, in relation to human rights, see the Proceedings of the 'Colloque sur les droits de l'homme des étrangers en Europe', Strasbourg, Council of Europe, 1985; 'Communication adressée par le Comité européen sur les migrations (CDMG) à la Commission contre le racisme et l'intolérance'; Doc. CDMG(94)31 of 28 November 1994.
19 For the European countries, see, for example, the study elaborated by the Swiss Institute of Comparative Law on 'Judicial measures existing in Member Countries of the Council of Europe aimed at fighting racism and intolerance', Doc. CRI(14)10.
20 See, for example, the programme elaborated by UNESCO for the International Congress on Education on Human Rights and Democracy (Montreal 8–11 March 1993), Doc. SHS-93/CONF.402/LD.2; 'L'apprentissage interculturel au service des droits de l'homme', Council of Europe, Doc. ICL-DH(91)1; and the recent European Youth Campaign against Racism, Xenophobia, Anti-semitism and Intolerance.

Bibliography

Abdelfattah Amor (1993), 'Application de la Déclaration sur l'élimination de toutes les formes d'intolérance et de discrimination fondées sur la religion ou la conviction', report on resolution 1993/25 of the UN Commission on Human Rights.
Anyanwu, K.C. (1985), 'Cultural philosophy as a philosophy of integration and tolerance', *International Philosophical Quarterly*, **25**, 277–287.

Crockett, H., Jr. (1976), 'On political tolerance: comments on the origins of tolerance', *Social Forces*, **55**.

Decaux, E. (1995), 'La lutte contre le racisme et la xénophobie', Premières rencontres européennes des institutions nationales de promotion et de protection des droits de l'homme, Decaux, Paris.

Eide, M.A. and M.T. Opsahl (1990), *Rapport général sur l'égalité et non discrimination*, 7th Colloquium on the European Convention on Human Rights, Oslo. Strasbourg, Council of Europe.

Elias, N. (1991), 'L'action du Conseil de l'Europe contre l'intolérance et pour les droits de l'homme', *L'Apprentissage interculturel au service des droits de l'homme*, Klagenfurt, Council of Europe.

Erdtsiek, J. (1955), 'Racism, xenophobia and the position of ethnic minorities', *Peoples*, Paris, UNESCO.

Ferrar, J. (1976), 'The dimension of tolerance', *Pacific Sociological Review*, **19**, (1), 63–81.

Haberstam, J. (1982–83), 'The paradox of tolerance', *Philosophical Forum*, 190ss.

Haeescher, G. (1989), 'Laïcité et droits de l'homme', *Colloque sur les droits de l'homme sans frontières*, Strasbourg, Council of Europe.

Kordig, C.R. (1982), 'Concepts of toleration', *Journal of Value Inquiry*, **16**, 59–66.

Marcuse, A. (1971), 'Critique de la tolérance', *Revue internationale de philosophie*, **95–96**.

Morsy, Zaghloul (1993), 'La tolérance aujourd'hui, analyses philosophiques', *Proceedings of the XIXth World Congress of Philosophy in Moscow, 22/28 August 1993*, Paris, UNESCO.

Sahel, C. (1992), 'Freedom of conscience', *Seminar of Council of Europe and Centre for Human Rights Studies*, University of Leiden, Strasbourg, Council of Europe.

Smith, A. (1994), 'The politics of culture: ethnicity and nationalism', *Companion Encyclopedia of Anthropology: Humanity, Culture and Social Life*, Tim Ingold (ed.) New York, Routledge.

Trifunouska, S. (1994), 'Multilateral responses to ethnicity, nationalism and racism in contemporary Europe', *Helsinki Monitor*, 79.

Trifunouska, S. (1994), 'L'Europe contre la discrimination; pour la démocratie et la la liberté', International Colloquium, 20–21 October 1994, Strasbourg, Council of Europe.

Woods, D.B. (1995), *Tolerance and Understanding Between Peoples*, Paris, UNESCO.

9 Terrorism and Human Rights

COLIN WARBRICK

Terrorism: Definition

In international legal studies of terrorism, no words are quoted more often or more appositely than those of Professor Richard Baxter, who said: 'We have cause to regret that a legal concept of "terrorism" was ever inflicted upon us. The term is imprecise; it is ambiguous; and above all, it serves no operative legal purpose.'[1] Unhappily, it also appears to be indispensable. Not even Professor Baxter's reputation and the cogency of his comment were enough to consign the term to legal oblivion. It intrudes persistently into debates and legal writing, but an international definition still remains elusive.[2] There are national definitions but sometimes they are not even consistent within a single jurisdiction, let alone with one another.[3]

Why the quest for an international definition has remained unfulfilled has a number of explanations, but one factor has been of great influence. If there be an identifiable concept of terrorism, a necessary, if not always sufficient, condition appears to be that there is conduct done with some political motive.[4] For those engaged in the exercise of power, what the motive is matters greatly: governments use force for the good motive of preserving public order, against 'terrorist' groups who use force for the bad motive of overthrowing the legitimate authorities; 'terrorist' governments use force for the bad motive of oppressing their people, against 'freedom fighters' who use force for the good motive of liberation. The term comports not just illegality but illegitimacy.[5] Those trying to escape the effects of partisan labelling of violent conduct in determining what counts as terrorism tend to narrow down the concept. For example, C. Gearty suggests that the word be 'limited to the use by subState factions of indiscriminate and petrifying violence in order to communicate a political message'.[6]

While there must be a political message, it does not matter what it is. This approach excludes the use of force by the authorities of a state as terrorism, whatever the claim made about the illegitimacy of a regime or the savagery with which it exercises its authority (not that the intention is to exclude condemnation of some exercises of official violence on other grounds).

'Terrorism' is not a term of art in international law, although it does tend to be used as a compendious term for conduct which states are required to criminalize by a variety of treaties.[7] While states have been able to reach agreement on these treaties (although participation in them varies widely and is by no means universal), even added together, they are not an adequate account of the phenomenon of terrorism.[8] What is missing is a similar agreement that attacks on the lives and security of individuals should be dealt with in the same way. Governments claim a legitimate right to use force against individuals for the purpose of maintaining internal order and repelling external attacks. They are not prepared, and indeed are unable, to forgo the right to use force in the same way that they have agreed to condemn (and, presumably, to forgo themselves[9]) hostage taking or hijacking aeroplanes. That is to say, the reason why violence is being used is a measure of its legitimacy. Further, the monopoly of violence is a mark of an effective government which is itself a claim of legitimacy in the international system. While not every act of violence by the government may be legitimate, in this sense, none of the violence of others is.

C. Gearty's understanding of terrorism, limiting it to 'subState' actors, avoids this difficulty. However, another obstacle to reaching international agreement about terrorism arises here. In modern international relations, one claim to justify violence in a particular cause and by non-state actors has gained wide if not universal support: the cause is self-determination; the actors are national liberation movements.[10] Of itself, this claim has no necessary connection with terrorism. However, experience has shown that, in their origins at least, many wars of national liberation have begun as low-intensity conflicts,[11] the only kind of operation the liberation movements could conduct against the militarily superior, imperial occupiers.

In practice, in this kind of conflict, incidentally or by design, the means of fighting are likely to have effects on the uninvolved population. Civilians may be killed deliberately because of their support for the regime; they may be killed deliberately but randomly by attacks on civilian targets, such as shopping centres or transport systems; they may be killed accidentally, as a result of 'collateral' damage from attacks on security forces or public property. The established power will categorize all these deaths as criminal and often as 'terrorist'. The liberation movement will say that some or all of them were legitimate acts of violence, as necessary steps to attain self-determination. The cause of colonial self-determination[12] enjoyed wide and strong support among states. These states would not agree to any definition of terrorism which might have inhibited activities which they deemed necessary for achieving liberation. It is true that an ambiguity remained as to whether liberation movements were entitled to resort to terrorism – General Assembly resolutions sometimes talked about 'any means whatsoever'[13] – but many states were prepared to condone that which other states declared to be terrorism.

These divisions began to dissolve during the 1970s. The inclusion in the Geneva Protocol I of wars of national liberation as international armed conflict had the effect of subjecting combatants to the restraints of international humanitarian law.[14] The members of the General Assembly and the Security Council were from time to time able to reach agreement on resolutions condemning terrorism. In 1994, the General Assembly approved the Declaration on Measures to Eliminate International Terrorism,[15] the first such resolution which made no reference to self-determination. It said:

> Criminal acts intended or calculated to provoke a state of terror in the general public, a group of persons or particular persons for political purposes are in any circumstances unjustifiable, whatever the considerations of a political, philosophical, ideological, racial, ethnic, religious or any other nature that may be invoked to justify them.

The change in emphasis reflects a growing concern that states are using terrorism as a weapon in inter-state conflicts,[16] as well as a recognition that the use of force in the cause of decolonization is now largely irrelevant. Although this represents an advance over previous disagreements, it passes by what is a significant segment of the activity commonly classed as terrorism, that is irregular violence against the government of a state to try to seize power or to change policy, or to achieve the secession of a portion of a state's territory and people.

In the traditional view of international law, activities of this kind were within the domestic jurisdiction of states. It is true that even localized activities are likely to have international repercussions. Safe havens across an international border where the security forces of the target state may not legitimately pursue them are of great advantage to the irregular fighter. The stronger or more effective those forces become in protecting domestic targets, the greater the temptation for the rebels to seek out interests of the state abroad, where they might not be quite so well defended. International cooperation to defeat such strategies remains of importance. But, unless one turns to the law of human rights, neither the right to use force nor the manner of it by either the government or the rebels is matter of international concern.

It has been the practice of international law to fix the legitimacy and legality of a government upon their effective exercise of authority, which includes the use of force to maintain order within its territory.[17] Governments characterize non-official violence within the state as criminal; that which attacks the institutions of the state may be treasonous as well as criminal. International law has treated this internal violence with indifference. Those who resorted to violence against the state violated no international rule and, if they made their project successful, were entitled to be regarded as the new government of the state or the government of a new state, if secession was the object of the force. If violence failed, those using it were liable to severe penalties imposed by the victorious government.

This simple picture has been complicated by a number of developments, some of them of longer standing than others. The legitimacy (if not the legality) of certain governments has come under scrutiny. Governments which violate on a wide scale human rights or which ignore the requirements of democracy may be challenged as having no or limited legitimacy.[18] There are neither firm legal rules nor authoritative institutions to determine which governments fail the test of legitimacy: the process of identification is highly political, though a wide consensus may exist about particular pariah regimes such as the apartheid governments of South Africa or the Saddam Hussein government in Iraq. As considered already, it has been argued that the people of a territory subject to colonial rule had a right to use force against the occupier as an aspect of the international law on self-determination. It is a small political step, though a large legal one, to posit a similar right against oppressive or undemocratic governments.[19] The transition from the political to the legal sphere of argument has been facilitated by claims that the right of self-determination itself has developed beyond the colonial context to embrace at least some of these examples.[20] The same problem would then arise as to whether there were any limits on the means allowed to those resisting the oppressive government. While we might recognize that the law may be changing, the transition is nowhere near complete and, for the time being, it is not necessary to work out the consequences if the change is accomplished.

Even if the law has not progressed so far as to deny the legality of oppressive regimes, the elaboration of international human rights law has provided an apparatus for measuring the legality of the way in which governments maintain their authority. International law no longer stands indifferent to the ruthless exercise of domestic force for the purpose of maintaining internal order. Where the conflicts attain a certain level, international humanitarian law imposes limitations on the way force may be applied by a government.[21] These limits may not be very extensive and the machinery for securing compliance with them is not strong, but they represent a fundamental shift in the nature of internal authority as seen from the outside. In internal conflicts of a sufficient magnitude to be covered by humanitarian law, the law of human rights applies as well, though its application may be modified to take into account the special circumstances of the conflict. Even where the disturbances have not reached this level of intensity, human rights law will apply and affect the way in which an internationally legal security policy can be maintained. This is as much the case for the government which has a firm democratic basis, and which ordinarily respects human rights, as it is for the oppressive regime.

These two matters together – the possibility of challenge to the legitimacy of the established order (or, at least, to the way it maintains its effectiveness) and the possibility of the legitimacy of some non-governmental bodies (including the legitimacy of some acts of violence by them) – continue to affect the political and legal background against which the response to terrorism must be considered. 'Terrorism', whatever its real meaning, is a term of deprecation: it necessarily carries with it the connotation of illegitimacy. Its very imprecision carries with it the possibility of utilization by opposite sides in the same conflict. For the governments of states, 'terrorism' has the virtue of drawing attention to the illegitimacy of non-state political violence: no act of violence of a rebel, a secessionist, even a person acting for humanitarian ends, is legitimate; those who perpetrate such violence have no protection against the law of that state, which may indeed subject them to a more stringent regime of criminal law and procedure than ordinary criminals. By this account, the bomb thrown by the rebel in a pitched battle with the military is no different from the bomb left in a supermarket or on a passenger train. On the contrary, the private fighter contests the right of the government to use any force against him while asserting the right to use (any) force to pursue the legitimate objective of overthrowing the illegitimate regime.

For non-governmental groups, this is not just a matter of rhetoric. Just as in colonial situations, what have come to be called 'low-intensity operations' are often the only way they can fight effectively against a government. Their very existence as viable units may depend upon coercion being applied to what one might loosely call 'non-combatants', civilians who do not actively support or even actively oppose their programme and activities. Compelling at least acquiescence may involve activities not so different from 'terrorism', however it is defined normally. If terrorism is illegitimate, and what these groups do can be effectively presented as terrorism, they are left without a legitimate form of fighting, however noble their cause. The reaction to the methods of national liberation movements shows that states as a whole are not prepared to accept the universality of this approach. Individual actions within a low-intensity campaign may amount to terrorism (hijacking aeroplanes, for instance) without making the whole guerrilla campaign 'terrorist' and the national liberation movement a terrorist organization.

A government confronted by a claim like this, particularly if the pattern of violence against it is beginning to enjoy some success, may find it difficult to respond. The ordinary methods of law enforcement become ineffective, while its military superiority is hard to bring to bear against a group of irregulars. Whether out of calculation or of frustration, a government may be tempted to merge the ordinary distinction between law enforcement and the maintenance of military security and employ its military machine in the service of maintaining order, while subjecting its soldiers to fewer restraints than those which attend the activities of policemen about the same business. This is counterterrorism. Thus terrorism and counterterrorism are linked by language and action: the language of the two sides is reciprocal: now it is the states who are called the terrorists, but the activity is in one respect the same: it impinges on the rights of individuals in serious and substantial ways.

Where the intensity of internal disorder reaches the level of an internal armed conflict, international humanitarian law will apply – Article 3 of the Geneva Convention and, to the extent that a state is bound by it or its provisions have become part of customary law, Protocol II to the Conventions. Resort to terrorism is specifically outlawed.[22] There have been attempts to draw analogies between internal armed conflicts and internal disturbances of lesser intensity to fix a similar obligation to desist from terror on both sides. This would establish minimum obligations when the state denied that the level of conflict had reached a level to bring it within Article 3, and also when disputes arose as to whether humanitarian law applied at all, as well as for all those incidents of a less serious kind. This approach has failed because states are concerned that, by admitting that the law of Geneva applies, even by analogy, they run the risk of conferring a degree of legitimacy on the group using force against it and that some use of force against the government will be regarded as justified and that some claim to privileged status as prisoners of war or political prisoners by the members of the groups will gain plausibility.[23]

A state's desire to maintain the maximum freedom of action by characterizing the situation as one within its domestic jurisdiction is common. For private groups, the obligations of compliance to qualify for the benefits of humanitarian law may impose such restrictions on the kind of operations they want to conduct as not to be worth any benefits they would gain: they seek legitimacy through what they hope will be a widely-shared perception of the political justification for the violence to which they resort. It should at this point be noted that some groups will claim legitimacy for acts of unequivocal terrorism, claiming perhaps that such activities gain necessary publicity for their cause.[24] So even if it were possible to reach agreement on what activities constituted terrorism by relying on humanitarian law, it is clear that some private group, not of course formally bound by such law, would not be prepared to accommodate it.

Human Rights

Function

If there is no international definition of terrorism, the initial characterization of an activity as 'terrorist' will be made by the national legal system and, for the remainder of this chapter, we shall use the term to cover any claims made by a state about activity hostile to it, so long as it is confined to C. Gearty's category of action by 'sub-State actors'.[25] Given that such actions will inevitably be criminal, why does the legislator need to attach an additional label to them? There is more than one answer to this question, but among them are the anathematization of the perpetrators, the establishment of stringent regimes of criminal procedure and possibly new offences to deal with those suspected of terrorist action and the extension of the role of the military into the maintenance of internal security. Among the effects of these measures are the shift of power from the legislature to the executive, the reduction in the accountability for the use of power, especially to the courts, and the generation of hostility not only to those convicted of offences but to their families and the supporters of the ends the defendants seek, whether or not they support their means.

It is here that the law of human rights has its relationship with terrorism, however the latter is defined. In view of what is to follow, it should be emphasized that the law of human rights gives no authority to individuals to use violence against the government of a state.[26] Indeed, those who resort to violence violate the human rights of their victims.[27] It is, of course, the case that it will not be possible to hold individuals accountable for violations of human rights at the international level, because the jurisdiction of international institutions over defendants is limited to states. However, the establishment of the International Criminal Tribunals for Yugoslavia and for Rwanda,[28] there being within the jurisdiction of each some serious violations of human rights, shows that the international system is capable of establishing machinery to hold individuals to account for breaches of human rights.

The function of the law of human rights in this field is to impose a brake on the introduction of laws, policies and practices which interfere with individuals' rights and which are justified as being necessary in the fight against terrorism. What matters is not how terrorism is defined but what the actual manifestations of threats to public order are within a particular national jurisdiction. The menace of violent acts against the state is and can be presented as such a serious matter that ordinary constraints against the implementation of harsh measures can be overcome. Furthermore, those who contest the legitimacy of repressive action run the risk of being portrayed as supporters of the terrorists. For them, to be able to rely on human rights standards has two advantages: the objectivity and, indeed, the 'bindingness' of those standards diminish, even if they do not totally eliminate, the charge of being partisan against the state when they demand that it respect human rights and, in the appropriate case, the possibility of appeal to international institutions for protection against violations of human rights obligations.

There is a substantial overlap between the law of human rights and international humanitarian law, especially as the intensity of any conflict increases. Reference to one set of standards or the other may not depend upon substantive difference between them in what they require of a state, but on who is invoking them (for example, the International Committee of the Red Cross (ICRC) as compared with an individual victim), against whom they are being used (is the state bound by one set of rules but not by the other?) and in what forum the claim is presented (is it a political claim for humanitarian relief or an individual, legal application brought, say, to the European Commission of Human Rights?). It is enough to note that human rights law will apply whatever the level of the internal conflict (although its application may be modified to consider the seriousness of the hostilities) and that human rights institutions sometimes take into account humanitarian law in deciding what human rights law demands of a state.

Application

Counterterrorism   The application of human rights law to moderate the response of governments to what they call 'terrorism' is one of the severest tests of the human rights idea. The demonization of the terrorist serves to justify treating him with less respect than the ordinary individual, a justification which can be rooted in the terrorist's own rejection of the standards of human rights, the rule of law and democracy, and in the damage his activities do to others. These are real concerns and, even if they are sometimes exaggerated by governments, they should not be diminished by proponents of human rights. The authorities will argue that an insistence on too strict an adherence to particular human rights standards will put at risk any prospect of enjoyment of them in the future, if the terrorist project succeeds. The case can be made for some measures of limitation on the exercise of individual rights or even for their temporary suspension. The first role of human rights law is to insist that the burden of demonstrating this necessity should rest on the state. The second is to indicate that, no matter what the necessity, some practices are utterly forbidden to the state: whatever the threat, it must fashion its security policy round these standards. It will be shown that these two matters are intimately linked together: the insistence on standards of due process contributes to ensuring that the absolute obligations upon states not to kill or torture are in fact adhered to.[29] In practice, human rights law serves as a protection against counter-terrorism getting out of hand.

Basic principles Although the distinction is not a scientific one, in the practice of human rights there is a difference between the way individual cases of human rights are treated and the responses to patterns of human rights violations. For the former, the emphasis is on discrete judicial or quasi-judicial procedures, ultimately leading to an internationally binding decision against the state, if a violation be established. For the latter, the mechanism is generally political, it may not be institutionalized and it will seldom lead to unequivocal conclusions. Nonetheless, patterns of violations are the aggregate of individual violations. Case law developed in individual applications is valuable in elucidating the wrongfulness in human rights terms of governmental policies, and policies which are commonly described in other ways are susceptible to analysis through the medium of specific human rights duties. The best example is the analysis of the phenomenon of 'disappearances' by the institutions of the Inter-American system.

Disappearance as a policy involves the abduction of individuals by unidentified persons (often officials working with the authority or connivance of their superiors) to unidentified places of detention (often secretly maintained by the state) to be tortured or killed.[30] The policy of disappearance has the advantage for the authorities of making the ascription of responsibility to the government, domestically or internationally, extremely difficult. Notably in the *Velasquez Rodrieguez* case,[31] the Inter-American Court of Human Rights held that the positive obligation under Article 1 of the Inter-American Convention on Human Rights included duties to investigate effectively and to pursue prosecution against those suspected of serious violations of human rights. In the particular case, the court found that there was evidence linking the disappearance to the authorities but 'even if that fact had not been proven, the failure of the State apparatus to act, which is clearly proven, is a failure on the part of Honduras to fulfil the duties it assumed under Article 1(1) of the Convention'.[32] This duty, which applies even to the acts of those not proved to be officials of the state, clearly applies to the acts of those who are and establishes the international accountability of the government for its counterterrorist policies, in addition to that which may arise out of mistaken or excessive implementation of them in a single instance.

It is worth remembering that human rights obligations are complex matters and that they are not of a uniform structure. In addition to the basic, negative obligation on state officials not to interfere with the rights of individuals (thus soldiers must not arbitrarily kill nor policemen torture), the state has a series of positive duties. They may be duties to make sure that the negative obligations are carried out effectively, so that states must ensure that their security forces are trained to exercise their power and plan to use it in ways commensurate with human rights.[33] In addition, there may be duties to take action to prevent the interference with an individual's rights by other private persons.[34] Each of these considerations is germane to counterterrorist policy. It is an almost invariable feature of them that they involve the disposition of lethal force in the maintenance of internal security to a greater degree than normal.

Whether it be because troops are employed in a domestic, civilian context for which their military training has been inappropriate or because the police are given unaccustomed firepower or relaxed rules of engagement, the dangers of excessive resort to lethal force are clear. For so long as it is feasible, the training and control of the security forces must ensure that there is no inadvertent slide into 'war' against the terrorists, when less severe means to deal with them are effective. The temptation to such excesses is all the more inviting if it is argued that the state has a positive obligation to protect individuals against the depredations of the terrorist groups, for then it appears that human rights law is the justification for public action, rather than a limit upon it.

Striking the balance in all but the clearest case, whether it be a matter of general policy or in an individual instance, comes close to limits of justiciability for an international body but it can insist that the state has procedures which show that the values protected by human rights are properly taken into account by those in charge of its security policy. Put in human rights terms, the state has a wide margin of appreciation about the necessity for the use of lethal force and an international supervisor is likely to be convinced of the legitimacy of state action if it can show that there are domestic procedures which give proper account to human rights.

A subsidiary question which is common to terrorist action is the extent to which human rights law imposes obligations on the way a state responds to the political demands of the terrorists. Does the state have a positive duty to accommodate all or any of the terrorists' demands? If the demand is for the release of fellow terrorist prisoners in exchange for the life of hostages, must the state concede if the threat to kill them is credible? If the demand is for a change of government or the right to secede in exchange for the cessation of a violent campaign, must the government give up power or territory? It would be extraordinary if such questions were matters of duty, but that a state does not have a totally free hand in treating with terrorists is the implication of the opinion of the European Commission of Human Rights in the case of *McFeeley*. There, IRA prisoners in Northern Ireland refused to leave their cells, even to use the lavatories, as a protest against the prison authorities' refusal to concede their demand for special status. The conditions in which they lived, if the responsibility of the authorities, would have been 'degrading' within the terms of Article 3 of the European Convention on Human Rights. Allowing that the government was not obliged to surrender to the demands, the Commission nonetheless said:

> the State is not absolved from its obligation under the Convention and Article 3 in particular, because the prisoners are engaged in what is regarded as an unlawful challenge to the authority of the prison administration. Although short of an obligation to accept the demands [...] the Convention requires that the prison authorities, with due regard to the ordinary and reasonable requirements of imprisonment, exercise their custodial authority to safeguard the health and well-being of all prisoners including those engaged in protest insofar as that may be possible in the circumstances. Such a requirement makes it necessary for the prison authorities to keep under constant review their reaction to recalcitrant prisoners engaged in a developing and protracted protest.[35]

This is a potentially far-reaching obligation which extends beyond the very particular facts of that case. If a state has such a duty with respect to the terrorists themselves, as was the case here, it would seem that it should have a similar obligation where the rights of innocent persons are at stake.

Human rights obligations are not all of the same quality. Some are expressed in absolute or almost absolute terms, such as the right not to be tortured. Others are qualified by narrowly defined exceptions, like the grounds for arrest or detention set out in Article 5(1)(a) of the

European Convention. Still others allow for interference for defined purposes with a legal basis and which satisfy a test of necessity, such as the limitations on the rights of freedom of expression set out in Article 19(3) of the International Covenant on Civil and Political Rights and Article 10(2) of the European Convention on Human Rights. Human Rights agreements generally provide for derogation in times of national emergency and state expressly that the guarantee of rights does not serve as a protection for 'any State, group or person' to engage in activity which will undermine the enjoyment of the protected rights of others.[36]

The differing structure of these standards means that the way a state will seek to justify its action in response to what it calls the terrorist threat will vary according to the particular provision alleged to be violated. If the obligation is an absolute one, there are essentially two questions: (1) Has the applicant discharged the burden of proof upon him about his factual allegations? (2) If he has, do these facts constitute conduct contravening the applicable rule?

This kind of inquiry is, in practice, limited to claims that persons have been subjected to torture or inhuman or degrading treatment or punishment. There may be serious differences about whether certain kinds of treatment amount to a violation of the rule. In the *Ireland* v. *UK* case, the European Commission and European Court of Human Rights assessed differently the 'five techniques' of sensory deprivation used against detainees in Northern Ireland. The Commission found there to be torture; the Court held that there was inhuman treatment.[37] Nonetheless, both bodies agreed that Article 3 of the Convention had been violated. Once they had reached that decision, the means of interrogation could not be justified by reason of the terrorist threat, given the absolute nature of the duty under Article 3.[38]

This kind of dispute is rare. More commonly, the state contests the factual basis of the claim. Because ill-treatment will almost invariably have occurred while a person is in the hands of the security forces, often in conditions of great secrecy, establishing his version of events against the denial of it by the state can confront an individual with an almost impossible burden of proof, especially if, as the European Court said in the *Ireland* v. *UK* case, the seriousness of allegations of breaches of Article 3 requires that an applicant make them out 'beyond reasonable doubt'.[39] In recognition of this, the European Court of Human Rights has been prepared to draw conclusions from objective evidence such as medical confirmation of injury which attribute responsibility to the state in the absence of a satisfactory explanation from the authorities.[40] This follows the approach of the Inter-American Court and of the Human Rights Committee in cases where it was faced with obduracy, if not outright non-cooperation from defendant states.[41]

This forensic device is not, of course, a complete answer and it may encourage states to keep their interrogation centres even more remote from view. A high premium, therefore, rests on the recognition of rights of access to prisoners by their lawyers and by doctors on a continuing basis throughout their custody and on fostering the development of mechanisms like those established under the United Nations and European Conventions against Torture, which allow for independent inspection of places of imprisonment, even in emergencies.[42]

Access to lawyers for persons suspected of terrorist offences who are in detention is important to secure the legitimacy of custody and to protect the right to fair trial, quite apart from any possible role it has to help prevent mistreatment. Limiting these rights and instituting a species of executive detention is a common feature of counterterrorist policies, explained by the difficulty of demonstrating to a court evidence sufficient to justify detention in normal circumstances or of obtaining adequate evidence to secure convictions through the ordinary criminal process. Executive detention is a device which may be justified by relying on the emergency derogation provision, but states may wish to avoid doing this if their strategy is to maintain that terrorist activity is criminal rather than political and can be dealt with by modified procedures which will, notwithstanding the changes, still comply with human rights obligations.

A prominent example of this is the system of 'Diplock Courts' introduced to deal with terrorist offences in Northern Ireland. Lord Diplock was charged by the government with devising a form of trial which was compatible with Article 6 of the European Convention, but which met the perceived obstacles to obtaining convictions by the existing procedure. Lord Diplock's solution was to abolish the right to jury trial for these offences (itself not a requirement of the Convention) and to modify the rules of evidence, especially on the admissibility and weight of confessions. There have been no successful challenges to the fairness of these procedures.[43]

The British government has been less successful in demonstrating the legitimacy of an extended period of detention for terrorist suspects immediately after arrest, before they are brought before a judge. National law allows up to five extra days of judicially unauthorized detention following the approval of the executive, beyond the two days allowed under the ordinary law. In the *Brogan* case, the European Court held that detention without the applicant being brought before a judge for only a little over four days violated Article 5(3), despite the government's argument that a longer period was necessary because of the background of terrorism.[44] The judgment is a strict one, because four days' detention will generally be considered compatible with Article 5(3) in ordinary circumstances.

Where the human rights standard expressly allows for some interference with an individual's right, states will be able to use the terrorist threat as justification for their actions – the interference will be said to be necessary for the prevention of crime or the preservation of public order. Nonetheless, the supervisory organs have a role to play and should not defer to any innovations which a state deems necessary. In *Klass* v. *Germany*, the European Court said, reviewing a law authorizing telephone tapping:

> Being aware of the danger such a law poses of undermining or even destroying democracy on the grounds of defending it, [the Court] affirms that the Contracting States may not, in the name of the struggle against espionage and terrorism, adopt whatever measures they deem appropriate.[45]

The supervisory authorities can discharge their responsibility by requiring that any special procedures are provided for by a law which states its limits with a sufficient degree of precision and which is not so wide as to amount to unfettered discretion, and by insisting on substitute measures of control of the exercise of any power if the national authorities deem it necessary to dispense with judicial review. These are limitations which are commonly ignored by anti-terrorist legislation.[46]

Emergencies The supervisory institutions have not always endorsed the claims of states that their anti-terrorist policies or practices are compatible with their human rights obligations. States sometimes then have a choice whether or not to invoke an emergency derogation provision.[47] This requires them to demonstrate that the terrorist activity poses a threat to the organized life in the state. If the state is able to satisfy the human rights body that there is an emergency, it may seek to justify its otherwise unacceptable regime on the grounds that it is 'strictly necessary to meet the exigencies of the situation'. Following the judgment in the *Brogan* case, that extended pre-trial detention without judicial supervision was incompatible with Article 5(3) of the European Convention, the British government issued a notice of emergency declaration with respect to the situation in Northern Ireland and successfully justified the law under Article 15 of the Convention.[48] The *Brannigan* judgment has been criticized, both for its acceptance of the government's claim that there was a situation of sufficient seriousness – the government and the court based their conclusion on a summation of all the loss of life, injury and damage through the 20 years of the disturbances in the Province, rather than on a review of contemporary events – and on the necessity of the period of pre-trial detention. It was suggested that it was in precisely such circumstances that detainees were most vulnerable to mistreatment and that the measures referred to by the government were practically ineffective to protect against the risk of excessive interrogation practices.

The European Court did not follow the line of the Inter-American Court of Human Rights in finding that judicial guarantees could not be dispensed with in an emergency because of their importance in protecting detainees.[49] The Inter-American decision was a little easier for that court to come to, because of the different text of the American Convention. All emergency derogation provisions contain a list of rights from which there may be no departure, whatever the seriousness of the emergency. Article 27 of the American Convention is more elaborate than most and, in addition to its list of non-derogable rights, it includes 'the judicial guarantees essential for the protection of such rights'. In the terrorist context, procedural guarantees are essential, not only as a protection against mistreatment during detention but also to prevent abusive or excessive recourse to powers which generally will confer a wider than normal discretion on the executive.

The *Brannigan* case raised an important question about the termination of the emergency. The experience in Northern Ireland is far from untypical.[50] Even with the ceasefire, the British government has been unwilling to repeal its emergency legislation, although there have been many administrative accommodations to the new situation. The unjustified continuation of an emergency derogation power is capable of challenge. There may be another consequence when a state relies on an exceptional regime to combat terrorism: extraordinary measures may become ordinary. Not only is there a temptation to persist with them longer than necessary, but they may be extended to other problems faced by the state or even introduced into general law.[51] The danger of this 'authoritarian drift' is hard to guard against. If the claim for special powers has been sustained to combat the threat of terrorism, why should not similar powers withstand scrutiny if they are used, say, against drug trafficking or organized crime, which may cause comparable threats to public order?[52]

Amnesties   Terrorist campaigns end in a variety of ways. Because they are fought for political ends, those ends may be achieved. Equally, the forces of the state may prevail and defeat the terrorists. Such 'clean' results are rare. The search for political objectives may end in compromise. The defeat of the terrorists may be the result of a vigorous counterterrorism policy which has ignored the constraints of human rights. A day of reckoning may arrive when those who have violated human rights have lost power or have been captured. What, if any, are the obligations of those now in control?

The problem of impunity or amnesty laws for human rights violators as part of a political settlement arises with increasing frequency.
No two cases are quite the same. It does not seem excessive to interpret the basic obligation in a human rights treaty as imposing positive
duties on a state to punish those responsible for egregious violations
of human rights.[53] On the other hand, it must be acknowledged that
the process of reconciliation within a state may require that a line be
drawn under past events, no matter how shocking. It has been suggested that a carefully drawn amnesty law, which has democratic
sanction, may not be contrary to the positive duty of the state.[54] As a
substitute, the establishment of an objective record of period by a
'truth commission' may serve both to propitiate public opinion and
to satisfy the state's international obligations.[55] Once again, the characterization of any of the activities as 'terrorist' is not likely to help. It
is the perception of them in the changed circumstances which will
decide whether the polity is minded to proceed further against the
perpetrators or not.

Conclusion

'Terrorism', however normally defined, presents a serious test for those
states committed to the ideas of human rights. There are good reasons
for acting severely against those who involve themselves in such activity, reasons which go beyond the ordinary need to deal with crime and
threat to public order. Violence for political purposes is particularly
unjustified where there are non-violent political channels for ventilat-
ing grievances. A state which is committed to human rights is, amongst
other things, committed to a responsive political system. Those who
resort to political violence are attacking the foundations of the system
which protects and acknowledges human rights. Even if their ultimate
objectives are benign, their methods are unacceptable. The state can
represent them as its enemies and, since the terrorists' objectives include the spreading of fear among the public at large, any success of
their campaign may understandably result in popular support for
strong governmental reactions. The exaggeration of the actual threat to
the security of the state to justify a special regime for dealing with it
may then be resorted to by a government wishing to show that it is
'doing something' about the phenomenon, as well as being politically
popular. It compensates for the necessarily mundane gathering of intelligence and the control of terrorism through ordinary measures of
the criminal process and it assuages some of the discontent which
arises when preventative measures have dislocating or inconvenienc-
ing consequences for the public at large, through increased security
and the taxation necessary to pay for the measures.

There are, though, dangers for a government in pursuing this strategy of exaggerated response. One is that it may defeat its purpose by enhancing the status of the terrorists, who will claim that the special regime shows that they are not 'ordinary' criminals: if special means are needed to deal with them, they will say, their violence is not criminal and neither are they. The claims that they are 'political prisoners' or even prisoners of war become more plausible. Adherence to the standards of human rights is one answer for the state. If it treats terrorists and terrorism within the confines of its human rights obligations, the state's claim that they are the perpetrators of criminal violence retains its credibility. The decision to have recourse to emergency powers of course weakens this stand, but does not undermine it altogether. One consequence of recourse to the label of 'terrorism' is that the terrorist is portrayed as being beyond the law so that (practically) any measures of dealing with him can be justified because he puts himself outside the protection of the law by reason of the objectives he seeks or the means he uses to pursue them.

The importance of the human rights idea here is not as a mere guide to prudence for state policy but as an imperative bar to the adoption of certain security measures and as requiring a high level of justification for others. It is to stop the state declaring open season on the terrorist. Even convicted terrorists have rights, terrorist suspects have more rights and those who support the terrorists' ends but not their means have even more rights. These are significant restrictions for the state to bear, because it is clear that some terrorist movements can be defeated if the state is ruthless enough, while others can survive, even if they cannot gain their ultimate ends, if the state is constrained in the counterterrorist methods which it may employ. Nonetheless, so much may be demanded if the state is to remain faithful to its human rights obligations. This is a matter of principle, but there are pragmatic considerations which support it also. The obligation to assess policy against human rights standards requires a continuing and less political review of the measures adopted. It is some guard against ineffective or disproportionate measures. It is a protection against what is sometimes the terrorists' aim of inducing an excessive response from the state, disproportionate in the sense that impact of policy is felt hard on those who, while not supporting the terrorists initially, can be swayed into some degree of support for them.

Governments are inclined to argue that too strict an interpretation of their human rights obligations will inhibit the fight against terrorism, with ultimately much more serious consequences for the enjoyment of human rights. The institutions are alive to this possibility. In *Fox, Campbell and Hartley* v. *UK*,[56] the European Court said: 'Certainly Article 5(1)(c) of the Convention should not be applied in such a manner as to put disproportionate difficulties in the way of the police authorities of the Contracting States in taking effective measures to counter organized terrorism.' Much turns on that 'disproportionate'. States nearly always insist that their security forces have behaved proportionately and particularly object to what they see as decision making with hindsight by international bodies. The human rights idea does not allow total submission to what the state deems necessary. If states take human rights law seriously, they will accommodate its prescriptions not only in their laws but in the training of their forces and the planning of their operations, so that the risk of a difference between their view and that of the courts will be diminished.

If human rights have any distinctive quality, it is that they are rights which carry extra weight against public interests and even the ordinary rights of others, including the organs of the state. The role of a state bound by human rights obligations and by those bodies charged with their supervision is not simply to balance one claim against another. It is to find ways of reconciling other rights and interests with a proper respect for human rights, which may only be interfered with to the extent that is necessary and proportionate, if indeed any interference is allowed at all. Because terrorism is really (or can be made to appear to be) a serious threat to public order and even to the survival of the state, and because meeting terrorism can be unspectacular and prolonged, the political imperative 'to do something' about terrorism may result in measures which conflict with human rights but enjoy democratic support. Other measures, equally threatening to human rights, may actively contribute to 'defeating' terrorism.

When there is popular or military endorsement for counterterrorist policies, human rights institutions face a severe task. If they take the state policies on, they run the risk of non-formal or purely formal compliance. If they endorse the balance struck by the state, international human rights protection may dissolve in circumstances when it is most necessary. Stuck, as has been suggested, between the oscillating poles of 'apology and utopia',[57] the institutions will not satisfy their state and human rights audiences all the time. But the temptations for states to compromise with their commitments are demonstrably strong: if the institutions cannot seek to set the limits beyond which states must not yield to these inducements, then no-one can. It is a formidable responsibility.

Notes

1 R.Baxter, 'A sceptical look at the concept of terrorism', *Akron Law Revue*, **7**, (2), 1974, 380–91.

2 See J. Murphy, 'Defining terrorism: a way out of the quagmire', *Israel Yearbook of Human Rights*, **19**, 1989, 13–53.

3 See A. Schmid and A. Jongman, *Political Terrorism*, Amsterdam, North-Holland, 1988.

4 It is for this reason that attempts to deal with terrorism by isolating only the objective factors of the conduct itself are too wide. Hijacking may be undertaken for reasons of personal gain, hostage taking for reasons of private revenge: both would be caught by 'terrorist' treaties but neither would be properly or usefully described as terrorism. See below, note 7.

5 See A. Roberts, 'Ethics, terrorism and counter-terrorism', *Terrorism and Political Violence*, **1**, (1), 1989, 48–69.

6 C. Gearty, *Terror*, London, Faber & Faber, 1991, p.25. Dr Gearty is a lawyer as well as a political scientist.

7 The treaties listed in General Assembly resolution 49/60, the Declaration on Measures to Eliminate Terrorism are the Tokyo Convention, 1963 (Crimes on Aircraft); the Hague Convention, 1970 (Aircraft Hijacking); the Montreal Convention, 1971 (Attacks on Aircraft); the New York Convention, 1973 (Attacks on Diplomats); the New York Convention, 1979 (Hostage-Taking); the Vienna Convention, 1980 (Protection of Nuclear Material); the Montreal Convention, 1988 (Attacks at Airports); the Rome Convention and Protocol, 1988 (Attacks on Ships and Fixed Platforms); and the Montreal Convention 1991 (Marking of Plastic Explosives). In general, see A. Cassese, 'The international community's "legal" response to terrorism', *International and Comparative Law Quarterly*, **38**, (3), 1989, 589–608.

8 This is the limitation of the approach commended by T. Franck, 'Porfiry's proposition: the role of legitimacy and exculpation in combating terrorism', in Y. Dinstein (ed.), *International Law at a Time of Perplexity*, Dordrecht, Martinus Nijhoff, 1989, p.149.

9 Whether 'terrorism' in this treaty sense by state officials is exclusively caught by the treaties is one of the issues in the Lockerbie case (Case concerning Questions of the Interpretation and Application of the 1971 Montreal Convention Arising from the Aerial Incident at Lockerbie (*Libya Arab Jarahiryia* v. *UK*) *International Court of Justice Reports. Provisional measures*, 1992).

10 H. Wilson, *International Law and the Use of Force by National Liberation Movements*, Oxford, Clarendon Press, 1988.

11 F. Kitson, *Low-Intensity Operations: Subversion, Insurgency, Peace-Keeping*, London, Faber & Faber, 1971.

12 And the rights of the Palestinian people and the overthrow of apartheid.

13 For example, General Assembly Res. 3103 (XXVIII).

14 C. Greenwood, 'Terrorism and humanitarian law – the debate over Additional Protocol I', *Israel Yearbook on Human Rights*, **19**, 1989, 187–207.

15 General Assembly Res. 49/60.

16 This is not the concern of the present work, but see R. Eriksson, *Legitimate Use of Military Force against State-Sponsored International Terrorism*, Maxwell Air Force Base, Alabama, Air University Press, 1989.

17 J. Crawford, *The Creation of States in International Law*, Oxford, Clarendon Press, 1979, pp.42–7.

18 D. Geldenhuys, *Isolated States: a Comparative Analysis*, Cambridge, Cambridge University Press, 1990 (especially Part II).

19 Neither T. Franck, 'The emerging right to democratic governance', *American Journal of International Law*, **86**, (1), 1992, 46–91 nor L. Damrosch, 'Politics across borders: non-intervention and non-forcible influence over political affairs', *American Journal of International Law*, **83**, (1), 1989, 1–50 advocates the legitimacy of the use of force in support of democracy.

20 See C. Tomuschat, 'Self-determination in a post-colonial world', in C. Tomuschat (ed.), *Modern Law of Self-Determination*, Dordrecht, Martinus Nijhoff, 1993.

21 See K. Hailbronner, 'International terrorism and the laws of war', *German Yearbook of International Law*, **25**, (1), 1982, 169–98.

22 Protocol II, Article 4(2)(d): 'prohibited at any time and in any place whatsoever'.

23 T. Stein, 'How much humanity do terrorists deserve?', in A. Delissen and G. Tanja (eds), *Humanitarian Law of Armed Conflict: Challenges Ahead*, Dordrecht, Martinus Nijhoff, 1991, p 567, *inter alia* referring to the debates of the International Law Association.

24 For discussion of terrorist strategy, see G. Wardlaw, *Political Terrorism: Theory, Tactics and Counter-Measures*, 2nd edn, Cambridge, Cambridge University Press, 1989.

25 Ibid.

26 This is without prejudice to whether another state may have a right of humanitarian intervention; see N. Rodley, *To Loose the Bands of Wickedness*, London, Brassey's (UK), 1992.

27 In the *Ireland* v. *UK* case, A/25 para. 149, the European Court of Human Rights said, 'it is not called upon to take cognizance of every single aspect of the tragic situation prevailing in Northern Ireland. For example, it is not required to rule on the terrorist activities in the six counties of individuals or groups, activities that are in clear disregard of human rights'.

28 Security Council resolutions 827 and 955.

29 Inter-American Court of Human Rights, Judicial Guarantees in States of Emergency (Art 27(2), 25 and 8 American Convention on Human Rights), Advisory Opinion OC-9/87, Series A No. 9.

30 General Assembly Res. 47/133, Declaration on the Protection of All Persons from Enforced Disappearances.

31 *Velasquez Rodrieguez* v. *Honduras*, Series C No. 4, 1988.

32 Ibid., para. 182.

33 *McCann et al.* v. *UK*, European Court of Human Rights, A/324 (1995).

34 Ibid., App No. 9837/82 47 DR 27 (no claim on the facts for injury caused by terrorists). To discern the existence of a duty is by no means to decide that questions of its breach will be justiciable.

35 *McFeeley* v. *UK*, App No. 8317/78, 20 DR 44, 81.

36 European Convention on Human Rights, Article 17; see *Lawless* v. *Ireland* (Merits), A/3 (1961).

37 A/25 (1978).

38 *Ireland* v. *UK*, A/25, paras 162–4, 1978; also *Tomasi* v. *France*, A/241/A, para. 115, 1992.

39 *Ireland* v. *UK*, A/25, para. 161.

40 *Tomasi* v. *France*, A/241/A, para. 110, 1992; but note *Klaas* v. *Germany*, A/269, paras 28–9, 1993, in which the court appears to restrict the principle to persons in places of detention.

41 For example, Alemeida de Quinteros, No. 107/1981, in *Selected Decisions of the Human Rights Committee under the Optional Protocol*, Vol. 2, p.138.

42 See the Report of the UN Committee against Torture with respect to Turkey and the government's reply, in which it argued that to comply with the recom-

mendations of the Committee would 'curb the efficiency of the fight with terrorism', *Human Rights Law Journal*, **14**, (11–12), 1993, 426–9.

43 For a full consideration, see J. Jackson and S. Doran, *Judge Without Jury: Diplock Trials in the Adversary System*, Oxford, Clarendon Press, 1995.

44 *Brogan* v. *UK*, A/145-B, 1988.

45 A/28, para. 49.

46 For Turkey, see C. Rumpf, 'The protection of human rights in Turkey and the significance of international human rights instruments', *Human Rights Law Journal*, **14**, (11–12), 1993, 394–407.

47 In general, see J. Oraa, *Human Rights in States of Emergency in International Law*, Oxford, Clarendon Press, 1992; and J. Fitzpatrick, *Human Rights in Conflict: the International System for Protecting Human Rights during States of Emergency*, Philadelphia, University of Pennsylvania Press, 1994.

48 *Brannigan* v. *UK*, A/258-B, 1993, on which see S. Marks, 'Civil liberties at the margin: the U.K. Derogation and the European Court of Human Rights', *Oxford Journal of Legal Studies*, **15**, 1995, 69.

49 Habeas Corpus in Emergency Situations, Advisory Opinion OC-8/87, 1987.

50 See C. Gearty and J. Kimbell, *Terrorism and the Rule of Law: A Report on the Laws relating to Political Violence in Great Britain and Northern Ireland*, King's College, London, CLRU, 1995.

51 For example, the introduction of modifications to the right to silence, first in Northern Ireland and then in English law. See *Justice. The Right to Silence Debate: the Northern Ireland Experience*, London, 1994; Criminal Justice and Public Order Act 1994, pp.34–7.

52 For a general consideration, see D. Charters (ed.), *The Deadly Sin of Terrorism: Its Effect on Democracy and Civil Liberty in Six Countries*, Fredricton, University of New Brunswick, 1994, especially pp.211–27 (but note that this is concerned with international terrorism).

53 *Velasquez Rodrieguez*; see above, note 31.

54 See J. Kolkott, 'No impunity for human rights violations in the Americas', *Human Rights Law Journal*, **14**, 1993, 153, and the literature there cited.

55 T. Buergenthal, 'The UN Truth Commission for El Salvador', *Vanderbilt Journal of Transnational Law*, **27**, (2), 497–544; P. Hayner, 'Fifteen Truth Commissions – 1974 to 1994: a comparative study', *Human Rights Quarterly*, **16**, 1994, 597.

56 A/182 para 34, 1990.

57 S. Marks, (op. cit., note 48), 90–94. The reference is to M. Koskenniemi, *From Apology to Utopia*, Helsinki, Likimiesliiton Kustannus, 1989.

Bibliography

Amnesty International (1993), *Getting Away with Murder: Political Killings and 'Disappearances' in the 1990s*, London, Amnesty International.

Fitzpatrick, Joan (1994), *Human Rights in Conflict: the International System for Protecting Human Rights during States of Emergency*, Philadelphia, University of Pennsylvania Press.

Friedlander, Robert (1979–92), *Terrorism: Documents of International and Local Control*, 6 vols, New York, Oceana.

Gearty, Connor (1991), *Terror*, London, Faber & Faber.

Laqueur, Walter (1987), *The Age of Terrorism*, Boston, Little Brown.

Oraa, Jaime (1992), *Human Rights in States of Emergency in International Law*, Oxford, Clarendon Press.

Roht-Arriaza, Naomi (ed.) (1995), *Impunity and Human Rights in International Law and Practice*, New York, Oxford University Press.

Vercher, Antonio (1992), *Terrorism in Europe: An International Comparative Legal Perspective*, Oxford, Clarendon Press.

Walker, Clive (1992), *The Prevention of Terrorism in British Law*, 2nd edn, Manchester, Manchester University Press.

Wardlaw, Grant (1989), *Political Terrorism: Theory, Tactics and Counter-Measures*, 2nd edn, Cambridge, Cambridge University Press.

Wilkinson, Paul (1986), *Terrorism and the Liberal State*, 2nd edn, London, Macmillan.

PART III
CHALLENGES

10 Human Rights and Scientific and Technological Progress

C.G. WEERAMANTRY

Introduction

It is a truism that we live in an age dominated by technology. Technology is a new source of power. It gives to those who command it power over other members of society, which is in many ways more fundamental and far-reaching than any power known before in the long history of humanity. It gives more control over the human environment, over human society, over the human body and over the human mind than was available to the most powerful potentates of the past.

It follows that this new dimension of power, like all other dimensions of power, must be subject to law. However, so fast has been the progress of technology, and so pervasive its influence, that law and lawyers have been quite unequal to the task. They were late in responding to the new challenge, by which time the new technologies had already raced ahead, well nigh out of legal control. When at last they got down to the task, lawyers found that none of the legal concepts, legal methodologies, legal structures and legal personnel, all of which had been fashioned to meet the needs of a time when power meant largely physical power, when trespass meant largely physical trespass, when assault meant largely physical assault, were geared to face the new challenges thus confronting the law.

By way of a simple illustration of the outmoded nature of legal concepts, let us take the law of trespass, which was fashioned to meet a situation of unlawfully entering another's territory. The law could handle that species of wrongdoing. However, when it suddenly became apparent that trespass could be committed without so much as setting foot in another's domain, and by such techniques as tapping telephone calls, bouncing sound waves off a window pane or breaking a computer code, the law was not ready with the appropriate armoury of new concepts to challenge these new weapons of intrusion. The law is devising them still. But even as the law fashions new concepts and remedies, new technologies render those new remedies outmoded even before they see the light of day. Such are the problems which confront us today. These will grow exponentially as we move into the new century, a century dominated by information technology.

Parallel to this growth of technology has been the growth of the corporate empires which own them. Since sophisticated technology is expensive and needs great wealth to generate and control it, the vast business corporations of today tend to become its proprietors. Those corporations, whose financial power in many instances exceeds that of many a nation-state, give technology an added dimension of power – the combination of technological and economic strength. Together they represent a phalanx of power which is well beyond the ability of the individual to resist.

Yet another dimension to this phalanx of power is the alliance which has been forged between technology, economic power and the military establishment. Technology, at its highest levels, becomes invaluable for purposes of war and, consequently, strikes an alliance with the military establishment in many countries. Each helps and sustains the other, for the military need the improved weapons which technology can devise and the technologists need the political and economic support which come from the military establishment. As a result, we are faced with the phenomenon of the military–industrial complex, regarding whose growing power President Eisenhower warned the American people, in his farewell speech. The world is facing globally the dangers that Eisenhower spoke of in a domestic context.

Problems in Domestic Law

The inadequacies of national legal systems to deal with the problems of modern technology may conveniently be considered under the heads of legal structures, legal procedures and legal concepts.

The inadequacy of legal structures is illustrated from time to time in trials before domestic courts where scientific complexities are placed before judges and juries who do not necessarily enjoy the benefit of a scientific training. Days of expert scientific evidence are placed before judges and juries who often find themselves quite out of their depth, but are yet required to render a decision. For example, in a murder case, the analysis of bloodstains may require a knowledge of the most advanced developments in immunology and protein chemistry. Such instances demonstrate how the right to a fair trial may sometimes be jeopardized by the extreme sophistication of scientific evidence today.

In former times, as special fields of law developed, special courts or divisions emerged with special experience in those fields. The increasing frequency with which science-related matters will surface before the courts has led to suggestions that judicial bodies should similarly comprise special divisions of judges with a scientific background who would be better equipped to handle sophisticated scientific evidence.

Judicial procedures are largely adversarial. Two parties present opposing viewpoints to the court and the court decides, upon a balance of probabilities, which of the two contending parties should win the day. This is not the best method to determine the human rights impact of a new piece of technology. Existing judicial structures are therefore not the appropriate agencies for making such determinations. In addition, they are hampered by archaic and formalistic rules of procedure which require evidence to be produced in a certain manner and which penalize a party not following the rules, by shutting out the evidence that party proposes to tender. Moreover, current procedures are expensive and dilatory.

For all these reasons, the courts are not geared to predict the future impact of a given piece of technology. They are not structured to make projections into the future. Other agencies must be found to determine these matters on behalf of the community.

Suggestions have been made to this end from time to time, such as human rights committees, watchdog agencies of the public to monitor new technologies, technical impact assessment boards and interdisciplinary committees. All of these must be studied for their usefulness in this regard. It should, in short, be realized that the traditional reliance on judicial mechanisms for the protection of the public against the invasion of their rights by modern technology is becoming increasingly inadequate. Since their traditional structures and procedures are not geared to the assessment of scientific material or its impact upon the community, the courts cannot be watchdogs of human rights in this regard.

As with legal structures and procedures, so also with legal concepts. They have been tailored by generations of lawyers to meet the needs of formalistic and individually based legal systems. For example, the concept of absolute ownership of property can be very damaging to human rights, for it enables owners of property to treat it as their private preserve, without due regard to the social obligations which ownership imposes. This is particularly so in relation to land, for the law has vested immovable property with many of the attributes of movable property. Movable property belongs to its owner in the absolute sense that the owner can damage or destroy it at his will. To apply these concepts to immovable property is to invite the owner of land to neglect the social responsibilities which go with the ownership.

Such attitudes have resulted in the environmental devastation we see all around us. The notion of absolute rights of private property is totally inconsistent with the notion of intergenerational fairness, which is a human rights concept only now beginning to emerge.

Before the first Land Commission in the British Solomons (1919–24), a Pacific Islander, giving evidence, poured scorn on the concept that land could be treated 'as if it were a thing like a box', which one could buy and sell like merchandise, pointing out that land was treated in his society with more respect and with due regard to the rights of future generations.[1] Such a view of property rights, particularly concerning land, could have saved the world from many environmental problems which cause immense concern today.

Similar considerations apply to the concept of absolute freedom of contract, which needs to be adapted to the requirements of the technological age. Modern technology gives vast power to global conglomerates who make commercial bargains in all parts of the world for the sale and use of their technology. The bargains are between parties of vastly unequal bargaining power, with one party desperately needing the technology which only the other can offer. The result can sometimes be very damaging to human rights.

Problems in International Law

Just as the rapid progress of technology poses grave new problems for domestic law, it poses new problems also for international law. The problem here is of a somewhat different kind for, despite all its limitations, domestic law can legislate to meet a new need, and can impose the will of the legislature upon its subjects. International law is not equipped with such a direct mechanism for formulating a binding rule of law. International law operates only through treaties, customary law, general principles of international law, decisions of tribunals and the writings of jurists. It will be seen that it becomes difficult for international law to lay down specific rules on such matters. The closest approach it can make to laying down rules after the manner of domestic legislation is an international treaty, but an international treaty needs the consent of every state which is to be bound, and takes a great deal of negotiation to achieve.

International law is thus even slower to respond to the threats posed by technology to human rights. Furthermore, states which have a vested interest in the particular technology under discussion will tend to oppose any international attempt to regulate it. A treaty binding that country will therefore be difficult to obtain.

It may be possible to build up a sufficient body of international opposition to the development or extension of a new technology through international conferences which evolve a kind of consensus in condemning a particularly damaging kind of technology. It is often through such international conferences that a feeling emerges in the international community that a particular technology needs to be controlled. Discussions may then take place in the General Assembly of the United Nations and an international instrument (declaration) may emerge.

Whether such a General Assembly declaration has the status of customary international law is a question that international lawyers have long debated. Some hold that it has no legal force whatever, but others view such widely accepted declarations as 'soft law' which, in due time, receives recognition as a rule of customary international law.

This brief discussion will show how difficult it is to regulate internationally such technology-related dangers as threats to the ozone layer, atmospheric and marine pollution, and threats to endangered species. The fact that hundreds of bird and mammal species and tens of thousands of plant life species are threatened with extinction does not seem to be sufficient to overcome these barriers to the formulation of new principles of international law.

However, international lawyers are conscious of the need for haste in the formulation of new rules of international law and are sometimes able to achieve these with remarkable speed, as in the case of the new rules of international law which were rapidly created for the handling of matters relating to outer space. Also international law has gone some way towards regulating many areas of technological danger, as, for example, in regard to nuclear technology or computer privacy. International lawyers are constantly discussing ways in which the formulation of rules of customary international law can be speeded up to meet such challenges.

Concerns of the Developing World

The deep concern felt by the developing world in regard to the misuse of science and technology was reflected at various conferences commencing in the 1970s. One of the best known of these was what is called the 'Poona Indictment', which was adopted at a meeting of the World Order Models Project held in Poona, India, in July 1978. The declaration, entitled *The Perversion of Science and Technol-*

ogy: An Indictment,[2] stated that it was 'an indictment of the way in which science and technology had become instruments of a global structure of inequity, exploitation and oppression'. It referred, *inter alia*, to drug testing among poor populations, and the employment of 50 per cent of all research scientists in the world in military research and development. Among specific areas referred to were the indiscriminate fishing methods used by mechanized trawlers, deforestation resulting in flooding of land and silting of rivers, and the drive to sell the products of modern technology, regardless of whether they served a real social need. The Poona Indictment stressed the need to direct scientific enterprise towards the needs, skills and knowledge of the majority of the underprivileged peoples of the world and discussed the lack of inclination among scientific elites in the developed and developing worlds to discuss the critical issues mentioned in this declaration.

Such statements, indicative of the deep concern felt in the developing world at the direction of growth of science and technology, have far-reaching human rights implications. True, some of the concerns thus expressed in the 1970s have attracted a measure of attention from the scientific community, but many of them still remain unaddressed. Global studies of the impact of technology on human rights need to take note of this dimension of the problems posed by modern science and technology.

Since the Poona Indictment, there have been many international conferences dealing with global issues of desertification, pollution, dumping of shoddy goods and the like, but the competing interests involved in furthering these technologies and in containing them pose a continuing problem.

United Nations Responses

In the late 1960s, the United Nations awakened to the dangers posed to human rights by recent advances in technology. The International Conference on Human Rights, held in Tehran in 1968, was the first to address these issues. The Proclamation of Tehran stated that 'while recent scientific discoveries and technological advances have opened vast prospects for economic, social and cultural progress, such developments may nevertheless endanger the rights and freedoms of individuals and will require continuing attention'.[3]

The Conference recommended to the organizations of the United Nations family that they undertake studies in regard to the following:

1   respect for privacy in view of recording techniques;

2   protection of the human personality and its physical and intellec-
      tual integrity in view of the progress in biology, medicine and
      biochemistry;
3   the uses of electronics which may affect the rights of the person,
      and the limits which should be placed on its uses in a democratic
      society;
4   more generally, the balance which should be established between
      scientific and technological progress and the intellectual, spir-
      itual, cultural and moral advancement of humanity.[4]

There were many reasons for the late awakening of the United
Nations system to this danger. Not the least of these was a lack of
immediacy, as compared with other and seemingly more urgent issues confronting the newly independent states which were emerging
from colonial rule. There was also a widely shared view that extremely sensitive political issues could arise in this area,[5] such as
possible allegations of the use of scientific and technological development for purposes of state control.

Once the United Nations system began to interest itself in this
field, it went on to concern itself with a varied range of the threats
from new technology, and both the Secretary-General and various
specialized agencies prepared a series of reports upon the subject.
Among the subjects studied were computerized data systems and
electronic communications techniques which might affect rights of
privacy; biochemical and medical advances, such as artificial insemination and psychotropic drugs; and the harmful effects of automation
and mechanization of production.

The problems under consideration were not of course without
their continuing political overtones. For example, just as it could be
argued that it was necessary to protect the individual against intru-
sions or controls by the state based upon the new technology, so also
it could be argued that science and technology could be used by
powerful states to violate the integrity of weaker states, interfering
with national liberation movements and exploiting their natural resources. In fact, such a political shift to the debate, switching the
emphasis from individual domestic protections to supranational state
obligations, occurred in 1974, when the Soviet Union, in association
with the German Democratic Republic, Hungary and Poland, among
others, brought to the General Assembly a draft declaration on the
use of scientific and technological progress in the interests of peace
and for the benefit of mankind.

On 10 November 1975, the General Assembly, by its Declaration
on the Use of Scientific and Technological Progress in the Interests of
Peace and for the Benefit of Mankind, called on all states to prevent
the use of scientific and technological developments to limit or

interfere with human rights and basic freedoms. The Declaration noted: 'while scientific and technological developments provide ever-increasing opportunities to better the conditions of life of peoples and nations, in a number of instances they can give rise to social problems, as well as threaten the human rights and fundamental freedom of the individual'.

One of the articles of this Declaration noted the responsibilities of states: 'to extend the benefits of science and technology to all strata of the population and to protect them from possible harmful effects of the misuse of scientific and technological developments'.

The Western countries abstained from voting on the Declaration. All states were required, in terms of this Declaration, to 'refrain from any acts involving the use of scientific and technological achievements for the purposes of violating the sovereignty and territorial integrity of other states, interfering in their internal affairs, waging aggressive wars, suppressing national liberation movements or pursuing a policy of racial discrimination'.[6]

These political overtones did not, however, obscure the importance of the problem. They rather highlighted its gravity and urgency, for they made it evident how far-reaching and many-faceted the impact of technology could be. Despite all this effort, the international community's mechanisms and conceptual tools designed to attain this object are proving inadequate to the challenge. Extensive thought and international cooperation are required in order to make inroads upon this problem.

The UN Commission on Human Rights took this concern further and initiated continuing studies on this much neglected area of possible violation of human rights. By resolution 1986/9 of 10 March 1986, entitled 'Use of Scientific and Technological Developments for the Promotion and Protection of Human Rights and Fundamental Freedoms', it invited the United Nations University (UNU) to study both the positive and negative impacts of scientific and technological developments on human rights and fundamental freedoms. The UNU responded to this request by appointing an interdisciplinary and cross-cultural group of experts, under its auspices, to study the problems involved. This resulted in a volume, *Human Rights and Scientific and Technological Development*, which looked at the problem from a global perspective and examined the normative and institutional responses to it by the international community. It also looked at some specific problems, such as the structure of the scientific enterprise, and issues connected with the environment. This study was taken further, from the generic to the specific, in another volume, *The Impact of Science on Human Rights: Global Case-Studies*,[7] through case studies of the impact of a variety of different types of technology in specific country settings.

One country from each geographical area was selected for this study. The resulting studies of agricultural technology in Thailand, industrial technology in Poland, medical technology in The Netherlands, weapons technology in Ethiopia and a variety of technologies in Venezuela, offer many insights, based on specific practical experiences, regarding the nature and genesis of the problems encountered, and on means which may be considered for their solution.

A growing body of literature is addressing this problem, which may truly be described as perhaps the fastest growing area of modern human rights, for there is scarcely an aspect of life in our time which has not been affected importantly – and sometimes fundamentally reshaped – by modern technology.

We shall now proceed to consider some of these areas of danger under the separate heads of the human body, human society and the human environment.

The Human Body

The Preamble to the Universal Declaration of Human Rights commences with a reference to the inherent dignity of all members of the human family and provides more specifically that all human beings are born free and equal in dignity and rights (Article 1); that no one shall be subjected to torture or to cruel, inhuman or degrading treatment or punishment (Article 5); and that everyone has the right to recognition everywhere as a person before the law (Article 6). Article 29(1) recognizes the importance of the free and full development of human personality. What are the technologies which erode this high recognition of human dignity through their impact upon the human body?

A vast range of biotechnological developments comes immediately to mind: human experimentation, foetal experimentation, sale and hire of organs, torture techniques, psychosurgery, personality tests, the use of untested drugs, genetic engineering, selective breeding and preselection of sex are but some of these. Sperm and ova banks, *in vitro* fertilization, embryo transplantation, foetus farms – all of these raise important ethical and human rights issues.

The problem here is that research on the human body for therapeutic and preventive purposes must always go ahead. On the other hand, as more knowledge is acquired, new possibilities open up for the use of that knowledge for unethical purposes, or for purposes whose ethical value is debatable.

The author's personal experience of speaking on these matters around 20 years ago to medical audiences led him to sense, at the time, that the intrusion of non-medical personnel such as lawyers into the arena of medical activity was unwelcome. The point of view was strongly expressed that doctors, no less than other human beings, are concerned members of society and could be trusted to use their specialist knowledge in the best interests of society; the area they were in charge of was a specialist area and they were the best judges of how their specialist knowledge could be used ethically.

In the past 15 or 20 years, that attitude has changed remarkably. Today, discussion of ethical issues in the medical field by non-medical persons, such as lawyers, ethicists and theologians, is welcomed. Major hospitals have set up interdisciplinary committees involving such personnel, to function alongside doctors in order to assist them in reaching decisions on difficult issues. Universities have set up ethics committees to exercise control over such areas as medical experimentation and psychological research. In short, constant vigilance is required to ensure that new advances in medical technology are kept within ethical guidelines.

Advances in medical technology, as in biotechnology, can spill over from the realm of pure science to the realm of commerce and, at that stage, the areas of possible abuse multiply. Organ transplants, extremely valuable as a new scientific technique, can become the subject of commercial exploitation. The sale of organs is sometimes organized on a commercial basis, with intermediaries and advertisements luring people from the poor world into the rich world to donate organs such as a kidney for a price which seems attractive to the poor person concerned. The donor can indeed live without a kidney, and is prepared to undergo the resulting inconvenience for the affluence that this brings him in his own society. Worse abuses are now taking place, as has been claimed recently in regard to destitute street children being rounded up in big cities for the alleged purpose of using their organs. Examples such as these show that the problems are becoming of urgent concern, both nationally and internationally.

Likewise, in regard to the human mind, invasive techniques such as psychosurgery were the subject of much abuse until, comparatively recently, professional controls in this regard were somewhat tightened. Instances of unwanted brain surgery in the United States, for example, have proliferated to the point of becoming a matter of grave national concern.

The possible invasions of human dignity and of the integrity of the human body are too varied and unforeseeable to catalogue in any single study.

Human Society

Concern about the damaging impacts of information technology upon society date back to the early 1970s. In 1972, President Nixon expressed his concern in a nationwide radio broadcast regarding the vast amount of information held in computer banks concerning 150 million US citizens. The President observed: 'Adequate safeguards must always stand watch so that man remains the master and never becomes the victim of the computer.' During the period which has elapsed since this warning, computer power has grown exponentially.

With the trend towards centralization, there is a tendency for a merger of various data banks in which such information is held. A pooling of data contained in income tax records, customs records, police records, health records, credit records, motor registration records and the like can give any government a vast dossier of information about each individual citizen. In addition, there are records held by public authorities, such as universities or national insurance schemes, which can add to the information available, providing many details which the individual concerned may prefer to keep private. Moreover, the growth of commercial organizations operating multinationally means that their thousands of employees and customers also run the risk of a pooling of data concerning themselves in a central data bank which is often beyond the control of national laws of the individual employee or customer.

As a result, major problems arise with regard to protection of the citizen against the abuse of this information, for information is power, and whoever holds a complete dossier of information about every facet of a person's life has power over that person. Moreover, there is the problem of trans-border data flow, that is the flow of data concerning citizens of a country which escapes beyond national borders and thereafter remains free from the control of the country to which that individual belongs. Trans-border data flow has attracted much attention, particularly from the OECD countries which have adopted strict guidelines regarding the control of such personal data.

The lack of the necessary controls, in regard to the vast bulk of the world's citizens, poses grave human rights problems, sometimes summarized in the term 'the new information tyranny'. Both governments and corporate establishments can be the entities which abuse such information power.

The preceding paragraphs deal with tyranny through information concerning a citizen. There is also the growing danger of the monopolization of the means of mass information by governments or media groups. This constitutes another aspect of tyranny through information, for it enables the controllers of the media to determine what information will reach the average citizen and what will not.

They are thus able to mould public opinion, for the public can only form its opinions on the basis of the information it receives. A newly emergent human right is the right to information. Citizens are entitled to a full and free flow of information (subject, of course, to certain obvious safeguards in the public interest), concerning matters of importance in the running of their daily lives. Selective, incomplete or distorted information can be a real threat to the exercise of all the other human rights which a citizen enjoys in a free society – including even the right to vote, for this presupposes the right to proper information. The right to health can be similarly damaged by incomplete information regarding food, drugs or environmental dangers.

Yet another form of tyranny, which modern technology is rendering easier to achieve than before, is through the perfection of methods of psychological and physical torture. Many governments across the world have been documented as resorting to torture as an instrument of government. New techniques are being perfected and new forms of psychological and physical torture, strange to say, are still being devised. Amnesty International has considered this problem at great length and has referred to it as an 'epidemic of torture' practices which is sweeping the world. Among the new instruments of torture are drugs which induce certain psychological reactions such as horror or fear or disorientation, and finely-graded electrical shock. There is also pharmacological torture, where the victim does not know which drugs, of a range of drugs causing predictable unpleasant symptoms such as temporary paralysis, will be administered to him. Psychological tortures used for in-depth interrogation are other developments. All of these impose a heavy responsibility on the medical profession (especially those connected with prisons and the army) to refuse to be party to the use of such techniques, and to report them when they do occur.

Another aspect of high technology which has adverse social implications is the way in which technological secrets are jealously guarded. While the possessor of technology is entitled to protect the intellectual property associated with it, there is often a shrouding of the research results, and the impact assessments of that technology, thereby preventing the public from being able to assess whether it is useful or otherwise.

In a related area, problems can arise regarding patent rights in new discoveries or inventions, with implications for basic human rights. Let us take, for example, the right to health and, as a perhaps fanciful illustration, the creation of a drug which cures cancer. To what extent does the creator of the drug have the right to fix exorbitant price levels, placing the drug beyond the reach of the global public? Likewise, problems can arise regarding patent rights in agricultural products such as 'miracle grains', disease-resistant species of essential crops and newly created hybrids. In all of these, the inventor or the creator or the owner of the patent has rights which must be respected. At the same time, one cannot ignore the interest of the community in the product. A proper balance needs to be struck, but the principles and mechanisms for achieving such a balance need further study.

In regard to the impact of technology on society, another trend to be noted is the spread of sophisticated technology to various terrorist movements, both domestic and international. The devices available to terrorist organizations keep increasing in sophistication and some organizations even maintain their own research laboratories for furthering and refining their weapons of attack. Terrorist organizations are sometimes in communication with each other, thereby enabling a pooling or exchange of the technical knowledge in their possession. These are all problems awaiting concerned domestic and international attention.

The Human Environment

It is not necessary to delve deeply into this area, which has been the subject of much popular attention. The depletion of the ozone layer, the extinction of fauna and flora, the felling of rain forests, desertification, the pollution of the atmosphere, of lakes, rivers and seas – all these are proceeding apace. Major international conferences, such as the 1992 Rio Conference on the Environment, bring together all the Member States of the United Nations community for the purpose of addressing these problems. They make some progress but, by and large, the solutions, if any, are only partial and the problems grow in intensity from year to year.

Oil spillage, discharges into the ocean of radioactive and other toxic wastes, unregulated depletion of marine species from plankton to whales, destruction of coral reefs – all of these cumulatively can affect the global food chain, apart from their damaging effects upon the right to a pure and healthy environment.

New technologies make massive deforestation a much easier operation than ever before. The loss of tree cover caused by uncontrolled felling of forests has an impact in at least three major ways. In the first place, it raises the carbon dioxide levels of the atmosphere which otherwise the forests might have absorbed. Secondly, it erodes the valuable topsoil on which agriculture depends. Studies reveal that tens of thousands of millions of tons of topsoil have been irreversibly lost in this fashion. Thirdly, it raises the water table, for the deep roots of trees no longer suck out the water and pump it into the atmosphere, with the result that the water table rises, carrying its salt layer to the surface and turning green belts into arid wastes.

Similar analyses could be made of many other activities connected with science and technology. Mining, for example, converts once attractive landscapes into barren moonscapes, unless a special effort is made to restore the land to a usable condition. Fortunately, in several countries, modern legislation requires the miner to restore land to a usable condition after mining.

Reference should also be made to the vast increase in the manufacture and use of new chemicals. Nearly one thousand new chemicals, many of them untried, come on the market each year, swelling the ranks of the nearly 100 000 chemicals already in use. The World Health Organization estimates that 75–85 per cent of cancers are triggered by environmental agents, such as industrial chemicals. Herbicides, such as Agent Orange, are thought to have caused cancer, sterility and deformities.

Chernobyl has brought to the attention of a concerned world public the massive human rights deprivations which can follow from nuclear reactor accidents. The chance of such an accident in one of the hundreds of reactors across the world cannot be discounted. Thermal pollution, acid rain, depletion of the ozone layer and the greenhouse effect are all manifestations of the problems which the present generation is bequeathing to succeeding generations.

Modern international law and human rights are developing the notion of intergenerational rights owed by one generation to its successors. Those other generations, not yet being in existence, are not recognized by most legal systems as bearers of rights and, consequently, their interests tend to be totally neglected. The recognition of this new human rights concept can reduce the damage caused to future generations by the self-centred orientation of current legal systems.

An Ethic for Scientists

The scientific enterprise has functioned hitherto on the basis that truthfulness of scientific reporting is the prime value. The primary principle which governs the scientific ethic is the principle of loyalty to truth. The emphasis on this ethical aspect has tended to cloud the importance of other ethical issues.

The medical profession has been an exception in this regard, for the Hippocratic oath has from very early times set before the medical practitioner certain ethical standards which he or she is expected to observe over and above the mere standard of scientific loyalty to truth. However, the Hippocratic code is a very rudimentary ethical code, totally inadequate to the vast new problems which today raise issues of an ethical nature. Even more importantly, it is to be noted that most other bodies of scientists do not owe loyalty to any formulated ethical code. The computer scientist, the engineer, the microbiologist, the physicist, the chemist – all of these, despite the vast social implications of their research, lack an ethical code which binds them to the observance of certain ethical values.

It is true that today an awareness of the need for such ethical codes is growing, and that such bodies as associations of engineers, or computer workers, are working out some basic ethical codes which practitioners of the relevant disciplines are expected to observe. These codes are still largely rudimentary and, by and large, not obligatory in their nature. Consequently, a researcher engaged on some work which may well be damaging to human rights is not required to take this factor into consideration in deciding whether or not to pursue that kind of activity. Therefore scientists engaged in work which can be very damaging to the environment, or weapons scientists engaged in perfecting some new lethal weapon, are not obliged, under the present dispensation, to consider the human rights implications of their work.

Notable exceptions do of course exist, as where scientists engaged on recombinant DNA experimentation imposed a moratorium on their own research in the fear that a newly synthesized microbe of unknown lethal potential could be created which could decimate the human race. In such notable instances, which are indeed exceptional, ethical principles have been translated into practical restraints on scientific research.

The human rights implications of damaging technology are, however, so great as to make it a matter of urgency that the importance of an ethical code for scientists be brought home to practitioners in all branches of science. It is no longer adequate for the scientist to say that he or she is a concerned human being like everyone else and can be depended upon to bear in mind any possible damage to society resulting from the work in hand. This has not worked in the past and it will not in the future. One recalls contemporaneous accounts of the jubilation shown by the scientists at Los Alamos when news was brought to them of the successful detonation at Hiroshima of the nuclear weapon they had created.[8]

A view heavily stressed in the 1960s was that the purpose to which science was applied was outside the boundaries of science itself. As observed in a well-known book of that period on scientific enterprise, 'Purpose, aesthetics, [...] ethics – these are outside the boundaries of science.'[9] Whatever may be the correctness of this observation within the purely scientific operations involved, it should not cloud the vision of the scientist regarding the purpose of his research. It is essential for him to bear in mind that it is the same set of technical rules which would be used, whether for the construction of a hospital or for that of a torture chamber. It will not do for the scientist to give of his expertise, shutting his eyes to the end result for which that expertise is used.

Law School Curricula

Since it is clear that the twenty-first century will be one dominated by technology and that, consequently, there will be a heavy proportion of science-related disputes coming before the courts for determination, it is a matter of some urgency to attune future lawyers to the interface area between technology and human rights. Most law school curricula are totally lacking in this regard and serious thought needs to be given to this future need by authorities in charge of legal education.

Taking this idea into the realm of continuing education, it will perhaps be important to give thought to the organization of a series of workshops where lawyers and scientists interact on these issues. In the biomedical field, this is already happening, but there is not much evidence of similar movements in regard to other fields of science.

The idea should also be considered of the establishment of institutions for the study of humanistic science, with an emphasis on those branches of science pertaining to life and the life sciences. A prototype of this kind of institution is the Mitsubishi Kasei Institute of Life Sciences in Tokyo, which emphasizes the humanistic aspects of science and promotes cross-disciplinary and public understanding of the interrelationship between science and society. Major technological enterprises, as well as governments, could take the initiative in this regard.

Another important step is the orientation of lawyers towards the problem of the impact of technology on human rights. It would be useful if organizations of lawyers, which traditionally set up subcommittees dealing with different aspects of their activities, were alerted to the need to establish a bar special committee in each country to review the current relationship between technology and human rights there, and to alert the community to any possible dangers. The American Bar Association's Standing Committee on Law and Technology, and its quarterly journal, *The Jurimetrics Journal*, could be used as a prototype for such efforts.

Technology and Human Rights Education

If a serious effort is to be mounted to preserve communities from the adverse effects of technology upon their human rights, it is vital that technology and human rights education go hand in hand. Training young people in technology is, by itself, insufficient. Along with that training there must also be the requisite input of human rights education, enabling them to see the interrelationship between technology and human rights, with particular reference to their own societies.

It is perhaps important that, at the vocational colleges, institutes of technology and universities, courses on technology be supplemented by the relevant human rights perspectives. Most courses in the sciences do not currently contain a segment on human rights. Human rights are important, not merely from the standpoint of attuning the minds of decision makers to the human rights nuances of their decisions on science and technology. Human rights also become relevant in the sense of the right of access to information which bears upon this technology. Very often, the technical information essential to a proper decision regarding the use of a product is not easily available. This is sometimes even so in regard to the decision maker himself, because a wall of secrecy relating to the impact of that technology comes between him and his decision. A classic instance of the withholding of technical information relating to a given product is the withholding of scientific information relating to the adverse impact of tobacco smoking. This information was kept away from consumers for many years. This illustration will indicate how important it is, in connection with science and technology, that there be a well recognized right of access to the relevant information.

If decision makers are often kept away from relevant information, it is quite evident how easy it is for the actual consumer to be denied the relevant scientific information relating to the product he or she is invited to use. It is vital that those in charge of decisions relating to science and technology insist on a free flow of the requisite technological information to the prospective users of the product, be they industrialists or the humble farmer in the field. It is only through such a free flow of information that the community would eventually have a guarantee that the proper decision has been made in regard to the acceptance or otherwise of a given technology.

Choice of Technology

Science and technology are often perceived as being inexorable in their development. Science floods into whatever areas its course of development dictates, and there is no element of choice which can direct or deflect its course.

While it is indeed true that science is often unstoppable in its relentless progress, this circumstance must not obscure the areas of conscious choice which are still available. Science cannot develop in every direction opened up by each new development, for the cost of modern science is extremely high and there are just not enough resources to permit of research in every direction where advances seem feasible.

This perspective becomes particularly important in the context of the developing world, where there is often a belief that, since the spread of technology is inexorable, there is no choice, especially for a poor country, over the nature of the technology which it is to receive or develop. On the contrary, there is very often an area of choice available to the recipient country as to which of several competing technologies it will opt to receive or develop.

There is here a danger, in that the decision makers in developing countries tend often to belong to elitist groups within those countries, which have common interests and shared perspectives with similar groups in the developed world. Consequently, where there is a choice, that choice is often made in consonance with the desires of privileged groups in a developing society rather than in accordance with the needs of the larger section of the population. This occurs despite the fact that the latter group may be in dire need of a technology suited to their particular condition rather than that of the affluent minority.

Readers wishing to pursue this aspect further are referred to S. Chamarik's observations in the chapter on 'Technological self-reliance and cultural freedom' in *Human Rights and Scientific and Technological Development* (see note 5). Such studies emphasize the need for self-reliance in the choice of technology. Many of these societies are, in fact, inheritors from the days of their colonial past of the technologies which were brought to them by the colonial power. With independence, the capacity to make an independent choice of technology is acquired but, for the reasons stated, that choice may not be fully exercised. In the words of S. Chamarik: 'Notwithstanding all the nationalistic claims, however, the fact remains that these national elites' aspirations and goals are closely associated with and strongly inclined toward the western master culture.'[10] The rural and traditional sector bears the heaviest the burden of a false choice and, as S. Chamarik observes:

> It is in this light that the existing state and future prospects for human rights in developing countries should be understood and assessed. The implications obviously go far beyond the issues between North

and South. They certainly involve more than the conventional set of human rights, as developed from the standpoint of the rising mercantile and industrial capitalist classes within the cultural context of the industrial West.[11]

The concept of appropriate technology has been worked out with these problems in view. There is not the space here to deal with the various facets of current thinking about appropriate technology. Appropriate technology, though a useful concept, needs to be carefully applied. Some of the problems attending the concept are the lack of a comprehensive approach, the lack of a future orientation, the creation of false hopes, an inadequate rate of change, the lack of institutional infrastructure, the lack of information on alternative technologies and the lack of people's participation.[12]

Examples of inappropriate technologies in the agricultural sector are the indiscriminate use of insecticides and herbicides, applied to the wrong extent, by the wrong method, or through failure to explore other methods which might be appropriate. So also are the use of inappropriate fertilizers which tend to reduce the proper use of natural elements, such as compost, hay and rice husk.[13]

The correct choice of technology is important also in the field of pharmacology, where very often expensive products developed for affluent societies are accepted almost as a matter of course by societies which cannot afford them, without a proper scrutiny of their suitability for the recipient community or the availability of alternatives.

In all of these examples, there is a commercial interest involved which has great resources at its disposal for pushing the sales of its product. Unless the technological elites in the receiving country are adequately equipped and motivated to make more disinterested evaluations, the human rights of the recipient agricultural community can be damaged.

Legislative Restructuring

Much of the legislation of the future will be science-oriented, or at least have some interface area with technology. Most legislatures of the world, as at present structured, do not have a built-in scientific resource for consultation regarding legislation which involves the use of technology in a manner which may have social implications. Nor do most legislators have the necessary background of scientific expertise to comprehend fully the implications of science-related legislation. As a result, many legislators tend to be over susceptible to the influence of lobbyists, who give them a scientific perspective from the standpoint of those who wish to promote the legislation, or those who wish to oppose it. Lobby groups are very powerful and have at their command great resources which can rarely be matched by the expertise available to individual legislators. An in-house repository of scientific expertise could be useful in this regard, so that legislators would be able to obtain a disinterested opinion in relation to proposed legislation before the lobbyists get to work. Also it may be possible for lawmakers with a scientific training to pool their resources and give the benefit of their own expertise when such matters come up for discussion.

Even more importantly, impact-assessment boards should be set up to which legislation which will have an effect upon society and upon human rights can be referred. Such impact-assessment boards or technology-assessment boards, as they are commonly called, would need to be interdisciplinary, and it would help legislators if a given piece of legislation could be cleared with such a board before it passes into law.

Another source of guidance on these matters is the creation of centres in each country for the study of scientific policy. Each country would know its particular technological needs and the likely impact of a given technology upon its society and environment. It would help greatly if such studies could be made prior to the passing of legislation, rather than delay them until legislation has passed into law and then becomes difficult to alter.

A Scientific Ombudsman

A problem of growing importance in the field we are considering is the moral responsibility of individuals who are engaged in a scientific enterprise which may have an adverse impact upon human rights. Quite often, workers in a project are faced with moral problems in regard to some research they are called upon to do and, consequently, would like to discuss this moral aspect or bring it to the notice of the public. They tend often to be inhibited from doing so because of the fear of adverse repercussions upon their employment prospects. The principle should be well established that a moral concern felt by such a worker should not be suppressed for fear of repercussions, but that the worker should be encouraged to discuss this matter and seek advice. In extreme cases, it may even be necessary to alert the public.

Disputes could arise as a result of such concerns and it would be useful to have an entity, set up officially or unofficially, to which such matters could be referred and which could also adjudicate in the event of complaints of victimization for whistle-blowing activity.

The matters discussed in this chapter and the suggestions made are but a representative sampling from the enormous slate of issues which demand discussion. Every community needs to be alerted to the intricate interrelationship between advancing technology and human rights. Decision makers and professionals, in particular, need to be sensitized to this problem and to have it very much in mind when called upon to make decisions, directly or indirectly, involving a technological element. All too often, decisions are made with a complete lack of awareness of the interlinkages which are the subject of this chapter.

As we move into the next century, every citizen will live increasingly under the dominance of technology. Unless these problems are addressed now, they may well be uncontrollable, and technology will reign uncontrolled even in areas where it nullifies important human rights. The price of freedom, it is said, is eternal vigilance. Here is an area where special vigilance is demanded, for the threats it poses are often unseen. They must be detected and addressed in time, but cannot be so addressed except by communities alerted to the presence of dangers surpassing in power and pervasiveness any which have been encountered in the long annals of the law.

Notes

1   P. Sack, *Land between Two Laws*, Canberra, ANU Press, 1973, p.33.
2   B. Weston, R. Falk and A. D'Amato, *Basic Documents in International Law and World Order*, St. Paul, MN, West Publishing Co. 1980, p.421.
3   United Nations, *Final Act of the International Conference on Human Rights*, Tehran, 22 April to 13 May 1968, p.5.
4   Ibid., p.12.
5   Sadako Ogata, 'Introduction: United Nations approaches to human rights and scientific and technological development', in C.G. Weeramantry (ed.), *Human Rights and Scientific and Technological Development*, Tokyo, UNU Press, 1990, p.3.
6   General Assembly resolution 3384 (XXX) (1975).
7   C.G. Weeramantry (ed.), *The Impact of Science on Human Rights: Global Case-Studies*, Tokyo, UNU Press, 1993.
8   R.W. Reid, *Tongues of Conscience*, London/Harmondsworth, Constable, 1969, pp.103–4.
9   Magnus Pyke, *The Boundaries of Science*, London, Pelican Books, 1963, p.201.
10 Ibid., p.46, citing A. Rahman, 'The interaction between science, technology and society: historical and comparative perspective', *International Social Science Journal*, 33, (3), 1981, 529; see also Susantha Goonatilake, *Aborted Discovery: Science and Creativity in the Third World*, London, Zed Books Ltd, 1984, chs 3 and 5.
11 S. Chamarik, 'Technological self-reliance and cultural freedom', in *Human Rights and Scientific and Technological Development* (op. cit., note 5), p.47.
12 For a fuller discussion of these, see Vittit Muntarbhorn, 'Technology and human rights: critical implications for Thailand', in *The Impact of Science and Technology on Human Rights: Global Case-Studies* (op. cit., note 7), pp.97, 114 ff.
13 Ibid., pp.113–14.

Bibliography

Alcorn, P. (1986), *Social Issues in Technology – A Format for Investigation,* Englewood Cliffs, NJ, Prentice-Hall.

Ellul, J. (1965), *The Technological Society,* New York, Alfred A. Knopf.

Goonatilake, S. (1982), *Crippled Minds: An Exploration into Colonial Culture,* New Delhi, Vikas Publishing House.

Goonatilake, S. (1984), *Aborted Discovery: Science and Creativity in the Third World,* London, Zed Books.

Goonatilake, S., Joan Gussow and Omawale (1984), *Food as a Human Right,* Tokyo, United Nations University Press.

Johnson, P. and A. Sasson (eds) (1986), *New Technologies and Development,* Paris, UNESCO.

Kirby, M.D. (1986), 'Human rights – The challenge of the new technology', *Australian Law Journal,* **60,** 170–81.

Ministry of Science, Technology and Energy (1988), *Science and Technology Policies: Evolution and Operation,* Bangkok.

Murphy, J.W. and J.T. Pardeck. (1986), 'Introduction', in J.W. Murphy and J.T. Pardeck (eds), *Technology and Human Productivity – Challenges for the Future,* New York, Quorum Books.

Ravetz, Jerome R. (1971), *Scientific Knowledge and its Social Problems,* Oxford, Oxford University Press.

Rosenfeld, Albert (1970), *The Second Genesis: The Coming Control of Life,* Englewood Cliffs, NJ, Prentice-Hall.

Rybczynski, Witold (1983), *Taming the Tiger – The Struggle to Control Technology,* New York, Viking Press.

Santikarn, Mingsarn (1981), *Technology Transfer,* Singapore, Singapore University Press.

Stewart, F. (1982), *Technology and Underdevelopment,* 2nd edn, London, Macmillan.

Toffler, A. (1979), *Future Shock,* London, Pan Books.

Weeramantry, C.G. (1983), *The Slumbering Sentinels: Law and Human Rights in the Wake of Technology,* Harmondsworth, Penguin.

Weeramantry, C.G. (1987), *Nuclear Weapons and Scientific Responsibility,* Wolfeboro, NH, Longwood Academic.

Weeramantry, C.G. (ed.) (1990), *Human Rights and Scientific and Technological Development,* Tokyo, United Nations University Press.

Weeramantry, C.G. (ed.) (1993), *The Impact of Science on Human Rights: Global Case-Studies,* Tokyo, United Nations University Press.

Winner, L. (1977), *Autonomous Technology (Technics-Out-of-Control) as a Theme in Political Thought,* Cambridge, MA, MIT Press.

Ziman, J.M., P. Sieghard and J. Humphrey (1986), *The World of Science and the Role of Law,* Oxford, Oxford University Press.

11 Globalization and Human Rights

VIRGINIA A. LEARY

Introduction: Globalization

Globalization is a pervasive phenomenon of our times. An important trend in international life, it affects people in all parts of the globe. One of the lesser noted impacts of globalization is its effect on human rights. Some of the rights of individuals and groups are enhanced by globalization, but it also has negative effects on human rights. While citing the positive aspects, this chapter focuses on the problems which globalization poses for the promotion and protection of rights, particularly the rights of workers and, most especially, the rights of women workers.

The term 'globalization' refers to the current transformation of the world economy: the reduction of national barriers to trade and investment, the expansion of telecommunications and information systems, the growth of off-shore financial markets, the increasing role of multinational enterprises, the explosion of mergers and acquisitions, global inter-firm networking arrangements and alliances, regional economic integration and the development of a single unified world market. The phenomenon of globalization is accompanied by increasing international mobility: the migration of workers, the growth of tourism and the increasing ease of international travel. Communication across borders has become easier with access to E-mail, the Internet and other communication channels.

Regional trading blocs such as the European Union and the North American Free Trade Agreement (NAFTA) and the Asia Pacific Economic Co-operation (APEC) promote trade liberalization. The establishment of the World Trade Organization enhancing and supporting the General Agreement on Tariffs and Trade (GATT) and other agreements adopted at the conclusion of the Uruguay Round has also contributed to trade liberalization. Going beyond the liberalization of trade in goods, the Uruguay Round added issues of agriculture and intellectual property to the more traditional GATT concerns.

The World Bank and the International Monetary Fund have imposed structural adjustment social policies on developing governments seeking their aid. These policies have required countries to cut food subsidies which aid the poor and to adopt labour practices that result in harm to workers. Under structural adjustment programmes, governments are less able to freely adopt economic and social policies; international financial institutions and transnational corporations are often the real influences in the adoption of such national policies. The free market ideology is pervasive and influential.

While these developments are viewed as means to improve the global economy, the persistence of serious social and economic problems is evidence that they are not a panacea. The Workers' Group of the ILO Governing Body pointed out in 1994 that there is generalized unemployment and underemployment throughout the world and social tensions are giving rise to internal political instability in many countries. They noted that there are:

> 1.1 billion people living in conditions of extreme poverty [...] countless millions unemployed and underemployed in the developing world, plus 35 million in industrialized countries; an estimated child workforce of between 100 and 200 million, often subjected to the most inhuman forms of exploitation; some 33 million held in servitude under different forms of forced labour; a growing migrant population of more than 100 million, about two in three of them so-called 'economic migrants' who have left their countries in search of work; and gross discrimination against women and ethnic groups.[1]

Most of these problems predate the advent of globalization, but increasingly it is being asked whether globalization is not exacerbating some of the conditions and whether an undue emphasis has not been put on free trade and the market economy to the detriment of consideration of social problems and violations of human rights arising from globalization.

The mixed record of globalization is cited in the Copenhagen Declaration and Programme of Action adopted at the World Summit for Social Development in 1995:

> Globalization, which is a consequence of increased human mobility, enhanced communications, greatly increased trade and capital flows, and technological developments, opens new opportunities for sustained economic growth and development of the world economy, particularly in developing countries. Globalization also permits coun-

tries to share experiences and to learn from one another's achievements and difficulties, and promotes a cross-fertilization of ideals,
cultural values and aspirations. At the same time, the rapid processes
of change and adjustment have been accompanied by intensified poverty, unemployment and social disintegration.[2]

Competitiveness: Decline of Labour Unions

Globalization has led to an intensification of international competitiveness. With the elimination of many barriers to free trade through
membership in GATT, countries are less able to erect tariff and non-
tariff barriers to protect their own markets and products. They are
forced to compete on the international market. The developed countries must compete with countries where labour and basic
commodities are cheaper. The developing countries must use their
comparative advantage and attempt to obtain access to the markets
of the developing countries.

The result is a 'race to the bottom' – a competition to have fewer
social benefits and lower salaries in order to compete on the international market. In the economically developed countries, international
competitiveness is leading to demands for the cutting of social ex-
penses such as costs of health care, unemployment insurance, welfare
of various kinds and day care programmes – and salaries. Each day,
in the United States, Canada and Western Europe, one may read of
'downsizing' – dismissing workers in order to cut labour costs and
increase the competitiveness of industry.

The situation in developing countries is characterized by the serious
problems of underemployment and poverty mentioned in the quota-
tion above from the Workers' Group of the ILO Governing Body.
While some few developing countries in Asia have recently developed
rapidly and are providing the main competition to the developed
country production, most developing countries remain locked in severe poverty and are not reaping profit from globalization.

In such an economic climate, the business sector has advantages
over organized labour, as pointed out in *Industry on the Move*, a
publication of the World Employment Programme of the ILO:

> Intensified international competition is putting pressure on business
> to adopt 'global best practice' production methods and on workers to
> accept greater flexibility in working time, pay and the tasks that they
> perform. Labour's power to influence the adjustment process has de-
> clined for various reasons: deconcentration of production units,
> increased use of decentralised bargaining and parallel sourcing and
> frequently high unemployment and weakened trade union power...
> The inescapable conclusion is that the balance of power has shifted in

favour of the business sector. However, in the more open world economic environment, this conclusion is of little help to most individual businesses, for whom the pressure to adjust has probably been increasing as much as in the case of workers and governments.[3]

In some developed countries, labour union membership is at an unprecedented low. In the United States, it has fallen to approximately 15 per cent of workers. The power of unions in the developed countries is much weaker than it was in the immediate past. In many developing countries, freedom of association for labour unions scarcely exists; obstacles of various kinds are placed in the way of organizing workers and, in certain countries, violence, torture, arbitrary killings and arbitrary arrests are routinely used to prevent workers from uniting to reclaim their rights.

Human Rights at Issue

Some of the benefits of globalization contribute to the enhancement of human rights. As pointed out at the World Summit for Social Development, increased trade often aids developing countries and thus contributes to the alleviation of poverty; increased communication permits countries to learn from each other. In the sphere of human rights, communication via E-mail and the Internet has permitted human rights advocates to call immediate attention to gross violations of human rights in their locality and to communicate with other human rights advocates throughout the world.

However, there are other less beneficent effects on human rights arising from globalization. The emphasis on competitiveness and economic development has had especially negative effects on such vulnerable groups as migrant workers, women workers and indigenous peoples. Globalization has been cited as a contributing factor in violations of the right to life, the right to protection of health, minority rights, freedom of association, the right to safe and healthy working conditions and the right to a standard of living adequate for health and well-being in many countries.

Workers' Rights and Globalization

The competitive pressures of the new international economy have had negative effects on the rights of workers. Low labour costs and low labour standards are important elements in the choice of location of branches or subsidiaries of transnational corporations or choice of suppliers for industrial development in the North. Textiles and other goods produced more cheaply in developing countries are taking over markets in the developed world. Governments thus have little or no incentive to improve working conditions – on the contrary, their competitive advantage depends on these conditions. Developing countries oppose the linking of labour standards to trade issues, pointing out that such linkages would take away their competitive advantage through cheap labour and low labour standards. Their argument is understandable since it is essential to increase the trade of developing countries; however, the cost falls on the most vulnerable elements in the developing countries: unskilled or semi-skilled labourers whose rights to organize labour unions, to engage in collective bargaining or to protest against unsafe working conditions are denied.

Louis Emmerij has referred to modern competition as all-out war between countries and firms, and pointed out that the 'resulting pressure on wages, social benefits and on labour standards in general is constant and getting more serious'.[4] In November 1995, in preparation for the meeting of APEC, 30 representatives from trade unions, human rights groups and non-governmental organizations from 14 APEC countries met in Kyoto to discuss the impact of globalization on human rights in the APEC region. The meeting, jointly sponsored by the Canadian-based International Centre for Human Rights and Democratic Development and the regional network Asia Pacific Workers' Solidarity Links, adopted the 'Kyoto Statement on Workers' Human Rights in the APEC region', which noted that

> rather than advancing the cause of rights, globalization has actually contributed to the erosion and suppression of basic internationally recognized human rights throughout the region ... While APEC calls for breaking down barriers to investment and trade throughout the region and the establishment of rules to facilitate capital mobility, internationally recognized human rights, including labour rights, profoundly affected by globalization, are being ignored [...] This is unacceptable.[5]

A common complaint of workers in developing countries has been the negative effect on working and social conditions resulting from the structural adjustment programmes imposed by the World Bank and the International Monetary Fund:

> Structural adjustment is a process of restructuring often characterized by an increased reliance on market forces and a reduced role for the State in economic management. This approach to restructuring started by shaping industry, investment and technology, and was then extended to the organization of manpower and labour. Initiated in the industrialized countries, it was then applied to developing countries. Structural adjustment programmes (SAPs) incorporate more market-

based approaches to the organization and delivery of public services, including the contracting out of public services, and coincide with or form an integral part of overall government policies on deregulation, privatization and trade liberalization. Unfortunately, SAPs, by their nature, lead to labour displacement and have a direct impact on employment, conditions of work and labour relations in the public sector. For these reasons, SAPs have encountered growing problems of implementation, not least because they have either ignored or failed to adequately address the social dimension of adjustment and the adverse impact on the workforce.[6]

The Workers' Group of the Governing Body of the ILO has pointed out that the international trade union movement is not opposed to the aims of structural adjustment but is strongly critical of the manner in which such programmes have been carried out, namely in not enlisting the aid of social partners in the planning. The workers attribute increased infant mortality, lower educational attainment, reduced real earnings, higher rates of accidents at work and increased levels of unemployment to poorly developed structural adjustment programmes and point out:

> it is alarming that in a significant number of violations of trade union rights before the [ILO] Committee on Freedom of Association, governments have sought to justify abuses – of collective bargaining rights in particular – on the grounds of the conditions imposed upon them by adjustment programmes.[7]

In several countries, conditions resulting from structural adjustment programmes have led to disturbances, including riots.

Women Workers: Export Processing Zones

Although unskilled workers in general are victims of globalization, the situation of women workers deserves particular attention. On the one hand, globalization has increased opportunities for women. Many women have entered the workforce through jobs in export processing zones or through becoming migrant domestic workers – both types of jobs created largely by globalization. Their work has contributed to family income and to a sense of independence and freedom for women workers. On the other hand, these jobs often lead to social disruption of the family and expose women to exploitation and, on occasion, violence and sexual abuse. As a group lacking in power and status in society, their human rights are frequently violated.

Economic development resulting from globalization produces dislocation of populations and migration pressure.[8] The disparity in economic development between countries and the need for workers in the more developed countries has resulted in large numbers of workers migrating across borders. In some cases, this movement is the result of organized recruitment and planned worker migration; in other cases, the movement is clandestine, resulting in large numbers of undocumented workers in developed countries. Women workers are often among the most numerous migrant workers, since there is high demand for domestic servants and for women in entertainment fields in more developed countries.

Women migrant workers are often drawn from the poorer segments of their own communities and are thus already in a situation of vulnerability. Their vulnerability is increased during their stay abroad: they are regarded as a form of cheap and exploitable labour, their passports are sometimes confiscated and, alone in a foreign country whose laws and customs they do not know, they are unable to find recourse against abuses. They are often working in countries where the status of women is low.

> Migrant women add their condition as women to the vulnerability of migrant workers. Abuses are particularly committed against women involved in domestic services or in the entertainment industry. Besides oppressive working conditions, with long working hours and very limited personal time, domestic workers suffer verbal and physical abuse and have to fight sexual harassment. Entertainers are victims of false promises, turned into waitresses and sometimes forced into prostitution.[9]

Several recent notorious cases of criminal actions against migrant women domestic servants who defended themselves against sexual abuse have publicized the dilemma in which such women find themselves. Whether abuses are flagrant or mild, the situation of migrant domestic women is frequently lacking in respect for human dignity. Their rights to security of person, to protection against rape, to organize and complain about working conditions are lacking. Few organizations exist to assist them.[10]

Although this section has focused on the situation of women migrant workers, it should not be overlooked that male migrant workers are often also subject to violations of their dignity and rights. In 1990, the UN General Assembly adopted the International Convention on the Protection of the Rights of All Migrant Workers and Their Families. The Convention applies to both men and women workers and their families and has no special provisions relating to women. As of January 1996, it had been ratified by only two countries, and countries which receive many migrant workers have shown little interest in ratification. Several ILO conventions and recommendations concern migrant workers,[11] but they also have received relatively few ratifications in comparison with other ILO labour conventions.

Export processing zones (EPZs) are an important manifestation of globalization. They are free-trade enclaves in the customs and trade regime of a country where foreign manufacturing firms produce mainly for export and benefit from a number of fiscal and financial incentives.[12] They are also referred to as 'free zones', 'special economic zones' and 'maquiladoras'. At least 70 countries (mainly developing countries) now have such zones. Low labour costs are one of the important incentives for government decisions to establish EPZs, since entrepreneurs may produce goods for exports with the cheap labour of the developing country, but without onerous customs and fiscal constraints. Textiles, clothing, footwear and electronics are the main goods produced in the zones. The zones have been encouraged by international and national institutions: the World Bank and United Nations Industrial Development Organization (UNIDO) have given technical and financial assistance to establish the zones and support has also come from the US Overseas Private Investment Corporation and the US Agency for International Development.[13]

While the majority of managerial and administrative posts in the zones are held by men, the majority of the unskilled and semi-skilled workers in most zones are women. The working conditions in the zones are thus of particular concern to women. The zones often provide higher salaries than corresponding jobs outside the zones and the women thus benefit from the higher wages. However, while wages are higher generally in the zones, other aspects of working conditions may be less satisfactory. In recent years, women in developed countries have campaigned for the abolition of restrictions on night work for women and other protective labour measures, on the grounds that they discriminate against women and prevent them from obtaining certain jobs. In recent years, ILO organs have debated this question at length and have concluded that night shift work is unsuitable for both men and women. In many EPZs, night work is common, since unrealistically high production targets arising out of competitive pressures make overtime and night work necessary for protracted periods. But it has been pointed out that night work for women in the zones causes particular problems:

> Work at night, whether on a shift or overtime basis, raises certain considerations that are perhaps more pronounced with respect to EPZs than in other contexts. The provision of transport and accommodation facilities, for instance, becomes critical, because the production workers generally live far from the workplace, in areas that may be poorly lit and with no public transport at the hours when they begin and finish work. Since not all employers provide these facilities, the question of personal security has assumed considerable importance.[14]

Faced with competitive pressures requiring night work, several governments of developing countries have denounced the ILO Convention on Night Work for Women, have not complied with its provisions, or have made clear their intention not to ratify it.

Safety and health issues are also of concern in the EPZs. Romero has written:

> The use of unsafe machinery, disregard of fire prevention rules, failure to install first aid facilities and supply protective gear and safety instructions to workers in a number of EPZs, remain widespread problems. In the worst cases […] they have led to tragic accidents with heavy death tolls. In the majority of cases, the Occupational Safety and Health laws apply to the zones and most EPZ host countries have ratified [ILO] Convention No. 81, the aim of which is to ensure, through regular inspections, that the norms guaranteeing the protection of workers in industrial workplaces are applied. However, problems persist and have in some contexts become worse, because of serious deficiencies in labour inspection services and the imposition of derisory sanctions with little or no dissuasive effects.[15]

Industrial relations issues are of concern in EPZs. By law, workers in nearly all the EPZs technically have the right to form and join trade unions, but the reality differs from the law. In many EPZs, union membership is very low. A number of reasons may account for the low number: young women make up the bulk of the workforce and tend to not be interested in union membership since they regard their work as temporary, relatively high wages discourage interest in unions, and there is the high turnover of labour. In addition to these factors, free union activities in the zones are often discouraged by governments. Zones are located in inaccessible areas with tight security, company unions are encouraged more than free trade unions, strikes are often forbidden and certain employers and EPZ authorities carry out anti-union activities.[16]

Working conditions in the zones appear to have improved somewhat with increasing publicity given to the problems. However, the conditions continue to impinge particularly on women workers. Again, competition plays an important part since companies often make veiled threats to relocate if labour becomes too expensive or conditions in the zones become too onerous.

The Rights of Indigenous Peoples

The international community has become concerned over violations of the rights of indigenous peoples in recent years, after many years of neglect. The United Nations Working Group on Indigenous Peoples has drafted a declaration on the rights of indigenous peoples, which is now being examined by a working group of the UN Commission on Human Rights and will eventually come before the General Assembly for adoption. The decade 1994–2003 has been declared the UN Decade for Indigenous Peoples. In 1989, the International Labour Organization adopted Convention No. 169, which revised an earlier convention with an assimilationist focus. The Convention becomes binding international law for states which ratify it.[17]

While violation of the rights of the indigenous has been taking place for centuries, the recent emphasis on economic development and international competitiveness has resulted in new onslaughts on their rights. The link between globalization and the rights of indigenous peoples, in their own eyes, was demonstrated by the choice of 1 January 1994, the date of the coming into effect of the North American Free Trade Agreement, for the uprising by Indians in Chiapas, Mexico, drawing attention to the violation of their economic and social rights.

Oil, uranium, minerals and timber are found throughout the world on indigenous lands, and prospectors and entrepreneurs have been permitted to encroach on them in the name of economic development.[18] Indigenous lands in many parts of the world have been trespassed upon in pursuit of traditional medicines which are then brought onto international pharmaceutical markets.

Economic development has resulted in serious violations of the right to health, the right to a healthy environment, the right to life and the cultural rights of indigenous peoples. International attention has been drawn to violations of the rights of the Yanomami Indians of Brazil (but without noticeable success in remedying them). The Inter-American Commission on Human Rights examined a complaint against Brazil in 1985 relating to the activities of independent prospectors and companies engaged in exploiting the mineral and timber resources of the Amazon regions inhabited by the Yanomami. The Commission found that the incursions, which included the construction of a highway through Yanomami lands, caused disruption of the social life of the Yanomami and introduced a number of diseases which decimated the population. The Commission also found that, in licensing and permitting these activities, Brazil violated provisions of the American Declaration of the Rights and Duties of Man relating, *inter alia*, to the right to life and the right to protection of health.[19]

The Challenge to Human Rights Non-governmental Organizations

Numerous human rights problems are exacerbated or caused by globalization as well as the structural adjustment programmes of the international financial institutions, yet non-governmental human rights organizations have been insufficiently active in focusing on these problems. Some organizations have limited mandates preventing consideration of problems arising from globalization; others consider their work as limited to civil and political rights; some shy away from the complexities of the international economy and concentrate on admittedly important and traditional problems such as torture and disappearances. Studies by human rights groups on links between trade and human rights are rare. Few organizations have expanded their mandate to include economic and social rights. Criticism of this lacuna in the human rights movement has led to some increased focus on economic and social rights by major organizations but, despite the rhetoric on interdependence and interrelationship of all rights, the dichotomy largely persists between the two sets of rights in the practical work of the organizations. Far more time and effort are spent on civil and political rights.

Nevertheless, some organizations have been notable exceptions. Two relatively new groups, the Centre for Housing Rights and Evictions (COHRE) and the International Human Rights Organization for the Right to Feed Oneself (FIAN) have been able to do exceptional work with a very limited number of staff and have demonstrated the link between globalization and violation of the right to housing and the right to adequate food. The International Commission of Jurists is one of the few organizations which have devoted efforts over a long period to the promotion and protection of economic and social rights. The New York-based Lawyers Committee for Human Rights has published a number of reports on workers' rights (both civil rights and economic or social rights) and has researched and published on the impact of the policies of the World Bank and the International Monetary Fund on human rights in a number of countries. Recently, Human Rights Watch – which formerly confined its work entirely to civil and political rights – has published reports concerning the right to housing in relation to the US position at the UN Habitat meeting and has shown increasing concern over social rights in the Asian region. A Center for Economic and Social Rights has been established in New York.

By and large, however, it has been non-governmental aid groups such as Oxfam, which carry out projects in developing countries, and grassroots organizations in those countries which have been most sensitive to problems arising from globalization. The labour movement has, of course, been calling attention to the problems of workers arising from globalization and structural adjustment on numerous occasions. But, in view of the relative weakness of the labour movement in some of the major countries, it has sometimes appeared to be a voice crying in the wilderness.

To the mutual harm of the labour movement and the human rights movement, the two movements have moved along parallel but separate lines. Although workers' rights are human rights, the international human rights movement devotes little attention to the rights of workers, despite the incorporation of workers' rights in the Universal Declaration of Human Rights, the International Covenant on Civil and Political Rights, the International Covenant on Economic, Social and Cultural Rights and numerous international labour conventions. Trade unions and labour leaders rarely enlist the support of human rights groups for the defence of workers' rights. A notable exception to the failure to work together is the International Labour Rights and Education Fund in Washington, DC, which brings together human rights activists, scholars and trade unions in defence of workers' rights.

Solutions

What should be done to improve the negative social situations arising from globalization? A number of international agreements, in particular the International Covenant on Economic, Social and Cultural Rights and the human rights conventions of the ILO, contain provisions relating to the protection of the rights most frequently in danger from globalization. The human rights movement and the labour movement should pay increased attention to these treaties and to promoting their implementation.

But enforcement of these treaties depends on 'mobilization of shame' and the willingness of states to conform to the evaluations of monitoring organs. The weakness of these enforcement mechanisms, although continually being improved, has led to calls for linking human rights, particularly labour rights, with trade. Threats to use trade sanctions have proved efficacious with regard to intellectual property and other actions deemed to be unfair competition. However, the linking of trade and labour rights is highly controversial. If sanctions are adopted unilaterally, they may easily serve as an excuse for protectionism. At the multilateral level, debates continue within the ILO, ranging the workers' movement against the employers' organizations and most states. The World Trade Organization is not at present considering the subject. For the moment, while debates continue, no immediate linking of trade and workers' rights internationally is foreseeable. Defining precisely which labour standards or workers' rights are fundamental is a first step towards any international movement on the subject, and this effort at clarification is currently being undertaken by the ILO.

With the financial assistance of a number of governments, the ILO has developed the International Programme for the Elimination of

Child Labour. The ILO works with national governments and with non-governmental organizations to develop programmes for the gradual elimination of child labour. The Programme takes into account the complexity of the problem of child labour and the necessity for thoughtful and consistent methods of remedying the problem. It deserves substantial continued support.

A number of corporations have adopted corporate codes of conduct dealing with labour and human rights:

> The most frequently cited example of company guidelines in this regard are the *Levi Strauss and Co. Business Partner Terms of Engagement and Guidelines for Country Selection,* which are directed to the company's contractors and suppliers. They cover, *inter alia,* occupational safety and health, freedom of association, wages and benefits, working time, child labour, forced labour and non-discriminatory hiring practices.[20]

Similar efforts are being made by the Reebok Corporation, the New York Skirt and Sportswear Association, the National Association of Blouse Manufacturers Inc., the Industrial Association of Juvenile Apparel Manufacturers and the Timberland Corporation. These efforts, if they become sufficiently widespread, will have a positive effect on social situations, but they frequently lack effective monitoring systems and need to be more widely adopted and enforced.

Labelling of items produced in conformity with good social practices is increasingly urged as a contribution to better social practices and protection of human rights arising from globalization. One of the better known efforts is 'Rugmark' – a mark establishing that carpets and rugs have not been made with child labour. Labelling has the value of permitting consumers concerned with social rights to influence production by using their purchasing power in support of good practices. Consumer boycotts or consumer-led efforts on occasion have substantial influence, but they are hard to mount and often run up against difficulty in verifying whether goods have been produced under good social conditions.

The World Summit for Social Development (1995) drew attention to the necessity of national and international attention being given to social problems. Unfortunately, it received relatively little media attention compared to other recent international conferences. The Copenhagen Declaration and Programme of Action resulting from the World Summit should be widely publicized and supported by human rights organizations. In the final analysis, only increased concern for social justice and human rights by corporations, labour unions, human rights organizations and governments will help to counteract the negative effects of globalization.

The need for social justice in the face of globalization was well expressed by Rubens Ricupero, the Secretary-General of the United Nations Conference on Trade and Development (UNCTAD) in his address to the World Summit:

> We have to demonstrate that there is life after globalization [...] faith in the future is synonymous with hope. And hope does not thrive with injustice. As national barriers fall and a single unified market begins to take shape, competition is exacerbated. Competition needs fair rules and strong arbiters [...] Partnership implies solidarity, standing shoulder to shoulder and helping those less equipped to cope with a more competitive global economy. The logic of competition has to be balanced by the logic of solidarity.

Notes

1   'The ILO towards the twenty-first century', submission of the Workers' Group of the ILO Governing Body to the Director-General concerning the future of the Organization, *Labour Education*, 1992–3, no. 3.

2   The Copenhagen Declaration and Programme of Action, World Summit for Social Development, United Nations, 1995, para. 14.

3   G. van Liemt (ed.), *Industry on the Move*, Geneva, International Labour Office, World Employment Programme, 1992, p.vi.

4   Louis Emmerij, 'Contemporary challenges for labour standards resulting from globalization', in Werner Sengenberger and Duncan Campbell (eds), *International Labour Standards and Economic Interdependence*, Geneva, International Labour Office, 1994.

5   'Kyoto Statement on Workers' Human Rights in the APEC region', available from International Centre for Human Rights and Democratic Development, 63, rue de Bresoles, Montreal, Quebec, Canada.

6   Hedva Sarfati, 'Trade Union Rights in the Context of Structural Adjustment: Transition to a Market Economy', IRRA 10th World Congress, Study Group No. 16, Industrial Relations in the Public Sector, Washington, DC, 4 June 1995.

7   'The ILO towards the twenty-first century' (op. cit., note 1), p.13.

8   For an extensive discussion of this subject see Graziano Battistella, *Human Rights of Migrant Workers, An Agenda for NGOs*, Quezon City, Philippines, Scalabrini Migration Center, 1993.

9   Ibid., p.ix.

10   Some organizations to assist migrant domestic workers exist in developed countries, such as the Association pour la défense des droits du personnel domestique in Quebec.

11   Convention concerning Migration for Employment (No. 97) and Migrations in Abusive Conditions and the Promotion of Equality of Opportunity and Treatment of Migrant Workers (No. 143), Recommendations concerning Migration for Employment (No. 86) and Migrant Workers (No. 151) and the Conventions concerning Forced Labour (No. 29) and the Abolition of Forced Labour (No. 105). The ILO also has a number of other conventions relating to women and work, most importantly, the Equal Remuneration Convention, 1951 (No. 100) and the Discrimination (Employment and Occupation) Convention, 1958 (No. 111), both of which have been ratified by more than 100 states. In 1996, the ILO

Conference adopted a Convention and a Recommendation on Home Work which has particular relevance for women. Women account for the vast majority of home workers and such work is often low-paid and escapes administrative control.

12 Ana Teresa Romero, 'Labour standards and export processing zones: situation and pressures for change', *Development Policy Review*, **13**, (3), September 1995, 247. The material in this section is mainly taken from this article.
13 Ibid., 249.
14 Ibid., 256.
15 Ibid., 259.
16 'These are well-documented in annual surveys carried out by the International Confederation of Free Trade Unions ... as well as in reports of the ILO's Committee on Freedom of Association and the Committee of Experts' (Romero, op.cit., note 12, 262).
17 As of June 1995, eight states had ratified the Convention and several others were in the process of ratification.
18 See Center for Economic and Social Rights, 'Rights Violations in the Ecuadorian Amazon', *Health and Human Rights*, **1**, (1), 83.
19 Resolution no. 12/85, Case no. 7615, Annual Report of the Inter-American Commission on Human Rights, 1984–5. See also Carol Hilling, 'Les Peuples Autochtones et La Commission Interaméricaine des droits de l'homme', *Recherches amérindiennes au Québec*, **XXIV**, (4), 1994, 37.
20 Romero (op.cit., note 12, 266).

Bibliography

Amjad, Rashid (1995), *To the Gulf and Back: Studies on the Economic Impact of Asian Labour Migration*, Geneva, ILO.
Battistella, Graziano (ed.) (1993), *Human Rights of Migrant Workers, An Agenda for NGOs*, Quezon City, Philippines, Scalabrini Migration Center.
Center for Economic and Social Rights (1995), 'Rights violations in the Ecuadorian Amazon', *Health and Human Rights*, **1**, (1).
Emmerij, Louis (1994), 'Contemporary challenges for labour standards resulting from globalization', in Werner Sengenberger and Duncan Campbell (eds), *International Labour Standards and Economic Interdependence*, Geneva, ILO.
International Labour Organisation (1992–3), 'The ILO towards the twenty-first century', submission of the Workers' Group of the ILO Governing Body to the Director-General concerning the future of the Organization, *Labour Education*, **3**.
Kyoto Statement on Workers' Human Rights in the APEC Region (1995), International Centre for Human Rights and Democratic Development, Quebec, Montreal.
Plant, Roger (1994), *Labour Standards and Structural Adjustment*, Geneva, ILO.
Romero, Ana Teresa (1995), 'Labour standards and export processing zones: situation and pressures for change', *Development Policy Review*, **13**, (3), September.
Sarfati, Hedva (1995), 'Trade Union Rights in the Context of Structural Adjustment: Transition to a Market Economy', IRRA 10th World Congress, Study Group No. 16, Industrial Relations in the Public Sector, Washington, DC, 4 June.
Sengenberger, Werner and Duncan Campbell (1994), *International Labour Standards and Economic Interdependence*, Geneva, ILO.
Van Liemt, Giesbert (ed.) (1992), *Industry on the Move*, Geneva, ILO, World Employment Programme.
World Summit for Social Development (1995), *The Copenhagen Declaration and Programme of Action*, New York, UN.

12 Education for Human Rights

VITIT MUNTARBHORN

Introduction

UNESCO's commitment to the promotion of education for human rights can be traced back to 1948, the year of the adoption of the Universal Declaration of Human Rights. However, it was in 1974 that its involvement with human rights education was concretized most visibly with the adoption of UNESCO's own Recommendation concerning Education for International Understanding, Cooperation and Peace and Education relating to Human Rights and Fundamental Freedoms. It called for the insertion of human rights into various levels of education and for the encouragement of 'action to ensure the exercise and observance of human rights, including those of refugees; racialism and its eradication; the fight against discrimination in its various forms'.[1]

In 1978, the International Congress on the Teaching of Human Rights held in Vienna advanced this further by highlighting the indivisibility of human rights – civil, political, economic, social and cultural – and propounded the following aims for human rights education:

1 fostering the attitudes of tolerance, respect and solidarity inherent in human rights;
2 providing knowledge about human rights, in both their national and international dimensions and the institutions established for their implementation;
3 developing the individual's awareness of the ways and means by which human rights can be translated into social and political reality at both the national and international levels.[2]

The Vienna Congress also voiced the need to teach human rights in an interdisciplinary form, integrating it into a variety of courses and disciplines.

This was reinforced in 1987 by the Malta International Congress on Human Rights Teaching, Information and Documentation which advocated, *inter alia*:

> the development of programmes of human rights teaching and education within the framework of formal and non-formal systems of education, duly taking into account: age, training level; professional orientation of the students; the major international instruments in the field of human rights; national and regional systems concerning human rights; and the experience of different countries in solving socio-economic, political, legal and other problems of ensuring the effective exercise of human rights and traditional freedoms.[3]

The scope of human rights education was broadened in 1993 by the Montreal International Congress on Education for Human Rights and Democracy, which established a key link between human rights and democracy. While emphasizing the role of formal and non-formal education on this issue, it called for more attention to education in specific contexts and difficult circumstances in regard to the following concerns: armed conflicts, displaced persons, states of emergency and military rule, the occupied territories, democracy in transition, children and post-Soviet societies. It noted the broad range of catalysts in human rights education, as follows:

> individuals, families, groups and communities, educators, teaching institutions and their boards, students, young people, the media, employers and unions, popular movements, political parties, parliamentarians, public officials, national and international non-governmental organizations, all multilateral and inter-governmental organizations, the United Nations Organization, in particular its Centre for Human Rights, specialized institutions of the United Nations system, in particular UNESCO and States.[4]

That impetus was further concretized later in 1993 by the World Conference on Human Rights, whose Declaration and Programme of Action advanced the relationship between human rights, democracy, peace and development, bearing in mind women's rights, with the following stipulations:

> 79. The World Conference on Human Rights calls on all States and institutions to include human rights, humanitarian law, democracy and rule of law as subjects in the curricula of all learning institutions in formal and non-formal settings.
> 80. Human rights education should include peace, democracy, development and social justice, as set forth in international and regional human rights instruments, in order to achieve common understand-

ing and awareness with a view to strengthening universal commitment to human rights.
81. Taking into account the World Plan of Action on Education for
Human Rights and Democracy adopted in March 1993 by the International Congress on Education for Human Rights and Democracy of
UNESCO, and other human rights instruments, the World Conference
on Human Rights recommends that States develop specific programmes and strategies for ensuring the widest human rights education
and the dissemination of public information, taking particular account of the human rights needs of women.[5]

In sum, education for human rights is 'essential for the promotion
and achievement of stable and harmonious relations among communities and for fostering mutual understanding, tolerance and peace'.[6]

Challenges

The above instruments attest to the fact that there is universal consensus on the value of human rights education and the need to
promote it. However, the realities facing the global and national
communities are more complex than they appear at first glance. Key
challenges for human rights education include universalization, interconnection, diversification and specification.

Universalization

In the past half-century, the world has witnessed the rise of a number
of universal standards in the form of treaties and declarations, and
related monitoring mechanisms, on human rights: for example, the
1948 Universal Declaration of Human Rights and the 1966 International Covenant on Civil and Political Rights, the International
Covenant on Economic, Social and Cultural Rights and the two optional protocols to the first Covenant.[7]

However, there are still marked inconsistencies between universal
standard setting and national implementation. A number of countries,
especially in Asia, have not acceded to the International Covenants
mentioned and other international treaties on the subject. For those
which have become parties to international instruments on human
rights, there are many discrepancies at the national level: many laws
and practices conflict with international standards. The situation is
aggravated by the fact that the texts of many international instruments
have not been translated into national and local languages, thereby
accentuating the gap between principle and practice.

There is also a trend among certain countries to advocate that
universal standards are subject to cultural variations. At times, this

kind of argument verges on 'ethnocentrism' which leads to the dilution of universal standards and undermines the spirit of human rights. This may equally lead to the distortion of human rights education to serve the ethnocentric approach rather than universalism.

A parallel challenge is the argument voiced by some countries which place emphasis on the rights of the community – communitarian rights – rather than on the rights of individuals. This is reinforced by various state claims of the individual's duties towards the community rather than his or her rights. While the interests of the community are important, the danger of this approach is that it may be used by vested interests to suppress dissent and democratic aspirations rather than to promote a holistic approach to human rights.

Interconnection

Internationally, it has long been established that civil, political, economic, social and cultural rights are interconnected and indivisible. In other words, there can be no 'bargaining' between a political right, such as freedom of speech, and a socioeconomic right, such as the right to an adequate standard of living.

However, one has noticed increasingly that some less than democratic countries favour fragmentation of human rights; they espouse economic, social and cultural rights rather than civil and political rights. On the other hand, it must be noted that some developed countries tend to emphasize civil and political rights rather than economic, social and cultural rights, thus giving rise to a degree of Eurocentrism or 'occidentalism'. These polarities are embroiled in increasing politicization which renders human rights education more difficult and fractious in certain settings.

On another front, the human rights discourse has been broadened in recent years. Lately, there has been greater focus on the linkage between democracy, development, peace and human rights, as witnessed by the document ensuing from the World Conference on Human Rights.[8] While verbally all countries agree upon the need to promote education interconnecting these concerns, practical implementation of all these elements based upon an integrated approach at the national and local levels tends to be nascent rather than well established. The challenge is to move away from 'gradualist incrementalism' towards 'accelerated activation'.

Diversification

There is general consensus that the teaching of human rights should cover a broad range of people and should be incorporated into a wide variety of subjects at different levels – not only legal courses but many other disciplines – while being culturally sensitive. While substantive courses on human rights are welcome, equally important is the need to infuse human rights information into all components of education, for example in courses on philosophy or home economics. Hence the diversification of human rights education. This rationale is reinforced by the following observation from the Montreal Congress on Education for Human Rights and Democracy:

> the need to diversify information, documentation and teaching materials and better orient them towards the needs of different categories of populations in various parts of the world. This could also help to avoid what was termed as a pre-conceived universalist (i.e. Eurocentrist) approach to human rights education still pervading at the level of action of many international governmental organizations and NGOs. In the effort towards diversification, the first need is to bring new actors on the scene, providing new sources of information and new approaches to its use for specific purposes.[9]

However, there are various obstacles facing diversification. As will be seen below, most substantive courses on human rights tend to be found at the higher level of education rather than at the primary and secondary levels. While there is a diversity of non-formal programmes worldwide, these programmes are often piecemeal and unsystematic, lacking in evaluation of their impact. Moreover, while much attention has been given to educating those who could otherwise be victims of human rights violations – 'the abused' – not enough emphasis has been placed on education provided for the potential 'abusers'. Where some human rights education is available to the latter, one is uncertain whether such education leads to a 'lip service' response or real behavioural change.

Specification

A clear trend internationally is towards the adoption of particular instruments which recognize the human rights of specific groups and persons. For example, there are now specific international agreements on the rights of women, children and migrant workers. Others, such as an instrument on the rights of indigenous peoples, are in the process of evolution. There is also a morass of international guidelines on specific groups and situations, for example rules concerning juvenile justice and standards concerning humane conduct towards those with HIV/AIDS. This trend of specification helps to emphasize the special needs of each category and overcome the generalities of earlier international instruments.

However, the proliferation of these standards poses a qualitative and quantitative challenge at the national and local levels, testing the scope of human rights education to the limit. At best, the specific needs of the various groups are catered to more concretely by means of more focused human rights education. At worst, capacity for reception of these standards leaves much to be desired. Where they exist, the targets for such reception are at times unmet owing to constraints concerning human and financial resources, insufficient room for popular participation and inadequate bases of technology and knowledge. This is compounded by lack of access by specific target groups to assistance and protection; the physical and mental distance between the state and these groups hampers compliance with and education for human rights in many communities.

Overview

The spread of human rights education across the globe can be analysed from the perspectives of formal and non-formal education. The former is taken to mean education in the formal system of schools, colleges, universities and the equivalent, while the latter implies education 'out of school', such as through non-formal courses given to specific groups beyond the school curriculum. For the purpose of simplification here, non-formal education can also be taken to cover family education and education via the mass media.

Formal Education

The insertion of human rights information into formal education varies according to the levels of such education. There is most direct insertion at the higher or tertiary level and least insertion at the pre-school, primary and secondary school levels, as seen below.

Pre-school, primary and secondary levels   In most regions of the world, human rights education at the pre-school, primary and secondary levels is nascent rather than well-established. There is a general lack of substantive courses on human rights, but at times human rights information is infused through other courses. In several settings there is emphasis on individual duties towards the state and the community, rather than on the human rights of individuals and groups. This is compounded by overcentralization of the educational system in many countries, and the gap between the haves and the have-nots, between male and female, between adult and child, between the majority and the minority, and between urban and rural areas.

Human rights education at the pre-school level has not been addressed sufficiently in all parts of the globe, and this is constrained by the fact that pre-school education is unavailable to the majority of the population in many countries. At the primary and secondary levels, much depends upon the discretion of the teacher to infuse human rights education via courses such as civic education, history and life experiences. At times there may also be specific courses on law and politics at the secondary level which bear upon some aspects of human rights. As the information given at these levels depends mostly upon the initiative of the teacher, a key concern is to what extent teacher training on human rights is provided. Across the globe, the general answer is that there is little teacher training available at present, although developed countries have committed more resources to provide such training at the present time.

In North America, evidence points to the discretion of the teacher in including human rights in the curriculum. The constraints faced by the teacher include lack of time, paucity of educational materials, insufficiency of training and hesitation to address the more sensitive human rights topics. The situation is exemplified as follows:

> The 1987 Canadian Human Rights Foundation nation-wide survey entitled *The Teaching of Human Rights in Canadian Schools* found that human rights teaching is not a required element of curricula in Canadian schools, nor is formal human rights education offered to teachers at the faculty of education level [...] For teachers desirous of dedicating classroom time to human rights issues, there was the lack of teacher-ready materials in the area.[10]

The situation in Canada has now improved as the result of more training programmes and educational materials being currently available to teachers.

At the secondary level of education, there have been some interesting experiments. For example, in the USA, the Californian authorities have developed a model curriculum to tackle issues of inhumanity and genocide, while the New York authorities have inserted human rights information into history and political movement courses.

In Europe, most references to human rights at the primary level are found in civics courses. There is now a trend in some countries towards revising the secondary school curriculum to insert more human rights information as part of civics courses, history, religion, geography, literature, languages and social sciences.

In the Middle East, Asia and the Pacific, references to human rights at the primary and secondary levels tend to be through civics courses. Australia has been innovative in this respect:

A range of positive initiatives have been taken by schools and education authorities concerning human rights education in the development of curricula for government and non-government schools, in such areas as non-sexist education, aboriginal studies and multicultural studies. Human rights issues are incorporated throughout syllabuses covering society and culture, legal studies, English, aboriginal studies, history and geography.[11]

The Philippines has probably the most developed programmes of human rights education for teachers in the Asian region. It has evolved a variety of materials to educate teachers for human rights dissemination, including modules to train teachers on international human rights standards as linked to the local situation and the national Constitution. One unit of these modules, geared to potential teachers, sets as its aims (1) to foster literacy in human rights as proclaimed in various international instruments and national official documents and the Constitution; (2) to appreciate the value of human rights and abhor any violations; (3) to show respect for human rights; to speak and act individually according to what is good and right; (4) to do what can be done as a member of a group to respect and protect human rights.[12]

Another unit cites the following objectives: (1) to be updated on the human rights situation, especially in the Philippines; (2) to be aware of the various obstacles to the full implementation of human rights; (3) to condemn human rights violations by reading and reacting to accounts and cases of such violations; (4) to be aware of what the public and private sectors are doing to promote and protect human rights; (5) to know why methodology for teaching human rights should include teachers' recognition of the rights of students, as well as teachers exercising their own rights.[13]

The cases discussed include the following: abuses committed in the name of martial law, conflicts between political opponents, conflict of cultures and religions, poverty, disease, insurgency and family ties. The courses use an active, participatory method encouraging participants to interview people and discuss their findings publicly.

By contrast with these innovations, it should be noted that many countries in the Middle East, Asia and Pacific are faced with cultural impediments, including the view that 'children should be seen and not heard'. There is a tendency in the more authoritarian settings to emphasize human duties rather than rights. Some countries, such as Thailand, which have advanced towards democracy, are still faced with an antiquated curriculum which emphasizes duties rather than rights, for example the duty to pay taxes, the duty of conscription, the duty to register births and deaths, without sufficient dissemination of human rights as espoused internationally.

In Central and South America, the situation is similar to the above; human rights tend to be infused via existing courses at the primary and secondary levels rather than by means of substantive courses on human rights. There is a key observation in this respect: 'Those countries whose governments tend to include human rights into their educational system show a greater will for democratizing their societies.'[14] However, there are major constraints on the dissemination process, including fragmentation of information and lack of conceptual and methodological clarity in the curriculum.

Africa is the least advanced region in regard to education at the primary and secondary levels. Where there are references to human rights, they tend to be via civics courses. The situation is seen as follows: 'Education for human rights continues to be generally neglected in Africa, particularly in the formal education sector [...] Subjects on human rights and democracy continue to be [...] subsumed in civics subjects at the primary and secondary levels.'[15]

While lack of financial resources is a concern, the issue of political intentions exists equally:

> The failure on the part of many African States to place emphasis on education for human rights and democracy can be attributed to many reasons (including the usual 'lack of adequate resources' reason) but from recent reports of clashes between the State authorities and universities and schools in many parts of the continent, it is apparent that in many African States severe limitations are still being imposed on academic freedoms.[16]

The future path of human rights education at the pre-school, primary and secondary levels in all regions is thus shaped by the political and social will of the state to advance the right to education, freedom of expression and pluralism in each society, as well as the allocation of resources, for the sake of people's participation and democratization.

Higher or tertiary level   In most parts of the world, substantive courses on human rights can be found at the higher or tertiary level, especially at law faculties in universities. The courses are optional or mandatory, although the trend still seems to favour optional courses. Substantive human rights courses tend to deal with international instruments and mechanisms, while courses on constitutional law or the equivalent may delve more into the local perspective linked with human rights. Increasingly, human rights are incorporated into a variety of courses in the political and social sciences beyond traditional courses found in the legal field, and this is evidence of the recent process of diversification.

More attention is now paid to specific groups who are disadvantaged, including women, children, minorities, migrant workers, refugees, displaced persons and indigenous peoples. This trend of specification implies that, in place of a single course on human rights, there may be several courses, ranging from a general human rights course on the international framework to more specific courses on disadvantaged groups, such as a course on women and/or refugees. There has also been a spread of human rights centres of research and education, especially in developed countries, some of which have a specific focus on the disadvantaged groups mentioned.

At universities, those teaching human rights have usually had some training or experience, whether in theory or practice. A number of teachers from developing countries have attended human rights courses in developed countries. A continual challenge is how to enable them to interlink the international human rights framework with national laws and practices, so as to ensure that the content of what they teach is relevant at the grassroots level. Added to this is the fact that the proliferation of international human rights standards complicates matters for teachers, particularly in developing countries. They may find it difficult to keep track of recent developments unless they have access to information bases and networks of an international kind. The current opportunities for retraining and in-service training for teachers, especially in developing regions, are limited, with negative consequences for the quantity and quality of the information available to them and imparted by them.

Most teachers from developing countries who have been trained in the West probably have to face the challenge of finding ways to avoid Eurocentrism, with its overemphasis on the international and regional human rights systems found in developed regions, especially in Europe. They also have to counter the tendency of underlining civil and political rights to the neglect of economic, social and cultural rights, and to ensure that there is a balance between rights and duties and between the interests of collectivities and individuals.

The teacher's own role is fostered or constrained by the very nature of the political system confronting him or her at the local level; in less than democratic countries, it is unlikely that the teacher would be able to teach human rights liberally, if at all, and he or she would be monitored closely by the authorities to convey a sanitized or official version of human rights. Moreover, the teacher continually has to address the question whether he or she can or should be actively involved in education 'for' human rights to promote changes in and beyond the classroom, as contradistinguished from education 'on' human rights which may prove to be merely passive and perfunctory.

On another front, there is the linguistic issue, which at times hampers human rights education where it seeks to convey in-depth information. Much of the international human rights literature and many of the international human rights instruments are not available in local language(s), especially ethnic languages, while the human rights information available in local languages and the research done at the field level are often inaccessible to the international community, as they have not been translated into the international languages. This gap creates a divide between international standard setting and identification of the roots of human rights and related practices at the national and local levels. It also prevents those teachers who are not proficient in international languages from having access to the international literature which could otherwise broaden the horizons of human rights education at the local level. This constraint may lead to the perpetuation of a parochial approach, rather than the burgeoning of a universalistic approach.

Turning now to the different regions of the globe, it is clear that the most extensive human rights education at the tertiary level is found in North America and Europe. There are a multitude of human rights courses and centres on these continents. This is exemplified by the following observation:

> The number of institutions offering human rights courses has grown in the past decade, and the diversity of disciplines offering such courses has also increased. Human rights courses at universities range from the study of legal and moral principles to detailed case studies of human rights violations, race relations and US foreign policy. Where human rights courses were almost the exclusive domain of law faculties a decade ago, social science, health and medical faculties and anthropology departments are beginning to offer them.[17]

The list of human rights programmes and human rights centres at North American universities is extensive, including the State University of New York, the American University, Columbia University, Tufts University, Minnesota University, Harvard University, Ottawa University, Yale University and Denver University.

In Europe, apart from the well-established International Institute of Human Rights in Strasbourg, there has been a proliferation of human rights centres in the past decade which offer both courses at the tertiary level and special courses as part of non-formal education. A recent list includes the following:

> Austrian Human Rights Institute; Danish Centre of Human Rights; Ludwig Boltzman Institute of Human Rights; Instituto Bartholomeo de la Casas; Abo Akedemie Institute of Human Rights; Centre de recherches et d'études sur les droits de l'homme et le droit humanitaire;

Norwegian Institute of Human Rights; Interdisciplinary Programme of Research on Root Causes of Human Rights Violations; Institute for the Sociology of Law, Lund University.[18]

In the Middle East, Asia and the Pacific, a variety of substantive human rights courses can be found, especially in the context of universities. Syria, Yemen, Kuwait and the Arab Emirates all have universities which provide courses on human rights or teach human rights via other courses such as constitutional law and political science. In Asia, there are various courses on human rights at the university level, such as in Japan, India, the Philippines and Thailand. As noted above, teacher-training courses at universities in the Philippines offer special modules on human rights evolved at the local level.

Another innovative example is the human rights course at Chulalongkorn University's Faculty of Law in Thailand, which places great emphasis on local realities, student participation and field visits, so as to sensitize the students to life situations and live cases. At the outset of the course, the students are asked to identify disadvantaged groups in the locality and are then requested to do research on such groups as part of a public dialogue. In recent years, the groups identified for research and discussion include women, children, workers, refugees, minority hill tribes, victims of projects affecting the environment, victims of coups, victims of suppression of mass media, slum-dwellers, prisoners, those with HIV/AIDS and street vendors. The student presentations on these groups are related to local laws and policies and the international framework of human rights. They are enlivened by videos concerning the various groups and are coupled with field visits, for example to a slum area, children's projects or a home for battered or needy women. The structure of the course follows a bottom-up approach: first, local situations are analysed, followed by their nexus with local and national laws, policies and practices, and finally the upward interaction with the international dimensions of the problem and related international instruments and mechanisms.

However, some countries in Asia, such as Brunei, do not yet have universities which offer courses on human rights.

Central and South America have a variety of tertiary institutions which offer courses on human rights either directly or indirectly. The situation is noted as follows: 'Some [of the course] addressed the introduction of human rights content as a subject in the educational system, as obligatory or optional courses. Others, at higher educational level, have introduced human rights material at a post-graduate level.'[19] The Inter-American Institute of Human Rights has been pressing for more integration of human rights into formal education at all levels, including higher education.

Africa's record on human rights education at the higher level lags behind that of other regions. While substantive courses on human rights can be found in some North African countries, such as Algeria, Morocco, Mauritania and Tunisia, other countries have not incorporated human rights education sufficiently at the higher level. The position is encapsulated as follows:

> Few, if any, African governments have formulated policies for the inclusion of this subject as a major part of the curricula of schools and universities. Subjects on human rights and democracy continue to be relegated to the fringes of other core subjects, such as international and constitutional law, at the tertiary level.[20]

Guinea can be cited as an exception to the above comment. At the university level, human rights is taught as part of courses given by administrators or visiting professors, and is part of a variety of law courses such as civil law and criminal law.[21] On a related front, the presence of the African Charter of Human and People's Rights and the African Commission on Human Rights is a continual reminder of the need to promote human rights education more extensively in the region with a view to preventing and remedying human rights violations.

Non-formal Education

In all regions of the globe, there are a multitude of initiatives on human rights education beyond the school setting, often propelled by non-governmental organizations. Of particular interest is the spread of courses and programmes aimed at difficult situations and specific groups who are the potential or actual victims of human rights violations, such as street children, their protectors and *animateurs*, such as non-governmental organizations, the mass media and community leaders. Some are also aimed at the power sector of society, such as civil servants, the military, parliamentarians and law enforcement personnel, who might otherwise abuse their considerable margin of discretion in dealing with the rest of the population. A variety of educational means and materials in multi-languages and multimodal forms, including cartoons, games, posters, leaflets, hotlines, radio, television and audio-visuals, have been evolved, highlighting the need to improve outreach programmes and diversify the methodology for teaching human rights and the production of related information.

While this development is welcome, the precise impact of human rights education at the non-formal level is hard to assess. Many of the programmes are piecemeal and unsystematic, and they do not have inbuilt evaluation mechanisms which can help in the appraisal of performance and impact. The coverage of the power sector mentioned above is also limited, while the private business sector has not been encompassed sufficiently by existing non-formal education. Other constraints identified by the Montreal Congress (above), especially in relation to human rights education in difficult situations and among specific groups, include the following: (1) the absence of political will of certain partners; (2) the dangers of marginalization of the process internationally as well as intranationally; (3) the absence of target group involvement in the development and use of material, processes and policies; (4) the potential use of unsuitable methodology; (5) the lack of training of many participants; (6) the insufficiency of coordination and cooperation between the national, regional and international levels; (7) the occasional tendency to confine human rights education to the legal profession; (8) the lack of a multidisciplinary approach; and (9) the resistance to change provoked by new relations based upon human rights.[22]

To these may be added the proliferation of international human rights instruments and related guidelines which renders the dissemination process more difficult owing to the changing mass of the information and making more difficult the access of the local population to such information. The test case at the present time is the interrelationship between human rights, democracy, development and peace. Existing non-formal programmes tend to cover one of these issues in its specificity rather than to delve into their interrelationship, the transverse nature of human rights and the interconnection between civil, political, economic, social and cultural concerns.

At the heart of all these challenges is the pervasive and intractable issue of how to promote the sensitization of conscience and behavioural change, especially through 'learning by doing'.

The experiences from the different parts of the globe highlight the above concerns. In North America, a variety of non-formal programmes can be found, at times promoted by the presence of human rights commissions, such as the Quebec Human Rights Commission. A network founded by Amnesty International helps to train teachers, while professional associations, such as the National Association for Social Studies, the National Association for the Advancement of Coloured Peoples, the American Association for the Advancement of Science, the International Political Association in the United States, Physicians for Human Rights, the American Bar Association and the Canadian Judicial Institute, have programmes on human rights training, research and/or networking. Trade unions are also involved to some extent in this process: for example, the Canadian Labour Congress, which has a course on women and human rights. However, the impact of human rights education on elements of the power sector, such as civil servants, is still limited, as witnessed by the following observation:

> There is introductory but inadequate human rights training for Federal Public Service employees in Canada and the US. External Affairs Canada, in conjunction with the Human Rights Research and Education Centre, began implementing courses for foreign service officers in 1987. Now employees of the Canadian International Development Agency also have access to a specialized course. In the US, human rights training is absent from the preparation of public servants before being sent to represent the signatory country in human rights violator countries.[23]

The slant towards education on civil and political rights is implied by the following comment: 'The human rights agenda of the West is still restrictively narrow, however. The agenda of poorer countries, which involves "linking personal freedoms and democracy with economic rights and economic emancipation", may fairly be applied to North America in the search for a more inclusive definition of human rights.'[24]

In Europe, there has been an increase in the training of power groups such as the police, military and civil servants, as seen in Denmark, Italy and the Netherlands. France has witnessed the spread of teacher-training courses on human rights. The presence of a regional human rights system in Europe propelled by the Council of Europe helps to promote human rights courses and programmes in the region. To this may be added the presence of the United Nations Centre for Human Rights in Geneva, which has both a publications and a training programme on a variety of issues.

A number of human rights programmes can be found in the Middle East, Asia and the Pacific. Various non-governmental organizations have held training courses for the police and judges in Egypt and the Lebanon. A number of courses on specific human rights issues, such as women's rights, street children, juvenile justice and children's rights, can be found in Asia. The Philippines has a wealth of experience in this regard. There have been several projects on street education and street children. A variety of leaflets have been produced on domestic violence, sexual harassment and children's rights. A very innovative programme is the training of the police and the military to respect children's rights when children come into conflict with the law and in situations where there is armed conflict.

In Thailand, in recent years, there has been a plethora of programmes on specific issues ranging from children's rights and women's rights to the role of civil servants, the police and the military in human rights issues. A non-governmental organization based in Bangkok, called ASIANET, has provided training for the Asia–Pacific region on children's rights and has produced a variety of educational materials, including a bilingual poster (Thai–English) on the Convention on the Rights of the Child in poetry form. Recently, it organized a training programme for law enforcement personnel and non-governmental organizations on juvenile justice, and its forthcoming programme is on AIDS and children's rights.

Australia has seen the growth of programmes with teachers, propelled by the Australian Human Rights and Equal Opportunity Commission. Public educational materials have been produced in areas ranging from women's rights to children's rights and the rights of indigenous peoples.

In Central and South America, a range of non-governmental organizations are active in promoting non-formal education. These include the Brazilian Peace and Justice Commission, the Latin American Association for Human Rights and the Peruvian Institute of Human Rights Education. They have initiated courses for teachers, civil servants and law enforcement personnel. A number of popular education programmes for the general population have also been available as part of human rights literacy efforts. Amidst this mass of constructive work, there are basic difficulties, in this observation: 'The profusion of education experience on human rights in Latin America is inaccurate, heterogeneous and lacking in references enabling its qualitative development, because human rights education sacrifices quality as a consequence of an inorganic diversity of actions.'[25]

On another front, Africa has seen gradual development of non-formal education on human rights in recent years. There have been some programmes for law enforcement personnel, and the initiatives are propelled by non-governmental organizations such as the African Centre for Democracy and Human Rights Studies and the Arab Institute of Human Rights. Legal aid is offered by the African Society of International and Comparative Law, while special programmes on women and the law are found in Zimbabwe. However, the spread of these programmes is hindered in several countries by the less than democratic nature of the state, armed conflicts and resource constraints.

Conclusions and Recommendations

In retrospect, it may be observed that human rights education tends to be found substantively at the tertiary level rather than at the preschool, primary and secondary levels in formal education. For the latter, there is limited infusion of human rights information; much depends upon the quality and the discretion of the teacher. Non-formal education has incorporated human rights more concretely in recent years, with more courses on difficult situations and specific groups. However, the diversity of these courses indicates a lack of systematization, coupled with inadequate impact assessment. The programmes to reorient the mind-set of potential abusers are nascent rather than well-established. The impediments upon human rights education in both formal and non-formal education include the following:

- inadequate incentives for teachers and insufficient teacher training on human rights;
- limited integration of human rights at the pre-school, primary and secondary levels of formal education and the presence of a unidisciplinary rather than an interdisciplinary response at all levels;
- incomplete vision tending to overemphasize civil and political rights to the neglect of economic, social and cultural rights, and vice versa, as well as insufficient linkage between human rights, development, peace and democracy;
- overemphasis on human duties in some settings;
- the top-down approach towards teaching methods and the information conveyed;
- the gap between international standards and practical implementation;
- too much learning by rote and a passive methodology;
- insufficient programmes in difficult situations and sensitive areas;
- inadequate monitoring and evaluation of programmes;
- insufficient attention to disadvantaged groups;
- limited access to information owing to overcentralization;
- the paucity of programmes which train the power sector to respect the rights of others;
- limited cross-cultural interchange between developed and developing countries (North–South) as well as between developing countries (South–South);
- undemocratic undercurrents against liberal education;
- repression of independent voices and non-governmental organizations;
- inadequate commitment of resources and lack of sustainability;
- insufficient popular participation from target groups in shaping course contents and form;
- limited networking between catalysts at the national and international levels.

Consequently, the path to the future, for UNESCO and others concerned with human rights education, must include the following agenda.

1   Provide more incentives to teachers and teacher training to encourage them to incorporate human rights directly through substantive courses on human rights and indirectly via other courses by means of infusion.
2   Integrate human rights more expressly and comprehensively into the educational curriculum.
3   Emphasize the interconnected nature of human rights and the interaction between human rights, peace, development and democracy.
4   Convey a balance between human rights and responsibilities in keeping with international standards and a sense of universalism.
5   Promote a more bottom-up approach to human rights education by analysing actual situations at the local level and using them as an entry point for human rights principles and international instruments.
6   Foster accession to human rights instruments and their implementation at the national level, coupled with more specific guidelines and training for law and policy enforcement, and translation of relevant instruments into national and local languages.
7   Utilize an active teaching methodology which sensitizes one's conscience and involvement, including more 'learning by doing', audiovisual techniques, artistic expression, field work and participation in community projects, while promoting multilingual information and multimodal methods.
8   Initiate more programmes in difficult situations and sensitive areas, for example more training on humanitarian law of armed conflicts near to and in potential or actual flashpoints.
9   Ensure that there is monitoring and evaluation of programmes so as to improve performance and impact.
10   Focus more on the needs of disadvantaged groups with a view to preventive, protective and rehabilitative action.
11   Increase training of the power sector, including the military, police, judiciary, religious leaders, parliamentarians, trade unions and the business community, and use media more effectively for this purpose so as to enhance respect for human rights.
12   Foster cross-cultural interchange between North–South and South–South, especially among the young, in order to encourage transnational understanding.
13   Propel democratization of human rights education as well as decentralization to improve access by distant communities.

14   Provide more protection for human rights teachers, *animateurs* and non-governmental organizations.
15   Commit more resources to human rights education and improve its sustainability by introducing social marketing and income generation to support the dissemination work, for example sponsorships from the business sector and sale of human rights materials to some sectors with a view to pooling the proceeds for future work.
16   Maximize popular participation, with more women's participation, in all programmes, whether in regard to planning or implementation and/or evaluation.
17   Improve networking between human rights teachers, *animateurs* and related institutions, for example via the UNESCO Associated Schools Project.
18   Facilitate greater access to information by means of traditional and modern forms of communication, including telecommunications and computer linkage.

This agenda should be activated by the adoption of a set time-frame for its effective implementation. This could take the form of a UNESCO Human Rights Education Plan of Action aiming, in the short term, at the year 2000 and, in the medium term, at the year 2010, as goals for the quantitative realization of one or more of the above recommendations.

The ultimate pursuit would thus be to accelerate the process of nurturing a universal culture of human rights in the dynamics of globalization.

Notes

1   Article 18(c).
2   Final Document of the UNESCO International Congress on the Teaching of Human Rights, Article 3, 1978.
3   *International Law: News and Information from Asia and the Pacific*, 2, (19), 1988, 8.
4   *Final Report of the International Congress on Education for Human Rights and Democracy, Montreal (1993)*, UNESCO, Paris, 1994, p.30.
5   *World Conference on Human Rights: The Vienna Declaration and Programme of Action (1993)*, New York, United Nations, 1993, pp.66–7.
6   Ibid., p.67.
7   *Human Rights: A Compilation of Human Rights Instruments*, United Nations, New York, 1988.
8   Op. cit., note 5.
9   Op. cit., note 4, p.12.
10   H. Gibbs and M. Seydegart, 'Education on human rights and democracy in Canada and the United States', background document of the UNESCO International Congress on Education for Human Rights and Democracy, Montreal, March 1993, p.2.

11   Report submitted by Australia in accordance with Economic and Social Coun-
      cil Resolution 1988(X) concerning rights covered by Articles 13–15 of the
      International Covenant on Economic, Social and Cultural Rights (Australian
      Government, Canberra, 1992, p.5). See also V. Muntarbhorn, 'Education for
      human rights and democracy in Asia and the Pacific', background document
      of the UNESCO International Congress on Education for Human Rights and
      Democracy, Montreal, March 1993, p.1.
12   A.C. Gaceta, *Human Rights Concepts Integrated into Foundations of Education*,
      Department of Education, Manila.
13   Ibid., p.3.
14   Asociación Latinamericana para los Derechos Humanos, 'Evaluation report
      1987–1992: human rights education in Latin America', background document
      of the UNESCO International Congress on Education for Human Rights and
      Democracy, Montreal, March 1993, p.2.
15   R. Stock, 'Education for human rights and democracy in the African region',
      background document of the UNESCO International Congress on Education
      for Human Rights and Democracy, Montreal, March 1993, p.1. See also Institut
      arabe des droits de l'homme, Tunis, 'L'éducation aux droits de l'homme et à la
      démocratie dans le monde arabe', background document of the UNESCO In-
      ternational Congress on Education for Human Rights and Democracy, Montreal,
      March 1993.
16   R. Stock (op. cit., note 15), p.1.
17   Gibbs and Seydegart (op. cit., note 10), p.4.
18   International Institute of Human Rights, Strasbourg, 'L'éducation aux droits de
      l'homme dans les pays d'Europe Occidentale – Progrès réalisés et difficultés
      rencontrées depuis 1987 (Congrès de Malte)', background document of the
      UNESCO International Congress on Education for Human Rights and Democ-
      racy, Montreal, March 1993, pp.3–4.
19   Asociación Latinamericana para los Derechos Humanos (1993, p.6).
20   Stock (op. cit., note 15), p.1.
21   Ibid., p.3.
22   *Final Report* (op. cit., note 4), p.38.
23   Gibbs and Seydegart (op. cit., note 10), p.8.
24   Ibid., p.16.
25   Asociación Latinamericana para los Derechos Humanos (op. cit., note 14), p.14.

Bibliography

Asociación Latinamericana para los Derechos Humanos (1993), 'Evaluation report
    1987–1992: human rights education in Latin America', background document of
    the UNESCO International Congress on Education for Human Rights and De-
    mocracy, Montreal, March 1993.
*Final Report of the International Congress on Education for Human Rights and Democ-
    racy, Montreal (1993)*, Paris, UNESCO, 1994.
Gibbs, H. and M. Seydegart (1993), 'Education on human rights and democracy in
    Canada and the United States', background document of the UNESCO Interna-
    tional Congress on Education for Human Rights and Democracy, Montreal, March
    1993.
Institut arabe des droits de l'homme, Tunis (1993), 'L'éducation aux droits de
    l'homme et à la démocratie dans le monde arabe', background document of the
    UNESCO International Congress on Education for Human Rights and Democ-
    racy, Montreal, March 1993.

International Institute of Human Rights, Strasbourg (1993), 'L'éducation aux droits de l'homme dans les pays d'Europe Occidentale – Progrès réalisés et difficultés rencontrées depuis 1987 (Congrès de Malte)', background document of the UNESCO International Congress on Education for Human Rights and Democracy, Montreal, March 1993.

Muntarbhorn, V. (1993), 'Education for human rights and democracy in Asia and the Pacific', background document of the UNESCO International Congress on Education for Human Rights and Democracy, Montreal, March 1993.

Police Handbook on the Management of Cases of Children in Especially Difficult Circumstances, Quezon City, Department of Social Welfare and Development, 1993.

Protection of Non-Combatants in the Philippines, Manila, UNICEF, 1993.

Stock, R. (1993), 'Education for human rights and democracy in the African region', background document of the UNESCO International Congress on Education for Human Rights and Democracy, Montreal, March 1993.

World Conference on Human Rights: The Vienna Declaration and Programme of Action (1993), New York, United Nations, 1993.

Index

303

World Bank 6, 266, 269, 272, 275
World Charter for Nature (1982)
    126, 127, 142, 143
World Commission on Culture and
    Development 24
World Commission on Environment
    and Development 126–7
World Conference on Education for
    All (Thailand 1990) 172
World Conference on Women
    (Beijing 1995) 5, 108
World Health Organization (WHO)
    20, 256
World Order Models Project 247
World Summit for Social Develop-

ment (Copenhagen 1995) 3, 9,
    144, 266–7, 268, 277
World Tourism Organization 109,
    112
World Trade Organization 265, 276
Wrésinski, Joseph 157, 166, 174, 175

xenophobia 181–92, 204–5, 213

Yanomami Indians 274
Yemen 292
Yugoslavia 32, 111, 225

Zanghì, Claudio 13, 199–217
Zimbabwe 296